OLD EDITION

The Acquisition of Private Companies

The Acquisition of Private Companies

Fifth Edition

WJL Knight LL B
Solicitor of the Supreme Court

Longman

© WJL Knight 1989

Published by

Longman Group UK Limited
21–27 Lamb's Conduit Street, London WC1N 3NJ

First published 1975
Fifth edition 1989

Associated Offices

Australia, Hong Kong, Malaysia, Singapore, USA

A CIP catalogue record for this book is available from the British Library.

ISBN 0-85121-438-X

Typeset by Kerrypress Ltd, Luton.
Printed in Great Britain by Biddles of Guildford Ltd.

Contents

v

Preface

The aim of this book remains the same—to provide a short guide for the practising solicitor who is engaged in the acquisition or disposal of a private company. I hope that the book will also continue to be of interest to accountants, bankers and others engaged in acquisitions.

Apart from updating, the major changes to this edition consist of the revision of the agreement for sale, and the introduction of a form of agreement for use when a corporate vendor is involved. In these precedents the deed of tax indemnity has been replaced by contractual provisions which vary the purchase price. Since the publication of the fourth edition, stamp duty on company acquisitions has almost disappeared as a subject with the abolition of capital duty and the statutory reliefs from stamp duty, and the introduction of stamp duty reserve tax. The chapter on stamp duty, which was once one of the longest in the book, has diminished accordingly. The pensions section in Chapter 1 has been substantially re-written, and a new section introduced into Chapter 3 which deals with some legal considerations relevant to stock market fund-raising operations. This edition also takes account of the Financial Services Act 1986.

Acquisitions are more and more a team effort and I am very fortunate in having colleagues at Simmons & Simmons who are prepared to spare the time to help me revise this book. My thanks are due to Roger Butterworth, Stephen Coleclough, Peter Freeman, Janet Gaymer, Paul Hale, Nicholas Heald, Howard Mather, Edward Troup and Michael Wyman. I am very grateful to Michael Boyd and Linda Endicott of Ernst & Whinney who revised the financial information contained in Chapter 7. I also wish to thank the quotations department of The Stock Exchange for reading the Class 1 circular and making very helpful suggestions.

I remain responsible for the errors and omissions. Subject to them, the law stated is that in force in England on 1 March 1989, although it has been possible to refer to subsequent developments, including the Companies Bill and the March Budget Statement.

London,   WJL Knight
April 1989

Table of Cases

xi

Table of Cases

Table of Statutes

Table of Statutory Instruments

Chapter 1

General Considerations

There are more than 900,000 active companies registered in Great Britain and of these only approximately 7,000 are public companies. Although these figures give no guide to the proportion of the nation's business which is carried on through private companies, they give some indication of the popularity of the private company as a vehicle for trade and investment.

This book deals (mainly, but not exclusively, from the point of view of a purchaser) with the legal aspects of transactions involving the acquisition of shares which represent the entire issued share capital of a company, or at least a controlling interest, where the selling shareholders are few enough to enable negotiations to be carried on with them individually. The company whose shares are to be acquired (which for the sake of brevity is called the 'target' throughout this book) in such a transaction may be a public company within the meaning of the Companies Act 1985, but is far more likely to be private. Public companies are recognisable as such by the inclusion in their name of the words 'public limited company' or the abbreviation 'p l c' and the privilege they enjoy is the right to issue shares to the public. All other companies are private companies, and a company with a limited number of shareholders will not normally need public company status, neither will it wish to be subject to the administrative burdens which the Companies Act 1985 imposes on public companies.

When those who trade or invest through the medium of a private company wish to dispose of their business they are faced with a choice of methods. The company itself can sell its assets, or the shareholders can sell their shares in the target. The latter approach tends to be popular, not only because it is a simpler transaction, involving a transfer of ownership only of the shares in the target, but also for tax reasons. A sale of shares will normally involve individual shareholders in a charge to capital gains tax on any gain realised, but if a company sells its capital assets the company will itself pay corporation tax on any net gains realised and it will then be difficult to pass the consideration to individual shareholders without further taxation (eg capital gains tax on a deemed disposal of their shares in a winding-up). Vendors will, therefore, often wish to sell shares rather than procure a sale of assets by the target, and a purchaser who wishes to preserve the benefit of tax losses available to the target will certainly buy shares rather than assets.

There is, however, one essential difference between purchasing the assets of a business and buying shares. A company is a person and has the capacity (to some extent limited by its memorandum of association) not only of owning assets but also of incurring contractual, tortious and, indeed, criminal liabilities. Therefore when acquiring a company, it is necessary to ascertain not only the nature and quality of the assets owned by the target, but also the nature and quality of its liabilities. Where the shares to be acquired represent the entire issued share capital of the target, the precise rights attaching to the shares themselves have little or no importance and it is necessary to concentrate not upon the shares which are being bought and sold but upon the target company itself.

Although investigation may go some way to establish whether or not the target owns the assets which it is said to own, the most intensive and searching enquiries cannot conclusively establish the extent of the liabilities which the target owes. It is therefore the practice for the purchaser to require warranties and indemnities from the vendors in respect of the target's affairs. These are considered in Chapter 2 and, insofar as they relate to taxation, in Chapter 5.

The regulations which affect a takeover bid for a listed company are not normally applicable to the acquisition of a private company. The City Code on Takeovers and Mergers applies to listed and unlisted public companies but only applies to private companies if:

(*a*) their equity share capital has been listed on The Stock Exchange at any time during the ten years prior to the relevant date; or

(*b*) dealings in their equity share capital have been advertised in a newspaper on a regular basis for a continuous period of at least six months in the ten years prior to the relevant date; or

(*c*) their equity share capital has been subject to a marketing arrangement as described in the Companies Act 1985, s 163(2)(*b*) at any time during the ten years prior to the relevant date (eg their shares have been dealt in on the Unlisted Securities Market); or

(*d*) they have filed a prospectus for the issue of equity share capital at the Companies' Registry at any time during the ten years prior to the relevant date.

In each case, the relevant date is the date on which an announcement is made of a proposed or possible offer for the company or the date on which some other event occurs in relation to the company which has significance under the Code.

The City Panel appreciates that the provisions of the Code may not be appropriate to all statutory and chartered companies or to all private companies falling within the categories listed above and will, therefore, apply the Code with a degree of flexibility in suitable cases.

The Code also applies if the transaction amounts to a reverse takeover of a listed company. A reverse takeover involves the acquisition for shares by a listed company of an unlisted one in circumstances in which the number of shares issued as consideration by the listed company is so great that a change in the control of the listed company results. In those cases the Panel claims authority and expects full compliance with the Code.

Although the rules and regulations of The Stock Exchange may affect the transaction, if the target is unlisted they will only apply if either the vendor or purchaser is a listed company (see Chapter 3).

Taxation apart, there is little legislation which has specific application to the transfer of ownership of private companies. The Stock Transfer Act 1963 prescribes a form of transfer which may be used and some sections of the Companies Act 1985 (notably s 151: see p 15) place restraints upon some aspects of the transaction; but there is, for instance, no legislation which implies any term into an agreement for the sale of shares. Schemes of arrangement under the Companies Act 1985, s 425, are rarely used as a method of acquiring a private company in the circumstances with which this book deals and equally rare is the application of s 428 et seq of that Act for the purpose of acquiring the shares of dissenting minority holders.

Since the coming into force of the Financial Services Act 1986 those who are concerned in a professional capacity with the sale and purchase of shares in private companies must consider whether they are carrying on investment business within the meaning of the Act and therefore need to be authorised under its provisions. Activities constituting investment business are described in Sched 1 to the Act, and those which might be relevant are para 12 (dealing in investments as principal or agent), para 13 (arranging deals in investments) and para 15 (advising investors or potential investors on the merits of purchasing or selling an investment). Paragraph 21 of Sched 1, however, provides that paras 12, 13 and 15 do not apply in relation to the acquisition or disposal of shares in a body corporate other than an open-ended investment company if (in summary) more than 75 per cent of the voting share capital of the company is involved in the transaction and the acquisition and disposal is between parties each of whom is a body corporate, a partnership, a single individual, or a group of connected individuals. For this purpose, a 'group of connected individuals' means people who are connected to the directors and managers of the target by being close relatives of them. 'Close relative' means a spouse, child, parent, brother or sister. If less than 75 per cent of the company is involved in the transaction, or if even one of the shareholders is not connected to a present director or manager (eg if one of them is a former director's widow) then the exemption will not apply and apparently, will not apply to those involved on either side.

Solicitors who advise on acquisitions can take some comfort from para 24 of Sched 1 which provides that para 15 (giving advice) does not apply to advice which is given in the course of a profession and the giving of which is a necessary part of other advice or services given in the course of carrying on that professional business. The paragraph goes on to provide that advice is not to be regarded as falling within the exemption if it is remunerated separately from other advice. It is to be assumed that para 15 is intended to catch advice given on the acquisition or sale of shares as an investment and not, eg, tax advice or advice about warranties and indemnities. In the case of an acquisition of a private company it is quite difficult to differentiate between the legal advice on the contract and commercial advice upon the merits of the shares as an investment. In this sense, the exception given in para 24 should be helpful. In any event, the problem does not exist for solicitors who are certified by the Law Society in its capacity as a recognised professional body as they are authorised persons. In their case, giving advice as to the merits of an investment in a private company in this context is likely to be 'incidental' within the meaning of the Solicitors Investment Business Rules 1988 and will not therefore constitute discrete investment business.

CONSENTS AND APPROVALS

There are many cases in which it is necessary or desirable to obtain some consent or approval before shares of a private company are acquired, and those which most commonly arise in practice are outlined below.

Consents required under contracts

Contracts entered into by the vendor, purchaser or, indeed, by the target, may render it necessary to obtain prior consent for the acquisition. For example, it may be a term of loans made to the target that they become repayable if control of the target changes. If the purchaser wishes the target to continue to enjoy the benefits of these loans, the consent of the lender must be obtained. If the target is a subsidiary of the vendor, the vendor may well have entered into loan agreements which contain clauses which restrict the disposal of a substantial part of the vendor's undertaking and assets and the consent of creditors or trustees for loan stockholders may be required. If the consideration for the acquisition is shares to be issued by the purchaser, the purchaser's advisers should consider whether the terms of any agreements entered into by the purchaser will be infringed by the issue of the shares. For instance, deeds constituting convertible loan stocks may restrict the issue of further share capital by the purchaser. It is, of course, not possible to give an exhaustive list of the consents which may be required under this heading because it will depend upon the previous contracts entered into by the vendor, purchaser and target. So far as the target is concerned, a warranty is often taken that no such contracts exist (see the Agreement for Sale, Sched 3, para 2 (25) on p 180).

Approval of purchaser's shareholders

If the purchaser is a company, the approval of its own shareholders may be required for the acquisition. If the consideration for the acquisition is the issue of shares in the purchaser, an ordinary resolution may be required to increase the share capital, and, unless the consideration shares can be issued under an existing general authority for the issue of share capital, an ordinary resolution will also be required to authorise the issue of the shares under the Companies Act 1985, s 80.

The statutory pre-emption rights conferred by the Companies Act 1985, s 89, which require new issues of shares first to be offered to existing shareholders, do not apply in cases where the shares are, or are to be, wholly or partly paid up otherwise than in cash (s 89(4)). It may, however, be the case that such a requirement is contained in the purchaser's articles or that there are some other relevant restrictions on the issue of share capital.

If shares in the target are sold to the purchaser by a director of the purchaser (or of the purchaser's holding company), or by a person 'connected' with such a director within the meaning of the

Companies Act 1985, s 346, shareholders' approval will normally be required under the Companies Act 1985, s 320, unless the value of the shares is less than the lower of £50,000 and 10 per cent of the purchaser's relevant assets. The Companies Act 1985, s 104, also imposes conditions (including the approval of shareholders) for the acquisition of 'non-cash assets' from subscribers of the memorandum of a newly incorporated public company within two years of its being issued with a certificate to do business, and from a member of a company registered or re-registered as a public company within two years from such registration or re-registration.

If the purchaser is a listed company, the approval of shareholders for the transaction may be required by the Quotations Department of The Stock Exchange if:

(*a*) the acquisition amounts to a 'Super Class 1';

(*b*) the transaction falls within Class 4;

(*c*) the accountants' report is qualified because of inadequate records; or

(*d*) the acquisition amounts to a reverse takeover.

These matters are dealt with in Chapter 3 (see p 89). If the purchaser is a public company which is itself the subject of a takeover bid, r 21 of The City Code on Takeovers and Mergers may require shareholder approval for an acquisition.

Special qualifications of the target

The target may have some qualification or accreditation which the purchaser desires to preserve; for instance, it will normally be necessary to obtain the consent of the committee of Lloyd's before shares in a Lloyd's broking company or underwriting management company can be acquired. Similar requirements can arise by statute. If the target is an insurance company the consent of the Secretary of State to a change in control may be required under the Insurance Companies Act 1982, Part II. If the target carries on investment business it will be sensible to check that its continued authorisation under the Financial Services Act 1986 will not be affected by the change of ownership.

The Financial Services Act 1986

Where the shares of the target are widely held, any circular offer to shareholders is likely to amount to an investment advertisement within the meaning of the Financial Services Act 1986, s 57 and, if that is the case, the circular may not be issued unless it is issued by an authorised person or unless its contents have been approved by an authorised person. This provision replaces s 14 of the Prevention of Fraud (Investments) Act 1958.

Article 3 of the Financial Services Act 1986 (Investment Advertisements) (Exemptions) Order 1988 (SI 1988 No 316) provides however that s 57 does not apply to an investment advertisement 'which is issued or caused to be issued by a body corporate . . . if the circumstances are that the body corporate issues or causes the investment to be issued to persons whom it reasonably believes to be members of, or the holders of [shares or debentures] in the body corporate and the advertisement contains no invitation or information which would make it an investment advertisement other than an invitation or information relating to [those shares or debentures]'. A similar, (but not identical) exemption was contained in s 14(3) (*a*)(iii) of the Prevention of Fraud (Investments) Act 1958 but the view was always taken that where a company circulated an offer on behalf of a bidder, the bidder committed an offence under the Prevention of Fraud Act by causing the document to be circulated. The exemption contained in the Order, however, does seem to be rather wider than the former exemption and it may be that bidders who arrange for the bid circular to be sent out by the target will obtain the benefit of the exemption, at least in the case of a cash bid. If the offer included investments as consideration, the exception would not apply, as the circular would then relate to investments other than those in the body corporate issuing the circular.

However, the cautious practitioner will note that the Financial Services Act 1986 (Investment Advertisements) (Exemptions) (No 2) Order 1988 (SI 1988 No 716) contains two exemptions which specifically address the problem of private company acquisitions and may conclude that the draftsman did not intend the exception under art 3 of the first Order to be used in these circumstances. Article 4 of the second Order allows a takeover offer if it is an offer for all the shares in, or the shares comprised in the equity or non-equity share capital, of a private company target. The conditions which must be satisfied before an offer comes within the scope of the order are quite complicated, but the principal ones are these:

(*a*) the terms of the offer must be recommended by all the directors of the target (other than any director who is also a director of the offeror);

(*b*) if the offeror holds 50 per cent or less of the voting rights of the target and makes an offer for debentures or for non-equity share capital then the offer must include or be accompanied by an offer made by the offeror for the rest of the shares comprised in the equity share capital; and (*c*) an offer for equity share capital must be conditional upon acquiring a 50 per cent or more of the voting rights.

The target must be a private company and the exemption will not apply if any shares comprised in the equity share capital of the target are or have at any time within the period of ten years immediately preceding the date of the offer been:

(*a*) listed or quoted on an investment exchange (in the United Kingdom or elsewhere); or

(*b*) shares in respect of which information has, with the agreement or approval of any officer of the target, been published for the purpose of facilitating deals in them, indicating prices at which persons have dealt or were willing to deal in them other than persons who were, at the time the information was published, existing members of a relevant class; or

(*c*) subject to a marketing arrangement which accorded to the company the facilities referred to in s 163(2)(*b*) of the Companies Act 1985; or

(*d*) the subject of an offer (whether in the United Kingdom or elsewhere) in relation to which a copy of prospectus was delivered to the relevant registrar of companies in accordance with s 41 of the Companies Act 1948, or s 64 of the Companies Act 1985.

For this purpose members of a relevant class are existing members or debenture holders of the target or employees or their family members.

It will be noted that if the target is resident in the United Kingdom and any of these conditions is not satisfied it is likely that the Takeover Code will apply to an offer for equity share capital (see p 2). The offer must be accompanied by advice from an independent financial adviser. The Order contains detailed requirements about the contents of the offer and these are referred to in the notes of the specimen offer in Chapter 7.

Article 5 of the Order gives a wider exemption for investment advertisements which are issued in connection with the sale or purchase of shares in a company which falls within Sched 1, para 21 to the Financial Services Act 1986 (see p 3), ie a transaction involving more than 75 per cent of the voting shares which is between parties each of whom is a body corporate, a partnership, a single individual or a group of connected individuals.

It should also be noted that under s 47 of the Financial Services Act 1986 it is a criminal offence punishable by a term of imprisonment not exceeding seven years, for any person knowingly or recklessly to make a statement, promise or forecast which is misleading, false or deceptive or dishonestly to conceal any material fact if that person makes the statement, promise or forecast or conceals the fact for the purpose of inducing another person ... to enter or offer to enter into an investment agreement (which will include an agreement for the acquisition of shares in a private company). The section is not confined to written statements.

Consents under the Taxes Acts

The purchaser will normally seek advance clearance under the Capital Gains Tax Act 1979, s 88, where the consideration for the acquisition is shares and it is expected that the vendors will thereby be enabled to 'roll over' their capital gains (see p 109). Other sections under which clearances may be sought, because of possible adverse tax consequences, are the Income and Corporation Taxes Act 1988, s 707 (see p 111) and s 776 (see p 116).

MERGER CONTROL AND COMPETITION LAW

Merger control and competition law are becoming more important factors in acquisition strategy. Consents and approvals may also be required under this head. Aspects of the subject are dealt with here under the headings: The European Communities, United Kingdom Merger Control, and United Kingdom Competition Law.

The European Communities

The consent of the Commission of the European Communities may be required under the Competition Law provisions of the EEC Treaty (the Treaty of Rome), which established the European Economic Community, or the ECSC Treaty (the Treaty of Paris), which established the European Coal and Steel Community. The Commission of the European Communities has sought to establish that mergers and acquisitions should be controlled at the Community level either by art 85 (which renders void agreements between undertakings which restrict competition subject to the possibility of exemption in certain circumstances), art 86 (which prohibits abuse of dominant position) or by a new merger control Regulation conferring express power on the Commission.

It has been established for some time that art 86 may apply where a company holding a dominant position within the EEC strengthens that position by acquiring control of another company to such an extent that it practically eliminates effective competition and affects trade between member states (see Case 6/72, *Europemballage Corp*

& *Continental Can Co Inc* v *EC Commission* [1973] ECR 215). This situation may not often occur, and the Commission has never formally exercised its powers under art 86 to prohibit a merger since *Continental Can*. However, a dominant position can be held to exist in a narrow market sector and it should not be assumed that art 86 applies only to very large companies. In cases where there is a real possibility of the acquisition falling within art 86, application can be made to the EEC Commission for a ruling. There is no prescribed form. The Commission cannot exempt a transaction from art 86 but it can issue a 'negative clearance' if the transaction falls outside the article.

Until 1987 it was assumed that art 85 could not apply to acquisition agreements which had the effect of merging the parties into a single economic unit (see, eg, Commission Decision *SHV/ Chevron* OJ 1975 L38/14). However, in Cases 124/84 and 156/84 *BAT and Reynolds* v *Commission* [1988] 4 CMLR 24 the European Court of Justice gave a ruling which indicated that art 85 could be applicable to partial mergers of businesses by means of the acquisition of shares where the two parties remained separate undertakings, or even, according to some commentators, to complete mergers. This ruling has encouraged the EC Commission to reconsider the possible application of art 85 to acquisitions (see, eg, the Commission's intervention in the consortium take-over bid for *Irish Distillers Group* (August 1988)).

At the same time there has been a renewed impetus to enact the long dormant draft merger control Regulation giving the Commission express powers to control mergers having 'a Community Dimension' and providing for compulsory pre-notification for mergers over a certain size, measured in combined worldwide turnover.

The result of this three-tracked approach (arts 85 and 86 and the proposed new Regulation) is to produce considerable legal uncertainty. If the merger control Regulation is enacted, this may clarify matters for acquisitions falling within its scope but for other acquisitions (eg where the combined turnover of the undertaking is below the threshold for pre-notification) art 86 remains theoretically applicable (if a dominant position exists) and the uncertainty over the application of art 85 will remain.

Quite separately from the question of the merging of the undertakings concerned, it is clear that art 85 may apply where restrictive covenants are taken from the outgoing shareholders (see Commission Decisions *Reuter/BASF*, OJ 1976 L254/40 and *Nutricia* OJ 1983 L376/22, confirmed by the European Court, Case 42/84 *Remia BV and others* v *EC Commission* [1985] ECR 2566).

If it is considered that there is a serious possibility that art 85 may be applicable, either to specific covenants or to the acquisition as a whole, the agreement should be submitted to the EC Commission on the prescribed Form A./B for negative clearance or art 85(3) exemption. A quick decision is virtually impossible but informal approaches to the Commission may assist.

Unlike the EEC, the ECSC has specific rules for mergers and acquisitions (which are referred to as 'concentrations'). Under art 66(1) of the ECSC Treaty, concentrations involving a coal or steel undertaking require, in principle, the prior authorisation of the Commission. Coal and steel undertakings are widely defined in art 80 of and Annex 1 to the Treaty and these definitions merit careful study.

It should be noted that in contrast to the EEC rules, there is no requirement that the concentration must be liable to affect trade between member states. Thus an acquisition affecting only the United Kingdom could still require authorisation under art 66(1). Moreover, even if less than a majority of shares in the target is to be acquired, authorisation may still be needed as a wide test of 'control' is laid down by an implementing decision (No 24–54).

The Commission has power to authorise individual transactions, and by art 66(3) can exempt entire classes of transaction from the authorisation requirement. The current exemption is contained in Decision 25–67 amended by Decision 2495/78 ECSC. The full text of the amended decision is published in the Official Journal 1978 No C255/2. No attempt is made here to describe its provisions in detail as they are very specific, but, in summary, tonnage and percentage thresholds are laid down for the turnover in coal or steel products of the undertakings involved; transactions involving amounts below these thresholds are exempted, although the Commission must be notified of them within two months of their taking effect. Certain minor transactions are free even of this requirement. The Commission has wide powers to order the separation of unauthorised mergers and acquisitions and to impose penalties.

Companies normally subject to the ECSC Treaty are likely to have had some experience of its requirements and possibly even of art 66. The Treaty may, however, be overlooked when a company not subject to the Treaty acquires a coal or steel undertaking. This is a trap for the unwary, particularly where the target only falls within the Treaty definition because of the activities of a small part of its organisation.

If the general exemption in Decision 25–67 is not applicable then an individual application must be made to the Commission for prior authorisation under art 66(2). The procedure is generally quicker than under the EEC Treaty.

United Kingdom merger control

The provisions of the Fair Trading Act 1973 which relate to merger control are set out in s 64 et seq. Under s 64 the Secretary of State may refer a merger to the Monopolies and Mergers Commission (the MMC) if it appears to him that it is or might be the fact that two or more enterprises, of which one at least was carried on in the United Kingdom or by or under the control of a body corporate incorporated in the United Kingdom, have ceased to be distinct enterprises and that either the merger creates or adds to a market share of one quarter or more or the value of the assets taken over exceeds £30 million (last increased by the Merger References (Increase in Value of Assets) Order 1984 (SI 1984 No 932)).

The provisions which determine whether enterprises cease to be distinct enterprises and the time at which they do so, can be found in ss 65 and 66 of the Act. An acquisition of one company by another will almost always meet the terms of the definition because two enterprises will be 'brought under common ownership or common control' (s 65(1)(*a*)). The 'market share' provisions will be found in s 64(2) and (3) and relate to the supply of goods of any description or services of any description in the United Kingdom or in a substantial part of the United Kingdom.

Section 65 of the Act provides that the assets taken over are the assets employed in or appropriated to the business of the target and that their value is the value at which the assets stand in the books of the relevant business less any relevant provisions for depreciation, renewals or diminution in value. In other words, it is necessary to look at the gross assets of the target and not only to the assets which are owned but also to the assets which are appropriated to the business and by s 67(3)) to any assets of the target which on the change in control are 'dealt with in the same way as assets appropriated to' the business of the target.

The Secretary of State is not only empowered to make a merger reference in respect of a completed merger but he also has the power to make a merger reference in advance where it appears to him that it is or might be the fact that arrangements are in progress or in contemplation which, if carried into effect, would result in the creation of a merger situation qualifying for investigation. The main ground on which mergers are referred to the MMC is the possibility that the merger will restrict competition. If a merger reference is made and if the MMC finds that the merger operates or may be expected to operate against the public interest, the Secretary of State may (but is not bound to) exercise the powers specified in Sched 8, Pts I and II (see s 73). The powers are very wide ranging and include power to make orders for divestment.

If the acquisition falls within the criteria which will allow the Secretary of State to refer the acquisition to the MMC, it is sensible, but not obligatory, to seek guidance in advance from the Office of Fair Trading. This can merely be informal consultation but there is also a more formal system of 'confidential guidance'.

Sections 57 and 62 contain special provisions governing the acquisition of newspapers; these sections should be noted carefully as, unlike the normal situation, failure to comply with the newspaper merger procedures is a criminal offence.

Changes to the Fair Trading Act to be introduced in 1989 include a voluntary pre-notification system which involves serving a 'merger notice' on the Office of Fair Trading. In straightforward cases, provided the acquisition has been publicly announced, the proposed arrangement will be deemed automatically cleared if nothing is heard from the Office of Fair Trading within 28 days. If the Office of Fair Trading needs more information it must say so, in which case the right to automatic clearance will lapse as it will if the full facts are not disclosed or if the acquisition is not made within six months. There is also provision for negotiation of undertakings to be given to the Secretary of State to avoid a reference and for the charging of fees for the operation of merger control procedures. It remains to be seen how these proposals will work in practice.

Until the new proposals are implemented, applications for guidance or clearance should continue to be made to the Secretary of the Mergers Panel, Office of Fair Trading, Field House, Bream's Buildings, London EC4A 1PR, and the procedures described in the guide published by the Office of Fair Trading, *Mergers — A Guide to the Procedures under the Fair Trading Act 1973* continue to apply. No decision with regard to a reference will be taken until after the acquisition has been made public (so that interested parties may have a chance to comment). Even after the acquisition has been made public the formula adopted is that the Secretary of State for Trade decides 'on the information at present before him' not to refer the proposed merger to the MMC. The words 'on the information at present before him' are intended to enable the Secretary to refer the merger if circumstances change. A decision is normally made within three weeks of the public announcement but the authorities are not always able to meet this deadline.

United Kingdom competition law

It is possible for an acquisition agreement to fall under the control of the Restrictive Trade Practices Act 1976. This Act applies to agreements or arrangements between two or more persons carrying on business within the United Kingdom in the processing, production or supply of goods, under which any two or more parties accept relevant restrictions. These include restrictions on prices or conditions of purchase and supply, restrictions as to the quantities or descriptions of goods produced and, of particular relevance in the acquisition context, covenants not to compete with a particular person or business. There is a parallel, and quite separate, system of control of agreements relating to services. The exchange of price information on goods (but not services) is also controlled.

The Restrictive Trade Practices Act only applies where two or more parties accept (ie undertake the burden of performing) restrictions. Consequently, an acquisition agreement under which the only restriction is a covenant by a sole vendor not to compete with the business he has sold will not be controlled by the Act. Such a covenant should not, of course, be unreasonable in scope or duration or it will be invalid at common law as being in restraint of trade. Multiple covenants by more than one vendor are, however, liable to be caught by the Act. To deal with this anomaly, new orders will exempt from this Act acquisition agreements containing vendors' covenants of reasonable duration. As no other restriction is allowed, these exemptions must be used with care.

If the Act does apply, particulars of the agreement must be furnished under Form RTP(C) (obtainable from the Office of Fair Trading) to the Director General of Fair Trading before the relevant restrictions take effect or, if their coming into force is delayed, within three months of the date of the agreement. Failure to do so renders the restrictions themselves void, gives a right of action to any injured third party and entitles the Director General of Fair Trading to apply to the Restrictive Practices Court for an order against the parties operating that agreement and any other agreement, particulars of which have not been furnished.

If particulars are duly furnished, the Director General will place the agreement on the register of restrictive agreements. Once this is done, he is obliged to refer the agreement to the Restrictive Practices Court unless:

(*a*) an EEC exemption or authorisation applies to the agreement, in which case the Director General has a discretion not to make a reference;

(*b*) the agreement has expired or been terminated;

(c) all the relevant restrictions have been removed (known as 'filleting' the agreement); or

(d) the restrictions are too insignificant to justify a reference. Here the Director General must obtain the approval of the Secretary of State for Trade.

One possible trap is that the removal of restrictions on only one of two parties who accept them does not render a registered agreement safe even though, as amended, it becomes an agreement with only one party accepting restrictions and thus would not have been registrable at all if originally executed in this form. The effect of this may be mitigated if, with the removal of the restrictions, the remaining restrictions are too insignificant to justify a reference.

Attempting to justify to the Restrictive Practices Court non-competition covenants in an acquisition agreement is not a profitable occupation for the parties. Restrictions are presumed to be against the public interest; the so-called 'gateways' through which restrictions must pass for the presumption to be rebutted are narrow and a final balancing test must also be satisfied. The incentive to avoid a reference to the court is strong as indeed should be the incentive to avoid falling within the scope of the Act at all. Multiple or mutual covenants not covered by the new exemptions and rendering the agreement registrable should therefore only be included after a scrupulous consideration of their utility.

Current proposals for reform of UK competition law include the complete repeal of the Restrictive Trade Practices Act and its replacement by an 'effects based' system more consistent with art 85 of the EEC Treaty. If implemented, this will radically alter the consideration of acquisition agreements from the point of view of UK competition law.

FINANCIAL ASSISTANCE BY THE TARGET

The Companies Act 1985, s 151 creates two offences relating to the giving of financial assistance in connection with acquisitions but allows a target, or its subsidiaries, to give financial assistance to a purchaser of the target's shares in a number of cases.

A substantial body of case law grew up around the predecessors to s 151, and in particular the Companies Act 1948, s 54, but because of the significant changes introduced by the Companies Act 1981 it is not safe to rely upon the previous authorities in connection with the interpretation of the present provisions. In one area, however, the authorities may continue to be of assistance. The civil consequences of breach of s 151 are not laid down by the Act so that, until he learns otherwise, it seems that the practitioner can reasonably proceed on the assumption that the law relating to the civil consequences of breach of the previous legislation will remain relevant.

One general point which should not be overlooked is that the articles of many companies will restate s 54 of the 1948 Act (see, eg, reg 10 of the pre-1981 Act Table A) and it may be necessary to change them before taking advantage of the new law.

The prohibitions

Subject to the exceptions which are dealt with below, s 151 provides that, where a person is acquiring or is proposing to acquire any shares in a company it shall not be lawful for the company or any of its subsidiaries to give financial assistance directly or indirectly for the purpose of that acquisition before or at the same time as the acquisition takes place (s 151(1)). It is further provided that, where a person has acquired any shares in a company and any liability has been incurred (by that or any other person) for the purpose of that acquisition, it shall not be lawful for the company or any of its subsidiaries to give any financial assistance directly or indirectly for the purpose of reducing or discharging the liability so incurred (s 151(2)).

'Financial assistance' is defined by s 152 as:

(a) financial assistance given by way of gift;

(b) financial assistance given by way of guarantee, security or indemnity, other than an indemnity in respect of the indemnifier's own neglect or default, or by way of release or waiver;

(c) financial assistance given by way of a loan or any other agreement under which any of the obligations of the person giving the assistance are to be fulfilled at a time when in accordance with the agreement any obligation of any other party to the agreement remains unfulfilled or by way of the novation of or the assignment of any rights arising under any loan or such other agreement; or

(d) any other financial assistance given by a company the net assets of which are thereby reduced to a material extent or which has no net assets.

For this purpose 'net assets' is defined by s 152(2) as the aggregate of the company's assets less the aggregate of its liabilities (including provisions as liabilities).

The first offence created by s 151, namely the giving of financial assistance for the purpose of an acquisition before, or at the same time as the acquisition takes place, is fairly easy to recognise. Clearly, if the purchase price of the target's shares is provided by the target, or by one of its subsidiaries, in one of the transactions defined to be financial assistance, then the section will be contravened. In practice, however, it is not these cases which give rise to problems. Far more common is the case in which the purchaser, whether by raising a loan or otherwise, incurs a future payment liability in order to take over the shares of the target and then, after the acquisition is completed and the target is under the purchaser's control, wishes to procure that the target enters into some transaction which has the effect of providing the purchaser with funds to meet the liability so incurred. It is this type of transaction which is specifically struck down by s 151(2) which provides that the target is forbidden to give financial assistance directly or indirectly for the purpose of reducing or discharging a liability incurred for the purpose of acquiring its shares.

For the purpose of s 151(2) any reference to a person incurring a liability is very widely defined, as by s 152(3), it must be read as including a reference to his 'changing his financial position by making any agreement or arrangement (whether enforceable or unenforceable and whether made on his own account or with any other person) or by any other means'. It is further provided that a reference to a company giving financial assistance for the purpose of reducing or discharging a person's liability is to be read as including a reference to the company giving financial assistance for the purpose of wholly or partly restoring the person's financial position to what it was before the acquisition took place. Read literally this could mean that a company which expends cash on an acquisition may not borrow from its new subsidiary after the acquisition if the purpose of the borrowing is to restore the financial position of the purchaser 'wholly or partly'. In such a case, of course, the provisions of s 153(2) will often be relevant (see p 20).

It may be helpful to envisage transactions which are caught by s 151, in a case in which a purchaser raises a loan to acquire the target's shares. If the target, or its subsidiary, in turn makes a loan to the purchaser and the proceeds are used to discharge the loan raised by the purchaser, then, if the purpose of the target's loan was to enable this to be done, the section will clearly be contravened. It is with less obvious cases that the difficulties arise. For example, it used to be thought that it was possible for a purchaser to sell assets to the target subsequent to an acquisition and use the purchase price to discharge a loan raised for the purchase of the target's shares. It was considered that, if the price paid by the target for the assets injected by the purchaser was fair, then there was no financial assistance given within the meaning of the Companies Act 1948, s 54. These ideas were changed when the point came before the court in *Belmont Finance Corp Ltd* v *Williams Furniture Ltd (No 2)* [1980] 1 All ER 393. In that case it was held that all parties to the sale of assets considered the price to be fair (although, as events turned out, the assets were bought by the target at a very substantial over value). In the Court of Appeal, Buckley LJ said (at p 402):

If [the target] buys something from [the purchaser] without regard to its own commercial interests, the sole purpose of the transaction being to put [the purchaser] in funds to acquire shares in [the target], this would, in my opinion, clearly contravene the section, even if the price paid was a fair price for what is bought, and a fortiori that would be so if the sale to [the target] was at an inflated price.

The judge went on to say that if the transaction was in the genuine commercial interests of the target, the fact that the target entered into the transaction partly with the object of putting the purchaser in funds to acquire its own shares or with knowledge of the purchaser's intended use of the proceeds might involve no contravention of the section, but he did not wish to express a concluded opinion on that point.

Unless the transaction falls within one of the specified categories of financial assistance in s 152, it seems that s 151 will not be infringed. The sale of assets by purchaser to target is not specifically prohibited and, so long as the assets are acquired at the same time as, or before, they are paid for (thus avoiding the effect of para (*c*) of the definition), such a transaction could fall only within para (*d*) as being 'any other financial assistance given by a company the net assets of which are thereby reduced to a material extent or which has no net assets'. It seems to follow that, if the price is fair (so that the net assets of the target are not reduced to a material extent by virtue of the transaction), such a sale will not amount to financial assistance. If, on the other hand, the assets are sold at a substantial over value so that the net assets of the target are thereby materially reduced, the transaction will be financial assistance and it will not matter if the parties believe the price to be fair (although, if the giving of financial assistance is not the main purpose of the transaction the parties' belief may be relevant for the purpose of considering whether or not it falls within the exemption given by s 153(2)) (as to which, see below).

If the liabilities of the target exceed its assets, all forms of financial assistance are forbidden whether or not they worsen the company's financial position and so, in the case of a purchase of assets by the target, it seems, on the assumption that the *Belmont* case is at least persuasive authority, that the fairness of the price will not be relevant in determining whether or not financial assistance is given. One or more of the exemptions may, of course, still be available.

If the target sells assets to the purchaser on terms that the purchase price is to be paid at some future date, it seems clear that the target will have given financial assistance because it will have fulfilled its obligations under the contract of sale 'at a time when in accordance with the agreement any obligation of any party to the agreement remains unfulfilled' (s 152(1)(*a*)(iii)). This transaction would appear to amount to financial assistance even though the price paid for the target's assets is equal to or exceeds fair market value. It is not thought that the giving of promissory notes or other forms of future payment obligation by the purchaser necessarily takes the transaction outside s 152(1)(*a*)(iii).

Where a purchaser has existing borrowings at the time of the acquisition, and borrows also for the purpose of the acquisition, it is not safe to take financial assistance from the target in order to reduce the purchaser's borrowings, even if the loan raised for the acquisition is not thereby repaid. Such a transaction would have the effect of restoring the purchaser's financial position to what it was before the acquisition took place (s 152(3)), by reducing the total level of the purchaser's borrowings. On the same basis, a transaction which would otherwise fall within the section does not escape merely because the purchaser has repaid the loan raised for the acquisition at some time before he receives the financial assistance from the target.

It is interesting to note that s 151(2) is only contravened if the financial assistance is given directly or indirectly 'for the purpose of reducing or discharging the liability' incurred in connection with the acquisition. Suppose the target were to give a guarantee, or otherwise to secure a loan raised by the purchaser for the purpose of the acquisition. This would not normally reduce or discharge the liability unless and until the guarantee was called or the security enforced and accordingly would, in a normal case, not be given 'for the purpose of reducing or discharging the liability'. The giving of a guarantee or security is specifically defined to be financial assistance by virtue of s 152, but it is not, on the face of it, easy to see that the giving of a guarantee or security *after* the acquisition is necessarily in breach of the section. The safe view, however, is that such a guarantee or security is prohibited by the section and such a transaction could well be attacked on other grounds, if it were not in the interests of the target.

The exceptions

Section 153 provides a number of exceptions to the prohibitions against giving financial assistance. So long as the assistance is given in good faith in the interests of the company, then no offence is committed if the company's principal purpose in giving the assistance is not to give it for the purpose of the acquisition. This exception also applies if 'the giving of the assistance for that purpose is but an incidental part of some larger purpose of the company'. A similar exception applies to the prohibition against giving assistance to reduce or discharge a liability incurred for the purpose of the acquisition.

In *Brady* v *Brady* [1988] 2 WLR 1308 the House of Lords considered the meaning of the 'larger purpose' exception. The case involved the reconstruction of a group of family companies with a view to their division between two sides of the family. As part of the scheme, one of the companies transferred a substantial part of its assets in order to give financial assistance in connection with the purchase of its shares. It was argued, however, that the 'larger purpose' of the transfer was that of the company's freeing itself from a management deadlock and enabling it to function independently under new ownership. Lord Oliver of Aylmerton, delivering the judgment of the House of Lords, said, at p 1327:

> . . . if [s 151] is not, effectively, to be deprived of any useful application, it is important to distinguish between a purpose and the reason why a purpose is formed. The ultimate reason for forming the purpose of financing an acquisition may, and in most cases probably will, be more important to those making the decision than the immediate transaction itself. But 'larger' is not the same thing as 'more important' nor is 'reason' the same as 'purpose'. If one postulates the case of a bidder for control of a public company financing his bid from the company's own funds — the obvious mischief at which the section is aimed — the immediate purpose which it is sought to achieve is that of completing the purchase and vesting control of the company in the bidder. The reasons why that course is considered desirable may be many and varied. The company may have fallen on hard times so that a change of management is considered necessary to avert disaster. It may merely be thought, and no doubt would be thought by the purchaser and the directors whom he nominates once he has control, that the business of the company would be more profitable under his management than it was heretofore. These may be excellent reasons but they cannot, in my judgment, constitute a 'larger purpose' of which the provision of assistance is merely an incident. The purpose and the only purpose of the financial assistance is and remains that of enabling the shares to be acquired and the financial and commercial advantages flowing from the acquisition, whilst they may form the reason for forming the purpose of providing assistance are a by-

product of it rather than an independent purpose of which the assistance can properly be considered to be an incident.

As Lord Oliver said, the concept of a 'larger purpose' is not altogether easy to grasp, or to apply to any particular set of facts. However, it does seem helpful if the transaction which involves the financial assistance is desirable for its own sake, from the target's point of view. Where a target purchases assets from the purchaser following completion of the acquisition, and the purchaser utilises the purchase price to reduce or discharge a loan raised for the purpose of the acquisition then financial assistance will be given in breach of s 151 if the target's net assets are thereby reduced to a material extent. If, however, there are good business reasons for acquiring these assets it may be possible to show that it was not the principal purpose of the target to reduce or discharge the liability, but rather to acquire the assets in question. This could therefore be a larger purpose, of which the giving of financial assistance could be thought to be merely an incident. In practice, it would obviously be helpful to show that there are compelling reasons to justify the target in making this purchase even though its net assets would be thereby reduced. The cautious practitioner would advise that the transaction be sanctioned pursuant to s 155 et seq where those sections can be brought into play.

In a typical vendor placing, the purchaser will make a payment to the bank or a broker who finds purchasers for the consideration shares which the purchaser issues to acquire the target. This is obviously financial assistance (although it is unlikely to reduce net assets to a material extent). It is suggested, however, that this would be a case where the company has a larger purpose, namely the acquisition of the target.

In addition to the exceptions which depend upon the motivation of the target, a number of transactions are (by s 153(3)) specifically exempted from the ambit of the section, irrespective of their purpose. These are:

    (*a*) a distribution of a company's assets by way of dividend lawfully made or a distribution made in the course of the company's winding up;

    (*b*) the allotment of bonus shares;

    (*c*) a reduction of capital confirmed by order of the court under the Companies Act 1985, s 137;

    (*d*) a redemption or purchase of shares made in accordance with the Companies Act 1985 Part V, Chapter VII;

    (*e*) anything done in pursuance of an order of the court under the

Companies Act 1985, s 425 (compromises and arrangements with creditors and members);

(*f*) anything done under an arrangement made in pursuance of the Companies Act 1985, s 582 (acceptance of shares by liquidator in winding up as consideration for sale of property); or

(*g*) anything done under an arrangement made between a company and its creditors which is binding on the creditors by virtue of the Companies Act 1985, s 60 (winding up imminent or in progress).

Of course, the dividend restrictions contained in the Companies Act 1985, Part VIII reduce the scope for paying substantial dividends in order to give financial assistance in connection with an acquisition. Practitioners should also bear in mind that payment of an abnormal dividend following an acquisition may have adverse tax consequences (see p 115).

Three further exceptions are also contained in s 153, namely:

(*a*) where the lending of money is part of the ordinary business of the company, the lending of money by the company in the ordinary course of its business;

(*b*) the provision by a company in accordance with an employees' share scheme of money for the acquisition of fully-paid shares in the company or its holding company (with a further exception for the purpose of facilitating transactions in shares); and

(*c*) the making by a company of loans to persons, other than directors, employed in good faith by the company with a view to enabling those persons to acquire fully-paid shares of the company or its holding company to be held by themselves by way of beneficial ownership.

None of these exceptions will, of course, have any relevance in the normal acquisition. For an attempt, which failed, to raise the first exception as a defence under the old s 54, see *Steen* v *Law* [1963] 3 All ER 770.

Relaxation for private companies

Section 155 et seq provides a 'whitewash' procedure to enable financial assistance to be given by private companies in cases which would otherwise be prohibited by s 151.

The following conditions must be satisfied:

(1) The assistance must be given by a private company in connection with the acquisition of its own shares or, if it is a

subsidiary of another private company, in connection with the acquisition of shares in that holding company (s 155(1)).

(2) The net assets of the company giving the assistance must not be reduced by giving the assistance or, to the extent that those assets are thereby reduced, the financial assistance must be provided out of distributable profits (s 155(2)). 'Distributable profit' is defined for this purpose by s 152(1)(*b*) and 'net assets' is defined by s 154(2) by reference to the company's accounting records. This restriction may well give rise to difficult decisions, particularly where the financial assistance is given by way of loan, guarantee or asset purchase. In many cases the attitude of the auditors will, in practice, be decisive.

(3) The procedure will not apply where the company is giving financial assistance in connection with the acquisition of shares of its holding company, and the company is also a subsidiary of a public company which is itself a subsidiary of that holding company (s 155(3)).

(4) The giving of the financial assistance must be approved by special resolution of the company, unless it is a wholly-owned subsidiary. It follows that a special resolution will not be required if all the shares of a private company target are acquired and financial assistance subsequently given by the target or its wholly-owned subsidiaries (s 155(4)). It may, however, be necessary to change the articles (see p 16).

(5) Where the acquisition of shares in question is or was an acquisition of shares in a holding company, that holding company and any intermediate holding company must also approve the transaction by special resolution. This does not apply to any company which is a wholly-owned subsidiary (s 155(5)).

(6) The directors of the company proposing to give the financial assistance (and, where the shares to be acquired are shares in its holding company, the directors of the holding company and of any intermediate holding company) must make a statutory declaration in the prescribed form which must give particulars of the assistance, identify the person to whom the assistance is to be given, and state that the directors have formed the opinion, as regards the company's initial situation immediately following the date on which the assistance is proposed to be given, that there will be no ground on which their company could then be found to be unable to pay its debts; and either:

(*a*) if it is intended to commence the winding up of the company within twelve months of that date, that the company will be able to pay its debts in full within twelve months of the commencement of the winding up; or

(*b*) in any other case, that the company will be able to pay its debts as they fall due during the year immediately following that date (ss 155(6) and 156).

The auditors of the company must enquire into the state of affairs of the company and report that that they are not aware of anything to indicate that the directors' opinion is unreasonable in the circumstances. The auditors' report must be annexed to the declaration (s 156(4)). Although the prescribed form does not contemplate it, there seems no reason why the directors should not make separate declarations.

(7) The financial assistance must not be given earlier than four weeks after the passing of any necessary special resolution (or the last of them) unless every member entitled to vote votes in favour (s 158(2)). This is a slightly odd formulation. The delay is presumably intended to give time for an application to the court under s 157. As holders of non-voting shares as well as the holders of voting shares may apply to the court within the four week period, an application could still be made even if all votes had been cast in favour. Moreover, the application must be made by the holders of not less than 10 per cent in nominal value of the issued share capital who did not vote in favour, so a single vote against could mean a delay of four weeks even though there is no possibility of an application to the court. The assistance cannot be given after the expiry of the period of eight weeks beginning with the date on which the statutory declaration (or the earliest of them) is made (s 158(4)).

(8) Any necessary special resolution must be passed on the same day as the making of the statutory declaration or within one week thereafter (s 157(1)).

(9) The declaration must be available for inspection by members of the company at the meeting at which the resolution is passed (s 157(4)), or the resolution is not effective. The declaration must be delivered to the Registrar of Companies with a copy of the special resolution (s 156(5)).

Section 157(2) permits an application to the court to cancel a special resolution if made by the holders of not less in the aggregate than 10 per cent in nominal value of the company's issued share capital or any class thereof, or, if the company is not limited by shares, by not less than 10 per cent of the company's members (but anyone voting in favour of, or consenting, to the resolution is not entitled to make the application). Substantial penalties are laid down for directors who make declarations without having reasonable grounds for the opinions contained therein.

Consequences of breach

Section 151 provides substantial criminal penalties for breach. If a company acts in contravention of the section, the company is liable to a fine and every officer of the company in default is liable, upon conviction on indictment, to imprisonment for up to two years, or a fine, or both.

It is reasonable to suppose that the civil consequences of breach will be similar to the consequences of contravening s 54 of the 1948 Act. These were severe. Those who were party to a breach could be called upon to compensate the company. The action could be brought either under the head of the tort of conspiracy or as a breach of a constructive trust (*Belmont Finance Corp Ltd* v *Williams Furniture Ltd* [1978] 3 WLR 712). The company could sue, even though it was a party to the conspiracy, if the essence of the transaction was to deprive the company improperly of part of its assets. An individual minority shareholder could sue on behalf of the company (*Wallersteiner* v *Moir* [1974] 1 WLR 991).

After some judicial dispute it was settled that security given in breach of the section was invalid (see *Victor Battery Co* v *Curry's* [1946] 1 Ch 242; *Selangor United Rubber Estates* v *Cradock (a bankrupt) and others (No 3)* [1968] 2 All ER 1073; and *Heald* v *O'Connor* [1971] 2 All ER 1105). A guarantee of indebtedness incurred by the target in breach of the section was void unless it amounted to an indemnity which, on its proper construction, was intended to apply even if the loan were unenforceable (see *Yeoman Credit* v *Latter* [1961] 2 All ER 295 cited in *Heald* v *O'Connor* at p 1110).

Where an executory contract contemplated a breach of s 54 it might nevertheless have been enforceable if the transaction could be carried into effect without infringing the section (see *Southwestern Mineral Water Ltd* v *Ashmore* [1967] 2 All ER 953). In that case the target was to provide security, by way of a debenture, for the payment of the purchase price for its shares. Had the vendors been prepared to waive the term of the agreement requiring the issue of the debenture they would have been at liberty to enforce the contract. They were not so prepared, however, and as the debenture was an integral part of the arrangement it was held that the agreement was unenforceable on either side. See also *Brady* v *Brady* [1988] 2 WLR 1308.

EMPLOYEES

It is often a term of an acquisition that key employees of the target enter into service agreements with the target on completion of the acquisition. The Agreement for Sale, cl 4(D) (see p 167), takes account of this. By itself, the acquisition of the target will normally have no effect upon existing contracts of service between the target and its employees. The acquisition will not constitute a transfer of an undertaking as defined in the Transfer of Undertakings (Protection of Employment) Regulations 1981 (SI 1981 No 1794), and these will not therefore be considered. It is only in the rare case where a contract of service has a specific provision relating to a takeover of the target that the contract will be affected. However, the purchaser should have in mind that in the event of a change in employer (eg upon a transfer of employment between companies in a group, but no change in the terms of employment other than the names of the parties) there is a statutory requirement to inform employees so transferred of the nature of the change within one month (Employment Protection (Consolidation) Act 1978, s 4).

In addition to individual contracts of employment, the purchaser should also consider whether there are any collective agreements between the target and a trade union or trade unions and whether the trade union or trade unions are recognised. Recognition of trade unions cannot now be compelled by statute. In the event of the target proposing to dismiss employees by reason of redundancy the target is under a duty to consult independent trade unions recognised by it and to inform the Secretary of State in relation to proposed redundancies (Employment Protection Act 1975, ss 99 and 100, as amended by the Employment Protection (Handling of Redundancies) Variation Order 1979 (SI 1979 No 958) with effect from 1 October 1979).

It is commonplace for changes in the target's employees to take place after an acquisition. Such changes may involve dismissal of the target's employees either actually or constructively, eg, where terms of employment are changed without an employee's consent and the employee resigns, accepting the breach of his contract of employment. Unlawful dismissal may be unfair (as defined in the Employment Protection (Consolidation) Act 1978, ss 54 and 55) or wrongful, that is constituting a breach of the employee's contract of employment at common law. If the target's articles provide that an executive director ceases to be an executive director upon the termination of his directorship (eg by an ordinary resolution of the target pursuant to the Companies Act 1985, s 303) it has been held that it will nevertheless be a breach of his service contract if the target removed him from office as a director (see *Shindler* v *Northern Raincoat Co Ltd* [1960] 1 WLR 1038).

The reasons for changes in the target's employees may include a decision to reorganise the target's management structure, prompted by economic or technical considerations or there may be circumstances which justify dismissal by reason of redundancy as defined in the Employment Protection (Consolidation) Act 1978, s 81, as amended by the Employment Act 1982, Sched 2. Where redundancy is involved the target may become liable to make redundancy payments under the Employment Protection (Consolidation) Act 1978. As redundancy payments will be calculated by reference to the length of an employee's continuous employment and age, a purchaser contemplating redundancies will wish to have details of the employee's length of continuous employment, age and remuneration for the purpose of calculating the amount likely to be due, together with details of any collective agreements or other agreements relating to redundancy entered into by the target. In ascertaining the employee's length of continuous employment the purchaser will have in mind the provisions which deem service to have continued notwithstanding a change in employer, eg upon the change in ownership of a business or upon a transfer of employment between associated companies in a group (see the Employment Protection (Consolidation) Act 1978, ss 151 and 153(4) and Sched 13).

In order to avoid a claim of unfair dismissal, the purchaser will need to bear in mind the general provisions for fairness of dismissal contained in the Employment Protection (Consolidation) Act 1978, s 57, as amended by the Employment Act 1980, s 6. The extent to which the target as employer of the employees concerned has in the particular circumstances (including the size and administrative resources of the target's undertaking) acted reasonably or unreasonably in treating the reasons for dismissal as sufficient reasons for dismissing the employees concerned will be particularly relevant. Where the reason for the dismissal is redundancy, particular attention will need to be paid to the selection of employees who are to be made redundant, so that there may be no unfair dismissal on the ground of redundancy as contemplated by the Employment Protection (Consolidation) Act 1978, s 59.

Where there has been an unlawful dismissal of an employee, such as a senior employee of the target, it will be necessary to calculate the amount which the employee would recover if he sued the target for damages for wrongful dismissal or for compensation for unfair dismissal. The following summary may be of assistance.

Damages for wrongful dismissal

The calculation of damages for wrongful dismissal normally falls to be made in relation to an employee with a fixed term contract of employment. It is first necessary to ascertain the unexpired period of the contract of employment or, if the contract is not for a fixed term, the length of notice which according to the contract the employee would have been entitled to receive and serve, if his employment had not been prematurely terminated. The relevant period for the assessment of the quantum of damages is from the date of dismissal down to the first occasion upon which the contract can be terminated by the target without the occurrence of a condition precedent which has not occurred (eg misconduct or illness).

It is then necessary to ascertain the value of the employee's entitlement (including fringe benefits which the employer is contractually bound to provide) throughout the unexpired period of employment or notice period (see *Beach* v *Reed Corrugated Cases Ltd* [1956] 1 WLR 807; *Bold* v *Brough, Nicholson & Hall Ltd* [1964] 1 WLR 201 and *Lavarack* v *Woods of Colchester Ltd* [1967] 1 QB 278). If the employee is entitled to commission, this must be taken into account if dismissal would result in a breach of a contractual obligation to provide the employee with an opportunity to earn the commission (see eg *Newman (RS) Ltd, Re, Raphael's Claim* [1916] 2 Ch 309). Where the employee has lost the use of a car provided by the target for his private purposes as well as for business the employee is entitled to be compensated. One method of assessing such a loss is to calculate the cost of purchasing and running a comparable car for the unexpired period of the contract of employment or notice period as appropriate. Loss of pension rights will need to be calculated. The terms of the employee's contract of employment and any relevant pension scheme will need to be reviewed. Loss of pension rights may be calculated in numerous ways. For example, a broker may be requested to establish the capital cost of purchasing an annuity to cover the difference between the pension receivable by the employee if he had retired at the end of the fixed term contract of employment or notice period and the pension to which he is actually entitled. Generally compensation will not be due for injury to feelings and reputation (*Addis* v *Gramophone Co Ltd* [1909] AC 488).

The employee's prospective earnings (if any) over the remaining term of the contract of employment or notice period should then be calculated. The employee is of course under a duty to mitigate his loss and, if he takes proceedings against the target and damages are not to be reduced, he will have to show that he has made attempts to obtain suitable alternative employment. This is the most difficult of all figures to quantify in advance. Each case must be considered on its merits; for example, highly qualified technical personnel will probably find it easier to obtain alternative employment than executives of advancing age with no special qualifications. It may be that the target itself, or, where the purchaser is a company, some other company in the purchaser's group will make the employee an offer of alternative employment. It is hard to generalise, but it should be remembered that an employee is not bound to accept employment of a lower status (see *Yetton* v *Eastwoods Froy Ltd* [1967] 1 WLR 104). He is, however, under a duty to take reasonable steps to seek out other similar employment as quickly as possible and all benefits received from alternative employment actually obtained or which ought reasonably to have been obtained must be taken into account.

By deducting the amount which the employee can reasonably be expected to earn in alternative employment from the remuneration that he would have received under the contract of employment, a net total entitlement will be ascertained. It is then necessary to make a deduction from this amount to account for the accelerated payment. This can be done by obtaining a quotation from a suitable insurance company for the capital cost of an annuity to provide the resulting net entitlement for the remaining term of the contract of employment. This may be used as the working figure. Further amounts may be deducted from this capital sum in respect of the possibility of serious illness which would have resulted in a premature determination of the employment and the employee's national insurance contributions. Unemployment benefits will be deductible (*Westwood* v *Secretary of State for Employment* [1984] IRLR 209).

The incidence of taxation must be taken into account. In *British Transport Commission* v *Gourley* [1956] AC 185 the court ruled that the object of awarding damages should be to put the plaintiff in the same position as if the particular wrong had not occurred. Accordingly a deduction should be made for tax. The taxation of payments by way of compensation for loss of office is governed by the Income and Corporation Taxes Act 1988, ss 148 and 188, and the Finance Acts 1988, s 74. The first £30,000 of a compensatory payment is not subject to tax in the hands of the employee. Any part of a compensatory payment which exceeds £30,000 is taxable in full as earned income. Where the compensatory payment exceeds the tax-free limit, the case of *Shove* v *Downs Surgical plc* [1984] 1 All ER 7 suggests that an attempt should be made to estimate the net amount which would have been received by the employee after deduction of tax from gross income had he continued to be employed. The net amount would represent his actual loss. The liability to tax on the damages should be taken into account so that the actual amount received equals so far as possible the net or actual loss suffered.

Compensation for unfair dismissal

Calculation of the amount which a leaving employee would recover if he presented a claim to an industrial tribunal alleging unfair dismissal by the target and claiming compensation (as opposed to re-engagement or reinstatement) will be by reference to the provisions contained in the Employment Protection (Consolidation) Act 1978, Part V, especially ss 72–76.

In the event of a finding of unfair dismissal an industrial tribunal has jurisdiction to make the following awards. The figures below are derived from the Employment Protection (Increase of Compensation Limit) Order 1989, the Employment Protection (Variation of Limits) Order 1989 and the Unfair Dismissal (Increase of Limits of Basic and Special Awards) Order, both of which came into force on 1 April 1989. In the past these limits have been revised annually.

Basic award

This award is calculated in the same way as a redundancy payment on the basis of the employee's age, period of continuous employment and pay. The rules for calculating a week's pay are in the Employment Protection (Consolidation) Act 1978, Sched 14, as amended. The maximum week's pay which may be used for the calculation is £172 per week. The maximum entitlement under this head is £5,160. Where the dismissal relates to trade union membership, the amount of the basic award is subject to a minimum (Employment Act 1982, s 4).

Compensatory award

The compensatory award is such amount as the tribunal considers just and equitable having regard to the loss sustained by the employee insofar as that loss relates to the unfair dismissal. *Norton Tool Co Ltd* v *Tewson* [1973] 1 All ER 183 is one of the authoritative pronouncements on the calculation of such compensation. Under this head fall to be considered matters similar, but not identical to, those already considered in relation to an amount which the employee would recover if he sued the target successfully for wrongful dismissal. The assessment of loss is calculated by reference to criteria which include the immediate and future loss of remuneration, the loss related to the manner of the dismissal, the loss of protection in respect of unfair dismissal deriving from length of employment, expenses, pensions and loss of certain fringe benefits. The employee is under a duty to mitigate his loss and a deduction may be made accordingly. If the employee received social security benefit during a period which coincided with the period following his dismissal, then the tribunal will not deduct such benefit from the amount of its award but will warn the employer not to pay over to the employee a prescribed amount of the total award. The prescribed amount represents the tribunal's estimate of the social security benefits and other similar payments likely to have been received by the employee. The employer will subsequently receive a notice from the Secretary of State stating whether the prescribed amount is to be paid to him or to the employee (Employment Protection (Recoupment of Unemployment Benefit and Supplementary Benefit) Regulations 1977 (SI 1977 No 674) as amended by SI 1980 No 1608). The maximum sum payable in respect of a compensatory award is £8,925.

Additional award

A tribunal may make a further award where an employer has failed to comply with an order to reinstate or re-engage the employee or where there has been a finding of an unfair dismissal for certain reasons (eg trade union activities). The maximum entitlements are £4,472 and £8,944 (Employment Protection (Consolidation) Act 1978 s 71).

Special award

A special award may be made where the dismissal relates to trade union membership (Employment Act 1982, s 5). The award is 104 weeks' pay or £12,550 whichever is the greater, subject to a maximum of £25,040. Where there is failure to reinstate or re-engage and the employer cannot show that it was impracticable to comply with the award, the tribunal may award up to £18,795 or 156 weeks' pay (the amount of which is not limited for this purpose) whichever is the greater.

Since certain of the items taken into account in calculating the compensation payable following an unfair dismissal will be the same as those taken into account in calculating the amount which the employee would recover if he sued the target for wrongful dismissal, an appropriate deduction may be made from the latter calculation. There is authority for the view that redundancy payments should be deducted from damages for wrongful dismissal but the position with regard to unfair dismissal compensation is not entirely clear. (See, eg, *Stocks* v *Magna Merchants Ltd* [1973] 1 WLR 1505 and *Basnett* v

Jackson (J & A) Ltd [1976] ICR 63). The amount of a basic award will be reduced by the amount of any redundancy payment award made by an industrial tribunal in respect of the same dismissal or in respect of any payment made by the employer to the employee on grounds that the dismissal was by reason of redundancy (Employment Protection (Consolidation) Act 1978, s 73(9)). If the amount of any payment made by the employer to the employee on the ground that the dismissal was by reason of redundancy exceeds the amount of any basic award which would be payable but for the above provision, that excess will go to reduce the amount of any compensatory award (Employment Protection (Consolidation) Act 1978, s 74(7)).

The calculation with regard to a claim for unfair dismissal will not have to be made at all if the leaving employee belongs to one of the classes excluded by statutory provision from having a right not to be unfairly dismissed (see the Employment Protection (Consolidation) Act 1978, ss 141 to 146). If a claim or claims by a leaving employee of the target are settled, then certain statutory provisions should be borne in mind. If it is contemplated that a payment by way of compensation for loss of office is to be made to a director, then the provisions of the Companies Act 1985, ss 312 to 316, will be relevant. Section 312 provides that a payment must be approved by the target in general meeting. Where the payment is made in connection with an acquisition, s 314 provides that unless it is approved by the selling shareholders before completion the payment will be held in trust for them by the director. The sections do not apply to a bona fide payment by way of damages for a breach of contract or by way of pension (including any 'superannuation gratuity or similar payment') (s 316(3)).

In *Taupo Totara Timber Co* v *Rowe* [1978] AC 537 the Privy Council held that an Australian equivalent of s 312 did not apply to payments to a director in connection with some employment held by him, nor to payments which the company was contractually bound to make. In addition, it may be relevant to consider the Companies Act 1985, s 320, which provides that a company shall not enter into an arrangement whereby the company acquires one or more non-cash assets of the requisite value from a director or connected person unless the arrangement is first approved by resolution of the company in general meeting. Having reference to the definitions of 'non-cash asset' and 'the transfer or acquisition of a non-cash asset' in s 739, it is arguable that the discharge of the target's liability for damages for breach of contract could amount to the acquisition of a non-cash asset by the company. It is suggested, however, that s 320 will not apply in a normal case. If the payment and the acquisition are not independent of each other, the payment may not be deductible in calculating the taxable income of the target (see *Snook (James) & Co v Blasdale* [1952] 33 TC 244; *Peters (George) & Co v Smith* [1963] 41 TC 264; and *Smith (George J) & Co v Furlong* [1969] 45 TC 384), and may involve 'financial assistance' by the target in breach of the Companies Act 1985, s 151 (see p 15).

If it is made a provision of the settlement agreement with the leaving employee that he is precluded from presenting a complaint to or bringing any proceedings before an industrial tribunal, eg, for unfair dismissal, such a provision will be void (Employment Protection (Consolidation) Act 1978, s 140). Accordingly, regard should be had to the procedures available under the Act whereby a conciliation officer may be requested to 'take action' in connection with any agreement to refrain from presenting a complaint of unfair dismissal as a result of which such an agreement may not be void (see especially ss 134(3) and 140(2)(*d*).)

PENSIONS

Purchasers should pay close attention to any pension arrangements for the target's employees. The purchaser will be concerned primarily with the funding of the pensions already accrued and the future pension contribution rate. The purchaser may also be concerned as to how the pension benefits compare with those provided under any existing pension scheme of the purchaser, particularly if the target's employees are to be transferred to it. The vendor will be concerned with retaining, or obtaining good value for, any surplus in the pension scheme and may also be concerned with protecting the target employees' pension expectations, at least for past service.

There are two main types of funded pension schemes: final pay and money purchase. A final pay scheme provides for each year of pensionable service a pension from normal retirement age of a sixtieth or some other specified fraction of final pensionable pay, being the level of pensionable pay at or near retirement. A money purchase scheme provides whatever pension can be bought for the employee on retirement with the pension contributions paid by or in respect of him and the investment return on those contributions. In addition both types of schemes will usually provide life cover and other ancillary benefits.

As no particular level of benefits is guaranteed under a money purchase scheme the only past service liability which can arise is for outstanding contributions and expenses. Unless there are to be completion accounts, the purchaser should obtain appropriate warranties. The purchaser should also consider whether the likely future pension contributions, when compared with those paid in the past, will have any material effect on profits because, for example, the scheme has only recently been established or contributions have not been paid on a regular basis or the target employees are to be offered membership of a final pay scheme of the purchaser. The purchaser should seek a warranty from the vendor that there is no commitment (whether legally enforceable or not) to provide any employee with a specific level of benefits. Sometimes money purchase schemes are used simply as a funding vehicle for providing 'final pay' type benefits. This may be apparent from the scheme rules and explanatory literature but not necessarily so. If a specific level of benefits has been promised the same funding considerations which arise in relation to final pay schemes should be addressed.

With a final pay scheme the purchaser should ensure that the liabilities in respect of service up to completion are fully funded. It is first necessary to identify those past service liabilities. It is then necessary to consider whether the available assets are sufficient to fund them. Since under a final pay scheme all pensionable service ranks for pension based on final pensionable pay at retirement or earlier termination of employment, it is generally accepted that the past service liabilities should be calculated by reference to projected final pensionable pay not at completion but at retirement or earlier termination of employment.

If the past service liabilities were to be based on final pensionable pay at completion the purchaser would be faced with funding not only the pension referable to service after completion but also any increase in the pension referable to service up to completion which is attributable to pay increases after completion. This would result in a significant increase in the contribution rate after completion, whereas, generally the contribution rate is fixed at a level which is intended, all other things being equal, to remain reasonably stable throughout the employees' remaining working lives. For accounting purposes this is now a requirement (see SSAP 24: Accounting for Pension Costs).

At the time of the transaction the ultimate final pensionable pay of the employees will not, of course, be known. Likewise the investment return which will actually be obtained on the current scheme assets will also be unknown. Therefore, in order to ascertain whether the current assets are likely to be sufficient to fund the past service liabilities it is necessary to make assumptions as to the rate of future pay increases and investment return and also as to a host of other unknowns, such as mortality and the rate of withdrawals from service before retirement. In addition, the value placed on the assets may differ from the market value so as to avoid the results being distorted by short term fluctuations in the stock market which are not really material given the long term nature of pension liabilities. Allowance may also be made for benefits which have historically been provided on a discretionary basis, such as periodic increases to pensions in payment and enhanced early retirement terms. If a practice, albeit discretionary, has been established, the purchaser may find it necessary to maintain it in the interests of good employee relations.

If the target has its own scheme, then whether or not the past service liabilities are fully funded can be determined by comparing the respective values of the past service liabilities and the scheme assets. Unless an actuarial valuation of the scheme has been completed recently or the scheme is relatively small, it is unlikely that there will be sufficient time prior to exchange to establish the position. The agreement for sale should therefore provide for an actuarial valuation of the scheme to be carried out after completion and for the vendor to make good any deficiency. The agreement should specify the actuarial assumptions and methods to be used. Expressions such as 'reasonable assumptions' are too vague to be meaningful. A provision along these lines is preferable to a funding warranty as it quantifies the vendor's liability.

Whether the vendor agrees to such a provision is, of course, a matter for negotiation. If the scheme is in deficit the vendor may argue that the contributions have been paid as recommended by the actuary and that any part of the contributions which are being paid to fund a previously discovered deficiency should, like salaries, be regarded as part of the liabilities of the target being acquired on an 'ongoing concern' basis: furthermore they will have been reflected in the accounts. Even if it is conceded that a valuation provision should be included, the actuarial assumptions and methods are likely to be the subject of much negotiation. A small difference in the assumptions may have a very significant effect. As the financial implications are unlikely to be apparent to the principals, the actuary should be asked to quantify as well as he can on the information available any differences which may become the subject of horse trading at the end of the day.

The vendor may also argue that any deficiency payment paid to the purchaser should be reduced to allow for any corporation tax relief which the target would obtain on paying an amount equal to the deficiency into the scheme (this relief may be spread over a period of up to five years if the deficiency exceeds the greater of £20,000 and the target's ordinary annual pension contributions — see IR12 (1979), para 5.4). The target should make any payment into the scheme. Corporation tax relief may not be available to the purchaser or the vendor if they make payments directly into the scheme as the payment would not be in respect of their own employees.

The vendor may argue for any surplus to be reflected in the purchase price. This is probably the only way in which he can obtain any benefit from it. Any attempt by the vendor to take over the target's scheme and then expel the target and its employees is likely to fail (*Re Courage Group Pension Schemes* [1987] 1 All ER 528).

If the target participates in a group 'final pay' scheme of the vendor it will be necessary to make alternative pension arrangements for the target employees and to arrange for a transfer from the vendor's scheme to their new scheme. The Inland Revenue will not allow the target to continue in the vendor's scheme on an indefinite basis after the target ceases to be a subsidiary of the vendor.

Typically the vendor's scheme rules will provide for the scheme to be partially wound up on the target ceasing to participate in it. Alternatively, the rules may just provide for leaving service benefits to be paid. A partial winding up involves the segregation of a portion of the scheme assets. The scheme rules will usually provide for the portion to be determined by the trustees or the actuary but sometimes the vendor as the principal employer under the scheme will also be involved. If an actuary is involved he should aim to achieve the greatest possible degree of fairness between the parties (*Re George Newnes Group Pension Fund* [1969] 98 J Inst of Actuaries 251). There are numerous methods which may be used to calculate the relevant portion including:

(*a*) the leaving service method which involves valuing the past service liabilities based on current final pensionable pay;

(*b*) the past service reserve method which involves valuing the past service liabilities allowing for future pay increases; and

(*c*) the share of fund method which involves dividing all the scheme assets between the continuing and leaving members in proportion to the respective values of their benefits.

The actuarial assumptions used may have a very significant effect on the results, particularly with leaving service and past service reserve methods.

The various methods were considered, obiter dictu, in *Re Imperial Food Limited Pension Scheme* [1986] 2 All ER 802. Under the Imperial scheme the employees' contributions were fixed and the employers' contributions varied according to what was required to meet the balance of the cost of the benefits. Two subsidiaries were sold and at the time the scheme was in surplus, the value of the scheme assets exceeded the value of the past service liabilities. The scheme rules provided for the segregation of such portion of the fund as the actuary considered appropriate. He used the past service reserve method. It was contended that he should have used the share of fund method, which would have produced a larger amount. The case was decided on the narrow point that the actuary's valuation could not be impeached as the method used was one which could be used by a competent actuary and there had been no mistake or improper motive. Walton J, in any event, considered that the past service reserve method adequately provided for the entitlements and expectations of the separating employees and strongly supported its use. He regarded the share of fund method as inappropriate because it involved applying part of the surplus (which he referred to as 'temporary surplus funding by the employing company') for the benefit of the separating employees, whereas the rights of the members under a continuing scheme are the same whether it is in surplus, strict balance or deficit. He considered that 'provided that the company is financially sound and there is no question of a discontinuance of the fund' the past service reserve method was appropriate in all three cases (although, if in deficit, it would be necessary for the actuary to be satisfied as to the strength of the company's covenant to contribute). The argument that out of fairness to the subsidiaries surplus should be made available as they had contributed towards it, was rejected as the financial position of the companies was not a relevant consideration and, even if it was, the subsidiaries' contributions had been at the ultimate expense of the parent company.

The judge did not say that a competent actuary could not use the share of fund method and so it appears that it is still open to a purchaser to argue for a share of any surplus.

Given the uncertainty as to the position under the vendor's scheme the purchaser should ensure that the agreement for sale specifies the method and assumptions to be used to calculate the transfer amount and contains a commitment from the vendor to pay or procure the payment of the same. The purchaser would not then be concerned as to the adequacy of the funding of the vendor's scheme or how any discretions under it are exercised. While any lesser commitment from the vendor may be commercially unacceptable to the purchaser, the vendor should bear in mind that the vendor's scheme trustees are independent of the vendor and are not bound to give effect to the pension provisions in the sale agreement. Any assurance from the trustees that they will make the proposed transfer would not be binding on them as it would be given before the transfer power becomes exercisable on the target ceasing to participate in the vendor's scheme. It may, however, be possible to commit the trustees by a formal alteration to their rules, although this would be unusual.

In order to reduce its exposure the vendor should require the amount payable by it to make good any shortfall in the payment (if any) made by the vendor's scheme trustees to be reduced to allow for any tax relief (see p 35) and also for any benefits retained in the vendor's scheme for the employees concerned.

Similarly, to cover the situation where the vendor's scheme trustees decide to pay more than that specified in the acquisition agreement, the vendor may seek a commitment from the purchaser to pay to the vendor an amount equal to any excess payment. Such a commitment would also deter the purchaser putting the target's employees up to claiming that they are entitled to a larger transfer under the vendor's scheme rules than provided for in the acquisition agreement.

The position is simpler where the group scheme of the vendor is a money purchase arrangement. The purchaser should, however, ensure that all employees are provided with vested benefits even if they have not qualified for them under the preservation requirements of the Social Security Act 1973 because they have completed less than two years of qualifying service. Unless within one year of normal pension age (or under normal pension age if below sixty) the target employees will have a statutory right to have their accumulated fund transferred to a new scheme (Social Security Pensions Act 1975, Sched 1A).

Usually the target continues participating in the vendor's scheme for a limited period following completion while alternative pension arrangements are made for the target's employees. The Inland Revenue will normally readily agree to a transitional period of up to a year. If the vendor's scheme is contracted-out of the state earnings related pension scheme it will be necessary for the target to obtain its own contracting-out certificate if previously it has been included in a holding company certificate of the vendor. Both the purchaser and the vendor may seek to include certain protective provisions in the sale agreement: the purchaser against the target being called upon to make payments other than reasonable contributions and expenses to the vendor's scheme and also against the benefits applicable to the target employees under the vendor's scheme being changed, and the vendor against the target causing any undue increase to the liabilities under the vendor's scheme. In this respect the vendor will, for example, be vulnerable if pay increases granted during the transitional period would rank for benefits under the vendor's scheme or if enhanced early retirement terms apply in the event of, eg, redundancy.

Where there is a transitional period in connection with a final pay scheme the past service liabilities can be calculated either as at completion or as at the end of the transitional period. The later date is simpler because it avoids the need for any adjustments in respect of the transitional period for investment return, contributions, the cost of insuring death in service benefits and other expenses; however, the earlier date helps to insulate each party from the effects of the other's acts after completion.

If any of the target's employees leave service during the transitional period a notional profit may accrue to the vendor's scheme, the profit being the amount (if any) by which the value of the transfer payment which would have been made in respect of the employee if he had remained in service and joined the new scheme exceeds the value of leaving service benefits. In the Imperial case Walton J described as 'totally absurd' a proposal that profits of that nature should be transferred to the new scheme since they relate to employees who never have anything to do with the new scheme.

On the target ceasing to participate in the vendor's scheme the employees will usually acquire a statutory right to a transfer value (based on their current final pensionable pay) which they may exercise by having it paid to the new scheme or, if they prefer, to a personal pension scheme or annuity policy. If the transfer to the new scheme is made without the statutory right being exercised, that right will also be transferred and will thereafter be exercisable against the new scheme trustees. Generally, the legislation does not prevent transfers being made in respect of employees in service without their consents where this is permitted under the scheme rules. The vendor's scheme trustees may, however, wish to protect themselves by requiring consents. In any event the employees' consents will be required to the deduction from pay of their contributions (if any) to the new scheme unless the deduction is authorised by their employment contracts (see Wages Act 1986, s 1).

It is beyond the scope of this book to delve into the technicalities of Inland Revenue approval and contracting-out of the state earnings related pension scheme. Suffice it to say both parties will need to take care to ensure that these requirements are met.

In addition to any funded pension schemes the target may have unfunded contractual commitments to provide pension benefits (eg under a service agreement). Unless these simply take the form of a promise to contribute to a personal pension scheme which the member has joined the contract should be approved by the Inland Revenue under s 591 of the Income and Corporation Taxes Act 1988. The target may also be providing pensions on a discretionary basis. The amount of damages payable in the event of a breach of warranty that there are no discretionary pensions is uncertain bearing in mind that, by definition, the pensions are determinable at will. The purchaser should therefore seek to provide in the agreement for sale that in calculating the loss flowing from any breach of warranty the target is deemed to be under a liability to continue any discretionary pensions.

The pensions checklist set out below will require adaptation to each particular case. It does not purport to be exhaustive but is designed to highlight some of the principal areas of potential concern to the purchaser. It is suggested that enquiries on the items listed should be made at the earliest possible stage, since the information obtained may enable the purchaser and its advisers to form a preliminary view of the state of the scheme or schemes and, in particular, to see if there are any obvious queries as to its funding. The purchaser should normally obtain actuarial advice and the checklist is not in any way suggested to be a substitute for such advice.

PENSIONS CHECKLIST

This checklist relates to every scheme or arrangement to which the target or any of its subsidiaries is a party and which provides 'relevant benefits' as defined by the Income and Corporation Taxes Act 1988, s 612, for any one or more present or former directors or employees or for their widows, widowers, children or dependants. The details listed below should be obtained in respect of each such scheme separately. Details of any ex gratia pensions should also be obtained.

1   Name of scheme

2   Documentation
2.1   Trust deeds and rules (including any amendments).
2.2   Explanatory literature.
2.3   Latest actuarial report.
2.4   Latest scheme accounts.
2.5   Letter of Inland Revenue approval.
2.6   Contracting-out certificate.
2.7   Memorandum and articles of association of any trustee company.
2.8   Insurance policies.

3   Scheme assets
3.1   List of scheme assets and their value.
3.2   Details of any self investment in target or vendor's group.

4   Membership data
4.1   List of members showing dates of birth, sex, pensionable service and pensionable earnings.

4.2 List of pensioners and deferred pensioners showing dates of birth, sex and pension entitlement.

5 Benefits
5.1 Discretionary increases to pensions in payment or in deferment over previous five years.
5.2 Other discretionary practices: redundancy, early retirement, long service bonus etc.
5.3 Any credit of additional pensionable service not fully vested.
5.4 Any backdating of pensionable service on joining the scheme for pension benefits.
5.5 Any benefit augmentations or special terms.
5.6 Do benefits accrue at a uniform rate or does the rate increase with age or length of service?
5.7 Are any employees provided only with life cover?

6 Contributions
6.1 Employer's contribution rate over previous five years.
6.2 Are contributions paid in arrears?
6.3 Anticipated future contribution rate.
6.4 Is the contracting-out incentive being paid?

7 Trustees
7.1 Names of the trustees.
7.2 In whom is the power of appointment and removal vested?
7.3 Who owns shares in any trustee company?

8 Employees
8.1 Does any employer (other than the target and its subsidiaries) participate in the scheme?

The checklist is, it is hoped, largely self-explanatory, but questions 5 and 6 require a special mention.

In question 5 it is important to ascertain full details of the benefits and discretionary practices so that the past service liabilities can be properly quantified. If pensionable service is backdated on joining the scheme there is a contingent liability in respect of employees who have not yet joined for which it can reasonably be argued that allowance should be made when determining the past service liabilities.

In question 6 the purchaser should know how the pension contributions have varied and the likely rate payable in future so that the effect on profits can be ascertained. If currently being paid the contracting-out incentive will be lost if the target's employees are transferred to a scheme which was contracted-out before 1 January 1986 (Social Security Act 1986, s 7).

SHARE PREMIUM ACCOUNT AND
PRE-COMBINATION PROFITS

In the context of acquisitions, the problems of share premium account and pre-combination profits have caused difficulty for many years. They are related problems and, before considering the law, it is necessary to understand their practical significance and why they are related. The merger relief now contained in the Companies Act 1985, s 131, resolves the problems in many cases but does not apply where, broadly speaking, less than 90 per cent of the target's equity share capital is owned by the purchaser after the acquisition. Having struggled to an understanding of the law, the practitioner then has to understand the accounting treatment of mergers and acquisitions, which, at the date of publication of this edition, is under review.

The Companies Act 1985, s 130, provides that where a company issues shares at a premium, whether for cash or otherwise, a sum equal to the aggregate amount or value of the premiums on those shares must be transferred to a share premium account. Once the share premium account has been set up, it cannot be used except for making bonus issues and paying certain expenses and may not be reduced without the consent of the court.

Shares are issued at a premium if they are issued for an amount in excess of their nominal value. When one company purchases the issued share capital of another in exchange for the issue of shares of the purchaser, then, on the assumption that the market value of the target's shares exceeds the nominal value of the consideration shares, the question will arise whether the consideration shares have been issued at a premium and, if so, what amount should be transferred to share premium account. Because of our accounting conventions, the question is directly related to the value at which the target's shares are brought into the purchaser's accounts. If the effect of s 130 is to oblige the purchaser to set up a share premium account of the difference between the nominal value of the consideration shares and the market value of the target's shares, it also means, in practice, that the purchaser is bound to bring the target's shares into its account at that same market value. This is called 'acquisition accounting'.

The purchaser may not wish to account for the transaction in this way because, on the assumption that the market value of the target's share capital is greater than the book value of the underlying net assets of the target, the difference will show up as goodwill in a consolidated balance sheet. This goodwill must then be written off against reserves (and share premium account is not available for this) or quantified through the profit and loss account, thus reducing reported profits.

In addition (and this is why the problem relates to the question of pre-combination profits), acquisition accounting may have the effect of reducing the ability of the purchaser to pay dividends. The purchaser's share capital will be enlarged by reason of the acquisition, while its distributable reserves will remain the same. Accordingly, the amount per share which may be distributed out of reserves will be decreased. The extra reserve produced by accounting for the acquisition on a valuation basis (ie taking the target's shares into the books at a valuation) is the share premium account and is not available for dividend. The fact that the target may have reserves available for dividend will not, of itself, affect the accounts of the purchaser and, if the new subsidiary pays dividends to the purchaser out of reserves which it had at the time of the acquisition, the purchaser will normally have to apply the proceeds to reduce the value of the target's shares in its accounts. Therefore, although payment of such a dividend may provide the purchaser with cash to fund a dividend of its own, it will not increase the purchaser's distributable reserves. Acquisition accounting can also produce an increased charge for depreciation.

Accounting for goodwill is dealt with in SSAP 22 and is in the course of amendment. The rules relating to the accounting treatment of mergers and acquisitions are contained in SSAP 23. Where 'merger accounting' is permitted, the purchaser can bring the target's shares into its accounts at the nominal value of the shares which it issues in exchange. Obviously this is only possible if the law permits, but the accounting rules are generally stricter than the legal requirements and sometimes require acquisition accounting where the law would permit merger accounting. Merger accounting is never mandatory, while the share premium account is a creature of statute. These issues are dealt with on p 46.

Share premium account

The law relating to share premium account is to be found in cases decided before the introduction of merger relief. In *Head (Henry) Ltd* v *Ropner Holdings Ltd* [1952] Ch 124 a holding company was formed to acquire the shares of two other companies whose share capital was taken by the holding company into its books at a valuation corresponding to that of the assets of the targets. The court held that the excess of the valuation over the nominal value of the consideration shares had to be credited to a share premium account. Harman J said (at p 128):

> Apparently, if the shares are issued for a consideration other than cash and the value of the assets acquired is more than the nominal value of the shares issued, you have issued shares at a premium.

This might be thought to be the end of the matter, but, before the decision in *Shearer (Inspector of Taxes)* v *Bercain Ltd* [1980] 3 All ER 295, there was a substantial body of legal opinion which contended that it was the directors of the purchaser who placed the fetters on their own wrists. Because the existence or otherwise of the share premium account arising as a result of an acquisition is directly related to the amount at which the target's shares are brought into the holding company's books, it follows, it was said, that it is the directors' decision as to that amount which is vital in determining the question. If the target's shares are brought in at an amount in excess of the nominal amount of the consideration shares, then the excess must indeed be credited to a share premium account; but there is no statutory provision which expressly requires the directors to bring the shares in at a valuation.

In *Craddock* v *Zevo Finance Co Ltd* [1944] 1 All ER 566 the Court of Appeal was asked to consider, for tax purposes, whether investments acquired by a dealing company in a reconstruction in exchange for the issue of shares should be brought into the purchaser's books at 'cost' (the nominal value of the consideration shares allotted) or at their market value (which was less). It confirmed the correctness of bringing the investments in at cost. Lord Greene MR said (at p 569):

> The propriety of the course adopted is manifest when the uncertainty as to the value of the investments . . . is borne in mind. It is, I think, true as a general proposition that, where a company acquires property for fully paid shares of its own, the price paid by the company is the nominal value of the shares. It is for those who assert the contrary to establish it, as could be done, for example, in the suggested case of a deliberately inflated valuation.

If the target's shares are brought in at an amount equal to the nominal value of the consideration shares it would not be consistent with any ordinary accounting practice to have a share premium account and it was therefore said to follow (because neither s 130 nor any other provision of the Act expressly requires the target's shares to be brought in on a valuation basis) that the section could not require a share premium account where the target's shares were, in fact, brought into the books at cost.

The difficulty with s 130 in the context of acquisitions is the difficulty that lies at the root of accounting for all acquisitions in exchange for the issue of shares. The shares which the purchaser issues as consideration for the acquisition are not, in its hands, money's worth (as Lord Greene pointed out in the *Zevo* case), and in truth, there is no cost to the purchasing company at all. The purchaser suffers an addition to its balance sheet 'liabilities' of the nominal amount of the consideration shares, but this liability is not one which the company can ever be called upon to meet unless it has assets available for the purpose. In a winding up, although the rights attaching to shares may require a division of surplus assets in a certain way, the mere number of shares in issue does not affect the amount of the assets which are available for distribution among the members.

Shearer (Inspector of Taxes) v *Bercain Ltd* [1980] 3 All ER 295 placed the matter beyond doubt. In that case an investment holding company acquired shares in two other companies valued at £96,000 in exchange for 4,100 shares of a nominal value of £1 each. It accordingly created a share premium account which, after deducting expenses, amounted to £91,717. It then received dividends from the two targets of £36,000, on receipt of which it wrote down the value of its investment in its subsidiaries from £96,000 to £59,950. The Revenue contended that these dividends could have been distributed by the holding company by way of dividend and raised a shortfall assessment. The holding company pleaded that under the relevant taxation legislation, it was subject to a 'restriction imposed by law' preventing distribution, in that it was obliged to create the share premium account and therefore had no distributable reserves. Walton J agreed, following *Head (Henry) Ltd* v *Ropner Holdings Ltd* and said (at p 301) that the matter would appear 'as plain as a pikestaff'.

Merger relief

The Companies Act 1985, s 131, excludes the application of s 130 where the company issuing the consideration shares

. . . has secured at least a 90 per cent equity holding in another company in pursuance of an arrangement providing for the allotment of equity of equity shares in that other company, or (*b*) by the cancellation of any such shares not held by the issuing company.

shares in the issuing company on terms that the consideration for the shares allotted is to be provided—(*a*) by the issue or transfer to the issuing company

'Arrangement' is defined by s 131(7) to mean 'any arrangement, scheme or arrangement (including an arrangement sanctioned in accordance with ss 425 or 582)'. The exemption also extends to cover shares issued, under the same arrangement, by the purchaser in exchange for the issue or transfer of non-equity shares in the target.

Accordingly, many share-for-share acquisitions will fall outside the terms of s 130 altogether and it will not be necessary (or indeed possible) to create a share premium account. Section 133 expressly provides that a sum corresponding to any amount representing premiums which, by virtue of s 131, is not included in the company's share premium account can also be disregarded in determining the amount at which any shares or other consideration provided for the shares issued is to be included in the company's balance sheet.

The purchaser is to be regarded as having secured at least a 90 per cent equity holding in the target in pursuance of an arrangement if as a result of any acquisition or cancellation of equity shares in the target in pursuance of that arrangement it holds equity shares in the target (whether all or any of those shares were acquired in pursuance of that arrangement or not) of an aggregate nominal value equal to 90 per cent or more of the nominal value of that company's equity share capital (s 131(4)). If the equity share capital of the target is divided into different classes, the section does not apply unless the requirements are satisfied in relation to each of those classes taken separately (s 131(5)). Equity share capital is defined by s 744 as any issued share capital except any part which, neither as respects dividends nor as respects capital, carries any right to participate beyond a specified amount in a distribution, and 'equity shares' is defined by s 131(7) as meaning shares comprised in equity share capital.

The accounting rules

The availability of merger relief means that merger accounting is possible, as a matter of law, in the majority of share-for-share acquisitions. However, the rules laid down in SSAP 23 are stricter. Merger accounting is only permitted if:
   (*a*) the business combination results from an offer to the holders of all equity shares and the holders of all voting shares which are not already held by the purchaser;

(b) the purchaser has secured, as a result of the offer, a holding of
   (i) at least 90 per cent of all equity shares (taking each class of equity separately) and
   (ii) shares carrying at least 90 per cent of the votes of the target;

(c) immediately prior to the offer, the purchaser did not hold
   (i) 20 per cent or more of all equity shares of the target (taking each class of the equity separately) or
   (ii) shares carrying 20 per cent or more of the votes of the target; and

(d) not less than 90 per cent of the fair value of the total consideration given for the equity share capital (including that given for shares already held) is in the form of equity share capital; and not less than 90 per cent of the fair value of the total consideration given for voting non-equity share capital (including that given for shares already held) is in the form of equity and/or voting non-equity share capital.

It will be noted that these rules differ from the merger relief rules set out in s 131. The purchaser who buys more than 20 per cent of the target's share capital for cash and then goes on to acquire the rest of the shares will qualify for merger relief under s 131 but will not qualify for merger accounting under SSAP 23. Conversely, the purchaser who buys less than 20 per cent of the target's share capital for shares and then goes on to acquire the rest for shares would not qualify for merger relief under s 131 on the first tranche of consideration shares issued, but only on the second. If the other conditions are met, however, merger accounting will be available.

If acquisition accounting is required in a case which qualifies for merger relief then a new, non-statutory reserve will be thrown up. Because this reserve is not share premium account it is possible to use it for writing off goodwill arising on consolidation.

One important point to note is that, where merger accounting is permitted, the consolidated accounts for the period in which the merger took place will show profits and losses of the target for the entire period without any adjustment in respect of that part of the period prior to the merger. Although this will not affect the legal position relating to dividends, it will of course have a significant effect upon the perceived results of the purchaser for the period.

Acquisition accounting will require that on consolidation the 'fair value' of the purchase consideration must be allocated between the underlying net tangible and intangible assets of the target. The Accounting Standards Committee has issued a lengthy discussion paper on this matter entitled *Fair Value in the Context of Acquisition Accounting*.

Pre-combination profits

The acquisition itself will not affect the ability of the target to pay dividends. If the target pays a dividend to its new holding company out of reserves arising from profits made prior to the acquisition, how is this dividend to be treated in the purchasing company's accounts? It is clearly a receipt of a capital nature and amounts to the partial realisation of a fixed asset.

Where acquisition accounting is used, pre-combination profits or losses of the target will be reflected in its assets at the time of the acquisition and, accordingly, distributions to the purchaser out of pre-combination profits will often be applied in the holding company's accounts to reduce the value of the target's shares. It may not, however, be appropriate to do this where it is unnecessary to provide for a diminution in the stated value of the target. If merger accounting is used it will rarely be necessary to provide for such a diminution. To the extent that it is not necessary to provide for a diminution in value of the shares of the target it appears that the amount of the distribution received will represent a distributable profit in the hands of the purchaser.

The general rule is that any surplus accruing on the realisation of a fixed asset can be distributed by way of a dividend so long as the value of the purchaser's remaining assets is fairly represented by, or in excess of, their book value (see *Lubbock* v *British Bank of South America* [1892] 2 Ch 198 and *Foster* v *New Trinidad Lake Asphalt Co* [1901] 1 Ch 208). Whether or not non-revenue profits can be distributed in any particular case is a matter legislated for by the articles of the company concerned, and by the Companies Act 1985, Part VIII. Section 280(3) includes realised capital profits in calculating profits available for distribution, except in the case of investment companies.

The Companies Act 1948, Sched 8, para 15(5), formerly contained a provision which was held, in *Shearer (Inspector of Taxes)* v *Bercain Ltd* [1980] 3 All ER 295, to prevent the distribution of pre-combination profits in any case, by providing that such profits must not be treated as revenue profits in the accounts of the holding company for any purpose. This restriction no longer applies.

In the case where acquisition accounting is used but merger relief is available, and the holding company credits to the investment the distribution paid out of the target's pre-combination profits, the question will arise as to whether an equivalent amount of the non-statutory merger reserve can be regarded as realised. This is a point on which there is, at present, no authority.

Chapter 2

Investigations and Warranties

The old common law rule of *caveat emptor*, although eroded beyond recognition in many fields, retains almost all its old force in relation to the acquisition of companies. Although the Financial Services Act 1986, s 47, provides that it is a criminal offence for any person to induce or attempt to induce another to enter into an agreement for the acquisition of securities by, inter alia, any dishonest concealment of material facts, it does not appear that any civil remedy based on the section (or its predecessors) has yet been awarded by the courts. No statutory provision implies into a contract for the acquisition of shares any term relating to the target's business and, although the Misrepresentation Act 1967, s 3, may have the effect of limiting the operation of clauses designed to exclude liability for misrepresentation, the provisions of the Unfair Contract Terms Act 1977 do not apply to any contract so far as it relates to the creation or transfer of securities (Sched 1, para 1 (*e*)). The ambit of this exception is not as clear as it might be, but it is generally thought that the parties to an acquisition are free to make their own bargain and the purchaser must do what he can, by investigation and contractual provision, to ensure that the target owns those assets that it is thought to possess and has no liabilities apart from those of which the purchaser is aware.

When a purchaser buys a business, as opposed to a company, it is at least theoretically possible to select the assets which he wishes to buy and the liabilities which he wishes to assume (but subject to the Transfer of Undertakings (Protection of Employment) Regulations 1981 (SI 1981 No 1794)). Although commercial considerations may require that, for the sake of maintaining the goodwill of the business, the purchaser accepts the liabilities of the business as they stand, these liabilities are taken over by contractual provisions which amount to an indemnity and which can be designed to exclude the liabilities which the purchaser does not want. A company, on the other hand, cannot so easily be fitted to the Procrustean couch. When a company is acquired, the liabilities of the target remain where they are unless creditors consent to their novation and no contractual provision between the vendor and purchaser can prevent the target being called to account for those liabilities after completion of the acquisition. Whatever warranties and indemnities the purchaser may take, the target is, and remains, liable to meet its obligations and no warranty or indemnity, however well drafted, will avoid the problem of obtaining reimbursement from a vendor who is unable or unwilling to pay. Even a retention of part of the purchase price as security for the warranties may not be adequate and will not recompense the purchaser for the loss of time involved in solving problems which he did not know he was inheriting.

Because a company is a person and has the capacity (only to some extent limited by its memorandum and articles of association) of freely incurring contractual, tortious, and even criminal liabilities, the purchaser's task of ascertaining the precise nature and quality of the assets, liabilities and profit potential of the target is by no means an easy one. His twin weapons are investigation and contractual protection, and it is with these that this chapter deals. In theory at least, nothing can afford complete protection and it is certainly true that neither investigation nor contractual protection on its own is satisfactory for the cautious purchaser. In practice, a balance is struck between the two, although much will depend upon the relative strength of the vendor and purchaser. The vendor who has suffered intensive investigations of the target will be less willing to give warranties and if time does not permit exhaustive investigations the purchaser will be more ready to insist upon wide ranging contractual protection. In cases where the executives of the target are not also substantial shareholders, problems can arise because those who can be expected to know about the target's affairs are, reasonably enough, reluctant to accept liability on warranties which may go far beyond the relatively small amount which they will realise from the transaction, while those who will realise a substantial amount claim that they cannot give warranties because they are unfamiliar with the target's affairs. In these cases investigation becomes of paramount importance.

It is worth making a general comment about the search against the target which the purchaser's solicitors will make at the Companies Registration Office as a matter of course. Incidentally, they will, if cautious, also make bankruptcy searches against individual vendors at the Land Charges Registry.

The company search should show an up-to-date copy of the memorandum and articles of association and should reveal the names of the directors and secretary and the names of the shareholders shown in the last annual return, together with any details of subsequent allotments of shares and particulars of any charges given by the target over its assets. The accuracy of the information given is not, however, guaranteed, because it is compiled by the target itself. To take an example, the file may be incomplete because of failure by the target to register changes in directors. Although this technically renders the officers of the target liable to a default fine, it gives no protection to a purchaser if it discovers after completion that the target has different or more directors than were thought. Neither will the information given necessarily be up to date, even though all relevant statutory provisions have been correctly complied with. For instance, the shareholders may have changed since the last annual return and, save in the case of fresh allotments, there is no obligation to bring the file up to date between returns. The position with regard to the registration of charges is dealt with on p 60.

It follows that, although the company search may provide useful information, it is merely an extract from a register which may be incorrect or out of date (without any infringement of the Companies Acts) and which affords no statutory protection to the share purchaser.

This chapter deals with accountants' investigations and reports, with some difficulties relating to the investigation of the target's title to its land, and, in general terms, with misrepresentation, warranty and indemnity. Taxation is a field apart and it is considered in Chapter 5.

THE ACCOUNTANTS' INVESTIGATION

Irrespective of whether the purchaser of the target is a listed company, it is quite usual for the former to instruct a firm of accountants, often the purchaser's auditors, to carry out an investigation into the target's affairs. The objective of such an investigation is to extract financial, commercial and administrative information from the target and to subject that information to close scrutiny so that the purchaser is provided with an expert, independent assessment of the target company and its activities.

A full acquisition report on a target company is not dissimilar from the type of report required by an issuing house which is sponsoring a company seeking a listing for its securities for the first time. In such a case, the issuing house requires a considerable amount of information regarding the company's affairs, both because it may be taking the risk of underwriting the issue and because of the need to preserve its reputation. However, these two types of report differ both from the accountants' report included in an acquisition circular issued to shareholders in accordance with the rules of The Stock Exchange and from that included in a prospectus. Both these latter reports are brief and are required to contain only a summary of the target's accounts covering a specified period, together with the accounting policies on which they have been based and the associated notes. They do not, for example, nor are they required to, include any commentary on how the company's profits were earned, whether it is sufficiently profitable, or what its future prospects might be.

The requirements for circulars relating to acquisitions are contained in The Stock Exchange's *Admission of Securities to Listing* (the *Yellow Book*), Section 6, Chapter 1. It should be noted that certain of the information required by the regulations relates to the acquiring company. In classifying an acquisition, and so determining which requirements have to be met, no distinction is generally made between acquisitions for cash and acquisitions for shares or other securities. Where, however, the acquisition would increase the shares of a class already listed by 10 per cent or more or debt securities of any amount are issued, then full listing particulars are required (see also Section 3, Chapter 1 and Section 6, Chapter 2).

The requirements of The Stock Exchange Council concerning accountants' reports are set out in Section 4 of the *Yellow Book*. In their report the accountants are required to express an opinion that the financial information given shows a true and fair view of the state of affairs of the target at the end of the period and of the results and source and application of funds for each of the periods reported upon.

Cases may arise in which the accountants reporting in respect of acquisitions are unable to report without qualification on the profits and net assets of the businesses of companies acquired, eg because of the absence of adequate records in regard to stock in trade and work in progress or other assets and liabilities. In such a case, the Council of The Stock Exchange reserves the right, before deciding to grant or maintain listing, to require that the approval of shareholders in general meeting be sought to any acquisition and will require this procedure in all cases in which it appears to the Council that the reporting accountants have been unable sufficiently to corroborate the amount of the net assets at the last balance sheet date or the amount and trend of profits for at least the last three years.

The Stock Exchange Council requires the information given in the accountants' report to be presented on the basis of historic cost accounting principles.

An example of a short form accountants' report on a target which could be included in a Class 1 acquisition circular is shown on p 336. The short form report is designed to inform the purchaser's shareholders solely about the trading record and asset position of the target. By contrast, the acquisition report is designed to inform the purchaser's management about the target, so that management is in a position to decide whether the proposed acquisition represents a sound commercial investment.

Because the scope of an acquisition investigation is wide and can cover the whole range of a target's business, the accountants will usually hold an early meeting with the purchaser in order to discuss the scope of the report. At this time the accountants should learn of any particular aspects of the target's business about which the purchaser has already been satisfied, and they should be forewarned of any areas which merit special attention.

If other professional advisers are involved at this stage, it is advisable that they too should be engaged in these discussions so that they can liaise and thus prevent unnecessary duplication of work. For instance, the accountants and the solicitors would both normally expect to enquire into the terms of any leases held by the target, and it is obviously not in the purchaser's interest to retain both these professional advisers to carry out such an examination. On the other hand, the accountants can often assist the solicitors by gathering for them information from the target's premises. Liaison between professional advisers should also ensure that all relevant areas are covered within the limitations imposed by the purchaser's timetable. The implications of this latter factor are too often overlooked but are most important because time constraints, imposed for one reason or another, undoubtedly limit the depth to which the accountants will be able to probe.

Before the accountants start their investigation they should be given clear instructions, in writing, from the purchaser. These instructions should refer specifically to any areas which they are required to examine in depth, such as the impact on the target of the wide-ranging legislation contained in the Financial Services Act 1986, and also to any areas specifically to be excluded from their investigation. The accountants should then seek access to the target. Usually this will have been agreed to by the target during the course of the negotiations and the accountants should make detailed arrangements with the management of the target accordingly. Confidentiality is an important factor and the accountants should be fully aware of the need to respect the wishes of the management of the target, not only because there may be other potential acquiring companies, but also because it may be harmful to the target's business if staff, customers and suppliers become aware of a possible change in ownership.

In general terms, the acquisition report should be designed to present the information which the purchaser requires (within the cost and time scale limitations imposed) at a time when it is of most use to the purchaser in influencing the course which the negotiations will take prior to their finalisation. The accountants should be mindful that a well presented report may be of little use if it is delivered to the purchaser late.

The report will include much financial information which will be historical and will have been audited by the target's auditors. At an early stage, the accountants will require access to the auditors' working papers, both to obtain an insight into the target's business and to establish the degree of reliance that can be placed upon the figures which depict the target's historical performance. Of course, the most recent financial information available may not, and probably will not, be audited and the accountants will have to make an assessment of the reliability of the unaudited management accounts. Generally they will do this through an examination of previous trends and by a comparison of previous management accounts with the audited accounts for the corresponding periods. It is important to appreciate that the accountants will not themselves conduct an audit of the target's affairs unless the purchaser's instructions, unusually, require them to do so. The accountants will perform an appraisal of the target's accounts, but will not necessarily verify the target's assets and liabilities independently or make an in-depth examination of the target's systems of internal control.

Much of the information required by the accountants should be readily available in one form or another at the target's principal place of business and can be obtained most easily by the management of the target company. Accountants therefore often find it convenient to leave with management a list of the basic information they require for the purpose of their report. This enables them to spend more of their time appraising and interpreting the information obtained than in finding it.

Accountants' acquisition reports can, of course, take a number of different forms, but a report should be tailor-made to suit the particular requirements of the purchaser and the business environment in which the target operates. It may be useful to consider the outline of an acquisition report, an example of which is set out below, in order to provide an indication of the content of a typical report on a small manufacturing target company.

ACCOUNTANTS' ACQUISITION REPORT

1   Introduction

This will normally recite the terms of reference under which the report is written; it should set out the scope of the work undertaken and refer to any general caveats relevant to the report as a whole. The prime sources of information should be identified and the reader's attention drawn to material areas not covered by the accountants' examination and to the reasons why these areas have been excluded.

2   History and business

2.1   *History.* A brief history of the target should be set out.

2.2   *Business.* Details of the target's present business with a description of its products, its principal operations and an assessment of its general position within the market in which it operates, within the context of the national economic situation, should be included.

2.3   *Growth.* An indication of the recent growth of the target and of its present size should be given, normally by reference to a brief summary of the net assets and profitability shown in its most recent audited accounts.

2.4   *Premises and locations.* The amount of work done will depend upon the division of work agreed with the solicitors. Certainly brief details of each property, its location and of any professional valuation should be included.

3   Corporate structure

3.1   *Capital structure.* Details of the target's present capital structure and of its present shareholders should be given.

3.2   *Group structure.* If the target comprises more than one company, information about the structure of the target group should be set out together with a description of the relationship between the subsidiaries and the parent company. Minority interests in subsidiaries should also be identified.

3.3   *Memorandum and articles of association.* This section should contain details of any unusual (but relevant) clauses in the target's memorandum and articles of association and details of share rights if relevant to the offer.

4   Management and personnel

4.1   *Directors and senior executives.* Details of the remuneration, including pensions and commissions, of the target's executives should be given, together with information on the terms of any service contracts and on any facilities granted to executives which may form part of their contracts of employment. The executives' qualifications should also be set out, and the accountants should make an assessment of the competence of the management if this is a part of their brief.

4.2   *Other employees.* The number of other employees should be analysed by department and location, and the basis on which they are remunerated should be shown. The facilities available to employees should be described and information given as to any known employee turnover statistics.

4.3   *Pension arrangements*. Details of pension arrangements for employees should be given and an assessment made of any unfunded liabilities.

4.4   *Succession and training*. The target's policy for management succession should be set out and an assessment made of any problems which the reporting accountants anticipate may arise. Details of the target's policies for staff and trade training schemes and the cost of such schemes should be included.

4.5   *Labour relations*. An assessment of the target's labour relations should be made, and any negotiating rights given to unions representing employees should be identified.

The reporting accountant may also comment on the likely reaction of executives and employees to a change in ownership of the business.

5   Operations and systems

5.1   *Research and development*. The level of, and need for, research and development in the target's business should be discussed together with any future plans for the commitment of manpower to research.

5.2   *Purchasing and sources of supply*. A description of the purchasing procedure should be given with an assessment of the effectiveness of the buying department. The principal suppliers to the target should be identified and the dependence upon individual suppliers for goods or services disclosed.

5.3   *Production*. The scale of production and the approach of management to present and future production problems should be discussed. The current manufacturing capacity and any bottlenecks should be referred to, as should the age of the plant, its serviceability, and the plans for its renewal and replacement. The degree of dependence on assembly or manufacturing at more than one location and on sub-contractors should be considered.

5.4   *Warehousing*. The procedures for receiving, storing and issuing stock should be assessed, and the adequacy and suitability of the warehousing facilities should be commented upon.

5.5   *Marketing, competition and selling*. In this section the target's major customers and competitors (which may often include the purchaser) should be mentioned. Details of any significant contracts with customers, of the selling prices and discounts offered by the target, of the sales force (or any appointed agents), of the dependence on export sales and the approach to exports, and of the advertising policy of the target should all be set out.

5.6   *Distribution*. A description should be given of the methods of distribution used, including the use of the target's own vehicle fleet, and whether the fleet is owned or leased. If a number of different transport facilities is used, the extent of the target's dependence on any one facility should be noted.

5.7   *Accounting.* This section should comprise a description and appraisal of the target's accounting systems and management accounting information.

6   **Taxation and indemnities**
The purpose of this section is to inform the purchaser of the target's outstanding corporation tax liabilities, when its corporation tax liabilities were last agreed with the Inland Revenue, compliance with VAT and PAYE legislation, and whether there are any close company or other tax problems associated with a change in ownership. Reference should be made to any indemnities recommended by the accountants which should be sought from the vendor of the target.

7   **Accounting policies**
This section should set out the accounting policies of the target in considerable detail so that the accounts can be properly understood. Any unusual accounting policies or any variations from best accounting practice should be highlighted.

8   **Turnover and profits**
This section should include not only the statutory published profit and loss account information but also a detailed breakdown of overhead expenses. An analysis of margins, variances and ratios covering the previous four- or five-year period should be included with a report on the performance of the target during that period.

9   **Assets and liabilities**
This section should consist of a complete description of each item in the target's balance sheet. A commentary on contingent liabilities and capital commitments should also be included.

10   **Source and application of funds**
A table showing the target's sources and application of funds during the period covered by the report should be summarised in this section.

11   **Future prospects**
According to the quantity and quality of information prepared by the target, the contents of this section may vary from a general discussion on the target's future, such as the effects of technological changes and trends in customer demand, to a detailed analysis of profit forecasts, cash flow projections and long term forecasts, and an assessment of their probable reliability.

12   **Miscellaneous**
12.1   *Borrowing facilities.* Details of the target's existing facilities should be

shown; the security given and the further security available should also be set out.

12.2 *Leasing commitments.* A summary of the target's commitments under leasing and hire-purchase agreements should be provided together with the nature and terms of the agreements.

12.3 *Insurance.* Details of the target's major insurance policies and of any deficiencies in insurance cover should be brought to the purchaser's attention.

12.4 *Government legislation.* An assessment of any relevant government enactments or guidelines affecting the target's operations should be included, whether or not the target has contravened such regulations, and whether a change in ownership would affect either the purchaser's or the target's position in relation to these regulations.

13   Summary and conclusions

This section should set out the main points included in the report, especially the matters of which the purchaser should be wary in its negotiations with the target.

The report, without summary and conclusions, should be discussed at an early draft stage with the target's management to ensure that all the facts presented in it are correct. This will give the target's management the opportunity to make representations to the accountants if it believes there are serious omissions or misplaced emphases in the report. The reporting accountants can then consider, but may not necessarily agree with, these representations before signing their report and presenting it to the purchaser. On reading the report the purchaser might ask for further work to be carried out; it is more likely that he will accept the report and find it an invaluable aid during the final stages of negotiations with the target's owners or management. A well constructed report also acts as a permanent record of the state of the target's affairs at the time of the purchase.

DIFFICULTIES WITH INVESTIGATION OF TITLE

If the target has significant interests in property or has properties which, although they have little or no market value are crucial to the continuance of the target's business, the purchaser's solicitors will either investigate title or ask for a certificate of title from the vendor's solicitors in addition to seeking the usual property warranties (see Agreement for Sale—Warranties 35 to 37). A certificate of title is often restricted in nature owing to the fact that the vendor's solicitors will themselves have to carry out a full up-to-date investigation before giving the certificate of title which time may not permit leading to restrictions in the scope of the certificate. In addition, there may be difficulty in persuading the vendor's solicitors to give a certificate in a form which the purchaser's solicitors consider sufficiently comprehensive to be of value to the purchaser and its financiers. For these reasons and since an investigation of title carried out by the purchaser's solicitors will often reveal matters affecting the value of the property interests, or matters relevant to the running of the target's business which, not being matters of title, may not be disclosed in a title certificate, it is usually helpful to a purchaser to have an investigation carried out by the purchaser's solicitors.

As no change in the ownership of the target's properties is involved in the acquisition, any such investigation (and, consequently, the giving of any such certificate) is considerably hampered. How far do these difficulties affect reliance upon such an investigation or certificate? A complete account of title investigation is beyond the scope of this book, but the following notes may be of interest. The tools of the title investigator are searches and inspection of title documents, and these will be considered separately. In addition to inspection by the purchaser's surveyor, inspection of the property itself by the title investigator is always desirable but rarely feasible either because it is simply impractical or for reasons of confidentiality. In addition, the title investigator will raise enquiries and requisitions of the vendor's solicitors. The replies to these should be annexed to the disclosure letter or incorporated by reference, and the accuracy of those replies warranted (see Warranty 36(f) on p 184). The purchaser's solicitors should resist attempts by the vendor's solicitors to circumvent this warranty by giving replies to the enquiries and requisitions which are qualified, eg 'Not so far as the vendor is aware, but no warranty is given', or 'The purchaser should rely on inspection and survey', where in the latter case for reasons of confidentiality this is impractical.

An investigation of title depends to a large extent on the quality and quantity of information supplied by the vendors, and the target and their directors and solicitors by way of title deeds (and inspection of the originals) and in replies to enquiries and requisitions. The purchaser requires protection against non-disclosure or inadequate disclosure of relevant property matters in that investigation and should require the normal property warranties (see Agreement for Sale, Warranties 34 to 35 on pp 183–184). The vendor should have nothing to fear from this if he has made full and proper disclosure of property matters since such disclosure will override the property warranties to the extent of that disclosure.

Searches

The intending purchaser or mortgagee of land who searches a statutory register is usually protected by his search. This protection, however, is not afforded if the ownership of the land remains unchanged.

Companies Registration Office

The Companies Act 1985, s 395 et seq, requires registration within twenty-one days of certain types of charges created by companies, but the list of charges required to be registered is by no means exhaustive and does not include, for instance, incumbrances such as leases or contracts for sale. In any event, a clear mortgage register gives no protection to the purchaser of shares. A registrable charge which is not registered is void only against a liquidator or creditor of the company and not against the company itself or its shareholders (see *Independent Automatic Sales Ltd* v *Knowles & Foster* [1962] 3 All ER 27). When a charge is rendered void against a liquidator or creditor the moneys secured thereby become automatically repayable so that non-registration may even affect the target (and thus the purchaser) adversely. It is also possible that a registrable charge has been granted, but has not yet been registered. Prior to the expiry of the statutory period, it seems that charge would be valid (see *Burston Finance Ltd* v *Speirway Ltd* [1974] 3 All ER 735).

Local authority searches including Land Charges Registry

Non-registration does not affect the enforceability of local land charges, but, if a local land charge is not revealed by a search because of non-registration or because of an error by the local authority, compensation may be payable under the Local Land Charges Act 1975. It is, however, only payable to a 'purchaser' which is defined by s 10(3) of the Act as any person who 'for valuable consideration . . . acquires any interest in land or the proceeds of sale of land . . .'. Although lessees and mortgagees are specifically included, a purchaser of shares does not fall within the definition and any person searching in this capacity will not obtain a right to compensation.

Land Registry

Under the Land Registration Act 1925, s 20, failure to register a registrable incumbrance will render it void, but only in the case of a disposition of the land in favour of a purchaser for value (including a mortgagee or lessee but, again, not including a purchaser of shares). A search by a person other than a purchaser of the land confers no priority period (see the Land Registration (Official Searches) Rules 1988 (SI 1988 No 629), r 10).

Land Charges Department

Again, official searches only protect purchasers of the land itself (Land Charges Act 1972, ss 4 and 11) and compensation for loss arising out of charges registered against estate owners prior to a good root of title will be payable only to such a person (Law of Property Act 1969, s 25). Failure to register such a charge created by the target will not affect its validity as against the target.

Other searches

Although no protection will be conferred on a purchaser of shares, it will usually be prudent for other searches to be made. Two examples are mining searches with British Coal for land in past or present mining areas, and searches of the relevant county council or London borough under the Commons Registrations Act 1965 for land in all areas.

Inspection of title documents

The title investigator will inspect the title documents in the target's possession and will require their production upon completion of the acquisition (see the Agreement for Sale, cl 4(c)(6) on p 166). How much protection does this afford?

Registered land

Inspection of a land or charge certificate held by the target or its mortgagee will show that the target is the registered proprietor of the land described. It is worth making a careful check that the target's name corresponds with that entered in the register when the entry was made. Although the Land Registry will accept the inclusion of a company number in the proprietorship register it is not obliged to do so, and name swaps between companies can have the effect of confusing the conveyancer. Although inspection of the land or charge certificate will yield that much information, and coupled with the Land Registry search on form 94C mentioned below will also assure the purchaser of shares that the Land Registry is not, at that moment, registering a disposition in favour of some other person (as the Registry normally requires land certificates to be deposited with it for that purpose—Land Registration Act 1925, s 64), the mere fact that there are no other encumbrances noted on the register does not mean that they do not exist. For example, overriding interests (see the Land Registration Act 1925, s 3(xvi) cannot be registered in any event and the purchaser's solicitors should enquire as to the existence of these in their enquiries and requisitions of the vendor's solicitors. Also, the registration of a caution, to protect a contract for sale or an option, does not require the production of the certificate at the Land Registry. In certain circumstances the Land Registry may dispense with production of the certificate (eg registration of a general vesting declaration—Land Registration Rules 1925 (SI 1925 No 1093), r 13). The safest course is to obtain from the target up-to-date office copy entries of the register together with a search in form 94C obtained immediately prior to completion which, while it confers no priority, will cover any adverse dealings affecting the title which have been lodged for registration at the Land Registry. Because the statutory search procedure does not give any priority, even unregistered incumbrances which should have been registered will continue to subsist after the completion of the share acquisition.

Unregistered land

Inspection of title deeds to unregistered land will not reveal oral leases, estate contracts or the unregistered land equivalent of overriding interests, neither will it give any protection against the existence of puisne mortgages (registered at the Land Charges Registry or not) or even against previous sales of the property or part not protected by endorsement of a memorandum on the retained title deeds (see *Claridge* v *Tingey, Re Sea View Gardens, Warden* [1967] 1 WLR 134).

As in the case of registered land, a check should be made that the target's present name corresponds with that applying at the date of the conveyance, lease or assignment of the land.

In practice, the conveyancing investigator to a large extent relies upon the efficiency of mortgagees or other incumbrancers. They will, the investigator hopes, have effected the necessary registrations or secured possession of the title deeds, in order to guard against subsequent dealings with the land by the target which would render their security or incumbrance void. The share purchaser should remember, however, that he is merely hoping that incumbrancers have donned some visible armour to protect themselves against weapons which are more powerful than those available to him.

MISREPRESENTATION, WARRANTY AND INDEMNITY

If a false statement of fact is made by the vendor to the purchaser about the target, what remedies does the purchaser have? Of all the questions with which this book deals, none is more difficult to answer, particularly in a brief space. Although there are few decided cases which specifically relate to company acquisitions, the basic problem—a false statement followed by a sale—has been one which has occupied the courts for centuries and it is surrounded by such a web of rules and classifications, many of which are only of historical interest, that any exposition of the modern law, however brief, is bound to reflect its complexity.

Until the decision in *Hedley Byrne & Co Ltd v Heller & Partners Ltd* [1964] AC 465 the law gave no damages for a non-fraudulent misrepresentation which was not a term of the contract between the parties. Not until *Esso Petroleum Co Ltd v Mardon* [1976] 2 WLR 583 (considered on p 70) did it become clear that the rule in *Hedley Byrne*, which gives damages for a negligent misstatement, can apply if the parties to the statement subsequently proceed to contract. The problem, therefore, was to distinguish between 'mere' representations giving no right to damages and representations which did form part of the contract between the parties. In this search the characterisation and classification of the offending statement was all important. Was it a mere recommendation of the object to be sold, a statement of opinion or a statement of fact? If it was a misrepresentation of fact, was it made innocently or fraudulently? Was it part of the contract between the parties (ie a warranty) or was it a collateral contract? It was necessary to answer these questions to determine whether the representee had a remedy at all and, if so, what his remedy was: was it rescission, an indemnity or damages? If damages, were they to be assessed on the tortious or contractual basis? Since the passing of the Misrepresentation Act 1967 many of these classifications have become less significant in terms of the net result to the representee. Nevertheless, the Act is grafted on to the law as it stood before 1967 and the classifications are with us still.

Non-contractual misrepresentation

The contract for the acquisition of a private company is a unique type of contract. Its operative terms are often straightforward, simply providing for a sale and purchase of shares. However, for the reasons noted on p 49, this simple contract is often accompanied by a long string of representations and warranties relating to the target. Because such contracts are normally negotiated between solicitors and are complex and carefully thought-out documents, it is perhaps less likely than in other fields that representations made by the vendor to the purchaser which do not appear in the written contract will be held to have induced the contract, thus giving rise to remedies.

If a false statement of fact does induce the contract then, whether the misrepresentation was made fraudulently, negligently, or innocently, the purchaser will have the right to rescind the contract even if the misrepresentation has become a term of the contract or the contract has been performed (Misrepresentation Act 1967, s 1). Rescission will not be possible if the contract has been affirmed by the purchaser; if the purchaser has taken some action since the contract which makes it impossible to put the parties back as they were before (eg if the target's business has ceased or changed substantially); or if any innocent third party would be prejudiced. If the misrepresentation is fraudulent, damages can be claimed in the tort of deceit, and if it is negligent within the meaning of the Misrepresentation Act 1967 (ie if the representor cannot prove that he had reasonable ground to believe and did believe up to the time the contract was made that the facts represented were true—s 2(1)), damages can be claimed under the provisions of s 2(1) of the Act. Section 2(2) of the Act provides that upon an action for rescission the court may declare the contract subsisting and award damages in lieu. The purchaser who is victim of an innocent misrepresentation may therefore, if the court thinks fit, be awarded damages instead of, but not as well as, rescission. The question of damages is considered on p 68.

It is the object of the Agreement for Sale (Chapter 6) to restrict liability to those representations given as warranties in the agreement or contained in the disclosure letter which qualifies the warranties. Clause 8(B) provides that the written agreement is the sole agreement between the parties and by Sched 7, para 1, the purchaser acknowledges that it has not entered into the agreement in reliance on any representations other than those contained in the agreement or the disclosure letter. It is the latter provision which is directly relevant to the question of representations. In *Alman and Benson* v *Associated Newspapers Group Ltd* [1980] Ch D (an unreported case available on *Lexis*), Browne-Wilkinson J held that a clause similar to cl 8(B) which provided that the written contract constituted 'the entire agreement and understanding between the parties with respect to all matters therein referred to' was not apt to exclude liability for representations. He said that:

If [the clause] were designed to exclude liability for misrepresentation it would, I think, have to be couched in different terms, for example a clause acknowledging that the parties had not relied on any representations in entering into the contract.

This, of course, is the effect of Sched 7, para 1. In deciding how far such provisions are effective it is necessary to refer to the Misrepresentation Act 1967, s 3 (as amended by the Unfair Contract Terms Act 1977). This section provides that:

> If a contract contains a term which would exclude or restrict—
> (*a*) any liability to which a party to a contract may be subject by reason of any misrepresentation made by him before the contract was made; or
> (*b*) any remedy available to another party to the contract by reason of such misrepresentation,
> that term shall be of no effect except in so far as it satisfies the requirement of reasonableness as stated in section 11(1) of the Unfair Contract Terms Act 1977; and it is for those claiming that the term satisfies that requirement to show that it does.

The Unfair Contract Terms Act 1977, s 11(1), provides that the requirement of reasonableness is that the term should have been a fair and reasonable one to be included, having regard to the circumstances which were, or ought reasonably to have been, known to, or in the contemplation of, the parties when the contract was made.

It is suggested that in a normal transaction, the inclusion in the contract of an acknowledgment by the purchaser that he has not entered into the contract on the basis of any representation other than those contained in the contract should be effective. If a representation has been made by the vendor, and the purchaser is relying upon it, then he has this opportunity to include it as an express warranty in the contract. If he does not do so, then in subsequent proceedings it will be difficult to show, having regard to the acknowledgment, that the contract was entered into in reliance upon the representation. It can be said that a provision of this nature is not subject at all to the Misrepresentation Act 1967, s 3, and that it is not the case that liability is excluded or restricted by the contractual provision, but that no liability arises because of the state of affairs of which the acknowledgment is a record. It is unlikely, however, that this argument will find sympathy with the court. In *Cremdean Properties* v *Nash* (1977) 244 EG 547, at p 551, Bridge LJ indicated that, in his view, exclusion clauses which purported to deny the very existence of a representation did not avoid the effect of s 3. Nevertheless, in a commercial transaction such as an acquisition, when the parties on each side are businessmen who take advice, it is difficult to see why the provision should not be regarded by the court as fair and reasonable in a normal case. In *Alman and Benson* v *Associated Newspapers Group Ltd* (see above) it was found as a fact that clauses similar to cl 8(B) of the Agreement for Sale (although not excluding liabilities for misrepresentation) are commonly included by skillful and reputable solicitors in share purchase agreements. It is suggested that a similar finding would have been made in relation to a provision such as Sched 7, para 1.

Vendors are well advised to seek to include an acknowledgment of this type in the contract. The acquisition of shares in the target will probably have been preceded by discussion and correspondence and it is reasonable to ask the purchaser to specify in the contract those representations upon which reliance is placed.

The purchaser may also have a remedy, in tort, if he enters into the contract in reliance upon a negligent misstatement. The rule in *Hedley Byrne & Co Ltd* v *Heller & Partners Ltd* [1964] AC 465 has been stated thus (Lord Denning MR in *Esso Petroleum Co Ltd* v *Mardon* [1976] 2 WLR 583, at p 595):

> If a man, who has or professes to have special knowledge or skill, makes a representation by virtue thereof to another—be it advice, information or opinion—with the intention of inducing him to enter into a contract with him, he is under a duty to use reasonable care to see that the representation is correct and that the advice, information or opinion is reliable. If he negligently gives unsound advice or misleading information or expresses an erroneous opinion and thereby induces the other side to enter a contract with him, he is liable in damages.

Liability under the rule in *Hedley Byrne* is not restricted to professional advisers (see dicta of Ormrod LJ in *Esso Petroleum Co Ltd* v *Mardon*, above, at p 601) and the above formulation seems wide enough to embrace a misstatement by a vendor whose knowledge of the target will of course be more extensive than the purchaser's. As a practical matter, however, the damages remedy for negligent representation given by the Misrepresentation Act 1967 probably renders this cause of action redundant (ibid, at p 602). For an analysis of the difference, see *Howard Marine and Dredging Co Ltd* v *Ogden (A) & Sons (Excavations) Ltd* [1978] 2 All ER 1134 at p 1144.

Contractual misrepresentation

A warranty is a subsidiary contractual term, breach of which will not entitle the innocent party to treat the contract as discharged but which will give rise to a claim for damages.

The warranties included in a contract for the acquisition of a private company are, for the most part, statements of fact and, as such, can be classed as representations. If a representation is made during negotiations and then appears in the written agreement, the party relying on it can still claim rescission of the contract if it proves to be false. The Misrepresentation Act 1967, s 1, provides that:

Where a person has entered into a contract after a misrepresentation has been made to him and—
    (a) the misrepresentation has become a term of the contract;
       . . . . then, if otherwise he would be entitled to rescind the contract without alleging fraud, he shall be so entitled . . . .

To enable the contract to be rescinded for misrepresentation, however, it seems on the face of the section that the misrepresentation must have been made to the purchaser before the contract was entered into. It can be said that if the representation appears only once in the history of the transaction, and is included in the written contract as a term of it, then the Act does not apply. Although the courts may be reluctant to draw this distinction, it is common practice to safeguard the purchaser by expressly including the right of rescission in the contract, at least for any breach discovered before completion (see the Agreement for Sale, cl 7(F), on p 169).

The drafting of warranties in an acquisition agreement will depend, in many respects, upon the type of business in which the target is engaged. The purchaser's solicitors will, after consultation with their client and their study of any accountants' report, attempt to obtain assurances with regard to those aspects of the target's business which are important to the purchaser. There are, however, many warranties which are standard for almost any type of acquisition. These general warranties will be aimed, in more or less detail, at ensuring that the latest audited accounts of the target are accurate and that the target has carried on its business in the normal course since the date of the last accounts without incurring any extraordinary liabilities. In addition, the purchaser will want details of other matters such as significant contracts, litigation etc. A full set of these 'standard' warranties is contained in the Agreement for Sale, Sched 3, para 2 (see p 174), which is drafted with a trading company in mind. It is unlikely that all these warranties will be appropriate to any individual transaction. Taxation is dealt with in Chapter 5.

It is the scheme of the Agreement for Sale to oblige the vendors to make disclosures which qualify the warranties by means of one specific disclosure letter, so that it will be possible to say, after completion, what was disclosed and what was not. For an example of the argument that can otherwise result, see *Levison v Farin* [1978] 2 All ER 1149. In that case Gibson J said, at p 1157:

A protection by disclosure will not normally be achieved by merely making

known the means of knowledge which may or do enable the other party to
work out certain facts and conclusions.

Purchasers will resist general disclosures, eg relating to board
minutes over a period of years, unless they have had an ample
opportunity of considering them.

If an accountants' report has been obtained, the vendors will often
wish to refer to it in the disclosure letter so as to ensure that all the
matters of which they have informed the accountants, and which
appear in the report, are regarded as disclosed. This can cause
difficulty in practice, because the purchaser may wish to resist
showing the vendors the report in its final form. It may be possible to
resolve the problem by agreeing that the report is regarded as
disclosed even though not seen by the vendors.

One difficulty which sometimes arises is the problem of
representations made to the vendors in connection with the
warranties. The vendors may ask the directors of the target to check
the warranties and to confirm their accuracy. Such a confirmation, if
incorrect, could give rise to a claim for negligent representation
which might fall on the target, either because the representation was
given on behalf of the target or because the directors are entitled to be
indemnified by the target. The purchaser will obviously not wish the
target to be liable in this way, and Sched 3, para 2(2) to the
Agreement for Sale (p 175) contains a disclaimer.

Damages for misrepresentation

The measure of damages is different in contract and tort. The
contractual measure aims to place the plaintiff in the position which
he would have enjoyed had the contract not been broken. The
plaintiff is therefore entitled to the loss of his bargain. The tortious
measure aims to place the successful plaintiff in the position in which
he would have been if the tort had not been committed (ie in the case
of a misrepresentation inducing a contract, as if he had not entered
into the contract at all).

If damages are calculated according to the contractual measure,
the purchaser is entitled to the difference between the market value of
the target's shares as they are and their value as it would have been if
the warranty had been true. Under the tortious measure, on the other
hand, the purchaser is entitled to the difference between the market
value of the target's shares as they are and the price paid. The
practical difference between the two approaches can be simply
illustrated. Suppose a balance sheet warranty is given and the target
has a liability which was not, but which should have been, disclosed

in the balance sheet; then the purchaser of the whole of the target's capital would, under the contractual measure, normally be entitled to recover the amount necessary to discharge the liability. It would not affect the position if the target possessed an unrelated asset, not taken into account in the calculation of the purchase price, which was worth as much as, or more than, the undisclosed liability. However, on the tortious basis, the existence of such an asset would affect the calculation and there would be no damage, if, despite the misrepresentation, the target was worth the price paid.

The foregoing is subject to one very important qualification. The measure of damages is calculated according to the value of the shares of the target and while the amount of the assets and liabilities of the target will certainly affect the value of those shares, the relationship may be neither simple nor direct. In a case where undisclosed liabilities, or a shortfall in assets, is small in relation to the target's business it may well be that the value of the target's shares is not affected at all. Where the target is bought for its profit earning capacity, and it can be demonstrated that the value of its shares was calculated by reference to earnings, then a shortfall in assets will normally only affect the value of the shares if the profit earning capacity of the target is affected. The purchaser will, however, normally expect to be reimbursed for undisclosed liabilities and shortfalls in assets, except when they arise within negotiated limits, and it is for this reason that the so-called 'pound for pound' clause is frequently found in the agreement for sale. See the Agreement for Sale, cl 7 (C) on p 168. This clause purports to say that, without affecting the purchaser's ability to claim damages on any appropriate basis, the vendors will pay to the purchaser an amount equal to any deficiency or liability of the target which arises from any breach of any of the warranties or which would not have existed or arisen if the warranties had been true. It should always be borne in mind that in a case where the value of the shares is calculated by reference to profits, and profits have been misstated, the purchaser's damages claim may well be a multiple of the shortfall.

Most of the litigation which has come before the courts relating to contracts for the sale of shares has been concerned not with breach of contract but with the tort of deceit following a fraudulent misrepresentation or under statutes which impose liability on company directors for misstatements or omissions in company prospectuses. In these cases the tortious measure applies and the plaintiff is entitled to the difference between the price paid and the value of the shares received and is not entitled to be compensated for the loss of his bargain (see eg *McConnel* v *Wright* [1903] 1 Ch 546, CA; *Doyle* v *Olby (Ironmongers) Ltd* [1969] 2 QB 158; and *Siametis* v

Trojan Horse (Burlington) Inc (1979) 25 OR (2d) 120 (High Court of Ontario)). Damages for non-contractual negligent misrepresentation awarded under the Misrepresentation Act 1967, s 2(1), will be ascertained according to the tortious rules, *F & H Entertainments Ltd* v *Leisure Enterprises Ltd* (1976) 120 SJ 331 and *Alman and Benson* v *Associated Newspapers Group Ltd* (1980) (an unreported case available on *Lexis*), although damages for innocent misrepresentation awarded in lieu of rescission under s 2(2) may perhaps be limited to an indemnity on the principles laid down in *Whittington* v *Seale–Hayne* (1900) 82 LT 49.

What measure will the courts apply when assessing damages for breach of a contractual representation? In *JEB Fasteners Ltd* v *Marks Bloom & Co* [1983] 1 All ER 583 the plaintiffs bought a manufacturing company without obtaining warranties. The accounts of the target for its first year of operations were inaccurate and the disappointed plaintiffs sued the accountants. It was held that the defendants had been negligent in the preparation of the accounts, but because the plaintiffs' motive for the acquisition was to obtain the services of the target's two directors the court held that the accounts had not affected the purchaser's judgment to any material degree in deciding to proceed with the acquisition and their claim was therefore dismissed. At p 587 Donaldson LJ said:

The plaintiffs did not take the usual precaution of requiring the directors of [the target] to warranty the accuracy of the audited accounts and the fact that there had been no material change in the profitability of the company since the end of the period covered by those accounts. Accordingly they cannot sue the directors for breach of warranty but must rely on a claim against the defendant auditors for negligent misstatement. Furthermore, the measure of damage is different. It is not the difference between the value of the company if the facts had been as stated in the accounts and its actual value, but the loss which the plaintiffs have sustained as a result of acting in reliance on the accuracy of the accounts.

These remarks are, of course, obiter dicta but they are a very helpful clarification of a question which had been rendered obscure by the difficult case of *Esso Petroleum Co Ltd* v *Mardon* [1976] 2 WLR 583. In that case Esso let Mr Mardon a petrol station, representing to him that the potential throughput was likely to reach 200,000 gallons by the third year of operation. That estimate had been made before the requirements of the planning authority were known. In fact, the planning authority had required that the petrol station be built backing on the main road and not facing it so that the gallonage actually achieved was far less. Although the actual configuration of the site was known to Esso at the time they let the site to Mr Mardon, already having made their representation, they did not revise their figure. The representation was made before the Misrepresentation Act 1967 came into force, but the Court of Appeal held that Esso were liable in damages both on the basis of the rule in *Hedley Byrne* and also because what they had said amounted to a contractual warranty. Although they had not guaranteed the throughput, the court held that Esso had by implication warranted that on a careful assessment they had estimated the throughput of the service station at 200,000 gallons in the third year. This warranty was broken because there was no such careful assessment based on the site as finally constructed. The court decided that the measure of damages was the same whether Mr Mardon's claim was founded on *Hedley Byrne* or breach of warranty. In a crucial passage Lord Denning said (at p 595):

Mr Mardon is not to be compensated here for 'loss of a bargain'. He was given no bargain that the throughput would amount to 200,000 gallons a year. He is only to be compensated for having been induced to enter into a contract which turned out to be disastrous for him. Whether it be called breach of warranty or negligent misrepresentation, its effect was not to warrant the throughput, but only to induce him to enter the contract. So the damages in either case are to be measured by the loss he suffered.

The key to *Esso Petroleum Co Ltd* v *Mardon* seems to be that the warranty found was that reasonable care had been used in making the representation as to the throughput. If this warranty had been true then the representation would not have been made at all and accordingly the plaintiff would not have been induced to enter into the contract. Since the tortious measure would also seek to put the purchaser into the position which he would have enjoyed had he not entered into the contract, it can be seen that in this case the two measures produce the same result.

It is not always the contractual measure which produces the highest damages for the purchaser. Suppose the purchaser buys a company in circumstances where only limited warranties are given. An example might be a management buy-out, where the existing management team purchases the shares of the target and the vendors refuse to give substantial warranties because, as they claim, the purchasers know more of the business than they do themselves. However, it might be that, in such a case, a warranty would be given as to, for example, the operation of a group pension scheme. If that warranty were misleading, damages on the contractual basis would compensate the purchaser for any corresponding diminution in the value of his shares. Suppose, however, that the purchase was a disastrous one and that there were very substantial undisclosed liabilities. The purchaser does not have the protection of the normal warranties and so therefore cannot claim against the vendors unless he can say that the existence of the warranty about the pension scheme induced him to enter into the contract and that he is therefore liable to be compensated for the damage he has suffered as a result, ie the difference between the price paid and the value received. If the purchaser could show that the statement in question amounted to a tortious misrepresentation (whether a negligent misstatement at common law or a negligent misrepresentation within the 1967 Act) which induced the contract then he could claim damages on the tortious basis; but what if the representation is not negligent, but nevertheless amounts to a contractual warranty as in the example above? Unfortunately there does not appear to be any clear authority and the cautious practitioner acting for a vendor on these occasions will do his best to limit the vendor's liability to the contractual measure. In the United States the law clearly restricts the plaintiff, in these circumstances, from recovering any loss which the defendant can prove with reasonable certainty the plaintiff would have suffered had the contract been performed. (See the Second Restatement of Contracts, s 349). For English authorities on the subject see *Cullinane* v *British 'Rema' Manufacturing Co Ltd* [1954] 1 QB 292, *Lloyd* v *Stanbury* [1971] 1 WLR 535; *Anglia Television Ltd* v *Reed* [1972] 1 QB 60 and *C & P Haulage* v *Middleton* [1983] 3 All ER 94. For recent authority on the duty of care owed by auditors to potential shareholders see *Caparo Industries plc* v *Dickinson* (1988) *The Times*, 5 August.

Although the above discussion has tended to emphasise the differences between the consequences of assessing damages on the contractual and tortious basis, in most cases the price paid is likely to be equal to the value of the shares as warranted; so the result of applying either measure to any particular breach of warranty is the same and argument does not focus on the practical effect of the difference. In *Levison* v *Farin* [1978] 2 All ER 1149 the target had made losses in the period between the date of the warranted balance sheet and the date of completion, and the vendors had given a warranty that between the balance sheet date and the completion date there would have been no material adverse change in the overall value of the net assets of the company on the basis of a valuation adopted in the balance sheet allowing for normal trade fluctuations. It was found that the disclosures which the vendors had made were not sufficient to avoid their liability under the warranty and damages were assessed in the amount of the diminution of the net assets of the target in the period between the accounts and completion, less the tax benefit which subsequently accrued to the target, and therefore to the purchaser, from the losses in the period (for which see p 141). Gibson J formulated the measure of damages in contractual language, saying (at p 1159) that it was true that the purchaser was entitled to receive the company with the warranty as to net asset value performed as at the date of completion. Given that the purchase price actually paid (the make up of which the judge investigated) was the same as the value of the target as it would have been had the warranty been performed, the application of either the tortious or the contractual basis would have produced the same result. In deducting the tax benefits from the damages Gibson J followed Viscount Haldane LC in *British Westinghouse Electric & Manufacturing Co Ltd* v *Underground Electric Railways & Co of London Ltd* [1912] AC 673, at p 689:

When in the course of his business [the plaintiff] has taken action arising out of the transaction, which action has diminished the loss, the effect in actual diminution of the loss he has suffered may be taken into account even though there was no duty on him to act.

In other words, although it was not suggested that the purchaser was under a duty to earn profits against which the tax losses could have been offset, the fact that he had received a benefit was taken into account and was not regarded as too remote.

Limiting clauses

Those who sell the share capital of the company with limited liability should not be confident that damages recoverable as a result of a breach of warranty cannot exceed the purchase price, even if the tortious basis of assessing damages is implemented. Although the purchaser cannot recover in respect of damage which could have been avoided if he had taken reasonable steps to minimise the loss caused by the breach of warranty, it is suggested that there is no reason to suppose that the purchaser must allow the target to be placed in liquidation. If the target owes a liability in circumstances in which the vendor should have disclosed this liability to the purchaser, so that he is in breach of, for example, a balance sheet warranty in not doing so, then, even if this liability exceeds the purchase price of the target's shares, the purchaser may have excellent reasons for providing the target with funds to meet the liability (and claiming reimbursement from the vendors) rather than allowing the target to be placed in insolvent liquidation. For example, abandoning the target might cause severe damage to the purchaser's commercial reputation or involve the purchaser in loss in respect of guarantees which he had given after completion. Indeed, by the time the liability comes to light the purchaser may well have provided further funds to the target by way of share or loan capital and these will now be required towards meeting the liability. All these matters may involve the vendor in a claim for consequential loss and vendors who wish to limit their liability to the amount of the purchase price should insist upon an express stipulation to this effect in the sale agreement.

Apart from clauses which place a limit on the vendor's liability, vendors often stipulate that no claim is to be made for breach of warranty unless the purchaser has given notice of the claim before the expiry of a specified period (see the Agreement for Sale, Sched 7, para 4, on p 216). Such an attempt to shorten the limitation period can be particularly useful if the vendor is old, as the existence of a potential liability for breach of warranty can cause difficulties in the administration of an estate. It is not always sensible for vendors to stipulate that proceedings must be commenced within a specified period, as this can force a purchaser who considers that he may wish to make a claim to issue a writ before the expiry of the period, exacerbating a situation which could perhaps otherwise have been resolved by negotiation. Other provisions which vendors commonly insist upon are clauses which limit the individual liability of a number of vendors who are each giving warranties and clauses which provide that no claims are to be made until the total liability under the agreement has exceeded a certain amount, thus sparing the vendors claims for small sums.

How far are limiting clauses of this type affected by the Misrepresentation Act 1967, s 3? The section only refers to misrepresentations made before contract. In the peculiar circumstances of an acquisition it is often the purchaser who prepares the draft contract which contains the warranties and it is, in practice, often difficult to say that vendors have given the representations until they actually sign the contract. If the limiting clauses are restricted only to the contractual terms it would seem, therefore, that they should not be affected by s 3, but recent trends in the courts to assimilate the law as it relates to contractual and non-contractual misrepresentation have yet to be fully worked out and the position may not be as clear as it appears. As noted on p 65, in the normal acquisition both parties are advised and it is difficult to see why these limiting clauses should not be regarded as reasonable by the courts in a normal case.

Joint and several liability

Warranties may be given for all the selling shareholders in the sale agreement, by those who are substantial shareholders, or by the directors of the target (or by any combination). When more than one person is liable on the warranties, the purchaser normally requires the liability to be joint and several. The purchaser is then able to bring proceedings against all or any of the warrantors as he wishes and to bring separate actions against each. For further detail about joint and several liability see Glanville Williams, *Joint Obligations* and *The Law Commission Report on Contribution* (1977 Law Com No 79).

Recovery of judgment against one of a number of joint or joint and several warrantors will not prevent proceedings against the others in respect of the same claim, although of course satisfaction of the judgment will discharge the whole liability. The plaintiff who brings successive actions will not, however, be able to recover costs in any action other than the first unless the court is of the opinion that there are reasonable grounds for bringing the action (Civil Liability (Contribution) Act 1978, s 3). If any of the warrantors should die, his personal representatives will be liable jointly and severally with the surviving warrantors. If the purchaser wishes to discharge one joint and several warrantor from his liability, he will take care to preserve his rights against the others. If one joint and several warrantor is effectively discharged (ie by release under seal or by accord and satisfaction), the other warrantors will also be released (*North* v *Wakefield* (1849) 13 QB 536). If the purchaser wishes to release one warrantor without the others, then unless all agree, the best that can be done is a covenant not to sue the warrantor who is to be released. A release which reserves rights against other warrantors will take effect as covenant not to sue.

If one joint and several warrantor is called upon to pay damages he may claim a contribution from the other warrantors who are liable in respect of the same damage. The right to contribution is governed by the Civil Liability (Contribution) Act 1978. The amount recoverable will be such as may be found by the court to be just and equitable having regard to the extent of the defendant's responsibility for the damage in question and may extend from nothing to a complete indemnity, but if the defendant's liability was limited by contract, he will not be liable to pay a contribution in excess of that limit (s 2). The joint and several warrantor who has made a bona fide settlement of the warranty claim can still claim a contribution (s 1(4)). The limitation period is two years from the date of judgment or the date when the compromise was agreed (Limitation Act 1980, s 10).

If vendors accept joint liability on warranties it may be sensible for them to stipulate between themselves that in the event of liability arising they will make payments to ensure that any liability (including costs) is borne in proportion to the number of shares sold by each of them. Agreements to contribution are not affected by the Act (s 7(3)).

Warranties by the purchaser

Cases arise in which the vendors seek warranties from the purchaser. The normal example is a case where the purchaser is issuing shares as consideration for the acquisition and the vendors intend to retain those shares. Because the acquisition of the purchaser's shares will represent a substantial investment by the vendors, they will seek warranties about the purchaser's affairs. Where the purchaser is listed or the subject of dealings on the Unlisted Securities Market, the warranties can normally be in a much shorter form than those which the purchaser will seek in relation to the target.

Unfortunately, the proposition in *Houldsworth* v *City of Glasgow Bank* (1880) 5 App Cas 317 may make the warranties ineffective. In that case the plaintiff sought to avoid his liability to make a contribution in the winding up of a company by claiming that he had been induced to take his shares by misrepresentation and, accordingly, that he had a claim as a creditor equivalent to the amount which he was obliged to pay as a contributory. The court held that he could not claim as a creditor in respect of the transaction under which he had become a member. This gives rise to a number of anomalies and difficulties and the cautious practitioner will conclude that the proposition is likely to affect warranties given by purchasers. In cases where the consideration shares are to be listed and represent more than 10 per cent of the shares of the purchaser listing particulars will be required and the vendors are likely to have a statutory claim for any misrepresentation contained in the listing particulars. In other cases, however, the warranties are of doubtful value although where there is a delay between contract and completion than a provision in the contract which allows the vendor to rescind for breach of warranty will be effective. If the vendors do rescind they may also, depending on the circumstances, have a claim for damages, but many practitioners doubt whether rescission is available after the shares have been issued to the vendors, as rescission at that stage will amount to a reduction of the purchaser's capital without the consent of the court.

Representations are currently being made by the Law Society's

Company Law Committee to change the law to remove the anomalies created by the *Houldsworth* decision.

Indemnity

Liability in respect of misrepresentation arises because of breach of a duty imposed by law or by contract, but liability under an indemnity arises not because of breach but because the parties have stipulated that one shall save another from loss in specified circumstances. Contractual provisions relating to tax are considered on pp 152 to 155. Indemnities are useful when the vendors have disclosed matters to the purchaser (so that the warranties are thereby robbed of their force) but the purchaser still demands contractual protection against the consequences of the matter in question, but see p 154 for a comment on the tax-effectiveness of indemnities.

Indemnities are normally strictly construed and liability under them will not go beyond that expressly stipulated. It is therefore common expressly to include liability for interest and costs incurred. Where indemnities are given by more than one person in the agreement for sale the liabilities are normally assumed jointly and severally. It may be sensible to provide that those giving the indemnity contribute between themselves to ensure that each vendor bears the liability in proportion to any benefit enjoyed by him.

Insurance

Insurance against liability under warranties and indemnities is quite often sought. Insurers will seek to exclude liability under warranties which look to the future (eg as to recoverability of debts) and, because they are insurers, will be extremely wary in accepting liability under a warranty which relates to the adequacy of other insurance policies (see, eg the Agreement for Sale, Sched 3, para 2(27) on p 180). They will also seek to exclude liability relating to any matter within the warrantors' knowledge at the date of the agreement or, of course, liability arising from fraud or dishonesty on the part of the insured. Tax avoidance schemes are also unpopular in this connection.

Although insurers should be consulted at an early stage, they may be wary of committing themselves to provide cover until after contracts have been exchanged. They require a report on the contract from their own solicitors (for which the proposers have to pay) before agreeing to cover. The following is a list of points which may be thought to be relevant in connection with such a report and serves as a useful checklist for vendors generally (even when not insured).

(1) Is there any 'pound for pound' clause? (see p 69). The effect of such a clause may be that damages might be claimed by the purchaser in circumstances where the value of the target as a whole is not diminished by the circumstances giving rise to the breach of warranty.

(2) Some of the warranties may be qualified with statements such as 'so far as the vendors are aware'. Does the contract provide that this implies due and careful enquiry by the vendors? (see p 165). This could mean that the vendors become liable under warranties so qualified, even though they are honestly ignorant of the circumstances giving rise to the liability.

(3) If accounts are warranted as 'accurate' the warranty is unlikely to be true, but it is unlikely that any claim would be made unless the deficiency is material. On the other hand, if accounts are warranted as making 'full' provision for all liabilities (including perhaps contingent or unquantified liabilities) then the warranty does not reflect accounting practice. Accounts normally only make provisions for material contingent losses which can be estimated with reasonable accuracy. (See Statement of Standard Accounting Practice 18.)

(4) A warranty that no liability has been incurred since a balance sheet date 'otherwise than in the normal course of trading' is quite restrictive as it would not cover, for example, replacement or repair of fixed assets or redundancy claims.

(5) Warranties under which plant or equipment is warranted as being in any particular condition or having any particular value are dangerous.

(6) A warranty under which the recovery of debts is guaranteed is not so much a warranty as in the nature of a guarantee.

(7) Warranties relating to management accounts or profit forecasts are dangerous and should be carefully considered. The vendors should be alert to spot whether or not management accounts are warranted in a roundabout way, for example by being annexed to the disclosure letter which is itself warranted as true (see p 189).

(8) Any warranty which says that a pension scheme is adequately funded is dangerous.

(9) A warranty under which insurance is said to be adequate causes underwriters (who are insurers themselves) to be on their guard.

(10) Any warranty which warrants the truth of written or oral information other than information contained in the disclosure letter is worrying.

(11) 'Sweeper' warranties under which the vendors warrant that all material facts have been disclosed are obviously wide-ranging.

(12) So far as tax warranties are concerned, official shortfall clearances are rare; capital allowances are often claimed; intra group transactions are quite common and book values are not normally equal to base costs. If warranties covering these points are given without qualification or disclosure, it is likely that insufficient work has been done by the vendors on tax disclosures.

(13) The sale agreement will contain a deed of tax indemnity or the more modern provisions relating to adjustment of the purchase price for tax claims (see p 153). Insurers will wish to check that the indemnity is limited to taxation arising before completion; that it is limited to claims falling on the target and does not cover claims against the purchaser arising otherwise than in respect of the target or the shares to be sold; that it excludes claims arising from transactions in the ordinary course of business since the accounts, claims in respect of which provisions have been made which are insufficient only by reason of any increase of rates of taxation or retrospective changes of the law, and claims which would not have arisen but for a voluntary act or transaction of the purchaser.

Is credit allowed for other provisions relating to taxation? Does the indemnity include requirements that notice be given of claims and that the indemnifiers be entitled to require that the target takes steps to minimise the loss? Is there a grossing up clause? (see p 154).

(14) The agreement should contain limitations on liability. Is there a minimum claim level (whether in the aggregate or in respect of any particular claim?) Is there a limit on total liability? (see p 74). Are there time limits within which claims are to be made? Are there provisions which limit liability to representations contained in the agreement and the disclosure letter? Does the payment of a claim under the indemnity provisions pro tanto satisfy a claim under the warranties?

(15) In preparing the disclosure letter, has care been taken to ensure that all items of the disclosure letter are not warranted 'correct', eg management accounts? Is it clear from the agreement that the disclosure letter does actually qualify the warranties? Surprisingly, it sometimes is not.

Chapter 3

Acquisitions by a Listed Company

The requirements of The International Stock Exchange of the United Kingdom and the Republic of Ireland Limited are set out in *The Admission of Securities to Listing* (the *Yellow Book*). The *Yellow Book* contains the listing rules made under Part IV of the Financial Services Act 1986, and reflects three EEC directives known as the Admission Directive, the Listing Particulars Directive and the Interim Reports Directive. These lay down minimum requirements for the admission of securities to listing, the content, scrutiny and publication of listing particulars as a condition of admission to listing and the continuing obligations of issuers after admission. Listing particulars will be required if shares are to be issued which will increase shares of a class already listed by 10 per cent or more, or if listed debt securities of any amount are to be issued. This book does not attempt to deal with listing particulars.

The directives make provision for the competent authority in each member state to impose additional requirements for these purposes. The Council of The Stock Exchange is the governing body of The Stock Exchange and the competent authority appointed under the Financial Services Act 1986. The Council has arranged for its functions as competent authority to be discharged by the Committee on Quotations, advised by the Quotations Department of The Stock Exchange.

The requirements concerning acquisitions or realisations of assets by listed companies and by their subsidiaries arise from the continuing obligations which a listed company owes to its shareholders and which are set out in the *Yellow Book*, Section 5, Chapter 2. The requirements relating to acquisitions and realisations are set out in Section 6, Chapter 1. The summary given in this chapter concentrates on the requirements in relation to the purchaser. The regulations apply to the acquisition and disposal of assets of all

80

kinds, but, in the context of this book, the comment in this chapter is limited to the acquisition of companies.

Classes of acquisition

Transactions are divided into four classes for the purposes of the regulations. If the acquisition is a Class 1 transaction, it will be necessary for the purchaser to make an announcement to the Company Announcements Office of The Stock Exchange and also to send a circular to shareholders. Very substantial acquisitions ('Super Class 1') will be subject to the approval of the purchaser's shareholders at a general meeting. A Class 2 transaction requires an announcement to the Company Announcements Office, but not a circular to shareholders, and a Class 3 transaction does not require announcement or circular unless all or part of the consideration is to be satisfied by the issue of securities for which listing is being sought, in which case an announcement must be made. Class 4 transactions are those which involve a past or present director or substantial shareholder, and in these cases it is normally necessary to obtain shareholders' approval. If the transaction is so large as to amount to a reverse takeover, the purchaser will normally be treated as a new applicant for listing.

It is therefore necessary to determine into which class the acquisition falls. The Committee may aggregate acquisitions that have taken place since either the publication of the last accounts of the purchaser or the issue of the last circular, whichever is the later. These aggregated transactions may then be treated as if they were one transaction if they were all completed within a short period of time.

Class 1

If the book value of the net assets of the target (excluding goodwill and other intangibles and after deducting loan capital and amounts set aside for future taxation) is in excess of 15 per cent of the book value of the net assets of the purchaser, the acquisition will fall within Class 1. If the assets of the purchaser include substantial intangible items, the Committee may relax the rule. A transaction will also fall within Class 1 if the net pre-tax profit of the target exceeds 15 per cent of the net pre-tax profit of the purchaser (excluding extraordinary items in each case) or if the value of the consideration for the acquisition exceeds 15 per cent of the purchaser's net assets or, if the consideration is equity share capital, it exceeds 15 per cent of the equity capital of the purchaser previously in issue (in which case listing particulars will be required).

Where the acquisition is made for equity share capital, and falls within Class 1 only because the market value of the equity share capital is more than 15 per cent of the assets of the purchaser, then the Committee will normally be prepared to deem such an acquisition to fall within Class 2, provided the other comparative figures are materially less than 15 per cent.

If the comparison of assets or profits shows a figure of 25 per cent or more then the acquisition is known as a 'Super Class 1' and must be made conditional on approval by shareholders in general meeting. In this connection an additional test will be applied for the purpose of comparing the purchaser with the target, based on the respective 'gross' capitals of each party. 'Gross' capital for this purpose will be calculated, for the purchaser, by aggregating its equity capital at its market value immediately prior to the announcement, its preference capital and debt securities (also at market value if listed), all other liabilities (other than current liabilities) including for this purpose minority interests and deferred taxation, and any excess of current liabilities over current assets. For the target a similar aggregation is made, save that the value of the consideration payable will be taken instead of the equity capital at market value. The aggregation is made on the basis that 100 per cent of the equity capital is to be acquired, whether or not such is the case.

Class 2

The transaction will fall within Class 2 if a comparison of the assets, profits, consideration, or capital, as described above, shows a relationship of 5 per cent or more but less than 15 per cent.

Class 3

The transaction will be a Class 3 acquisition if the net book value of the target's assets or the value of the consideration (whichever is the greater) is less than 5 per cent of the net book value of the assets of the purchaser and the net profits of the target are less than 5 per cent of those of the purchaser.

Class 4

An acquisition may fall within Class 4 if shares of the target are held by a director or substantial shareholder of the purchaser (or of any company in a group of which the purchaser forms part) or by any associate of such a director or substantial shareholder. This may apply even if the director or substantial shareholder is retaining his holding. The expressions 'director' and 'substantial shareholder' are defined to include persons who ceased to be directors or substantial shareholders within the last twelve months, and 'associate' is also defined (Section 6, Chapter 1, para 1.2). Whether or not the acquisition falls within Class 4 will depend on the extent of the interest involved. The Department should be consulted (through the brokers acting for the listed company) as early as possible.

An acquisition may also fall within Class 4 if any part of the equity share capital of the target has recently been, or is to be, acquired (whether by subscription or otherwise) by a director or an associate of a director.

Announcements

It will be seen that an announcement to the Company Announcements Office and to the press will be required in any case where all or part of the consideration for the acquisition is satisfied by the issue of securities of the purchaser for which listing is being sought. Otherwise, an announcement will only be required if the transaction falls within Classes 1, 2 or 4.

Six copies of the announcement should be given to the Company Announcements Office (through the listed company's brokers) for release to the market and consequently to the press and, if desired, direct to the press simultaneously. Where an announcement is required by the Rules, the information which it must contain is set out in Section 6, Chapter 1, para 4.2. Where an announcement is not required, but it is desired to make one, the announcement should include either details of the consideration (explaining how this is being satisfied, including the terms of any arrangements for payment on a deferred basis) or the value of the assets being acquired or disposed of. Any announcement about a transaction, however small, which does not state the value of the consideration or indicate the size of the transaction may mislead shareholders.

An announcement should be made as soon as possible after terms have been agreed (usually directly upon exchange of contracts).

Circulars

A circular to shareholders will be required if the transaction falls within Classes 1 or 4. The circular will normally take the form of a letter from the chairman or secretary, addressed to the shareholders, describing the transaction, with appendices containing an accountants' report on the target and giving further information required by The Stock Exchange.

Where it is necessary to convene a meeting of the purchaser's shareholders, eg because it is necessary to increase the purchaser's share capital or because shareholders' approval is required for some other reason, the circular will be sent out before completion of the acquisition and will contain the appropriate notice convening the meeting. In other cases it will normally be sent out after completion of the acquisition. In either case the circular will be designed to inform shareholders about the acquisition and must comply with The Stock Exchange requirements summarised below. For a specimen circular see p 334.

FORM OF CIRCULAR

1   Information about the acquisition

1.1   *Particulars of the target's business.* Particulars of the assets being acquired, including the name of the target, a description of the trade carried on, the value of the assets being acquired, and the net profits attributable to the assets being acquired (Section 6, Chapter 1, paras 3.6 and 4.2).

1.2   *Consideration.* The aggregate value of the consideration, explaining how this is being satisfied, including the terms of any arrangements for payment on a deferred basis (Section 6, Chapter 1, para 4.2). A statement that an application has been or will be made to the Council of The Stock Exchange for any consideration shares to be admitted to the Official List (Section 3, Chapter 2, para 2.1).

1.3   *Accountants' report.* An accountants' report on the target must be included covering the last five audited financial years. The requirements of the Committee concerning accountants' reports are set out in Section 4, and particular requirements relating to property companies are set out in Chapter 1 of Section 10 (Section 6, Chapter 1, para 3.6).

1.4   *Effect of the acquisition.* The benefits which are expected to accrue to the purchaser as a result of the transaction and the effect of the acquisition on earnings or assets and liabilities of the purchaser should also be stated (Section 6, Chapter 1, paras 3.6 and 4.2).

1.5   *Taxation.* In the absence of a statement that income tax and apportionment clearances as appropriate have been obtained, a statement that appropriate indemnities have been given and a statement that inheritance tax indemnities have been given (Section 3, Chapter 2, paras 3.13 and 3.14).

2   Information about the group

2.1   *Name and office.* Name of the purchaser, registered office and head office if different from the registered office (Section 3, Chapter 2, para 1.1).

2.2   *Changes since latest accounts.* Statement of any significant change in the financial or trading position of the purchaser group which has occurred since either the end of the last financial year for which annual accounts have been published or the publication of the latest interim financial statement, or an appropriate negative statement (Section 3, Chapter 2, para 5.10).

2.3 *Significant litigation.* Information on any legal or arbitration proceedings pending or threatened against any member of the purchaser group which may have or have had during the previous twelve months a significant effect on the group's financial position or an appropriate negative statement (Section 3, Chapter 2, para 3.15).

2.4 *Borrowings.* Indication as at the most recent practicable date (which must be stated) of the following, on a consolidated basis if material:

(a) the total amount of any loan capital outstanding in any member of the purchaser group and loan capital created but unissued, and term loans, distinguishing between loans guaranteed, unguaranteed, secured (whether the security is provided by the issuer or by third parties) and unsecured;

(b) the total amount of all other borrowings and indebtedness in the nature of borrowing of the group, distinguishing between guaranteed, unguaranteed, secured and unsecured borrowings and debts, including bank overdrafts and liabilities under acceptances (other than normal trade bills) or acceptance credits or hire purchase commitments;

(c) all mortgages and charges of the group; and

(d) total amount of any contingent liabilities or guarantees of the group.

An appropriate negative statement must be given, where relevant, in the absence of any such loan capital, borrowings and indebtedness and contingent liabilities. As a general rule, no account should be taken of liabilities between undertakings within the same group, a statement of that effect being made if necessary (Section 3, Chapter 2, para 5.16).

2.5 *Working capital.* A statement (which will relate to the purchasing group as enlarged by the acquisition) that in the opinion of the directors of the purchaser the working capital available to the group is sufficient, or, if not, how it is proposed to provide the additional working capital thought by the directors to be necessary. Where cash forms a substantial part of the consideration for a transaction falling within Class 1, the Department will require a letter from the purchaser's brokers confirming that they are satisfied that the statement as to the sufficiency of working capital has been made by the directors after due and careful enquiry and that persons or institutions providing finance have stated in writing that such facilities exist (Section 6, Chapter 1, para 3.8 and Section 3, Chapter 2, para 2.19).

2.6 *Material contracts.* A summary of the principal contents of each material contract (not being a contract entered into in the ordinary course of business) entered into by any member of the group within the two years immediately preceding the publication of the circular, including particulars of dates, parties, terms and conditions, any consideration passing to or from the purchaser or any member of the group, unless they have been on view in the last two years, in which case it will be sufficient to refer to them collectively as being on view.

In cases where it is contended that contracts cannot be offered for inspection without disclosing to trade competitors important information, the disclosure of which might be detrimental to the interests of any of the parties, application may be made to the committee to dispense with the offer of such documents for inspection (Section 3, Chapter 2, para 3.16).

2.7   *Prospects.* Information on the group's prospects for at least the current financial year including special trade factors and risks (Section 3, Chapter 2, para 7.6).

2.8   *Profit forecasts.* Where a profit forecast appears in the circular the principal assumptions, including commercial assumptions, upon which the directors have based their profit forecasts, must be stated. The accounting policies and calculations for the forecast must be examined and reported on by accountants and their report must be set out. The company's broker must report in addition whether or not they have satisfied themselves that the forecast has been stated by the directors after due and careful enquiry, and such report must be set out (Section 3, Chapter 2, para 7.2).

2.9   *Substantial interests in shares.* The name of any person other than a director, so far as known by the purchaser, who, directly or indirectly, is interested in 5 per cent or more of the purchaser's capital, together with the amount of each such person's interest or, if there are no such persons, an appropriate negative statement (Section 3, Chapter 2, para 3.9).

3   Directors' interests

3.1   *Interests in share capital.* Interests (distinguishing between beneficial and non-beneficial interests) of each director relating to listed securities and which:

     (*a*) have been notified to the purchaser pursuant to the Companies Act 1985, ss 324 or 328; or

     (*b*) are required pursuant to s 325 of that Act to be entered in the register referred to therein;

or an appropriate negative statement.

In the case of companies not subject to the Companies Act, the interest of each director, including his spouse and children under 18, whether or not held through another party, in the share capital of the company, together with any options in respect of such capital (Section 3, Chapter 2, para 6.6).

3.2   *Interests in transactions.* All relevant particulars, including the consideration passing to or from any member of the group, about the nature and extent of any interest of directors of the purchaser in transactions which are or were unusual in their nature or conditions or significant to the business of the group, and which:

     (*a*) were effected by the purchaser during the current or immediately preceding financial year; or (*b*) were effected by the purchaser during an earlier financial year and remain in any respect outstanding or unperformed;

or an appropriate negative statement (Section 3, Chapter 2, para 6.5).

3.3 *Service contracts.* Details of directors (including proposed directors), existing or proposed service contracts with any member of the group, excluding contracts expiring or determinable by the employing company without payment of compensation (other than statutory compensation) within one year, except contracts previously made available for inspection in accordance with Section 5 and not subsequently varied, or an appropriate negative statement (Section 6, Chapter 1, para 4.2 and Section 3, Chapter 2, para 6.4).

3.4 *Emoluments.* If the total emoluments receivable by the directors of the purchaser will be varied in consequence of the transaction, all particulars of the variations; if there will be no variation, a statement to that effect (Section 3, Chapter 2, para 4.14).

4   Experts' consents

In the case of a statement or report attributed to an expert, a statement that the expert has given and has not withdrawn his written consent to the issue of the circular with the statement included in the form or context in which it is included (Section 3, Chapter 2, para 1.8).

5   Documents for inspection

A statement that for a period (being not less than fourteen days) at a named place in the City of London (or such other centre as the Committee may determine) as well as at the registered office of the purchaser, the following documents (or copies thereof) where applicable may be inspected:

(1) the memorandum and articles of association of the purchaser;

(2) any trust deed or other document constituting debt securities which are to be issued as consideration for the acquisition;

(3) material contracts;

(4) directors' service contracts;

(5) the acquisition agreement;

(6) all reports, letters or other documents, balance sheets, valuations and statements by any expert any part of which is extracted or referred to in the circular;

(7) a written statement signed by the auditors or accountants setting out the adjustments made by them in arriving at the figures shown in any reports and giving the reasons therefor; and

(8) the accounts of the purchaser or, in the case of a group, the consolidated audited accounts of the purchaser and its subsidiaries for each of the two financial years preceding the publication of the circular together with, in the case of a United Kingdom company, all notes, reports or information required by the Companies Act.

Where any of these documents are not in the English language, there must be available for inspection translations either notarially certified or made by a person certified by a solicitor qualified to practice in any part of the United Kingdom to be in his opinion competent to make such translations (Section 3, Chapter 2, para 3.17).

Drafts of the circular should be submitted to the Department by the brokers acting for the listed company as soon as possible. It should be noted that, where the acquisition is made in consideration of securities for which listing is being sought, listing will not be granted until the circular has been approved even if listing particulars are not required. If (as is often the case) completion of the acquisition is conditional upon listing being obtained, the completion date should be set bearing this in mind. The Agreement for Sale in Chapter 6 contains a clause making completion conditional on listing.

Shareholders' approval

The approval of shareholders to the transaction will normally be required by the Department if:
(*a*) the transaction is a 'Super Class 1' (see p 82);
(*b*) the transaction falls within Class 4;
(*c*) the accountants' report is qualified because of inadequate records; or
(*d*) the acquisition amounts to a reverse take-over (ie if the assets or profits of the target are larger than those of the purchaser (including subsidiaries) or if the transaction would result in a change of control of the purchaser, eg through the introduction of a new majority shareholder or group of holders).

The Committee will require that a very substantial acquisition or reverse takeover be subject to the approval of shareholders in general meeting. The acquiring company will normally be treated as a new applicant for listing. Listing for the company's securities will be suspended until after the shareholders' approval has been obtained. Listing will then be cancelled prior to the publication of listed particulars, following which the company's securities will normally be restored to listing.

When the following conditions are satisfied, the company will not be treated as a new applicant, and listing will normally be restored before shareholders' approval has been obtained but only after full information has been published:
(*a*) the target is of a similar size to the purchaser;

(*b*) the two companies are in a similar line of business;

(*c*) the enlarged group is suitable for listing; and

(*d*) there will be no material change in the board or voting control or in the management.

If there is a possibility that shareholders' approval should be obtained by virtue of the Department's rules, the Department should be approached before exchange of contracts as it will be necessary to determine whether completion of the acquisition should be made expressly subject to shareholders' approval in the contract. In these cases the circular giving the required information will be sent to shareholders before completion of the acquisition and will include a notice of meeting and a proxy card complying with the Department's requirements.

Shareholders' approval may also be required, in an indirect way, if it is necessary to increase the capital of the purchaser to make the acquisition. In these cases the Department will require a statement that no issue will be made which will effectively alter the control of the purchaser without prior approval of shareholders if 10 per cent or more of the voting capital will remain unissued after completion of the acquisition. In calculating the 10 per cent, shares reserved for options or the exercise of conversion rights are disregarded.

Using shares to fund an acquisition

When a listed company makes an acquisition the purchaser frequently wishes to use its own shares to fund the price. The vendors may be willing to accept some shares in the purchaser as consideration, but more often than not they require cash. There are essentially two methods of using shares in the London market to raise cash for an acquisition: the rights issue and the placing. Which method is used will depend upon a number of considerations, and market reaction will often be the most important, but the following part of this chapter deals with a number of points which arise under the heads of timing, accounting, stamp duty, and the r 520 notice.

As used in this chapter, a 'rights issue' means an offer to existing shareholders of new shares for cash on renounceable provisional letters of allotment, while a placing means a sale of new shares to selected persons. A placing may be a 'vendor placing' in which the new shares are allotted to the vendors as consideration for the acquisition and then sold by them to the placees, or it may be a 'cash placing' in which the new shares are placed for cash which is used to pay the price. Although the legal and accounting results are different, the net economic effect to the vendors of these two types of placing is the same. It is common practice, at least in the case of a large placing, to offer some or all of the shares to be placed to existing shareholders, with the placees taking those shares which the existing shareholders do not want. This type of offering does not, however, turn the issue into a rights issue. The Association of British Insurers has said that its members will expect an offer to existing shareholders where the issue amounts to more than 10 per cent of the purchaser's existing capital or involves a discount of more than 5 per cent on the market price of the consideration shares.

It is obvious that a rights issue and a cash placing can be used to raise more money than is needed for the acquisition, while the vendor placing will only raise the purchase price. On the other hand the rights issue is not suitable for the smaller acquisition, involving, as it does, a fairly major market operation. There are a number of variants on the basic theme of rights issue or placing, including the so-called 'vendor rights issue' where the consideration shares are allotted to the vendors and then offered to the purchaser's shareholders on an underwritten basis. This chapter, however, deals only with the basic types of transaction.

Timing

Timing is important for a number of reasons and in a number of ways. The vendors will want the cash consideration at completion, and, normally, as quickly as possible. However, the timing of the announcement of the issue is no longer subject to control, following the general consent issued under the Control of Borrowing Order 1958 (SI 1958 No 1208) on 14 March 1989 which exempts any transaction from the order, except transactions by local authorities.

Issues in the London market to fund acquisitions are invariably underwritten. That is to say they are not announced until a securities house has entered into a commitment to take the securities. In the case of a rights issue, the underwriting will be in the classic form and underwriters will agree to take rights shares not taken up, which cannot be sold in the market at or above the offer price. In the case of a placing the securities house will agree to find purchasers of the new shares from the vendors or, in the case of a cash placing, subscribers for the new shares to be allotted by the company direct to the placees. The period from the entering into of this commitment, normally on the announcement of the issue, and the date when the shares are finally taken up is the underwriting period and underwriters will receive a fee according to its length. A typical fee structure might be 2 per cent of the amount of the issue for the first thirty days of the underwriting period and one-eighth of 1 per cent for every week or part of a week thereafter. With this in mind, the purchaser will wish to keep the underwriting period as short as possible.

Where the sole or main purpose of a rights issue is to fund an acquisition, it is likely in practice that a meeting of the purchaser's shareholders will be required to approve the acquisition (if it is Super Class 1—see p 82) or to increase share capital and grant the directors authority to allot under s 80 of the Companies Act 1985—see p 5. The resolutions to carry these matters into effect are ordinary resolutions and fourteen clear days' notice will be required (although the articles of the purchaser should be checked). The acquisition agreement will be conditional on these matters and on the admission of the new shares to the official list. Because the provisional allotment letters are negotiable documents they cannot in practice be issued until the conditions of the issue have been satisfied, so the steps are: sign the acquisition agreement, announce and post circular to shareholders, wait fourteen days, hold shareholders' meeting, complete acquisition (having borrowed the money to do so), post provisional allotment letters, wait twenty-one days, collect proceeds, repay borrowings.

In the case of a placing the underwriting period is shorter, even where some or all of the new shares are offered to existing shareholders. Such an offer need not made on renounceable documents and can therefore take place during the notice period for the meeting, so the steps are: sign the acquisition agreement, announce and post circular to shareholders containing offer, wait fourteen days, hold a shareholders' meeting, complete the acquisition and placing simultaneously.

In the case of a cash placing it will often be necessary to pass a special resolution to disapply pre-emption rights under s 89 of the Companies Act 1985 (see p 5). This requirement will extend the notice period to twenty-one clear days and therefore increase the underwriting period. Most listed companies pass a general disapplication of s 89 at their annual general meetings, but this will only normally cover new shares up to 5 per cent of their issued capital, in accordance with the published wishes of the investment committee of the Association of British Insurers, and is unlikely to be sufficient to fund a major acquisition.

It is obviously important, in order to keep the underwriting period to a minimum, to ensure that the rights issue does not require a s 89 disapplication. The scheme of s 89 et seq is not to require a disapplication if there is an offer to existing shareholders which complies with the statutory procedure, but there are a number of points to watch. First, a statutory offer must remain open for twenty-one clear days which does not start until the offer is made. Where the offer is sent by post it is deemed to be made at the time at which the letter would be delivered in the ordinary course of post (s 90(2)). This poses obvious difficulties in the case of foreign shareholders, and indeed the impossibility of knowing when a letter would be delivered to them in the ordinary course of post makes it imperative to find another way of communicating the offer to them. This problem is compounded by the fact that certain jurisdictions, notably the United States and Canada, have securities laws which prohibit the making of offers in those jurisdictions without regulatory filings. Luckily s 90(5) provides that where a holder has no registered address in the United Kingdom, the offer may be made by publishing it in the *London Gazette*. It is the practice therefore to make the offer by these means but, in addition, to send the documents for convenience to foreign shareholders unless prohibited from doing so by the local law.

Another point to watch in the statutory procedure is the treatment of fractions. It is the normal practice to aggregate fractions and sell them in the market, but s 89 provides that the offer must be made to shareholders in proportions which are 'as nearly as practicable' equal to the shares held by them. Where the computer will do it, this seems to require allocations to be rounded up and down as appropriate. The sale in the market of the shares resulting from the aggregation of fractions amounts to a cash issue, but this will normally be covered by the general disapplication obtained at the purchaser's latest annual general meeting.

Accounting

An issue of shares for cash, whether as a rights issue or as a placing will involve a share premium account of the difference between the net price and the nominal value of the shares. These matters are discussed on pp 42 to 48. The acquisition will be accounted for on an acquisition basis and, if the price paid exceeds the fair value of the assets of the target, goodwill will arise on consolidation, which cannot be written off against share premium account. It will normally be possible, however, to reduce capital by writing down the share premium account. This will involve a special resolution which must be sanctioned by the court. The purchaser will not wish to extend the underwriting period by including the special resolution as one of the matters to be dealt with at the extraordinary general meeting convened to approve the acquisition, but it is possible to convene a separate extraordinary general meeting by notice included in the same circular.

In a vendor placing it will normally be possible to obtain merger relief under the Companies Act 1985, s 131. If the acquisition is accounted for on a merger basis no goodwill will arise, and if it is accounted for on an acquisition basis the difference between the nominal value and the fair value of the consideration shares will show up as a non-statutory reserve against which goodwill arising on consolidation can be written off.

Stamp duty

With the abolition of capital duty the stamp duty costs of the acquisition itself will not be increased by a rights issue or a cash placing. However, in the case of a vendor placing, a further transaction in securities is involved, namely a sale of the shares from vendors to placees, and this will be subject to stamp duty reserve tax (see p 99). In a case where the issuing house arranging the placing acts as a principal, and agrees to buy the shares from the vendor and sell them on to the placees there will be a double charge to stamp duty reserve tax unless the transaction is within the Finance Act 1986, s 89A. Section 89A will exempt the agreement to sell to the issuing house if:

(a) the agreement is part of an arrangement, entered into as part of its business, under which it is to offer the securities for sale to the public;

(b) the agreement is conditional on admission of the securities to listing;

(c) the consideration under the agreement is the same as the price at which the issuing house is to offer the security for sale; and

(d) the issuing house sells the securities in accordance with the arrangement referred to in (a).

There can be doubts about the applicability of s 89A in many cases, either because the securities are not offered to 'the public' but to a small class of persons or because part of the placing takes place after the listing has become effective, so that the agreement to place is not in fact conditional upon listing. These problems can be avoided if the issuing house acts as agent for the vendors in placing the shares rather than as principal, and the vendor placing agreement on p 312 is prepared on this basis.

A vendor placing may also add to the stamp duty costs of the acquisition itself. Many cases arise in which the target owes substantial sums to the vendor. Such a debt may exist before the acquisition or may be created as a result of the payment of a substantial pre-sale dividend (see p 117). In this case the purchaser is normally required to pay for the shares and to put the target in funds to repay the indebtedness resulting from the payment of the dividend and its lending back. In order to raise the money to repay the indebtedness by means of a vendor placing and to obtain merger relief under the Companies Act 1985, s 131, it will be necessary to capitalise the debt owing from target to vendor in the form of equity share capital. Paying money to the target to repay the indebtedness does not involve a stamp duty charge (see p 98), but purchasing share capital does. A vendor placing will therefore increase the cost of the acquisition to the purchaser by 0.5 per cent of the value of the debt which has to be capitalised.

The rule 520 notice

Even after the Council of The Stock Exchange has granted permission for the admission of the new shares to the official list, the listing will not become fully effective until a notice is posted (or, these days, screened) under rule 520 of the rules of The Stock Exchange (see *Yellow Book*, Section 1, Chapter 1, para 8). The notice will not be posted until after the shares have been allotted. There has only been one case in which, after the permission had been granted, the notice was not posted, but underwriters will normally insist that their commitment is conditional upon the posting of the notice.

This gives rise to practical difficulties. In the case of a vendor placing the purchaser cannot allot the consideration shares until completion of the acquisition, but the vendors will not complete until they get their cash and the placees will not pay until the listing is fully effective. The normal procedure is for The Stock Exchange to post the notice the morning after they have been notified of the allotment, but vendors are understandably reluctant to part with the target on one day, and wait until the following day until they are paid. In that case they bear the risk of something happening which means that the notice is not posted. Such an event is almost inconceivable, but the consequences are severe, and a vendor who has stipulated for cash will not run any risk, however slight, of ending up with unlisted shares in a purchaser with a problem.

The normal way out of this conundrum is to go through all the completion procedures but for the parties' solicitors to hold the completion documents overnight subject only to the posting of the rule 520 notice. The consideration shares are allotted subject to completion, The Stock Exchange is informed of the allotment and posts the notice, whereupon the acquisition automatically completes simultaneously. In a case where there is a delay between contract and completion it is necessary for the acquisition agreement to provide that completion is conditional not merely on the grant of permission for the admission of the consideration shares to the official list, but upon the listing becoming fully effective.

Much the same procedures can be applied in the case of a cash placing, but the considerations in a rights issue are somewhat different. The underwriters will still insist on their commitment being subject to the posting of the rule 520 notice, but the notice will not be posted until after the provisional letters of allotment have been despatched. It will not be acceptable for the letters of allotment to be expressed as being subject to completion of the acquisition, as the rights letters are negotiable and of value, but on the other hand, where the purpose of the issue is to raise the purchase price, shareholders are entitled to be assured that the acquisition has been completed. In such a case it would create a major problem if the issue went ahead without the acquisition. One solution is for the purchaser to take the overnight risk. As the rights issue proceeds will not be available for some weeks after all the conditions of the acquisition have been satisfied there is no question of using the issue proceeds to complete the acquisition and it will normally be completed with borrowed funds. The rights letters are then mailed immediately, the notice is posted the following morning and the underwriters are fully committed thereafter. If something goes wrong overnight and The Stock Exchange fails to post the notice the purchaser is left with a new subsidiary and a large overdraft.

There is one last twist to this tale. There used to be useful section in the Companies Act 1985 and its predecessors (s 86) which provided that where a prospectus stated that an application had been made for listing and the listing was not granted the allotment was void. This section has now been repealed and not replaced by anything in the Financial Services Act 1986. The result is that, in the event of a failure to post the rule 520 notice, the allotment is still valid. As the notice has not been posted when the rights letters are despatched, it is theoretically possible for this to happen and good practice to include a statement in the provisional letters of allotment, that they will lapse if the rule 520 notice is not posted. This degree of conditionality is acceptable, particularly because the condition will normally have been satisfied by the time the letters have been received. In some cases it might be possible to take advantage of this by completing the acquisition in escrow, in the same way as described above for a vendor placing, mailing the letters, and releasing the documents from escrow when the rule 520 notice is posted. Then, if the notice is not posted, the allotment letters lapse, the underwriters are off the hook and the acquisition does not complete. In this case, of course, it is necessary for the acquisition agreement to be conditional not merely on the grant of permission for the admission of the relevant securities to the official list, but upon the listing becoming fully effective.

The Unlisted Securities Market

Where the purchaser has securities traded in the Unlisted Securities Market then it must refer to the terms and conditions of entry to the Unlisted Securities Market in connection with the acquisition. The purchaser's obligations arise under paragraph 5 of the general undertaking which such companies are required to give to The Stock Exchange. In general terms, the requirements are similar to those of the *Yellow Book*, but are less onerous. Reference should be made to the following tests in order to classify transactions:

(*a*) the value of the assets acquired compared with the assets of the purchaser;

(*b*) net profits (after deducting all charges for taxation and excluding extraordinary items) attributable to the assets acquired, compared with the profits of the acquiring or disposing company;

(*c*) the aggregate value of the consideration given or received, compared with the assets of the purchaser;

(*d*) equity capital issued by the purchaser as consideration for the acquisition compared with the equity capital already in issue.

Notification to the Department is required when comparison in any of the above cases gives a result of 5 per cent or more. The notification should be in the form of an announcement including details of the assets acquired, how the consideration was satisfied, the value of the assets and the profits attributable to those assets.

If comparison in one or more of the above cases shows results of 25 per cent or more, the transaction is considered to be sufficiently material to call for not only an announcement but also a circular to be sent to shareholders. The requirements and the contents of such circulars are contained in Section D of the document *The Stock Exchange Unlisted Securities Market*. Circulars are required irrespective of whether the consideration was in cash or securities. The Department must be consulted in advance where the relative tests amount to 100 per cent or more, or where a change of control might result.

Transactions which involve a director, substantial shareholder or past substantial shareholder of the company (or any other company being its subsidiary, holding company or a subsidiary of its holding company) should be subject to prior approval of the company in general meeting and the issue of an explanatory circular. This also includes transactions with associates of any of the foregoing. Where it is proposed to enter into such a transaction, the Department must be consulted as soon as possible, and prior to any contract being entered into.

Rights issues and the offering of shares to existing holders in a placing will be excluded from the operation of Part III of the Companies Act 1985 where the shares are listed—see Sched 4 to the Financial Services Act 1986 (Commencement No 3) Order 1986 (SI 1986 No 2246), but at the time of publication, Part III will apply to such offers by a USM company and it will therefore be necessary to file a prospectus. Part III will be replaced by Part V of the Financial Services Act 1986, when it comes into force.

Chapter 4

Stamp Duty and
Stamp Duty Reserve Tax

Stamp duty is chargeable under the head 'conveyance or transfer on sale' on transfers of registered shares from vendor to purchaser. Unless stock transfer forms are presented for stamping within 30 days a penalty is payable, and the company secretary will be liable to a £25 fine under the Stamp Act 1891, s 17, if he registers a transfer which is not duly stamped. The exemptions which apply to transfers of property certified at £30,000 or less do not apply to share transfers. Duty is payable by the purchaser and is chargeable at the rate of (£0.50 per £100 (or part) of the consideration.

Loan capital is generally exempt from stamp duties. However, where the purchaser agrees to pay to the vendor the amount of any indebtedness which is due from the target to the vendor, the amount of the indebtedness repaid may be treated as consideration for the shares in the target (see Stamp Act 1891, s 57). An undertaking by the purchaser instead to procure repayment by the target will not be regarded by the Stamp Office as falling within s 57, unless it is plain that the target does not have sufficient resources to make payment. In such circumstances, the indebtedness could be reconstituted as loan capital and assigned to the purchaser against payment of the amount involved.

Duty is charged on so much of the consideration as is ascertainable at the date the transfer is stamped. Where the consideration is, for example, to be determined following the preparation of completion accounts, the transfer may be presented for stamping within the thirty day period and the duty paid subsequently, once the amount of the consideration has been determined. However, this is subject to the operation of the 'contingency principle'. In treating consideration as ascertainable, all contingencies are ignored. Accordingly, if there is a specified maximum amount of consideration or, in the absence of a maximum, a minimum amount, this will be treated as the consideration payable and the duty calculated accordingly.

The contingency principle applies in 'earnout deals' where part of the consideration given for the purchase of shares is deferred and becomes payable only if profit targets are met. The level of future profits is unascertainable, and so this consideration should not be liable to duty, but if it is subject to a maximum amount stamp duty will become payable on the transfer of the shares to the purchaser by reference to that maximum. Should the profit targets not be met, so that the full consideration does not become payable, the stamp duty cannot be reclaimed.

Where the deferred consideration is to be satisfied in shares, it is possible to argue that part of the consideration received by the vendors is the right to the future allotment. This right is a chose in action (see *Marren (Inspector of Taxes)* v *Ingles and Others* (1980) 54 TC 76) and as such is not dutiable consideration at all. However, in many cases the purchaser will retain the option to satisfy the deferred consideration in cash, and this may be regarded by the Stamp Office as sufficient to make the transfer stampable in respect of the deferred consideration as well.

Part IV of the Finance Act 1986 introduced a new tax, the stamp duty reserve tax, which is chargeable where there is an agreement to transfer 'chargeable securities' which is not completed within two months by a duly stamped instrument. Where the agreement is completed later, but within six years, repayment of the stamp duty reserve tax may be obtained if the duly stamped instrument of transfer is presented to the Stamp Office. Despite its name, stamp duty reserve tax is a tax distinct from stamp duty, and unlike stamp duty it is directly assessable. 'Chargeable securities' are defined by the Finance Act 1986, s 99(3) to include stocks, shares, loan capital and units under a unit trust scheme, but the definition does not include shares in companies incorporated outside the United Kingdom (unless recorded in a register kept in the United Kingdom), bearer shares or most forms of loan capital. Renounceable letters of allotment are, however, subject to the tax (Finance Act 1986, s 88(2)).

Although bearer shares are subject neither to stamp duty on sale (since ownership passes by renunciation or delivery and no instrument of transfer is created) nor to stamp duty reserve tax on the agreement to sell, it is unlikely that bearer shares will generally come to replace registered shares since, on issue, duty will be payable under the head 'bearer instrument' of an amount equal to three times the transfer duty (ie £1.50 per £100 (or part) of the consideration given for the issue). Under s 60(4) of the Finance Act 1963 the company issuing the bearer shares is liable to pay the duty. Following the abolition of capital duty, the issue of bearer shares is no longer prohibitively expensive and it is possible that they may be of use in limited circumstances, in particular where a number of successive sales, which would otherwise be subject to stamp duty or stamp duty reserve tax, is envisaged.

Although the charge to stamp duty reserve tax is potentially of very wide scope, it will not, in practice, usually be of concern in relation to the acquisition of shares in a private company. An exception may occur where a purchaser company intends that on completion the shares in the target should be transferred into the beneficial ownership of another company within the purchaser's group. Unless the acquisition agreement contains provision for the purchaser to substitute the other company to complete the agreement, a direct transfer of the shares from the vendor to the purchaser's subsidiary must not be taken, as there is no relief from stamp duty reserve tax equivalent to that from stamp duty afforded by the Finance Act 1930, s 42 (see below). Instead, in order to avoid stamp duty reserve tax on the acquisition agreement, it is necessary for there to be two transfers, first, from the vendor to the purchaser and, secondly, from the purchaser to its associated company. Relief under the Finance Act 1930, s 42 may then be claimed in respect of the latter transfer, and the acquisition agreement will not be subject to stamp duty reserve tax, as it will have been duly completed by a stamped instrument.

Capital duty was formerly payable upon certain increases in the capital of a company and was therefore relevant to company acquisitions where the consideration took the form of an issue of shares in the purchasing company. Capital duty was introduced by Part V of the Finance Act 1973 on the entry of the United Kingdom into the European Community in compliance with Council Directive 69/335/EEC of 17 July 1969, the provisions of which ceased to be mandatory from 1985. Capital duty was repealed in the United Kingdom by the Finance Act 1988, s 141 with effect from midnight on 15 March 1988. Where exemption from capital duty under the provisions of the Finance Act 1973, Sched 19, para 10 had been provisionally obtained prior to that date, the relief will be confirmed provided that the circumstances in which the relief may be lost had not arisen at that date. Despite the repeal of capital duty, it remains necessary to comply with the requirements of the Companies Act 1985, s 88 and to make returns of allotments to the Registrar of Companies together, where appropriate, with the duly stamped contract or written particulars where the contract is not reduced to writing.

In the previous editions of this book it has been necessary to consider at some length the various reliefs from stamp duty, as well as from capital duty, available where the consideration for the acquisition was or included the issue of shares in the purchasing company. As part of the reform of stamp duties in 1986 which included the introduction of stamp duty reserve tax and the reduction of the rate of stamp duty chargeable on transfers of registered shares, these reliefs were repealed. It will now usually be impossible to avoid a charge either to stamp duty or else to stamp duty reserve tax.

Exemption from stamp duty may be available if the vendor and the purchaser are companies associated within the meaning of the Finance Act 1930, s 42. To meet this requirement, the vendor or the purchaser must be directly or indirectly the beneficial owner of not less than 90 per cent of the issued share capital of the other, or not less than 90 per cent of the issued share capital of each of the vendor and the purchaser must be directly or indirectly in the beneficial ownership of a third company. It is apparent that this exemption may be available in the case of the reorganisation of a group of companies, but is unlikely to apply to an acquisition of a company at arm's length.

Relief from stamp duty is available for certain reconstructions or reorganisations falling within the provisions of the Finance Act 1986, ss 75, 76 and 77 and in respect of transfers by way of gift (see Finance Act 1985, s 82 and the Stamp Duty (Exempt Instruments) Regulations 1987 (SI 1987 No 516)), but consideration of these lies outside the scope of this book.

Chapter 5

Taxation

Almost every aspect of taxation can apply, in some way, to the acquisition of a private company. Detailed discussion of all possible revenue considerations is outside the scope of this book, and the purpose of this chapter is to mention (in more or less detail) problems which often arise in practice.

The chapter is divided into two main parts: tax payable by vendors, and taxation of the target. Further sections deal with the impact of *Ramsay* and *Furniss* v *Dawson*, with taxation warranties and other contractual provisions and with the tax treatment of payments under them. The changes announced in the 1989 Budget are referred to where relevant but the chapter does not contain any detailed consideration of the Finance Bill, which includes a number of anti-avoidance measures.

The chapter does not deal with the taxation treatment of any reconstruction or reorganisation which the vendor or the vendor's group may undertake as a preparatory step to any sale. Nor is there any detailed consideration of the impact on corporate and personal tax planning of the changes to tax rates contained in the Finance Act 1988. Readers should, however, note that these changes have overturned much conventional wisdom as to the optimum method of structuring a transaction and every transaction should be approached afresh. Consideration will have to be given to proposals which formerly would have seemed heretical, such as constituting part of the consideration as dividends or remuneration. The changes have had an equally dramatic effect on anti-avoidance legislation, most of which is framed with a view to preventing the conversion of income into capital. Nevertheless, sections on those provisions are retained in this chapter as they are still of concern in some cases and will, of course, be of renewed importance if the differential between income and capital gains tax rates is re-introduced.

TAX PAYABLE BY VENDORS

Tax will normally be payable on any gain made by the vendors on the sale of their shares in the target. Where the gain is not part of a trade an individual will, subject to any exemption or special charge which may be applicable, pay capital gains tax on the gain. Corporations will pay corporation tax on the gain whether or not it forms part of their trade, but, if it does not form part of their trade, the tax will normally be assessed under the same rules as apply to capital gains tax. Corporation tax on capital gains is currently payable at the rate of 35 per cent, while capital gains tax is payable at the individual's marginal rate of income tax (currently either the basic rate of 25 per cent or the higher rate of 40 per cent) but under the Capital Gains Tax Act 1979, s 5 exemption is granted, to individuals only, on the first £5,000 of total chargeable gains (less allowable losses) in the year of assessment. For the purposes of computing the gain an indexation allowance is granted for both individuals and companies by the Finance Act 1982, s 86 et seq (as amended by the Finance Act 1985, s 68 et seq and the Finance Act 1988, Sched 8, para 11).

The indexation allowance is calculated from March 1982, or the date of acquisition if later, on the greater of the acquisition cost and the market value of the asset on 31 March 1982 if held at that date. Expenditure allowable under the Capital Gains Tax Act 1979, s 32 also qualifies for indexation. Acquisition costs have generally been rebased to 31 March 1982, although special provisions apply to ensure that neither chargeable gains nor allowable losses are thereby increased (see Finance Act 1988, s 96). While the rate of tax applied will be the same, an individual vendor will generally, because of the availability of the indexation allowance and rebasing to 31 March 1982 (and, in appropriate cases, retirement relief), be concerned to obtain a capital gains tax rather than an income tax treatment (but see pre-sale dividends below).

Several matters which should be considered when advising vendors are outlined below, classified as follows:

(*a*) the non-resident vendor:
(*b*) transfer of assets on retirement;
(*c*) consideration payable by instalments;
(*d*) share for share exchanges;
(*e*) the Income and Corporation Taxes Act 1988, s 703;
(*f*) the Income and Corporation Taxes Act 1988, s 776;
(*g*) pre-sale dividends;
(*h*) sale of debts.

The non-resident vendor

An individual is chargeable to capital gains tax if he is resident or ordinarily resident in the United Kingdom. It is beyond the scope of this book to examine in detail what constitutes 'residence' or 'ordinary residence' or to deal with the complicated cases which arise in connection with visitors to the United Kingdom. It is worth, however, making a few points.

(1) In order to escape liability for capital gains tax it is normally necessary to be neither resident nor ordinarily resident in the United Kingdom for the whole of the year of assessment in which the disposal is made. In the case of the sale of shares in a private company, the disposal will be made when an unconditional contract is entered into for the disposal, or, if there is no unconditional contract, on the date of completion. If an individual is ordinarily resident in the United Kingdom, he will not escape capital gains tax simply by departing for the whole of the year of assessment in which the gain is made and then subsequently returning. If he has an intention to return, even if he is physically absent through the whole of the year, he will still be 'ordinarily resident'.

(2) Where a vendor intends to live abroad permanently, it can be worth ensuring that the gain does not arise in a year of assessment for any part of which he has been resident in the United Kingdom. There are, however, valuable extra-statutory concessions. If a person claims that he has ceased to be resident and ordinarily resident in the United Kingdom, and can produce some evidence of this (eg that he has sold his house here and set up a permanent home abroad), his claim is usually admitted provisionally with effect from the date following his departure. Normally, this provisional ruling is confirmed after he has remained abroad for a period which includes a complete tax year and during which any visits to this country have not exceeded three months in aggregate. If, however, he cannot produce sufficient evidence, the decision on his claim will be postponed for three years and will then be made by reference to what actually happened in that period. During the three intervening years, his tax liability is computed provisionally on the basis that he remains resident in the United Kingdom. His liability is adjusted, if necessary, when the final decision is made at the end of three years. When a person leaves the United Kingdom and is treated on his departure as not resident and not ordinarily resident in the United Kingdom he is not charged to capital gains tax on gains accruing to him on disposals made after the date of his departure. (See Extra-Statutory Concession D2 and the Inland Revenue booklet *Residents and Non-residents Liability to Tax in the United Kingdom*, paras 16

and 17.) The Revenue is not obliged to apply the Extra-Statutory Concession if there is any tax avoidance motive and, particularly where the intention to dispose of the shares is formed while the vendor is still UK resident, its use should be approached with care. (See *R v IRC, ex p Fulford-Dobson* [1987] STC 344.)

(3) It is worth noting that 'professional trustees' resident in the United Kingdom are treated as non-resident where the settlor was not resident, ordinarily resident or domiciled in the United Kingdom at the time of the settlement (Capital Gains Tax Act 1979, s 52(2)).

(4) Special provisions may apply to non-residents who carry on a trade, profession or vocation in the United Kingdom through a branch or agency or who are dual resident companies.

Transfer of assets on retirement

The Finance Act 1985, s 69 and Sched 20, grants valuable relief from capital gains tax to the owner of a family business selling after reaching retirement age or who has been forced to retire through ill health. The first £125,000 of gains and half the next £375,000 of gains will be free of capital gains tax if they arise on a 'material disposal of business assets' by a person who has reached the age of 60 or who has retired through ill health before that age (s 69(1)). A 'disposal of business assets' includes a sale of shares (s 69(2)(c)).

The provisions are complex and will need to be reviewed in each case. The qualifying conditions applying to the company and applying to the disposal are summarised below.

Conditions applying to the company

A disposal of business assets is 'material' if throughout a period of one year ending with the 'operative date' the vendor *either* owns the business then owned by the company *or* the company is a 'family company' of which the vendor is a full time working director and the company is either a trading company or the holding company of a trading group (s 69(5)).

A 'family company' is a company in respect of which the vendor can exercise 25 per cent of the voting rights or, if not less than 51 per cent of the voting rights are exercisable by him or a member of his family, not less than 5 per cent are exercisable by the vendor himself. 'Family' means husband or wife of the vendor and relatives of the vendor or the vendor's husband or wife; 'relative' means brother, sister, ancestor or lineal descendant. Uncles, aunts and cousins do not count. A 'trading company' is defined as any company whose business consists wholly or mainly of the carrying on of a trade or trades. The holding company of a trading group also qualifies for relief; a 'trading group' is defined to mean a group of companies (being the parent and its 51 per cent subsidiaries) the business of whose members taken together consists wholly or mainly of the carrying on of a trade or trades.

A 'full time working director' is defined as a director who is required to devote substantially the whole of his time in a managerial or technical capacity to the service of the company or, as the case may be, the companies in the group taken together.

Qualifying conditions for disposal

The conditions relating to the company need to be fulfilled in relation to each vendor who seeks relief and if the period ending with the 'operative date' on which they are fulfilled exceeds ten years the full relief is obtained. For the purposes of calculating this period separate periods during which the vendor carried on a business may be aggregated provided that not more than two years elapse between any two qualifying periods. If the conditions are fulfilled over a shorter period than ten years (with a minimum of one year) relief is reduced pro rata.

For the purposes of the relief the 'operative date' is the date of the disposal or, if earlier, either the date on which the company ceased trading (provided the vendor had reached sixty or retired through ill health prior to such cessation) or the date on which the vendor retired from a full time working directorship. If the operative date is the date of retirement the company must continue to qualify as a family company carrying on a trade and the vendor must continue as a director of the company to devote at least ten hours per week to the service of the company (or of the group) in a technical or managerial capacity until the date of sale or cessation of trade.

The amount of the gain available for relief will be restricted by reference to the chargeable business assets of the company (or the group) at the time of the disposal. Relief is given on that part of the gain which bears the same proportion to the total gain as the value of the 'chargeable business assets' bears to the value of the 'chargeable assets' of the target (or the group). Every asset is a chargeable asset except those on the disposal of which no chargeable gain would arise (Sched 20, para 7(3)). Examples of a non-chargeable asset would be tangible moveable property of less than £3,000 and debts (not being debts on securities). 'Chargeable business assets' means assets (including goodwill but not including investments) which are assets used for the purposes of a trade carried on by the company by a member of the group. Special rules apply in the case of groups to exclude investments in subsidiaries from the definition of chargeable assets and to apportion the value of assets in subsidiaries which are not wholly owned.

A number of detailed rules exist making provision for disposals by trustees, for aggregating several disposals and in relation to assets which have been owned by the vendor's spouse.

A vendor who has obtained relief under the Capital Gains Tax Act 1979, s 85, on an exchange of shares in the target for shares in the purchaser will not be entitled to retirement relief on a disposal of the consideration shares (unless they qualified for relief in their own right) even though a disposal of shares in the target would have been eligible for relief. The Finance Act 1985, Sched 20, para 2, allows such a vendor to elect within two years of a share for share exchange (or of any reorganisation of capital falling within the Capital Gains Tax Act 1979, s 77) for the provisions of s 78 not to apply to the exchange. The exchange will therefore be treated as a disposal for capital gains tax purposes and retirement relief will be available if the other conditions for relief are fulfilled.

Consideration payable by instalments

It is often the case that some part of the consideration payable for the acquisition of a private company will be payable after completion. Examples include the case where part of the consideration is retained as security for warranties and cases where the consideration is based on profits yet to be earned. In these cases it is necessary to consider the impact of capital gains tax upon the arrangements which are proposed.

It is the normal rule (Capital Gains Tax Act 1979, s 40(2)) that capital gains tax is payable on the disposal by reference to the total consideration receivable. Consideration is brought into account without a discount for postponement of the right to receive any part of it and, in the first instance, without regard to a risk of any part being irrecoverable or to the right to receive it being contingent. The Capital Gains Tax Act 1979, s 41(1)(c) specifically provides that no allowance will be made for any contingent liability in respect of a warranty or representation made on the disposal by way of sale of any property other than land, although, if the contingent liability becomes enforceable, adjustments are made. A retention as security for warranties will not therefore normally affect the capital gains tax computation.

The Capital Gains Tax Act 1979, s 40(1), applies where consideration is payable by instalments over a period exceeding eighteen months beginning not earlier than the time when the disposal is made. Liability to tax may be deferred if the vendor satisfies the Board of Inland Revenue that he would otherwise suffer undue hardship. The Board may allow the tax to be paid by instalments over a period not exceeding eight years and ending not later than the time at which the last of the instalments of consideration is payable. The vendor has to show hardship and it seems that this will normally be shown if he cannot pay the tax out of the resources made available to him by the transaction. The paragraph only applies where the consideration is truly payable by instalments. For instance, if the consideration is paid by means of a 'vendor placing' and the vendor then deposits part of the consideration with the purchaser, even though that part of the consideration might only be returnable at some future date, the consideration does not appear to be payable by instalments within the meaning of the paragraph.

Where consideration is calculated by reference to profits earned after completion (sometimes called an 'earnout'), or is otherwise indeterminate in amount, the computation is more difficult. In these cases the practice of the Revenue is to value the contingent right to receive the consideration and to charge tax by reference to the aggregate of the consideration actually received and the value of the contingent right. The contingent right is itself a chargeable asset and in *Marren (Inspector of Taxes)* v *Ingles and Others* (1980) 54 TC 76 it was held that this right was disposed of when the vendor received the future consideration, thus giving rise (in that case) to a further chargeable gain. The Capital Gains Tax Act 1979, s 20(1), provides that there is a disposal of assets by their owner where any capital sum is derived from assets, even though no asset is acquired by the person paying the capital sum. It was argued on behalf of the taxpayer that this subsection was confined to cases where no asset was acquired by the person paying the capital sum and, of course, in cases relating to deferred consideration an asset (ie the shares in the target) is so acquired even though it is acquired before the final consideration is paid. The House of Lords rejected this argument, holding that the section applies whether or not assets are acquired by the person paying the capital sum. See also *Marson (Inspector of Taxes)* v *Marriage* (1979) 54 TC 59. It has been suggested that, if there is a limit on the total consideration payable, or if the amount to be paid is definite although payable at an indeterminate time, it may be that *Marren* v *Ingles* does not apply, and s 40(2) does, so that tax is to be calculated by reference to the full amount, not the value of the contingent right. This area is one of some uncertainty and although some clarification has been given where the deferred consideration consists of shares or debentures (see below), in many cases the treatment will depend on the view taken by the vendor's Inspector of Taxes.

A further consequence of *Marren* v *Ingles* is that deferral of the charge to capital gains tax by means of roll-over relief (see share for share exchanges below) will not be available to the extent that the consideration shares are to be issued at some future date, since the contingent right to an allotment of shares does not amount to an issue of shares within the Capital Gains Tax Act 1979, s 85.

In order to avoid the problems arising from *Marren* v *Ingles*, it has become common to issue shares or other securities of the purchaser to which special rights attach, in place of a simple covenant to pay. These securities are issued to the vendor at completion and carry rights to ensure that their value falls to be determined by reference to the earn-out formula. The Revenue have indicated that where, under the sale agreement, a right is created to an unascertainable amount (whether or not subject to a maximum) which is to be satisfied wholly by the issue of shares or debentures, then they will, if the vendor so elects, treat that right as a security for capital gains tax purposes, so that roll-over relief will be available. If, however, the deferred consideration is to be satisfied or may be satisfied in cash, then the value of the right to the deferred consideration will be brought into the capital gains tax computation. (See Extra-Statutory Concession D27.) Since many purchasers will require to retain the right to satisfy the deferred consideration in cash, the scope of this concession may be limited in practice.

It may however be possible to use similar arrangements involving the retention by or issue to the vendor of special shares in the target carrying a right to a dividend or to be repurchased by the target on the basis of the earnout formula in order to defer a charge to tax until receipt of the earnout consideration.

Share for share exchanges

Where the consideration for the acquisition is the issue of shares or debentures by a purchaser company, capital gains tax otherwise payable on the sale of shares in the target may be deferred. The relevant provisions are contained in the Capital Gains Tax Act 1979, ss 77–91.

If the provisions apply, no tax is payable on the exchange and the new shares are treated in the hands of the vendors as if they had been acquired at the time when, and for the consideration for which, the shares in the target were acquired; in other words the gain (or loss) accrued at the time of the exchange is 'rolled over' into the consideration shares or debentures. In order to obtain roll-over relief it is necessary that the purchaser either holds, or as a result of the exchange will hold, more than one quarter of the ordinary share capital of the target before the exchange takes place. 'Ordinary share capital' is defined for this purpose (by ICTA 1988, s 832(1)) as 'all the issued share capital (by whatever name called) of the company, other than capital the holders of which have a right to a dividend at a fixed rate but have no other right to share in the profits of the company'.

Alternatively the exchange must take place as the result of a general offer made to members of the target or any class of them (with or without exceptions for persons connected with the purchaser), the offer being made in the first instance on a condition such that if it were satisfied the purchaser would have control of the target.

The consideration shares or debentures must be issued to the vendors. For the purposes of the Capital Gains Tax Act 1979, s 85 'issue' includes 'allot' (Capital Gains Tax Act 1979, s 64(2)) and consideration shares or debentures may therefore be issued on renounceable letters of allotment without prejudicing the availability of relief although, of course, any subsequent renunciation will result in a disposal of the shares for capital gains tax purposes.

The Capital Gains Tax Act 1979, s 87, imposes an overriding condition on the application of roll-over relief in these circumstances. The condition is that the exchange is effected for bona fide commercial reasons and does not form part of a scheme or arrangements of which the main purpose, or one of the main purposes, is avoidance of liability to capital gains tax or corporation tax. This condition, however, does not affect relief available to any vendor who (together with persons connected with him) does not hold more than 5 per cent of, or of any class of, the shares in or debentures of the target. It is open either to the purchaser or to the target to apply for clearance and, if the Board of Inland Revenue notifies the applicant that it is satisfied that the exchange will be effected for bona fide commercial reasons and will not form part of any such scheme or arrangements, the condition is deemed satisfied. Clearance has been refused in cases where the consideration shares or debentures have been intended to overcome the difficulties described above connected with deferred consideration and *Marren* v *Ingles*. It seems possible that clearance will, in future, be more difficult to obtain where the consideration shares or debentures in effect represent deferred consideration which would not fall within the terms of the Extra-Statutory Concession D27. If the overriding condition imposed by s 87 operates to defeat roll-over relief, the section provides that tax assessed on vendors and not paid within six months from the date when it is payable is recoverable within two years from any other person who holds all or any part of the consideration shares or debentures that were issued to the vendor and who acquired them without there having been a chargeable disposal for capital gains tax purposes or who acquired them from the vendor in the circumstances referred to in the Capital Gains Tax Act 1979, s 44(1) (disposals between spouses), or ICTA 1970, s 273 (disposals between members of a group of companies).

On a subsequent disposal of the new holding the calculation of the tax payable can be complex, particularly where only part of the new holding is disposed of and the shares in the target were originally acquired at different dates and at different prices. The basic rules are to be found in the Capital Gains Tax Act 1979, s 65, and (in relation to shares held on 6 April 1965) Sched 5, para 13, and (in relation to shares acquired after 6 April 1982) the Finance Act 1982, ss 88 and 89, and the Finance Act 1983, Sched 6.

Vendors who have reached retirement age and who wish to avail themselves of the reliefs conferred by the Finance Act 1985, s 69, should consider carefully before they sell the shares in their family business in exchange for shares in the purchaser so as to obtain roll-over relief, as the retirement relief will not be applicable to the sale (as there is no disposal) and may not be available on a subsequent disposal of the consideration shares, if these do not themselves qualify for relief. In these circumstances, the vendor may elect that roll-over should not apply (see p 107).

The Income and Corporation Taxes Act 1988, s 703

The Income and Corporation Taxes Act 1988, s 703 and succeeding sections are concerned, as the headnote to Part XVII of the Act states, with 'tax avoidance'. The sections provide the Revenue with powers enabling them to serve notices cancelling income tax advantages arising from a very wide range of transactions involving securities, although it appears that s 703, when originally enacted as the Finance Act 1960, s 28, was intended only to provide the Revenue with power to counteract 'dividend stripping'.

It is instructive to remember what dividend stripping was. If a company had large revenue reserves and the owner of shares in the company was in a position to have these paid out by way of dividend, he would wish to avoid income tax on the dividend. He would therefore sell the shares 'cum dividend', receiving a purchase price equal to the value of the securities including the potential dividend. The purchase price would not be subject to income tax but would only be chargeable to any relevant capital gains tax in his hands (before 1965, of course, there was no capital gains tax). The purchaser would be a person or company who would not suffer the same rate of tax on the dividend and, once the dividend had been declared to the purchaser, the purchaser would then sell the shares back to the original owner at their 'ex dividend' price. If the purchaser of shares was, for instance, a dealer in securities, the loss which the purchaser made on selling the shares back to the original owner at a low price would be allowable for income tax purposes and be available to offset the tax chargeable on the large dividend he had received in the meantime. Payment of the dividend therefore caused the purchaser no tax disadvantage, whereas the original owner had converted the dividend into capital and obtained a tax advantage.

The powers conferred on the Revenue by s 703 to counteract dividend stripping have been used to counteract a wide range of tax advantages deriving from the sale of private companies. In order for the Revenue to be able to serve a s 703 notice the following conditions have to be satisfied (s 703(1)):

(*a*) one of the circumstances mentioned in s 704 must have occurred;

(*b*) there must be a transaction in securities;

(*c*) in consequence of the transaction the taxpayer must be in a position to obtain, or have obtained, a tax advantage;

(*d*) the taxpayer must be unable to show that the transaction or transactions were carried out either for bona fide commercial reasons or in the ordinary course of making or managing investments and that none of them had as their main object, or one of their main objects, to enable tax advantages to be obtained.

Two cases in point which illustrate the potential application of the section to private company acquisitions are those of *IRC* v *Cleary* (1967) 44 TC 399 and *IRC* v *Brown* (1971) 47 TC 217. The facts in the *Cleary* and *Brown* cases were broadly the same. In each case, the taxpayer had arranged for the sale of the shares owned by him or her in one company to another company controlled by the taxpayer and his or her associates. Were it not for the section, the taxpayer would have been charged only to any applicable capital gains tax on the sale. In both cases, however, the taxpayer paid income taxes on the consideration received. (For the quantum of the tax advantage see *Bird* v *IRC* [1988] 2 WLR 1237, HL.)

In order to understand the cases, it is necessary to analyse them in the light of the conditions for the application of the section given above.

Condition (a)

Had any of the circumstances mentioned in s 704 occurred? In both cases the part of s 704 which was relevant was s 704D which states the relevant circumstances in effect as follows:

(1) That in connection with the *distribution* of *profits* of a company to which this paragraph applies, the person in question . . . receives [a consideration which either—

(i)   is, or represents the value of, assets which are (or apart from anything done by the company in question would have been) available for distribution by way of dividend, or

(ii)   is received in respect of future receipts of the company, or

(iii)   is, or represents the value of, trading stock of the company and the said person so receives the consideration that he does not pay or bear tax on it as income].

(2) The companies to which this paragraph applies are—

(*a*)   any company under the control of not more than five persons; and

(*b*)   any other company which does not satisfy the condition that its shares or stocks or some class thereof (disregarding debenture stock, preferred shares or preferred stock), are authorised to be dealt in on a stock exchange in the United Kingdom, and are so dealt in (regularly or from time to time),

so, however, that this paragraph does not apply to a company under the control of one or more companies to which this paragraph does not apply.

Reading s 704D in the light of nature it is impossible to conceive that it applies to the circumstances of the *Brown* and *Cleary* cases, but the words shown in (author's) italics are given extended and artificial meanings by s 709(3) which provides that, in s 704:

(*a*)   references to profits include references to income reserves or other assets,

(*b*)   references to distribution include references to transfer or realisation (including application in discharge of liabilities).

It is therefore possible to render the opening words of s 704D so that they read: 'That in connection with the *transfer* of *assets* of a company to which this paragraph applies'.

In both the *Brown* and *Cleary* cases the purchaser company was one to which the paragraph applied and it had transferred assets (ie it had paid cash) to the taxpayer.

In the *Cleary* case the purchaser company had sufficient reserves and cash to pay a dividend of an amount equal to the purchase price and it was therefore held that the consideration was 'assets which are (or apart from anything done by the company in question would have been) available for distribution by way of dividend'. In the *Brown* case the company had sufficient standing to the credit of its profit and loss account to pay a dividend equal to the cash element of the consideration, but its current liabilities exceeded its current assets by £3,000. It therefore had to borrow the amount of the cash consideration from a bank. Megarry J took the view, affirmed on appeal, that as the company had reserves available for distribution there was no legal impropriety in its borrowing the money to effect that distribution. The money once borrowed was, therefore, 'assets available for distribution'. Even though a prudent or cautious financier might not have paid a dividend in such circumstances, it was legally possible and that was sufficient.

Condition (b)

In neither case was there any difficulty on this point. The sale of shares in a company is obviously a transaction in securities (which in any event is defined to include a sale by s 709).

Condition (c)

Did the taxpayer obtain a tax advantage? In *IRC* v *Parker* (1966) 43 TC 396 Lord Wilberforce indicated that a taxpayer obtains a tax advantage if he receives something which is not subject to income tax but which, if he had received it in another way, would have been. In both the *Brown* and *Cleary* cases, if the purchaser company had declared a dividend, the taxpayer would have received it. It did not declare a dividend but used its assets to pay the consideration for the shares acquired from the taxpayer. In both cases, therefore, the taxpayer received cash as consideration for shares when, if it had been received by way of dividend, it would have been subject to income tax. The tax advantage was therefore obtained. (See also *Anysz* v *IRC* and *Manolescue* v *IRC* (1977) 53 TC 601 and *Williams* v *IRC* (1980) 54 TC 257.)

Condition (d)

In neither case was the taxpayer able to show that the transactions were carried out for bona fide commercial reasons and that none of them had, as their main objects, to enable tax advantages to be obtained. In the *Brown* case Russell LJ said (on appeal—(1971) 47 TC 217, at p 239) that:

[The] evidence amounts to no more than saying that the taxpayer and his wife wanted some money and entered into the transaction to get it. Now it seems to me that you do not show that a transaction of sale of securities for full consideration to a company already owned by yourself is a transaction to be entered into for bona fide commercial reasons merely by saying that it is such a sale transaction and that you wanted the money.

In considering the application of s 703 to acquisitions, the potential application of s 704C should not be overlooked. This section applies if the taxpayer receives a consideration which represents the value of assets which are (or would have been) available for distribution as dividend, 'in consequence of a transaction whereby any other person . . . receives . . . an abnormal amount by way of dividend'. In *Emery* v *IRC* [1981] STC 150 the target owned valuable properties which it sold for a profit of £244,000. The taxpayer then sold his shares in the target to an investment company for £223,409 payable by instalments and subsequently sold his right to receive those instalments to a wholly owned subsidiary of the purchaser for the same price. The target then paid a dividend of £260,500 to the purchaser. It was held that the vendor had received the consideration in consequence of an operation whereby the purchaser received an abnormal dividend and accordingly the consideration was treated as income.

In *IRC* v *Garvin* [1981] STC 344 the facts were similar but there the House of Lords held that there was no sufficient connecting link between the sale of the shares in the target and the declaration of the dividend. The fact that the purchaser acquired the whole of the share capital of a target with substantial undistributed profit did not by itself form sufficient ground for holding that such acquisition was the cause of the subsequent distribution of those profits by the target. The court held that the word 'whereby' in s 704 imported some causal connection between the transactions and the subsequent receipt of the abnormal dividend. In that case the Revenue attempted also to bring s 704D into play, by contending that the consideration was received 'in connection with the distribution of the profits' of a company to which s 704D applied. The targets were under the control of five or fewer persons at the time they were sold, but there was no evidence that they were so controlled at the date of the distribution. The court held that the relevant date was the day of the distribution of profits and accordingly that s 704D did not apply.

It is fair to say that in both these and the *Brown* and *Cleary* cases there was an element of tax avoidance. In each case the vendors entered into a series of transactions with a view to obtaining as capital that which could more easily have been obtained as dividend. If an acquisition has this result then it must be prudent to utilise the clearance procedure given in s 707. In the *Brown* case Megarry J said:

Having provided reasonable safeguards for the bona fide or ordinary transaction, I do not think that the legislature has given any indication of intending to use kid gloves in these cases.

In the light of the Finance Act 1988 changes to the taxation of income and capital gains, the potential for obtaining a tax advantage (condition *(c)*) is reduced and so the importance of this section may have been diminished. However, the rebasing to 1982, the indexation allowance, the individual's annual exemption and the possibility of deferral of the charge to tax through roll-over or other reliefs may make a capital gains tax treatment preferable, so that the prudent practitioner will continue to give consideration to the section.

The Income and Corporation Taxes Act 1988, s 776

This section attempts to counter tax avoidance by the realisation of gains in a capital form on a disposal of land which, if realised in another way, might be assessed as trading income. The section can have the effect of taxing as income under Case VI of Schedule D capital gains realised on the sale of shares in a company.

The section applies (s 776(2)):

(*a*) if land or any property deriving its value from land has been acquired for the sole or main object of realising a gain from disposing of the land; or

(*b*) if land is held as trading stock; or

(*c*) if land is developed with the sole or main object of realising a gain from disposing of the land when developed.

If a gain of a capital nature is obtained from the disposal of the land either by the person holding or developing the land or by any connected person (as defined by the Income and Corporation Taxes Act 1988, s 839) or, indirectly, by any person who is a party to any arrangement as respects the land which enables a gain to be realised, the gain may be taxed as income.

The section is very widely drafted. In particular s 776(4) provides that land is disposed of if, by any one or more transactions or by any arrangement or scheme, whether concerning the land or property deriving its value from land, the property in the land or control over the land is effectually disposed of. Accordingly, the sale of a land owning company or a company which controls a land owning company could fall within the section.

Under s 776(10) there is an exemption in respect of a disposal of shares in a company which holds land as trading stock or a company which owns directly or indirectly 90 per cent or more of the ordinary share capital of another company which holds land as trading stock, provided all the land so held is disposed of in the normal course of its trade by the company which held it and so as to procure that all opportunity of profit in respect of the land arises to that company. This exemption does not extend to 'arrangements' or 'schemes' for realising gains by indirect methods or by a series of transactions, which are caught by s 776(2)(ii). Although there is a procedure under s 776(11) for obtaining a clearance, this is rarely used, since the Revenue have proved reluctant to confirm such clearance, so that application merely serves to put the Revenue on notice. For recent cases see *Chilcott* v *IRC* (1982) 57 TC 446, and *Sugarwhite* v *Budd (Inspector of Taxes)* [1988] STC 533.

Pre-sale dividends

If the target has significant distributable reserves, a UK resident corporate vendor will be able to reduce its capital gain on the sale of the target by procuring the payment of a dividend by the target prior to the sale. In the hands of a UK resident company such a dividend is free of corporation tax (ICTA 1988, s 208) and such a payment allows the purchase price of the target to be reduced while the vendor still receives the same total consideration, including the dividend. Because the purchase price of the target's shares is reduced, the capital gain is, of course, lower. Measures were announced in the 1989 Budget intended to reduce the scope for avoidance of tax on capital gains by companies on disposal of subsidiaries. However, a pre-sale dividend paid out of the target's 'normal' profits and reserves remains effective.

A pre-sale dividend will normally be paid under the terms of a group election under ICTA 1988, s 247 (see p 130) and no liability to advance corporation tax (ACT) will arise. Both purchaser and vendor will wish to satisfy themselves that a valid group election is in force at the date of payment of the dividend. The group election ceases to apply when the purchaser ceases to be the beneficial owner of the target (s 248(4)) so that where the parties wish to make the payment under a group election it will be necessary to pay the dividend prior to exchange of contracts. For group relief purposes, 'arrangements' for the transfer of beneficial ownership can affect the ability of purchaser and target to surrender group relief (ICTA 1988, s 410: see p 132), but these provisions do not apply to group elections and accordingly the election will remain in force while the beneficial ownership of the target is with the purchaser notwithstanding that arrangements exist for its sale. The vendor should not enter into an exclusivity agreement with the purchaser. The agreement not to seek another purchaser while negotiations proceed could amount to a fetter on the vendor's beneficial ownership of the target within *Wood Preservation Ltd* v *Prior* [1969] 1 WLR 1077. The purchaser who agrees to a pre-sale dividend will wish to be sure that the target is not going to become liable to pay ACT in respect of the dividend and will, for safety's sake, also wish to ensure that the terms of the sale agreement give the target an effective indemnity against that liability if it should arise.

In some circumstances however it may be desirable to make the dividend payment outside the group election. This will be the case where the vendor can use the ACT to frank its own dividend (ICTA 1988, s 239) and if the purchase price is adjusted to allow for the interest cost of the ACT payment over the period prior to its recovery by the target the result can be satisfactory for both parties. Section 247 provides that it is for the target to choose whether or not to pay the dividend within the group election and on the face of the section it seems that the choice must be made while the group election remains in force.

In practice, the target may not have sufficient funds to pay the dividend and therefore it will be necessary for the vendor to lend an equivalent amount to fund the payment. The sale agreement will provide that, at completion, the purchaser must put the target in funds to repay this loan. Because the purchase price will have been reduced by the amount of the dividend, this will not involve any additional cash outlay on the purchaser's part (and may indeed reduce his liability to stamp duty on the acquisition). Where the parties wish to make the payment under a group election then of course it is necessary that the dividend is 'received' while the election remains in force, and if no money is to pass (because the dividend is immediately to be re-lent) then the question will arise whether the mere crediting of accounts is a sufficient receipt. On the authority of *Garforth (Inspector of Taxes)* v *Newsmith Stainless Ltd* (1978) 52 TC 522, the crediting of an account is probably sufficient, but the prudent practitioner will ensure that cheques are passed from target to vendor and vice versa. The Companies Act 1985, s 153(3), specifically provides that a distribution of a dividend is not prohibited by s 151 which prohibits financial assistance by the target in connection with the sale of its own shares (see p 21).

Since the Finance Act 1988 a pre-sale dividend may also prove beneficial for individual vendors, for whom the ACT paid in respect of the dividend represents a basic rate income tax credit. As a £75 dividend carries with it a £25 tax credit, further tax of only £15 need be paid to satisfy liability to tax at 40 per cent, thus giving an effective tax rate of 20 per cent (£15 out of £75) on the cash dividend. Of course, no group election is available for individual vendors so this route will only be of use if the target can utilise any ACT payable on the dividend. This may well be the case as privately owned companies tend not to have paid significant dividends so that mainstream corporation tax in past years will be available against which ACT can be recovered.

Because these transactions involve the payment of an abnormal dividend in connection with a transaction in securities the practitioner will consider whether or not ICTA 1988, s 703, is in point. If time permits the parties may well seek a clearance under s 709 but it is suggested that the section ought not to apply. These transactions have the effect of turning capital into income rather than the reverse, and represent an extraction of profit from the target which could have taken place at any time while the target belonged to the vendor. It is a curious effect of the Finance Act 1988 that it is now in certain circumstances less tax efficient to receive capital rather than income—the mischief that s 703 was designed to prevent! By the Capital Gains Tax Act 1979, s 26(7), it is specifically recognised that the payment of a dividend to a company in the same group is a permitted means of reducing the value of an asset and accordingly is not caught by the provisions of s 26, which counteract value shifting arrangements. A pre-sale dividend cannot be used to create a capital loss for corporation tax purposes (ICTA 1970, s 281).

As a matter of company law, it will be necessary to consider the provisions of the Companies Act 1985, Part VIII, to ascertain the distributable reserves of the target. Under s 270, the distribution must be justified by reference to the company's accounts and in some cases it may be necessary to prepare interim accounts. Last, but not least, falls to be considered the duties of the directors of the target. It is, of course, their duty to act in the interests of the target and in some cases it may be appropriate for them to seek assurances from the vendor or the purchaser that the target will have sufficient working capital following payment of the dividend.

Sale of debts

It is not uncommon for the target to owe debts to the vendors. Normally, these can be dealt with by the purchaser placing the target, at completion, in funds to repay the debt, but, if the debts are too substantial for the target to bear the cost of repaying or refinancing them, the only practical solution may be for the vendors to assign the debts to the purchaser. In such a case, it is likely that the target's business has not been successful and such assignments commonly occur as part of a transaction which realises a capital gains tax loss for the vendors. In this case, any loss which the vendors realise on a sale of the debt will not normally be allowable for tax purposes, since a debt, unless it is a debt on a security, is not a chargeable asset. The relief in respect of loans to traders contained in the Capital Gains Tax Act 1979, s 136, may be of assistance, but it is quite limited in scope. In particular, it does not apply where the borrower and lender are companies in the same group (s 136(3)(*c*)) or where the lender assigns the loan (s 136(3)(*b*)). Can the vendors convert the debts, before the sale, into securities, so as to realise a capital gains tax loss when they sell? At least part of the answer is given by *Harrison* v *Nairn Williamson Ltd* (1977) 51 TC 135.

In that case the taxpayer company received a holding of preferred shares in a subsidiary company in replacement of a holding of loan stock worth considerably less than its nominal value. In computing its allowable loss arising on a subsequent sale of the preferred shares, the taxpayer company claimed to bring into account the full amount paid for the subscription of the loan stock. It was held, however, that the Capital Gains Tax Act 1979, s 19(3) (now s 29A), applied to the acquisition of the loan stock by the taxpayer company because it was acquired 'otherwise than by way of a bargain made at arm's length'. Accordingly, the acquisition cost of the loan stock (and hence the preferred shares) was its market value at the date of its subscription and the allowable loss was restricted to the difference between the market value and the sale consideration.

It was argued for the taxpayer company that s 19(3) did not apply, because there was no 'disposal' of the loan stock by the target, only an acquisition by the taxpayer company, but the Court of Appeal did not agree. In any event the new section (s 29A) clearly applies in such a case unless the consideration is of an amount or value lower than the market value of the asset. This last condition stops the market value rule applying to give a higher base cost than the actual consideration in these cases.

It follows that debt reconstructions of this nature made shortly before a sale are unlikely to have the effect of making losses on debts allowable in full for capital gains tax purposes. The same will apply if new shares were issued as a rights issue, providing funds to repay the debt (see *IRC* v *Burmah Oil Co Ltd* (1981) 54 TC 200 and the second proviso to the Capital Gains Tax Act 1979, s 79(1)). The question of what is or has been considered is not a reorganisation of share capital within the Capital Gains Tax Act 1979, s 78 *Young Austen Young Ltd* [1987] STC 709).

If the vendor waives debts due from the target he should take care to apportion part of the sale consideration to the waiver. If all the consideration is attributed to the shares, the vendor may find he has translated what should be a capital loss into a capital gain. In *Aberdeen Construction Group Ltd* v *IRC* (1978) 52 TC 281 the taxpayer company narrowly avoided such a fate. See also *Booth (EV) (Holdings) Ltd* v *Buckwell (Inspector of Taxes)* (1980) 53 TC 425 where the vendor was bound by the allocation of consideration stipulated in the sale agreement although a different allocation would have produced a more favourable result.

TAXATION OF THE TARGET

This part of the chapter deals in outline with some of the aspects of the target's affairs which, in practice, often arise in connection with acquisitions, namely:

(a) the close company target;
(b) the target in a group;
(c) tax losses;
(d) advance corporation tax carry forward;
(e) value added tax;
(f) inheritance tax.

The chapter concludes with a general discussion of the contractual protection which a purchaser may seek.

It will be seen that tax problems and considerations can arise not only because of the target's past transactions but also because of the acquisition itself, which can give rise to tax charges on the target or loss of relief or allowances.

The close company target

Although the competition is stiff, the provisions of the taxing statutes which relate to close companies are some of the most intricately drafted legislation extant. The 1989 Budget envisages their repeal and instead a special tax regime will apply to close companies whose income consists mainly of investment income ('close investment companies'). What follows is intended as a brief summary of the existing legislation (which applies to accounting periods commencing before 1 April 1989). This legislation will continue to be relevant as apportionments can be made up to six years (and in some cases longer) after the end of the accounting period.

Most resident targets will be close unless they are part of a listed group. Close companies are defined by ICTA 1988, s 414, and the target will be close if it satisfies either the 'control test' in s 414(1) or the 'apportionment test' in s 414(2). By virtue of s 414(5), however, the target will not be close if it is controlled by a resident 'open' company (ie a company which is not close).

Under the control test, the target is close if it is under the control of five or fewer participators or of any number of participators who are directors. The words 'control', 'participator' and 'director' are given extended meanings by ss 416 and 417 which prevent most attempts to 'open' a company which would otherwise be close.

A person is taken to have 'control' of a company if he 'exercises or is able to exercise or is entitled to acquire' control, whether direct or indirect, over the company's affairs, and in particular a person is taken to have control if he possesses or is entitled to acquire:

(a) the majority of the share capital or issued share capital of the company or of the voting power in the company; or

(b) such part of the issued share capital as would entitle him to the greater part of the income if it were distributed; or

(c) rights which entitle him to receive the greater part of the assets of the company on a winding up.

Where two or more persons together satisfy any of the conditions of control they are taken to have control of the target, so that if it is possible to point to any five or fewer participators (or any number of participators who are directors) who together have control, the target will be close. For this purpose rights or powers of nominees or 'associates' (relatives, partners, co-trustees and co-beneficiaries) are attributed to participators. 'Participator' is so defined that almost any person who could have control over or an interest in a company's affairs (alone or together with others) falls within the definition. In particular it includes those who possess or are entitled to acquire share capital or voting rights in the target; any loan creditor of the target (widely defined but excluding banks lending in the ordinary course of business—s 417(9)); any person who possesses or is entitled to acquire a right to receive or participate in distributions etc; and any person who is entitled to secure that income or assets will be applied directly or indirectly for his benefit (s 417(1)).

'Director' includes any person occupying the position of director by whatever name called, any person in accordance with whose directions or instructions the directors are accustomed to act and any person who is a manager and owns or controls alone or with associates 20 per cent or more of the ordinary share capital of the target (s 417(5)).

The target satisfies the apportionment test if on the assumption that it is close, more than half of any amount falling to be apportioned under ICTA 1988, ss 423–430 and Sched 19 (see below) could be apportioned between five or fewer participators or among any number of participators who are directors.

This book deals with companies whose controllers are few enough to enable negotiations for an acquisition to be carried on with them individually. In such a case, if the target is resident, the definitions are cast so widely that it is almost bound to be close unless it is controlled by a company which is not a close company. If a parent company of a group is close, all its subsidiaries will normally be close, but if the parent company of a group is open (otherwise than by reason of foreign residence), the companies which it controls (directly or indirectly) will escape closeness via s 414(5). In practice, if the target is open, it is most likely to be open because the ultimate holding company of the group of which it forms part has shares listed on The Stock Exchange and falls within s 415, which takes most listed companies out of the net of closeness.

In deciding whether or not a target is close, the trail does not stop at these shores. If the target is controlled directly or indirectly by non-residents, it is necessary to look at their structure to decide whether or not they would be close if they were resident, as under s 414(6) foreign companies which would be close if resident here are treated as close in determining the status of resident companies which they control.

If the target is close four potential heads of tax liability appear:

(*a*) shortfall apportionment;

(*b*) loans to participators;

(*c*) payments which are treated as distributions; and

(*d*) inheritance tax apportionment.

If the target or the purchaser is close the 'first business loans' provisions of ICTA 1988, Sched 19 may be significant.

Shortfall apportionment

In recent years the rules relating to shortfall apportionment have been substantially relaxed, and with the exemption (by the Finance Act 1980) of trading income from apportionment the subject has lost much of its importance. Nevertheless, it is still the case that if a company is close on the last day of its accounting period it can be treated by the Revenue as having distributed its income for that period when it has not in fact done so. The object of the legislation is to prevent the accumulation of income by individuals in companies which they control, thus avoiding the higher rates of taxation. While in many cases there is now little difference in the taxation applying to distributed and undistributed income, the application of the apportionment rules is mandatory and these provisions will continue to be of concern.

The relevant provisions are contained in ICTA 1988, ss 423–430 and Sched 19 which oblige the inspector to 'apportion' the income of a close company among the participators. If an apportionment is made, ACT (subject to the rules in s 430) falls to be paid by the target and higher rate tax by the participators by reference to the amount apportioned. Section 429 provides that, if the tax assessed on the participators is not paid, the tax may be assessed on the target.

A purchaser of the target's share capital will therefore wish to know that there is no likelihood of a shortfall apportionment in respect of accounting periods ended before completion, because any such apportionment could result in a tax charge falling on the target after completion.

The amount of income which would normally fall to be apportioned is the excess of 'relevant income' for the accounting period over distributions made in respect of the accounting period. In the case of non-trading companies and in other special cases, however, wider powers are given to the Revenue (ss 423 and 424).

'Relevant income' is defined by Sched 19, para 1, and, in the case of a company which is a trading company or a member of a trading group (defined by Sched 19, para 7), is so much of its 'distributable income' for that period as can be distributed without prejudice to the requirements of the company's business (including such requirements as may be necessary or advisable for the acquisition of a trade). The trading income of such a company is exempt from apportionment. Higher standards apply in the case of companies which are not trading companies. For any company the limit of 'relevant income' is its 'distributable investment income' plus 50 per cent of its 'estate or trading income' (Sched 19, para 2).

The rules relating to the computation of relevant income are contained in Sched 19, paras 1–6. Distributable investment income is subject to apportionment except in the case of a trading company or member of a trading group which can show that distribution would prejudice the requirements of its business. A number of allowances are available to other companies.

In the case of a group of companies all of which are close, shortfall apportionment can apply throughout the group (income being apportioned and sub-apportioned until it reaches the individual participators in the holding company).

Under Sched 19, para 3, the distributions of a company for an accounting period are taken to consist of any dividends declared in respect of the period and paid during the period or within a reasonable time thereafter. If there is danger of a shortfall apportionment and if the purchaser is an open company, it will therefore be possible to declare a dividend within a reasonable time after completion (payable to the new owner) which will avoid a shortfall apportionment in respect of an accounting period ended before completion. 'Reasonable time', for once, is not defined, but the limit used to be eighteen months after the end of the accounting period (ICTA 1970, s 291) and it is understood that a dividend paid within this period will be regarded as paid within a reasonable time. Any such dividend can often be paid without incurring liability for advance corporation tax because of a group income election made pursuant to ICTA 1988, s 247.

Schedule 19, para 16 provides for shortfall clearances. A trading company, a member of a trading group or a company with estate or trading income may at any time after the general meeting at which accounts are adopted forward to the inspector a copy of the accounts and the directors' report. The inspector may, having received the accounts, call for further information and, once he is satisfied, he must intimate within three months whether or not he proposes to make an apportionment in respect of the company for the accounting period covered by the accounts. Purchasers may find that the target has agreed a required standard of distribution with the inspector and, if time is too short to obtain a clearance or if for other reasons this is not desired, any agreement with the inspector will assist the purchaser in assessing the risk of an apportionment. In all cases, whether clearances have been obtained or not, it is normal to take an indemnity from the vendor in favour of the target in respect of apportionments made by reference to income in accounting periods ended before completion.

Loans to participators

Under ICTA 1988, s 419, a loan by a close company to an individual participator (including 'associates', certain companies and participators in any company controlling the lender) can give rise to a liability on the lender to make a payment equivalent to advance corporation tax on the amount of the loan. The payment is not in fact ACT and does not, therefore, fall to be set off in computing the lender's liability to mainstream corporation tax.

The section extends to cover cases where the participator incurs a debt to the close company or a debt due from the participator to a third party is assigned to the close company. Debts which participators incur for the supply by the close company of goods or services in the ordinary course of trade are not included unless the credit given exceeds six months or is longer than that normally given to the company's customers. The section does not apply to loans made in the ordinary course of a business carried on by the close company which includes the lending of money, and there are limited exemptions for full time employees or directors who do not have a 'material interest' in the close company (5 per cent: see ICTA 1988, s 187(3)). Outright misappropriation of the company's funds cannot be regarded as an act of the company and is therefore not a loan or advance for this purpose (*Stephens (Inspector of Taxes)* v *Pittas (T) Ltd* [1983] STC 576).

By s 419(4) relief is given where the loan is subsequently repaid, although if payment of tax has not been made under s 419 the Revenue will normally seek payment of interest on any such amount for the period from the date on which payment should have been made to the date relief becomes available. Under s 421 an individual can incur a charge to higher rate tax if the company releases or writes off the loan. Section 422 applies the provisions to loans made by companies which are controlled by close companies but which are not themselves close, eg because they are non-resident. Section 419 will then apply as if the loan had been made by the close company itself.

If the target is close, the purchaser will require a warranty to the effect that no such loans have been made by the target or by companies controlled by the target.

Payments treated as distributions

Under ICTA 1988, s 418(2), expenditure incurred by a close company in providing for a participator's living or other accommodation, entertainment, domestic or other services or 'other benefits or facilities of whatever nature' is treated as a distribution by the company. This does not apply to benefits provided for individuals who are taxed on benefits in kind in any event (directors or employees earning more than £8,500) and does not apply to provision for relatives of any pension or gratuity given on death or retirement of a director or employee.

If the target is close the purchaser will require a warranty to the effect that the target is not liable to be treated as having made a distribution within this section as a result of any event prior to completion, as otherwise ACT on the deemed distribution can become payable by the target.

Inheritance tax apportionment

Under the Inheritance Tax Act 1984, ss 94 and 202, a close company is liable to pay inheritance tax in respect of transfers of value made by it. The section provides for apportionment among the participators according to their respective rights and interests in the company immediately before the transfer and if the company does not pay the tax, the persons to whom amounts are apportioned are liable to pay. If the target is itself a participator in a close company it can become liable to apportioned inheritance tax under s 202(2) even though its liability may (if the target is close) be sub-apportioned among the target's own participators by virtue of s 94(2). Purchasers will therefore normally require a warranty or indemnity covering liability under s 202.

First business loans

The Income and Corporation Taxes Act 1988, Sched 19, para 8(1), provides that certain expenditure is to be regarded as available for distribution and is not to be regarded as applicable to the requirements of the company's business. Among the expenditure so regarded is:

(a) any sum expended or applied, or intended to be expended or applied, out of the income of the company—

  (i) in or towards payment for the business, undertaking or property which the company was formed to acquire or which was the first business, undertaking or property of a substantial character in fact acquired by the company, or

  (ii) in redemption or repayment of any share or loan capital or debt (including any premium thereon) issued or incurred in or towards payment for any such business, undertaking or property, or issued or incurred for the purpose of raising money applied or to be applied in or towards payment therefor, or

  (iii) in meeting any obligations of the company in respect of the acquisition of any such business, undertaking or property.

These provisions are presumably aimed at those who incorporate their businesses taking only a few shares and leaving the balance outstanding on loan account to be repaid out of profits. They can cause problems in connection with an acquisition. If the target has a 'first business loan' this will obviously increase the likelihood of a shortfall apportionment. A first business loan can arise by virtue of the acquisition itself if the purchaser is a close company which has raised a loan to pay for the acquisition, and the purchaser was formed to acquire the target or the acquisition represents the first 'business undertaking or property of a substantial character in fact acquired by' the purchaser. This will typically be the case in management buyouts where the acquisition is made by a 'Newco' incorporated for the purpose by the management. The purchaser may be hoping that dividends paid by the target after completion of the acquisition can be applied in paying interest on and repaying principal of the loan, but will the provisions of para 8 have the effect of disallowing any such application for the purpose of computing relevant income? If they do have this effect, dividends paid to the purchaser will be apportioned among the participators even though they are in fact all applied in payments to the lender in respect of the 'first business loan'.

Schedule 19, para 1(3), provides that in determining relevant income for shortfall apportionment purposes regard is to be had to 'such requirements as may be necessary or advisable for the acquisition of a trade'. Paragraph 8 only applies to restrict relevant income for the purposes of para 1(2), so by this ellipsis the 'first business loan' provisions do not apply to loans made for the purpose of acquiring a controlling interest in a trading company or a company which is a member of a trading group (except in the case of acquisitions from associated companies—para 9). Accordingly, where the target is a trading company para 8 should not cause problems in relation to the repayment of a loan raised for its purchase. Because the trading income of a trading company or a member of a trading group is exempt from apportionment, it seems that such a company can repay the principal of a first business loan out of trading income without danger, but if the target does not carry on a trade, eg if it is an investment company and is not a member of a trading group within para 7(2)(*a*), and if the purchaser repays the loan otherwise than out of trading income exempt from apportionment, para 8 can still have unfortunate effects.

Para 8 applies to sums expended or applied, or intended to be expended or applied 'out of the income of the company'. The meaning of these words was considered in *Morris Securities Ltd* v *IRC* (1940) 23 TC 525 and in *Hanstead Investments Ltd* v *IRC* (1975) 50 TC 419. In *Morris* the taxpayer company had acquired properties as a 'first property' and expended £13,000 towards payment for them in an accounting period in which the profit of the company amounted to £21,000. Although the £13,000 did not appear to be funded out of income but was in fact raised by increasing the company's overdraft, Lawrence J said:

> It is impossible to say that when a company has in fact made a bona fide profit of £21,000 and has discharged a liability that liability has not been discharged out of income.

In *Hanstead* the taxpayer company carried on the business of land dealing. The company bought land for £6,000 and sold the same land two days later for £49,000. Was the £6,000 purchase price 'expended or applied . . . out of the income of the company'? The Court of Appeal held that it was not, deciding that 'out of the income of the company' means income in the sense of profits. As the £6,000 fell to be deducted in computing the company's profit, it was not payable out of income. The *Morris* case was distinguished on the facts.

It seems therefore that although the purchaser of a non-trading target might contend that payments of interest on the loan raised to purchase the target were not, on the basis of the *Hanstead* case, made out of income, it will be difficult to show that repayments of principal fall outside the terms of para 8 if the purchaser's income (eg dividends from the target) exceeds the principal repaid.

The phrase 'business, undertaking or property' is not defined by the paragraph but 'property' would presumably include shares. The paragraph catches not only the original loan raised for the purpose of the acquisition, but any refinancing (para 8(5)).

Close investment companies

A company which is close and whose income consists mainly of investment income will, for accounting periods commencing after 31 March 1989, be liable to corporation tax at a special rate equivalent to the higher rate of income tax unless it distributes sufficient of its profits. Restrictions will also exist on the deduction and allowances such a company may obtain against tax.

The target in a group

The target may be a member of a group for tax purposes if it has subsidiaries or if it is itself a subsidiary of another company. It may be, of course, that the target has subsidiaries and is itself a subsidiary. In such a case the acquisition will carve a sub-group out of a larger group. Different provisions of the Tax Acts apply to different types of subsidiary. The statutes describe subsidiaries as '51 per cent subsidiaries', '75 per cent subsidiaries' or, occasionally, '90 per cent subsidiaries'. The relevant definitions are contained in ICTA 1988, s 838, and in the sections referred to below. The basic rules are that a company is a 51 per cent subsidiary of another if and so long as more than 50 per cent of its 'ordinary share capital' is owned directly or indirectly by that other, and a company is a 75 per cent subsidiary of another if and so long as not less than 75 per cent of its ordinary share capital is owned directly or indirectly by that other; however, it will only be a 90 per cent subsidiary if the other company owns not less than 90 per cent of its ordinary share capital *directly*. It is obvious from this that a company which is a 75 per cent subsidiary will always be a 51 per cent subsidiary and a company which is a 90 per cent subsidiary will be both a 75 per cent subsidiary and a 51 per cent subsidiary. However, if company A owns 100 per cent of the ordinary share capital of company B which in turn owns 100 per cent of the ordinary share capital of company C, company C will not be a 90 per cent subsidiary of company A (although it will be both a 75 per cent and a 51 per cent subsidiary of company A and a 90 per cent subsidiary of company B).

References to ownership are to beneficial ownership and references to indirect ownership are to ownership through another body corporate. Where all subsidiaries in a chain are wholly owned the top company indirectly owns all the share capital of the bottom company, but where some companies in the chain are only partially owned s 838 contains provisions for ascertaining the percentage owned by one company of another. The provisions are complex but they work out as might be expected. The definition of 'ordinary share capital' in s 832(1) is not, however, quite as might be expected. It means 'all the share capital (by whatever name called) of the company, other than capital the holders of which have a right to a dividend at a fixed rate but have no other right to share in the profits of the company'.

If the target is a member of a group many tax consequences ensue. The main points which may be significant in the context of an acquisition are dealt with below and these relate to: group income; group relief; surrender of ACT; and tax on capital gains.

Group income

Under ICTA 1988, s 247, a resident company which is a 51 per cent subsidiary of another resident company may pay dividends or interest to that other or to that other's 51 per cent subsidiaries without paying ACT in respect of the dividends or deducting tax at source from the interest under s 349(1) or (2) of the Act. Payments so made are called 'group income'. In order that a company may avail itself of this privilege the paying company and the receiving company must make a joint election to the inspector. The election comes into force three months after it is made (or earlier if the inspector is satisfied that it is validly made) but ceases to have effect if the companies become no longer entitled to make it. It follows from this that any purchaser will wish to ensure that any dividends or income paid or received by the target before completion and which were paid gross because of an election under the section were validly so paid. Under s 247(6) the inspector is empowered to make assessments or adjustments in the event that a company purports to make a payment gross under an election but the election is invalid.

If a target is a 51 per cent subsidiary of another company before the acquisition and proposes to pay a dividend before it is acquired, the dividend should be paid before any arrangements are entered into which might fetter the vendor's beneficial ownership (see *Wood Preservation Ltd* v *Prior* [1969] 1 WLR 1077) and certainly before contracts are exchanged, as references to ownership of share capital in the context of subsidiaries are to beneficial ownership and the target will therefore cease to be a 51 per cent subsidiary of the vendor at the latest when contracts are exchanged for the sale of the target's share capital. If there is an interval between contract and completion, the vendor will probably remain the registered shareholder and thus remain entitled to receive any dividend paid during that period (subject to the terms of the acquisition agreement), but the vendor will have ceased to be the beneficial owner of the target's share capital even if the contract is conditional, and in that case, for tax purposes, the target will have ceased to be a 51 per cent subsidiary of the vendor so that under s 248(4) its former group election will have become invalid on exchange of contracts.

The group income provisions apply where a company is a trading company or a holding company owned by a consortium (see s 247(9)). For group income purposes a company is not a 51 per cent subsidiary of another if, in tracing a chain of indirect ownership, one of the owners in the chain is not resident in the United Kingdom or holds the shares as trading stock (s 247(8)).

Following the 1989 Budget it is intended that the tests described above should be brought into line with those for group relief contained in ICTA 1988, s 413(7)–(10).

Group relief

Under ICTA 1988, s 402 group relief applies between companies resident in the United Kingdom if one is a 75 per cent subsidiary of another or if both are 75 per cent subsidiaries of a third. The ownership chain is broken if it goes through a company not resident in the United Kingdom or if shares are held as trading stock, but the rules are slightly different from the group income rules (cf s 413(3) and s 247(8)). Section 413(7)–(10) strikes at certain artificial arrangements.

If a company which is a member of such a group has incurred trading losses in an accounting period or has certain other amounts eligible for relief from corporation tax arising in that period, it may surrender the amounts to another company within the group which can utilise them to relieve its own tax liability in respect of a 'corresponding accounting period'. The company receiving the benefit of the relief (called the claimant company by the legislation) may pay the other company (the surrendering company) for the relief. It is provided by s 402(6) that payments for group relief are not taken into account for any tax purposes, either in respect of the claimant company or the surrendering company. Any payments for group relief have to be made 'in pursuance of an agreement' between the claimant company and the surrendering company and must not exceed the relief surrendered. The amount paid is usually equal to, or slightly less than, the corporation tax paid, so that, in effect, instead of paying tax to the Revenue the claimant company pays it to the surrendering company. Group relief can also be surrendered by companies owned by a consortium to the members of the consortium (and members of the same group as those consortium members) and vice versa (s 402(3)).

If the target itself is a company owning 75 per cent subsidiaries, it may well have been the claimant company or surrendering company in respect of group relief, but when it is sold still owning its subsidiaries then, so long as the target is not itself a subsidiary of any other company or is not owned by, or a member of, a consortium, the purchaser in effect buys the complete group and all the group relief arrangements will pass under the purchaser's control. The purchaser will be concerned to see, or to take a warranty to the effect, that all group relief surrenders and payments within the target group have been properly made, but at least the group relief arrangements will not have to be disentangled.

More difficult problems arise when the target is itself a 75 per cent subsidiary of another company or is owned by a consortium. In a case where the target has been surrendering or claiming group relief from companies which are not to be acquired at the same time as the acquisition of the target, it is necessary, at the time of the acquisition, to give some thought to the group relief arrangements. It is necessary to consider accounting periods completed before the acquisition and the accounting period current at the date of acquisition.

It is probable that the group relief arrangements in respect of some accounting periods completed before acquisition will not have been finalised because the tax computations remain to be agreed. If the target is a loss maker, it may well be necessary or desirable, after the acquisition has been completed, for the vendor to receive and pay for group relief in respect of accounting periods completed before the acquisition. In such a case the vendor will be anxious to ensure that it is able to obtain the benefit of the target's losses and the purchaser will wish to ensure that the target will be paid for them (and vice versa if the target is a profit maker obtaining the benefit of group relief surrendered to it by companies in the vendor group). In either case it will be necessary to have a written group relief agreement and to make arrangements for liaison between vendor and purchaser with regard to the tax computations. It was settled by *Chapman (AW) Ltd v Hennessey* (1981) 55 TC 516 that it is possible to make surrenders of group relief after the target has left the group.

Group relief in respect of the accounting period current at the time of the acquisition tends to be complicated. There is provision in s 409 for apportionment of group relief when companies join or leave a group during an accounting period but s 410 provides that if in any accounting period arrangements are in existence by virtue of which, at some time during or after the expiry of that accounting period, a target could leave a group, there can be no group relief between the target and the members of the group which it proposes to leave. The section seems to say that, if any such arrangements exist, the target shall be deemed never to have been a member of the previous group for group relief purposes, but the section is normally only applied back to the beginning of the accounting period during which the 'arrangements' came into existence. Taxpayers have, on occasion, successfully argued that relief is only derived from the actual date on which 'arrangements' came into existence although the Revenue is known to dispute this view.

'Arrangements' is a deliberately loose term and arrangements can come into existence before contracts are in fact exchanged. It may therefore be advantageous to the vendor if the target changes its accounting date so that an accounting period ends just before the arrangements arise (although pinning down the date when the arrangements arose can be difficult). Under s 409, the purchaser group will only have the benefit of group relief involving the target on and after the date upon which the beneficial ownership of the target's capital passes (profits and losses are apportioned on a time basis). An accounting period should not, however, be changed too lightly as there may well be many tax consequences that flow from such a change. The object of s 410 seems to be to prevent companies with large losses, arising or due to arise in an accounting period (caused perhaps by capital allowances), joining strange groups, surrendering their losses and leaving again under pre-existing 'arrangements'. It should be noted, however, that the section applies whether the target is a surrendering company or a claimant company. It should also be noted that the provisions apply to a company remaining within the selling group if the target has succeeded to its trade. Packaging a trade in a company for subsequent sale may therefore affect group relief between the company to which the trade formerly belonged and the other members of the group.

For a discussion of the meaning of the word 'arrangements' in this context and the wide meaning given to it see *Pilkington Bros Ltd* v *IRC* [1981] STC 705.

Surrender of advance corporation tax

Under ICTA 1988, s 240, a resident company can surrender ACT paid in respect of dividends to its resident 51 per cent subsidiaries provided they are 51 per cent subsidiaries throughout the accounting period in which the dividends were paid. The rules about following the ownership chain are the same as for group relief (see p 131).

A company may wish to surrender ACT if it cannot use it for setoff against its own liability to mainstream corporation tax. Under ICTA

1988, s 239(2), the amount of ACT which can be set against a company's liability for mainstream tax in any accounting period is limited to ACT which would have been payable on a distribution made at the end of that period, being a distribution which, together with the ACT payable in respect of it, is equal to the company's income and capital gains charged to corporation tax for that period. If a company has paid distributions in an accounting period which, when grossed up, exceed its chargeable profits, the excess is called surplus ACT and can be set off against tax in other accounting periods. Under s 239(3) surplus ACT can be carried back six years if a claim is made to that effect and under s 239(4) it can be carried forward indefinitely, but surrendering ACT under s 240 can enable it to be used by a subsidiary in a current accounting period. It should be noted that a surrender under s 240 applies to all ACT and not just to surplus ACT.

ACT surrendered to a subsidiary is treated as if it were ACT paid by that subsidiary subject to certain limitations. If it is surplus to the subsidiary's own requirements it cannot be carried back (although it is treated as the first amount to be set off against mainstream tax, leaving the subsidiary's own ACT free to be carried back or forward) and s 240(5) provides that ACT surrendered to a subsidiary may not be set-off against that subsidiary's mainstream tax for any accounting period in which, or in any part of which, it was not a subsidiary of the surrendering company. Section 240(1) prevents ACT surrenders between the target and the selling group in an accounting period during which arrangements are in existence for the target to leave the group. The section also strikes at certain artificial arrangements and is the ACT equivalent of the group relief anti-avoidance provisions contained in ICTA 1988, ss 410 and 413.

It is common for payments to be made by subsidiaries to surrendering companies in return for ACT surrendered. Such payments are treated in the same way as payments for group relief, and are not taken into account for tax purposes in calculating the profits or losses of the paying or receiving company (s 240(8)).

Where the target is a parent company and is not itself a subsidiary, the purchaser will be concerned to see that any ACT surrenders have been properly made, so that the tax computations have been correctly prepared. If the target is a subsidiary and has received the benefit of surrender of ACT from a parent which is not being purchased, the purchaser will wish to ensure that the target has not paid for, and will not become liable to pay for, any ACT which becomes irrecoverable under s 240(5) when the target leaves the vendor group. It should be noted that there is no provision for surrendering back any unusable ACT.

A number of anti-avoidance measures directed at the sale of subsidiaries with surplus ACT were announced in the 1989 Budget. These will be modelled on existing group relief and loss relief provisions.

Tax on capital gains

For the purposes of corporation tax on capital gains, groups are defined under ICTA 1970, s 272. (The provisions of the 1970 Act relating to companies' chargeable gains have not been consolidated in the 1988 Act.) A company and its 75 per cent subsidiaries form a group (although, following the 1989 Budget, the principal company in the group must also have an interest greater than 50 per cent, directly or indirectly, in the profits and assets of each subsidiary). As a general point, the provisions now considered will not cause great difficulty where the target is a parent company (sold with its subsidiaries intact) but is not and has not been a 75 per cent subsidiary of any other company. If, however, the target is or has been a 75 per cent subsidiary (whether or not it has subsidiaries itself), the provisions may give rise to unexpected liabilities.

Tax recoverable from other group members. Under ICTA 1988, s 347, if a chargeable gain accrues to a company which at the time is a member of the group and the company fails to pay its corporation tax assessed for that accounting period within six months of the due date, if the tax so assessed included any amount in respect of chargeable gains, an amount of that tax not exceeding corporation tax on the amount of that gain may be recovered from a company which was at the time when the gain accrued the principal company of the group and any other company which, within the two year period preceding the gain, was a member of the group and owned the asset disposed of or any part of it (or, where the asset in question was an interest or right in or over another asset, owned either asset or any part of either asset).

It should be noted that what can be recovered is corporation tax on the amount of the gain, so it seems that any allowable capital losses available to the company which should have paid the tax and which might have reduced the tax payable need not be brought into account when assessing the other group company.

It will be seen, therefore, that if the target is the principal company of a group, it may be made liable for its subsidiary's chargeable gains even if the subsidiary in question is not a subsidiary of the target at the time of the acquisition. Moreover, if the target owned an asset which was disposed of before the acquisition of the target to another member of the group (perhaps the vendor), the target can be made liable after the acquisition to account for tax on chargeable gains payable by a company with which it has then no relationship. Section 347(3) provides that the company paying tax assessed under s 347(1) can recover an equal amount from other group companies, but the purchaser is likely to want an express indemnity from the vendor.

A number of other provisions, notably those relating to the migration of companies and the taxation of gains of non-resident or dual resident companies, also allow tax to be recovered from other companies in the same group.

Section 347, incidentally, provides an interesting illustration of how groups work for these purposes. Suppose company D is a wholly-owned subsidiary of company C which in turn is a wholly-owned subsidiary of company B which in turn is a wholly-owned subsidiary of company A. Company D has two direct wholly-owned subsidiaries X and Y, so that the group looks like this:

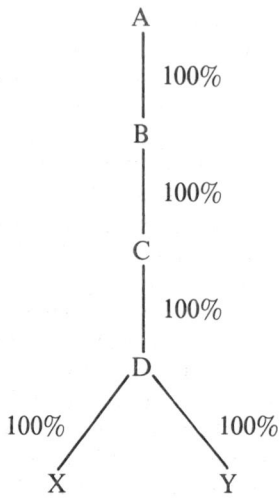

Y sells an asset to X which immediately disposes of it outside the group but fails to pay its corporation tax (including an amount in respect of chargeable gains) for the relevant accounting period. An amount of that tax not exceeding tax on the chargeable gain can then be recovered from Y, because it held the asset within the two-year period, and, it would appear, from all the other companies in the group, because they are all 'principal companies' of one of the groups of which X is a member. X is, in fact, a member of four groups: the D group comprising D, X and Y; the C group comprising C, D, X and Y; the B group comprising B, C, D, X and Y; and the A group comprising all the companies. If D owned exactly 75 per cent of the 'ordinary share capital' of X and Y, and C owned 99 per cent of D, X and Y would not be 75 per cent subsidiaries of A, B, or C, but the groups would be the same. Section 272(1)(*b*) includes in a group 75 per cent subsidiaries of any group member.

Intra-group transfers. Under ICTA 1970, s 273, transfers of chargeable assets within a group do not give rise to any immediate charge to tax. The section provides that both parties to the transfer are treated as if the asset were acquired for a consideration of such amount as would secure that on the transferor's disposal, neither a gain nor a loss would accrue. In other words, the consideration is assumed to be the disposing company's base value including any indexation allowance (Finance Act 1982, Sched 13, para 2(3)). To take a simple example, suppose that company B acquires an asset at a cost of £10,000 which subsequently increases in value to £20,000. Company B is then acquired by company A and becomes its 75 per cent subsidiary. A transfer of that asset from company B to company A will be deemed to be made at the price (ignoring indexation allowance) of £10,000 irrespective of the asset's worth and of what company A actually pays company B for it. Suppose company A pays the market value, ie £20,000. When company A sells the asset to a third party at a price of £30,000 the chargeable gain would be £20,000 (ie £30,000 less £10,000) even though company A has actually paid £20,000 for the asset. By s 273(2) certain disposals fall outside the terms of the section. Examples are the disposal of a debt and the disposal of an interest in shares in a company in consideration for a capital distribution. This means that the liquidation of a subsidiary will involve a chargeable disposal of its shares by the parent (see the Capital Gains Tax Act 1979, s 72).

Section 273 also does not apply where the transaction is treated by the Capital Gains Tax Act 1979, ss 78 and 85, as not involving a disposal (s 273(2A), inserted by the Finance Act 1988, s 115). This is an important provision and ensures that where, for example, shares in a subsidiary are hived down to a second subsidiary on a share-for-share basis that second subsidiary acquires those shares at current market value while the consideration shares received by the parent in the share-for-share exchange will have the original base cost of the shares transferred. These statutory provisions reverse the decision in *Westcott* v *Woolcombers Ltd* [1987] STC 600.

Section 273 is obviously useful, as assets can be switched around within a group of companies without incurring an immediate liability to tax on any chargeable gains, but in the context of an acquisition it can cause problems. The section may mean, for instance, that an asset owned by the target has a lower base value for tax purposes than its actual cost. If the target has acquired that asset from a company which was in the same group at the time of the acquisition, on any subsequent disposal of that asset outside the group the purchaser may be aggrieved to find that the target's tax bill is higher than he thought (see the example given above). A general warranty is therefore taken to cover this point (the Agreement for Sale, Sched 4, warranty (22)).

The section may also in conjunction with the 'value shifting' provisions of the Capital Gains Tax Act 1979 s 26 (amended as envisaged in the 1989 Budget) affect the liability to capital gains tax arising on the disposal of shares in a subsidiary from which assets have been transferred.

Companies leaving a group. In the early days of capital gains tax it was possible to make use of what is now s 273 to avoid the charge to corporation tax on capital gains by means of what became known as 'the envelope trick'. If company Y owned an asset which had grown substantially in value it could transfer that asset to a new 75 per cent subsidiary, X, formed for the purpose in exchange for the issue of shares by X. The shares of X were deemed acquired by Y at their current market value (ie the actual value of the asset at the time of the transfer), but s 273 applied to the transfer of the asset. Y could then sell the shares of X to a purchaser so that dominion over the asset passed without any charge to tax on capital gains. X was the 'envelope' in which the asset was placed before it was sold.

To prevent this form of tax avoidance what is now the Income and Corporation Taxes Act 1970, s 278, was enacted. This provides that if company X, called 'the chargeable company' by the section, leaves a group owning an asset which it has acquired within the last six years from company Y which was at the time of the acquisition a member of the group which X is leaving, X is treated as if, at the time of the acquisition from Y, it had sold and immediately reacquired the asset at its market value. Under s 278(6) X's assessment to corporation tax for the accounting period in which it acquired the asset from Y is reopened and recomputed. It should be noted that the provisions of the Finance Act 1988, s 96 and Sched 8, which allow for the rebasing of acquisition costs to the market value as at 31 March 1982, will not apply where X acquired the asset from Y prior to 6 April 1988. Instead, where the asset was acquired by the group on or before 31 March 1982, the gain that would otherwise be chargeable under s 278 is to be reduced by one-half (Finance Act 1988, s 97 and Sched 9).

The section also applies if, at the time when X leaves the group, it does not itself own the asset in question, but the asset is owned by an 'associated company' of X which is also leaving the group. For the purposes of the section, two or more companies are associated companies if, by themselves, they would form a group (s 278(4)). The section does not apply, however, if X and Y both leave the group together and are associated companies (s 278(2)). The section applies not only to the original asset which X acquired but also to any replacement asset if any gain on the asset has been rolled over into that replacement asset under the Capital Gains Tax Act 1979, ss 115 to 121.

References to companies ceasing to be a member of a group are construed in accordance with s 272(3) which provides that a group remains the same group so long as the same company remains the principal company of the group and, if at any time the principal company of a group becomes a 75 per cent subsidiary of another company, the group of which it was the principal company before that time is regarded as the same as the group of which that other company (or one of which it is the 75 per cent subsidiary) is the principal company. A company does not cease to be a member of a group for the purpose of the section if it ceases to be a member of a group by being wound up or dissolved or in consequence of another member of the group being wound up or dissolved.

Section 278 is difficult to construe. Assume a group which looks like the diagram below:

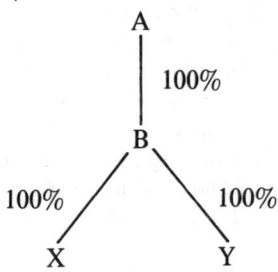

The following permutations (among others) are possible.

(1) If X is the target, X will leave the B group (B, X and Y) and will leave the A group (all the companies) and the section will therefore apply to any asset which X owns at the time of the acquisition and which was acquired from any of the other companies within the six year period. If Y sold the asset to X, it will not help if Y is bought by the same purchaser at the same time. X and Y are not associated companies because, by themselves, they do not form a group.

(2) If B is the target and is sold with its subsidiaries intact, B, X

and Y will leave the A group. Prima facie the section will apply, again, to any asset which X owns and has acquired within the six year period from any of the other companies, but if the asset has been acquired by X from B or Y it seems that the section will not in fact apply, because of s 278(2). Two or more associated companies (B, X and Y) are ceasing to be members of a group (the A group) at the same time and the section does not have effect as respects an acquisition by one from another of those associated companies. B, X and Y are associated because, by themselves, they form a group. If X has acquired the asset from A then, of course, the section will apply.

(3) If B is the target and X owns the asset which it has acquired from B, which in turn acquired it from A within the six year period, although the acquisition by X from B is not in point (because of s 278(2)) the section will still apply to B as the chargeable company because B is leaving the group having acquired the asset from A and 'an associated company' (X) is also leaving the group owning the asset. B and X are associated because by themselves they form a group (s 278(4)(a)). However, if A sold the asset to Y rather than B and Y sold it to X, will the section still apply when B, X and Y leave the group? It does not apply to X because its acquisition from Y is taken outside the charge by s 278(2). Y no longer owns the asset, so the section will only apply to Y if the asset is now owned by a company which is Y's 'associated company' and which is also leaving the group. It is possible to argue that X is not associated with Y because *by themselves* they do not form a group, although they do if B is added. This is an odd result and one that presumably was not intended by the draftsman. Where a sub-group leaves a larger group it is clear for the purposes of the exemption in s 278(2) that each of the members of the sub-group is associated with each other member, but it is not clear that the same result is obtained from construing the reference to 'associated company' in s 278(3).

(4) If A is the target, no company will leave any group and the section will not apply.

(5) It should be noted that the section applies if X leaves a group owning an asset which it acquired from another company which was a member of that group at the time of the acquisition of the asset. The section does not in fact say that X has to be a member of the same group at the time the asset was acquired, although this is clearly the intention. Suppose that X and Y were quite unrelated at the time of the acquisition of the asset by X from Y but subsequently B acquired X's share capital so that X became a member of the B group. If X is the target and is sold by B within the period of six years from the date of X's acquisition of the asset from Y, the section appears to apply because X is ceasing to be a member of the B group and, at the time of

the acquisition of the asset, Y was a member of the B group. Normally, of course, this will not matter because the section only supposes the asset to have been sold and reacquired at market value at the time of the acquisition, and if X and Y were unrelated the sale was probably at market value, so that X's base value will be high and no further tax will be payable. It is possible, however, that X acquired the asset at an undervalue (eg pursuant to an option granted some time before) and in that case the section would appear to produce a charge to tax even though s 273 had never applied to the asset in question.

Under s 278(5) tax assessed on the chargeable company can be recovered, if it is not paid within six months, from any company which was the principal company of the group which the chargeable company left (or which is the principal company at the date of the assessment) and also from any company which owned the asset in question on the date for payment of the tax or when the chargeable company ceased to be a member of the group. It is difficult to believe that this provision is as wide as it appears. If X leaves the group owning the asset and then sells it at arm's length to an unrelated third party and X is subsequently assessed for tax under s 278, it seems from the section that if the third party is a company it can be charged to tax. Innocent purchasers will hardly regard as sufficient the right to indemnity from X which is conferred by s 278(5).

Tax losses

If a company has incurred a loss in carrying on a trade, it may claim to have the loss set off for tax purposes against profits, of whatever description (including chargeable gains), made in the accounting period in which the loss is sustained or in the preceding accounting period. Alternatively, the company may carry forward the loss against any trading income from the trade in succeeding accounting periods until the loss is exhausted (ICTA 1988, s 393). If a target has trading losses otherwise eligible for carry forward, the purchaser will wish to know whether the change in ownership of the target's shares will affect the availability of these losses for set off against future profits made by the target. The Income and Corporation Taxes Act 1988, s 768, which is considered below, has the effect of preventing such a carry forward in many cases, but s 768 is in addition to, and not in substitution for, a considerable body of authority on this question.

Although the acquisition of shares in the target will not itself affect the target's trade, the target's business may change following the acquisition as its affairs come under new control. In each case it is a question of fact whether or not the old trade has been discontinued and a new trade has been commenced. If this has occurred, any losses incurred in the old trade are not available for carry forward against the profits of the new, because the new trade is not 'the trade' within the meaning of s 393.

Before the enactment (originally in the Finance Act 1969) of what is now s 768, many cases came before the courts which concerned changes in a target's business at the same time as the acquisition of its shares.

In *Ingram (JG) & Son Ltd* v *Callaghan (Inspector of Taxes)* (1968) 45 TC 151 the target's trade consisted of manufacturing rubber goods. For a period of nine months the company ceased to manufacture rubber goods but sold similar products made of plastic which had been made by another company. At the end of this nine month period the target was acquired by the purchaser and thereafter manufactured and sold similar products but now made of plastic. It was held on appeal that the target's trade had been permanently discontinued and a new trade set up. Losses made in the manufacture of rubber goods were therefore not available to be carried forward to be set off against the profits of the manufacture of the plastic goods.

In *Gordon and Blair Ltd* v *IRC* (1962) 40 TC 358 the target was a brewer. Shortly before the acquisition it had ceased to brew its own beer and entered into arrangements with the eventual purchaser to the effect that the purchaser would brew the beer which was then sold by the target under the target's brand name. It was held that the target's former trade had ceased when it ceased to brew beer and a new trade had been commenced. Similar cases relating to changes in a trade prior to or following an acquisition are *Tryka Ltd* v *Newall (Inspector of Taxes)* (1963) 41 TC 146 and *Seaman (Inspector of Taxes)* v *Tucketts Ltd* (1963) 41 TC 422.

In all the cases cited above it was held, on the facts, that the changes in the target's trade had amounted to a discontinuance, but it is not every change in the nature of a trade which amounts to a discontinuance and therefore means that losses cannot be carried forward. The expansion of an existing trade is not necessarily regarded as a new trade and a trade may be suspended for some time and then revived. In *Robroyston Brickworks Ltd* v *IRC* (1976) 51 TC 230 the target manufactured and sold bricks and had been making losses for a number of years. In March 1968 the target ceased brick production and by August 1968, when the purchaser acquired it, had sold off its entire stock of bricks and its plant and machinery, paid off its creditors and gradually dispensed with the services of the remaining employees. Following the acquisition the target commenced manufacturing bricks at the purchaser's brickworks. The Court of Session held that the target's trade had only been suspended and that accordingly losses accrued prior to the transfer of the trade from one works to another were available to the set off against future profits. Cases such as this are now likely to be caught by s 768.

Section 768(1) has the effect of disallowing carry forward if:

(a) within any period of three years there is both a change in the ownership of the company and (either earlier or later in that period, or at the same time) a major change in the nature or conduct of a trade carried on by the company, or

(b) at any time after the scale of the activities in a trade carried on by a company has become small or negligible, and before any considerable revival of the trade, there is a change in the ownership of the company.

By s 768(4) 'major change in the nature or conduct of a trade' includes:

(a) a major change in the type of property dealt in, or services or facilities provided, in the trade; or

(b) a major change in customers, outlets or markets of the trade.

Section 768 applies even if the change is the result of a gradual process which began outside the period of three years referred to in s 768(1).

As a result, events which might not formerly have been held to amount to the discontinuance of one trade and the setting up of another will now, if coupled with a change of ownership, prevent losses being carried forward. In *Willis (Inspector of Taxes)* v *Peeters Picture Frames Ltd* [1983] STC 453 it was held that whether a change is 'major' is a question of fact and degree for the Commissioners and it seems that the word will not be construed literally, ie as relating to more than one half of the type of property dealt in or of the customers, outlets or markets.

Section 768(1)(b) deals with cases (such as the *Robroyston* case cited above) in which the target's trade has been suspended and its shares acquired during the period when the trade was suspended. Although suspension of a trade does not necessarily amount to a discontinuance, losses will not be available for carry forward in cases caught by the section.

The section contains machinery for enabling the inspector to ascertain the beneficial ownership of shares in the company for the purposes of ascertaining whether or not a change in the ownership of the company has taken place.

Section 769 defines a 'change of ownership'. The definition is fairly wide and certainly includes an acquisition of a controlling interest by a single purchaser. When the purchaser is already a shareholder in the target, however, it is worth checking the rules carefully, because not every sale and purchase of shares between shareholders results in a change of ownership. If the target is a 75 per cent subsidiary of another company and continues to be so after a change in the direct ownership of the target, that change of ownership is disregarded (s 769(5)). In other words, the transfer within a group of shares in a subsidiary will not normally trigger the section, but the sale of the parent company will mean a change of ownership of all of its 75 per cent subsidiaries (s 769(6)). Both these provisions provide means of tax avoidance and are to be amended following the 1989 Budget.

Capital allowances available to a trading company are treated as trading expenses (Capital Allowances Act 1968, s 73). If they go to increase the trading loss, s 769 will apply to prevent their carry forward in the same way as it applies to other trading losses. Neither s 393 nor s 768 restrict the purchaser taking advantage of any capital allowances unclaimed at the date of sale. It may therefore be advantageous to disclaim such allowances for periods prior to completion and to claim them in later periods when they can be used to reduce profits of the target or, by way of group relief, of the purchaser.

'Losses' which do not form part of a trade, eg an investment company's excess management expenses and charges on income (plus unused capital allowances), can be carried forward (ICTA 1988, s 75) and the carry forward is not restricted by s 768; neither are losses for the purposes of tax on capital gains subject to the restrictions (although see p 148 below for the possible application of *Ramsay* principles to restrict the utilisation of such losses). As noted above, trading losses may to a limited extent be set off against chargeable gains, but there is no reciprocal treatment, so that allowable capital losses may only be carried forward to be set off against chargeable gains.

As a general point it should be noted that trading losses, management expenses, charges on income and capital allowances are only capable of being surrendered under group relief arrangements in respect of the accounting period in which they are incurred (s 403). The purchaser acquiring a target with losses accrued in completed accounting periods can therefore only utilise these losses against profits or gains made in the target itself. Only losses accruing in future accounting periods will be available for group relief within the purchaser group (see s 409 for the treatment of the accounting period current at the date of acquisition and see p 132). Capital losses are not available for group relief at all.

Advance corporation tax carry forward

Surplus ACT can, under ICTA 1988, s 239(4), be carried forward indefinitely to be set off against a company's liability to mainstream corporation tax (see p 133). A target which was once profitable but has ceased to be so may therefore have a large amount of surplus ACT capable of being carried forward and set off against its mainstream corporation tax in future accounting periods. This can be attractive for a purchaser if the purchaser expects to be able to arrange for the target to become profitable again (eg by diverting business from another member of the purchaser group) as he will then have the benefit of the target's surplus ACT. The Income and Corporation Taxes Act 1988, s 245, however, prevents the carry forward of surplus ACT in similar circumstances as ICTA 1988, s 768 prevents the carry forward of tax losses (ie change of ownership coupled with a major change in the trade or a revival of the trade).

If s 245 applies, the date of the change of ownership is deemed to start a new accounting period and there is no carry forward into that and subsequent accounting periods. Section 768 only applies to trading companies, but, as surplus ACT can arise in investment companies, s 245 applies to them as well and defines 'major change in the nature or conduct of a trade or business' as including a change whereby the company ceases to be a trading company and becomes an investment company or vice versa and, if the company is an investment company, a major change in the nature of the investments held by the company. The section applies to ACT which the company is treated as having paid by virtue of ICTA 1988, s 240 (surrender of ACT to a subsidiary), as it applies to ACT which it has actually paid.

Anti-avoidance measures relating to the surrender or carry forward of surplus ACT were announced in the 1989 Budget.

Value added tax

In most cases the target will be liable to register for VAT and either will have a VAT registration in its own name or benefit from a group registration under the Value Added Tax Act 1983, s 29. If a group registration is not in force the purchaser's main concern will be that the accounts show full provision for any VAT liability and that in respect of transactions in the current accounting period all VAT has been fully provided for. It is also prudent to take specific warranties against certain VAT matters and these are provided for in the Agreement for Sale, Sched 4, warranty (47).

If a group registration is in force additional considerations arise.

The effect of a group registration is to enable all companies within the scope of that registration (and not all the companies in a group need be included) to make supplies from one to the other without accounting for VAT (Value Added Tax Act 1983, s 29(1)). The representative member is liable to account to or recover from Customs and Excise all VAT payable by or due to the group, but all the members of the group will be liable jointly and severally for any VAT due from the representative member. If the target and its subsidiaries include all the companies within the group registration then the purchaser will probably wish to continue with that registration and may in due course wish to include the acquired companies within its own group registration. If, on the other hand, the group registration includes companies in the vendor's group which the purchaser is not acquiring, the terms of the group registration will need to be amended. Whether the purchaser takes over the group registration will depend in part upon whether the representative member is included in the target and its subsidiaries or whether it is a company retained by the vendor. Agreement will have to be reached between the parties and arrangements made either to separate out the group members and apply for a new group registration for the target and its subsidiaries or for inclusion of the target and its subsidiaries in the purchaser's group registration. The tax indemnity in the Agreement for Sale, Sched 4 will cover any liability falling on the target or its subsidiaries for VAT attributable to any other member of the vendor's group registration.

Inheritance tax

Under the Inheritance Tax Act 1984, s 1, inheritance tax is charged on the value transferred by a 'chargeable transfer'. Section 3 of that Act defines a 'transfer of value' as (subject to certain exceptions) any disposition made by 'a person' which brings about a reduction in the value of that person's 'estate'. Section 2(1) defines a chargeable transfer as 'any transfer of value which is made by an *individual* [other than] an exempt transfer'. Consequently, although a company, being a person and having an estate, can make a transfer of value, no company can make a chargeable transfer. It follows that inheritance tax problems relating to the acquisition of companies at arm's length are mercifully few. However, a company can be liable to pay inheritance tax in the following exceptional circumstances:

(1) Under the Inheritance Tax Act 1984, s 202 (apportionment in the case of close companies: see p 126).

(2) Any company (whether open or close) may, like any other person, be liable to inheritance tax in respect of a chargeable transfer

by virtue of the Inheritance Tax Act 1984, ss 199 to 201, in any of the capacities listed in that section (other than those of transferor and settlor). Generally speaking, it is unlikely that any liability will arise unless the target has been involved in tax avoidance schemes. The liability may arise:

(*a*) if the target is a transferee of value;

(*b*) if at any time after the transfer in question there is vested in the target (beneficially or not) property to the value of which any inheritance tax is attributable or if the target is beneficially entitled to an interest in possession in such property (the liability will not arise if the target has obtained the property as purchaser or derives title from a purchaser, unless the property is subject to an Inland Revenue charge);

(*c*) if property (or income from it) which has become comprised in a settlement as a result of a chargeable transfer is applied for the benefit of the target;

(*d*) if a transfer has been made under the settled property provisions, and:

   (i) if the target is trustee of a settlement;

   (ii) if the target is entitled (whether beneficially or not) to an interest in possession in settled property; or

   (iii) if any settled property is applied for the benefit of the target at or after the time of the transfer in question; or

(*e*) in the case of a transfer on death:

   (i) if the target is a personal representative of a deceased person;

   (ii) if the target is trustee of a settlement in which was comprised property to the value of which inheritance tax is attributable; or

   (iii) if property (or income from it) which was comprised in a settlement at the time of the transfer in question, is applied for the benefit of the target.

The terms 'trustee' and 'personal representative' include anyone who has acted in relation to the property so as to become liable as executor or trustee.

It may be noted that, where a close company is entitled to an interest in possession in settled property, the participators in the company are treated as the persons beneficially entitled to that interest according to their respective rights and interests in the company (Inheritance Tax Act 1984, s 101).

In addition to an indemnity against liability under ss 199 to 201 the purchaser should also seek protection against diminution in the value of the target's assets through the imposition of the Inland

Revenue charge for unpaid tax under the Inheritance Tax Act 1984, s 237.

There is also the question of any adjustment to the burden of inheritance tax. There is, of course, nothing to prevent the parties to any transaction agreeing how the burden of tax is to be borne. Moreover ss 211 and 212 may give other persons rights against the target in this respect. In particular:

(a) under s 211(3) where personal representatives have paid inheritance tax arising on a death and an Inland Revenue charge is imposed on any property, the personal representatives may in certain circumstances require repayment to them of the tax by the person in whom the property is vested; and

(b) by virtue of s 212(1) and subject to certain exceptions, where a person is liable for inheritance tax attributable to the value of any property, he has the power, whether or not the property is vested in him, to raise the amount of the tax (either for payment or recoupment) by a sale or mortgage of, or terminable charge on, the property.

A purchaser may therefore wish to seek protection against any diminution of the assets of the target through any claims against the target in respect of adjustment of the burden of inheritance tax and in particular against any claims arising under ss 211 and 212.

RAMSAY AND FURNISS v DAWSON

The 'emerging principle' or 'new approach' in *Ramsay (WT) Ltd* v *IRC* (1981) 54 TC 101 and *Furniss (Inspector of Taxes)* v *Dawson* (1984) 55 TC 324 has created uncertainty in a number of areas which affect the purchase of private companies. The principle may affect the transaction itself and the taxation of the target both before and after the acquisition.

The limits of the principle have to some degree been resolved through the further cases which have now been decided by the House of Lords (*Craven* v *White, IRC* v *Bowater Property Developments Ltd, Baylis* v *Gregory* [1988] 3 WLR 423), but the extent to which the principle applies to stamp duty and to value added tax remains uncertain (*Ingram* v *IRC* [1985] STC 848). Some practical guidance to the circumstances in which the Revenue had indicated the principle would be sought to be applied prior to these decisions can be found in the correspondence with the Revenue in 1985 published by the Institute of Chartered Accountants in England and Wales (TR588).

Furniss v *Dawson* was, of course, itself a case relating to the acquisition of a private company. In cases where the parties are seeking to avoid tax the principle may apply to disregard steps inserted into the transaction for no commercial purpose other than the avoidance of tax. Purchasers will be concerned to know whether the target has been involved, in the past, in any transactions to which the principle might apply and a warranty should be sought (see the Agreement for Sale, Sched 4, warranty (19) should be sought. Vendors may wish to give this warranty 'to the best of their knowledge and belief' rather than accepting absolute liability.

If the target has accrued capital losses, the purchaser may wish, after the acquisition, to transfer assets to the target before they are disposed of, so as to ensure that gains are realised in the target against which the accrued losses can be off-set. It is understood that at least one case on this subject has been heard before the Special Commissioners but there are, as yet, no reported decisions. However, in the correspondence with the Institute of Chartered Accountants referred to above, the Revenue stated it would be unlikely that the principle would be invoked where the losses were a 'relatively insubstantial element in the acquisition, as evidenced by the circumstances in which they were utilised and the commerciality of the circumstances surrounding the acquisition'. While, therefore, a warranty as to the existence of capital losses may be given, no warranty should be given as to their availability to off-set any particular gain. It is considered that similar arguments will apply to the use of excess management expenses in investment companies.

CONTRACTUAL PROTECTION

No consistent and logical treatment of tax in agreements for the sale of private companies has yet evolved. Given the complexity and arbitrary nature of the legislation concerned, it is doubtful if it ever will.

Even though an accountants' investigation may have been commissioned, the purchaser is likely to require assurances in one form or another:

(*a*) that the target has complied with all appropriate tax legislation;

(*b*) that the latest accounts contain proper provision for taxation;

(*c*) that there are no surprises (perhaps in the form of disguised base values);

(*d*) that the target has not been involved in any of the transactions which anti-avoidance legislation or case law has rendered dangerous;

(e) that the target has all the reliefs and allowances which should be available to it; and

(f) that the target is not going to be visited with liability to pay tax assessed on others (eg liability to pay higher rate tax as a result of an apportionment of income under the provisions relating to close companies or liability under ICTA 1988, s 347, to pay tax in respect of chargeable gains incurred by other group members).

The purchaser's advisers will therefore wish to obtain warranties and indemnities from the vendors to cover all these eventualities. Faced with the bewildering array of potential liabilities it is possible to overreact. In a famous phrase Lord Davey remarked that 'every grocer's shop takes power to bridge the mighty Zambezi'. Those acquiring grocer's shops today are more inclined to suspect the proprietor of having issued quoted Eurobonds. It is a foolhardy purchaser, however, who does not seek to obtain as much information and protection as he reasonably can in respect of the taxation of the target. What form should this protection take? In relation to some taxation matters, warranties are clearly appropriate and in relation to others an indemnity is more suitable, but in many cases the selection of warranty or indemnity (or both) to cover a potential liability is largely a matter of taste.

Warranties should be taken with regard to the taxation attributes of the target's assets as indemnities will not normally be appropriate. The accounts will show the assets at a valuation. Is this valuation the same as the base value for the purpose of corporation tax on chargeable gains? There may be many reasons why it is not so and a simple example arises in connection with the replacement of business assets. Suppose the target has at some time in the past disposed of a branch office for £200,000 realising a capital gain of £100,000. It has not become chargeable to tax on this gain, because the whole of the consideration has been used to purchase a new office for £200,000. Under the provisions of the Capital Gains Tax Act 1979, s 115, the gain is 'rolled over' and the acquisition cost of the new offices is deemed to be not £200,000 but £100,000 so that upon the sale of the new offices for £300,000 a chargeable gain of £200,000 (not £100,000) will arise. This fact is not disclosed in negotiations and when the target comes to dispose of the office in due course the purchaser is aggrieved. He looks to his indemnities but finds they do not relate to gains made by the target after completion. Why indeed should the vendors indemnify the target against tax on gains made after completion when they will not have the benefit of these gains? The purchaser is, however, objecting to the fact that he was not aware of the amount of the contingent liability to tax which was inherent in the asset in question. A warranty that the base cost was the same as the value attributed to the office in the accounts would have given him a remedy against the vendors.

Warranties are also appropriate where the purchaser wishes to be assured that the target has or has not taken any particular action. A warranty that all taxation returns have been made accurately and on time and that all taxation has been properly and punctually paid is of obvious value. The purchaser will not wish to be involved with back duty claims with the Inland Revenue or with PAYE or value added tax audits, even in relation to quite small sums. The loss of management time can be substantial, particularly if key employees of the target leave as a result of the acquisition so that the facts have to be mastered by incoming staff. It may be said that the purchaser is adequately protected if the target is indemnified by the vendors against the tax due and against penalties, costs and interest relating to taxation, but in practice this is not the case. A more satisfactory result may well be achieved by asking for a warranty; if the vendors have knowledge of a dispute they are unlikely to deceive the purchaser by giving a false warranty (indeed if they do, they may consider their liability under the Financial Services Act 1986, s 47) and it is usually better for the purchaser to force a disclosure so that he knows the worst before the acquisition and can make appropriate arrangements (including perhaps a specific indemnity) to enable him to deal with the problem.

An indemnity is appropriate where the target is liable to pay tax arising from the income or gains of others. As explained above, under the Income and Corporation Taxes Act 1988, s 347, the target may be made liable for chargeable gains realised by other members of the same group. A warranty that no such chargeable gains had occurred would not normally be acceptable. The purchaser is not, in fact, concerned to see that the primary liability has not arisen; he is concerned to ensure that the target is properly indemnified against the liability. Indemnities are also useful when obtaining protection against liability under anti-avoidance sections. It is often simpler to take an indemnity rather than to attempt to draft a warranty. Of course, if it is likely that the target has entered into tax avoidance transactions then warranties may be more appropriate, as they may bring out disclosures.

In many cases, however, it will be a matter of taste whether a warranty or an indemnity is taken and the choice of warranties (in addition to the general indemnity) included in the Agreement for Sale (Chapter 6) is to that extent arbitrary. Neither does the selection pretend to be exhaustive or mandatory in all cases. The choice of what protection to demand must be left to the individual practitioner in the circumstances of the particular transaction with which he or she is concerned. For example, no specialised type of company (eg an insurance company) is considered.

Tax warranties

Examples of tax warranties are given in the Agreement for Sale, Sched 4, para 3. One basic warranty is that the provisions in the latest audited accounts are adequate. The warranties relate to general taxation matters ((1) to (4)); distributions and payments ((5) to (10)); losses ((11) to (13)); close companies ((14)); anti-avoidance clearances and elections ((15) to (21)); capital assets ((22) to (34)); miscellaneous matters ((35) to (39)); taxation of employees ((40) to (43)); and stamp duty, VAT and inheritance tax ((44) to (49)). It is unlikely that all the warranties will be appropriate in any particular transaction.

One problem in formulating suggestions is the question of how specific to make the warranties. Is it, for instance, satisfactory to take a simple warranty that the target has properly operated the PAYE system? Or is it desirable to go further and ask for a warranty that tax has been properly deducted from, for example, all payments as compensation for loss of office (ICTA 1988, s 148) and in respect of all benefits in kind (ICTA 1988, s 143)? Apart from the comfort of seeing the likely problem areas written down in the agreement, the advantage of being specific is that it focuses the minds of the vendors on the point in question and may lead to a disclosure. Most practitioners acting for purchasers will yield to the temptation to use general words and then go to the specific 'without prejudice to the generality of the foregoing'.

The drafting problem of general and specific wording also arises because one warranty tends to overlap with another. For instance, it is normal to take a warranty that the latest audited accounts contain full provision for all tax liability. This general warranty will overlap with many other specific warranties (eg that all claims for group relief have been properly made) but the advantage of the specific warranty remains. An element of repetition is inevitable.

Tax indemnity

The established method of giving tax indemnities has been for the vendor to indemnify the target itself by a deed given at completion containing perhaps both a general indemnity and specific indemnities, although specific indemnities are now less commonly required. Some practitioners preferred to include the indemnities in the sale contract and to indemnify the purchaser against any depletion or diminution in the assets of the target. However, for the reasons discussed below in the final section of this chapter, it has become usual to extend the benefit of a deed of indemnity to include the purchaser, so that payments made by the vendor to the purchaser in respect of tax liabilities of the target may fall to be treated for tax purposes as adjustments to the purchase price. The Agreement for Sale adopts this method and extends it. The Agreement contains, in Sched 4, paras 1 and 2 the vendor's agreement to make to the purchaser payments by way of reduction in the consideration in respect of 'relevant taxation claims' falling on the target (see p 189). The Agreement takes the process to its logical conclusion by excluding the target altogether from the benefit of the indemnity.

Schedule 4, para 2(A) contains a general indemnity designed to cover any liability incurred before completion which is not reflected in the audited accounts of the target, excluding only liabilities incurred in the ordinary course of business since the date of the last accounts (see the definition of 'relevant taxation claim' in para 1(6). The vendor will seek to add further exclusions as appropriate to the circumstances of the particular transaction.

TAX TREATMENT OF PAYMENTS UNDER WARRANTIES AND INDEMNITIES

If the vendor is called upon to make any payment to the purchaser or the target under the warranties or indemnities he will wish to be satisfied that any payment goes to reduce the consideration which he is treated as having received for the purposes of computing any capital gain. In respect of the warranties statutory provision is made in the Capital Gains Tax Act 1979, s 41(1)(*c*) which provides that:

In the first instance no allowance shall be made . . . for any contingent liability in respect of a warranty or representation made on a disposal by way of sale or lease of any property other than land.

The section goes on to provide that if any contingency subsequently becomes enforceable the capital gains tax computation will be adjusted accordingly. Where the disposal is for cash this will result in a repayment of tax or a discharge of any outstanding liability. The application of the section is however not clear where the consideration is one to which the Capital Gains Tax Act 1979, s 85 applies as no actual tax will have become payable as a result of the sale. In these circumstances it is understood that any payment under the warranties will serve to increase the base cost of the consideration shares on any ultimate disposal. In either event the purchaser's position, ie his overall acquisition cost of the target, will be adjusted correspondingly.

In the case of indemnities the position is less clear. Indemnities may be given to the target although provision may be made for the sums so indemnified to be paid to the purchaser (particularly in the case of a sale of less than a 100 per cent interest in the target). In the past the Revenue seems to have allowed any payments under the indemnities made to the target as a deduction against the vendor's consideration for the purposes of calculating the capital gain. The position is far from clear and it may nevertheless be open to the purchaser to argue that the fact that the company has received indemnities against specific matters cannot affect the position or reduce the amount which is treated as having been paid for the acquisition of the shares in the target.

Whatever the position of the vendor, it is, however, generally accepted that a right of indemnity enforceable by the target against the vendor is an asset for capital gains tax purposes falling within the Capital Gains Tax Act 1979, s 20 so that any amount received by the target will be subject to tax. This results from the decision in *Zim Properties Ltd* v *Procter* (1984) 58 TC 371 (and see also Inland Revenue Extra Statutory Concession, 19 December 1989) that a right to bring an action to seek to enforce a claim that was neither frivolous nor vexatious, where the right could be turned to account by negotiating a compromise yielding a capital sum, constituted an asset for the purposes of capital gains tax. The result of this is that the target's net of tax receipt from an indemnity payment would be reduced and in order to provide a full indemnity the payment would need to be increased. A vendor will, not unnaturally, be unwilling to gross up for tax any payment made to the target under an indemnity and the prudent vendor should, indeed, refuse to give any indemnity which has that effect. Since any payment made to the purchaser in respect of a tax liability of the target would seem not to be subject to tax in the purchaser's hands (although it would correspondingly reduce the purchaser's acquisition cost for the target's shares) the Agreement for Sale, Sched 4, paras 1 and 2 provides for the vendor instead to make payments to the purchaser by way of reduction in the consideration in respect of relevant taxation claims. If such payments are subject to tax in the purchaser's hands (which it is not thought to be the case) then it is submitted that it is appropriate for these to be grossed up and para 1(5)(ii) has this effect.

Cases arise in which provision must be made for a non-tax liability which is expected to fall on the target but which is unquantified at the time of the sale. As a condition of the sale the purchaser may insist that the target receives an indemnity against this payment, but if this liability is itself deductible in calculating the target's liability to tax, then it may be more satisfactory for the vendor to agree to make payment, as in respect of tax liabilities, direct to the purchaser. Not only will this have the effect of ensuring that this amount is deducted for the purposes of calculating the vendor's capital gains tax bill, but, because the target retains the benefit of the tax deduction, the payment from vendor to purchaser can be calculated by reference to the net, after tax, diminution in the target's assets.

Chapter 6

The Agreement for Sale

Two forms of agreement are set out in this chapter: a form for use by individual vendors and a form for use by a corporate vendor. Although the two forms are very similar, the differences are such as to make it convenient for the reader to set out both forms in full, rather than to include a note of the differences. These agreements are not so much agreements as collections of useful clauses. It would be rare indeed to find all the provisions of these agreements incorporated in a contract for the sale of a private company.

Where the purchaser is a public company and the consideration includes an allotment of shares in the purchaser, then attention must be paid to the provisions of the Companies Act 1985 which impose conditions upon the allotment by a public company of shares which are paid up otherwise than in cash. Unless the transaction is exempt, the non-cash consideration must be valued by an independent person who must make a report to the purchaser, with a copy to the allottees. Failure to do this is visited with alarming consequences, namely, that the allottees become liable to pay for their shares in cash. The Companies Act 1985, s 103(3), exempts from these rules an arrangement providing for the allotment of shares on terms that the whole or part of the consideration is to be provided by the transfer of all or some of the shares, or of all or some of the shares of a particular class, in another company. This exemption does not, however, operate unless it is open to all the holders of the shares in the target to take part in the arrangement. In determining whether this is the case, shares held by, or by a nominee of, the purchaser are disregarded.

In a case where some of the shareholders are to sell their shares for cash and others are to sell for shares then, unless the transaction is structured so that each shareholder of the target can participate in the arrangement providing for the allotment of shares, an expert's report must be obtained. If, however, the shares which are to be acquired for cash are acquired in one transaction and the share for share transaction is carried through subsequently, it seems that an expert's report is not required as, in considering the second transaction (which is the one providing for the allotment of shares), the shares already acquired by the purchaser can be disregarded. The cautious practitioner will not, however, separate artificially what is, in truth, a single transaction in order to avoid an expert's report. In view of the Draconian consequences of failure to comply with the sections, it is safer to obtain the report.

The agreements contemplate a target with subsidiaries, and will therefore require amendment if there are none. Amendments will also be required if the consideration is paid wholly in cash. Where the consideration is shares in the purchaser, an additional engrossment should be signed for filing at the Companies Registration Office (Companies Act 1985, s 88).

The provisions concerning in the Fourth Schedule reflect the law at 1 March 1989 and do not take in account the provisions of the Finance Act 1989.

The notes to both agreements appear on p 291.

AGREEMENT FOR SALE—INDIVIDUAL VENDORS

CONTENTS

THIS   AGREEMENT is made the   day of
19

BETWEEN:

(1)   THE PERSONS whose names and addresses are set out in the first column
      of Part 1 of the First Schedule (hereinafter together called 'the
      Vendors'); and

(2)   PLC ('the Purchaser') a company registered in
      England under number   whose registered office is at

WHEREAS:

The Purchaser wishes to acquire the entire issued share capital of
            Limited from the Vendors on the terms of this Agreement.

NOW IT IS HEREBY AGREED as follows:

1   INTERPRETATION

(A)   Definitions
In this Agreement where the context admits:

(1)   'the Company' means   Limited a company registered
      in England under number   and incorporated on
      [19   ] as a private company limited by shares
      under the Companies Act(s)   ;

(2)   'Completion' means completion of the sale and purchase of the
      Sale Shares;[1]

(3)   'Consideration Shares' means ordinary shares of
      each in the Purchaser credited as fully paid;

(4)   'the Directors' means the persons named in Part II of the first
      schedule and 'the Continuing Directors' means the persons
      named in Part III of that schedule;

(5)   'the Disclosure Letter' means the letter dated the date hereof
      written by or on behalf of the Vendors to the Purchaser in agreed
      terms;[2]

(6)   'the Properties' means the properties particulars of which are set
      out in the list annexed to the Disclosure Letter;

(7)   'the Sale Shares' means the shares to be bought and sold pursuant
      to Clause 2;

(8)   'the Subsidiaries' means the companies listed in Part II of the
      second schedule; and

(9)   'the Warranties' means the warranties and representations set out
      in paragraph 2 of the third schedule, in paragraph 3 of the fourth
      schedule and in paragraph 8 of the sixth schedule.

(B) Construction of Certain References
In this Agreement where the context admits:

    (1)   words and phrases the definitions of which are contained or referred to in Part XXVI of the Companies Act 1985 shall be construed as having the meanings thereby attributed to them;

    (2)   references to statutory provisions shall be construed as references to those provisions as amended or re-enacted or as their application is modified by other provisions from time to time and shall include references to any provisions of which they are re-enactments (whether with or without modification);[3]

    (3)   where any statement is qualified by the expression 'so far as the Vendors are aware' or 'to the best of the Vendors' knowledge and belief' or any similar expression, that statement shall be deemed to include an additional statement that it has been made after due and careful enquiry;[4]

    (4)   references to clauses and schedules are references to clauses hereof and schedules hereto, references to sub-clauses or paragraphs are, unless otherwise stated, references to sub-clauses of the clause or paragraphs of the schedule in which the reference appears, and references to this Agreement include the schedules;

    (5)   references to any document being in agreed terms are to that document in the form signed on behalf of the parties for identification; and

    (6)   references to the Vendors include a reference to each of them.

(C) Joint and Several Liabilities
All warranties, representations, indemnities, covenants, agreements and obligations given or entered into by more than one person in this Agreement are given or entered into jointly and severally.

(D) Headings
The headings and sub-headings are inserted for convenience only and shall not affect the construction of this Agreement.

(E) Schedules
Each of the schedules shall have effect as if set out herein.

2   SALE OF SHARES

(A) Sale and Purchase
Subject to the terms of this Agreement each of the Vendors shall sell and the Purchaser shall purchase, free from all liens, charges, equities and encumbrances and together with all rights now or hereafter attaching thereto the number of ordinary shares of £   each set opposite his name in the second column of Part I of the first schedule which shares together comprise the entire issued share capital of the Company.

(B) Simultaneous Completion
The Purchaser shall not be obliged to complete the purchase of any of the Sale Shares unless the purchase of all the Sale Shares is completed simultaneously.

(C) Waiver of Pre-emption Rights

Each of the Vendors hereby waives any pre-emption rights he may have relating to the Sale Shares, whether conferred by the Company's Articles of Association or otherwise.

3   CONSIDERATION

(A) Amount [Consideration Shares]

The total consideration for the Sale Shares shall be the sum of £   ,
but subject to adjustment as provided in the fourth and fifth schedules. [The total consideration for the Sale Shares shall be the allotment to the Vendors of   Consideration Shares].

(B) Placing[5]

The total consideration for the Sale Shares shall be the allotment to the Vendors of the number of Consideration Shares which, when placed through placees nominated by the Purchaser shall produce payment to the Vendors of aggregate net proceeds of £   . The Purchaser shall arrange a placing to produce such aggregate net proceeds and shall procure the payment of that amount to the Vendors at completion against the renunciation by the Vendors of the allotment of such Consideration Shares as directed by the Purchaser. The Vendors warrant that they will renounce such allotment free from liens, charges, equities and encumbrances, and together with all rights attaching thereto, agree to confirm such warranty in favour of   and hereby grant authority to   to place such Consideration Shares on their behalf.

(C) Dividends etc

The Consideration Shares shall rank pari passu and as a single class with the existing ordinary shares of   each in the Purchaser, and shall carry the right to receive in full all dividends and other distributions declared, made or paid after the date of this Agreement [save that they shall not carry the right to participate in the [interim] [final] dividend of the Purchaser for the year ending   19   [declared on   ]].[6]

4   CONDITIONS AND COMPLETION

(A) Conditions[7]

Completion is conditional upon:

(1) the passing at a general meeting of the Purchaser of a resolution to increase the authorised share capital of the Purchaser to not less than £   and to authorise the directors of the Purchaser to allot the Consideration Shares;[8] and

(2) the admission by the Council of The Stock Exchange of the Consideration Shares to the Official List, and such listing becoming fully effective;[9]

and in the event that the above conditions are not satisfied on or before   19   this Agreement shall lapse and no party shall make any claim against any other in respect hereof, save for any antecedent breach.

(B)   Date of Completion

Subject to the provisions of this clause, Completion shall take place on
         19   at the offices of Messrs   .

(C)   Vendors' Obligations[10]

On Completion the Vendors shall:
   (1)   deliver to the Purchaser:
         (*a*) duly executed transfers of the Sale Shares by the registered
               holders thereof in favour of the Purchaser or its nominees
               together with the relative share certificates;
         (*b*) such waivers or consents as the Purchaser may require to
               enable the Purchaser or its nominees to be registered as
               holders of the Sale Shares;[11] and
         (*c*) powers of attorney in agreed terms.[12]
   (2)   procure the passing of a resolution of the board of directors of the
         Company resolving to register the transfers referred to in item
         (1)(*a*) subject only to due stamping;
   (3)   cause such persons as the Purchaser may nominate to be validly
         appointed as additional directors of the Company and the
         Subsidiaries and, upon such appointment, forthwith cause the
         Directors (other than the Continuing Directors) and the secretary
         or secretaries of the Company and the Subsidiaries to retire from
         all their offices and employments with the Company or the
         Subsidiaries, each delivering to the Purchaser a letter under seal
         acknowledging that he has no claim outstanding for
         compensation or otherwise and without any payment under the
         Employment Protection (Consolidation) Act 1978;[13]
   (4)   procure revocation of all authorities to the bankers of the
         Company and the Subsidiaries relating to bank accounts, giving
         authority to such persons as the Purchaser may nominate to
         operate the same;
   (5)   procure the resignation of the auditors of the Company and the
         Subsidiaries;[14]
   (6)   deliver to the Purchaser as agent for the Company and the
         Subsidiaries:
         (*a*) a certificate from Messrs   in the form approved
               by the Purchaser prior to the signing hereof as to the title of
               the Company or the Subsidiaries to the Properties;[15]
         (*b*) the title deeds to the Properties;[16]
         (*c*) all the statutory and other books (duly written up to date) of
               the Company and each of the Subsidiaries and its/their
               certificate(s) of incorporation and common seal(s);[17] and
         (*d*) certificates in respect of all issued shares in the capital of each
               of the Subsidiaries and transfer of all shares in any Subsidiary
               held by any nominee in favour of such persons as the
               Purchaser shall direct;[18] [and]
   (7)   deposit the sum of £   with the Purchaser on the terms
         of Clause 7; [and]

(8)   comply with clause 3(   ); [and]
(9)   procure the discharge of the guarantees and other obligations stipulated in the Disclosure Letter to be discharged at completion.

(D) Service Agreements

On Completion the Company and   shall enter into service agreements in the form of the draft(s) in agreed terms.[19]

(E) Purchaser's Obligations

On Completion the Purchaser shall [pay] [satisfy] the consideration for the Sale Shares as provided by clause 3 [and comply with the provisions of paragraph 3 of the seventh schedule] [any payment in cash to be made] by way of town clearing banker's draft made payable to   .

(F) Failure to Complete[20]

If in any respect the preceding provisions of this clause (other than sub-clause A) are not complied with on the date for Completion set by sub-clause B the party not in default (or, in the case of non-compliance with sub-clause D, the Purchaser) may:

(1)   defer Completion to a date not more than twenty-eight days after the date set by sub-clause B (and so that the provisions of this sub-clause F, apart from this item (1), shall apply to Completion as so deferred); or

(2)   proceed to Completion so far as practicable (without prejudice to its rights hereunder); or

(3)   rescind this Agreement.

5   PURCHASER'S RIGHT OF ACCESS[21]

From the date hereof the Purchaser and its accountants and agents shall be allowed access to all the premises and books of account of the Company and the Subsidiaries, and the Vendor shall supply any information reasonably required by the Purchaser relating to the Company and the Subsidiaries.

6   RESTRICTION OF VENDORS

(A) Covenants

Each of the Vendors undertakes with the Purchaser that he will not:

(1)   for the period of   after Completion, either on his own account or in conjunction with or on behalf of any person, firm or company, carry on, or be engaged, concerned or interested (directly or indirectly) in carrying on, the business of
(other than as a holder of less than 5 per cent of any class of shares or debentures listed on The Stock Exchange) within   ; and

(2)   for the period of   after Completion, either on his own account or in conjunction with or on behalf of any other person, firm or company, solicit or entice away from the Company or any of the Subsidiaries any person who at the date hereof is an officer, manager, servant, or customer of the Company or any of the

Subsidiaries whether or not such person would commit a breach of contract by reason of leaving service or transferring business.

(B) Reasonableness[22]
The restrictions contained in sub-clause A are considered reasonable by the parties, but in the event that any such restriction shall be found to be void but would be valid if some part thereof were deleted, or the period or area of application reduced, such restriction shall apply with such modification as may be necessary to make it valid and effective.

(C) Registration[23]
[Any provision of this Agreement, or of any agreement or arrangement of which it forms part, by virtue of which such agreement or arrangement is subject to registration under the Restrictive Trade Practices Act 1976 shall only take effect the day after particulars of such agreement or arrangement have been furnished to the Director General of Fair Trading pursuant to s 24 of that Act.]

7   WARRANTIES AND DEPOSIT

(A) Purchaser's Knowledge[24]
The Warranties are given subject to matters fairly disclosed in the Disclosure Letter, but no other information relating to the Company or the Subsidiaries of which the Purchaser has knowledge (actual or constructive) shall prejudice any claim made by the Purchaser under the Warranties or operate to reduce any amount recoverable.

(B) Warranties to be Independent
Each of the Warranties shall be separate and independent and, save as expressly provided, shall not be limited by reference to any other Warranty or anything in this Agreement.

(C) Damages[25]
Without restricting the rights of the Purchaser or the ability of the Purchaser to claim damages on any basis in the event that any of the Warranties is broken or proves to be untrue or misleading, the Vendor shall, on demand, pay to the Purchaser:
  (*a*)   the amount necessary to put the Company and each of the Subsidiaries into the position which would have existed if the Warranties had not been broken and had been true and not misleading; and
  (*b*)   all costs and expenses incurred by the Purchaser, the Company or the Subsidiaries, directly or indirectly, as a result of such breach.

(D) Pending Completion[26]
The Vendors shall procure that (save only as may be necessary to give effect to this Agreement) neither the Vendors nor the Company nor any of the Subsidiaries shall do, allow or procure any act or omission before Completion which would constitute a breach of any of the Warranties if they were given at any and all times from the date hereof down to Completion or which would make any of the Warranties inaccurate or misleading if they

were so given. In particular, without prejudice to the generality of the foregoing, the Vendor shall procure that items (*a*) to (*g*) of paragraph 2(22) of the third schedule shall be complied with at all times from the date hereof down to Completion.

(E)   Further Disclosure by Vendors

The Vendors shall forthwith disclose in writing to the Purchaser any matter or thing which may arise or become known to the Vendor after the date hereof and before Completion which is inconsistent with any of the Warranties or which might make any of them inaccurate or misleading if they were given at any and all times from the date hereof down to Completion or which is material to be known to a Purchaser for value of the Sale Shares.

(F)   Right of Rescission[27]

In the event of any such matter or thing as is mentioned in sub-clause (E) becoming known to the Purchaser before Completion or in the event of its becoming apparent on or before Completion that the Vendors are in breach of any of the Warranties or any other term of this Agreement the Purchaser may rescind this Agreement by notice in writing to the Vendor.

(G)   Application of Deposit[28]

Subject to the following provisions of this clause, the Purchaser may apply all or part of the deposit referred to in sub-clause 4C(7) ('the deposit') in recouping any amount lawfully due to it under or by reason of any breach of the terms of this Agreement and any amount so applied shall *pro tanto* satisfy the liability concerned.

(H)   Interest

The deposit shall be deposited by the Purchaser with bankers selected by it and any interest earned thereon shall accrue to and form part of the deposit and shall, accordingly, belong to the Vendor subject to the provisions of this Agreement.

(I)   Release

In the event that the Purchaser shall not have notified the Vendors in writing of any claim hereunder before   19   the deposit and accrued interest shall be released to the Vendors' solicitors Messrs whose receipt shall be an absolute discharge. In the event that the Purchaser shall have so notified any such claim, it shall use its best endeavours to quantify the amount claimed and any balance shall be so released on that date. Upon final determination of the total amount (if any) falling to be applied by the Purchaser under this clause, any balance of the deposit shall be released to the Vendors' solicitors provided that no amount shall be released before the said   19   .

8   PROVISIONS RELATING TO THIS AGREEMENT

(A)   Assignment

This Agreement shall be binding upon and enure for the benefit of the successors of the parties but shall not be assignable, save that the Purchaser may assign the benefit of the Warranties to any transferee of the share capital of the Company or any of the Subsidiaries.

(B)   Whole Agreement
This Agreement (together with any documents referred to herein) constitutes the whole agreement between the parties hereto relating to its subject matter and no variations hereof shall be effective unless made in writing.[29] This Agreement supersedes   .

(C)   Agreement Survives Completion
The Warranties and all other provisions of this Agreement, in so far as the same shall not have been performed at Completion, shall remain in full force and effect notwithstanding Completion.

(D)   Rights of Rescission
Any right of rescission conferred upon the Purchaser hereby shall be in addition to and without prejudice to all other rights and remedies available to it and no exercise or failure to exercise such a right of rescission shall constitute a waiver by the Purchaser of any such other right or remedy. Completion shall not constitute a waiver by the Purchaser of any breach of any provision of this Agreement whether or not known to the Purchaser at the date of Completion.

(E)   Release of One Vendor
The Purchaser may release or compromise the liability of any of Vendor hereunder without affecting the liability of any other Vendor[29A].

(F)   Further Assurance
At any time after the date hereof the Vendors shall, at the request and cost of the Purchaser, execute such documents and do such acts and things as the Purchaser may reasonably require for the purpose of vesting the Sale Shares in the Purchaser or its nominees and giving to the Purchaser the full benefit of all the provisions of this Agreement.

(G)   Invalidity
If any provision of this Agreement shall be held to be illegal or unenforceable, the enforceability of the remainder of this Agreement shall not be affected.

(H)   Payment to the Vendors
[Subject to clause 4(E)] any payment falling to be made to the Vendors under any provision of this Agreement may be made to the Vendors' Solicitors Messrs   whose receipt shall be an absolute discharge.

(I)   Notices
Any notice required to be given hereunder shall be in writing in the English language and shall be served by sending the same by pre-paid first class post, telex or telecopy or by delivering the same by hand, in the case of the Purchaser to its registered office and in the case of the Vendors to   . Any notice sent by post, as provided in this sub-clause, shall be deemed to have been served forty-eight hours after despatch and any notice sent by telex or telecopy, as provided in this sub-clause, shall be deemed to

have been served at the time of despatch and in proving the service of the same it will be sufficient to prove, in the case of a letter, that such letter was properly stamped, addressed and placed in the post and, in the case of a telex or telecopy, that such telex or telecopy was duly despatched to a current telex or telecopy number of the addressee.

(J)   English Law[30]

This Agreement shall be governed by, and construed in all respects in accordance with, English law.

9   Costs

Each party to this Agreement shall pay its own costs of and incidental to this Agreement and the sale and purchase hereby agreed to be made, provided that if the Purchaser shall exercise any right hereby conferred to rescind this Agreement the Vendors shall indemnify the Purchaser against expenses and costs incurred in investigating the affairs of the Company and the Subsidiaries and in the preparation of this Agreement.

AS WITNESS the hands of the parties or their duly authorised representatives the day and year first before written.

FIRST SCHEDULE

Vendors and Directors

Part I — Vendors

Name and Address   *Sale Shares*

Part II — Directors

Name of Director   *Company/Companies*
                                                            of which (s)he is
                                                            a director

Part III (Continuing Directors)

Name of Director   *Company/Companies*
                                                            of which (s)he is a
                                                            director

Part IV (Secretary)

Name of Secretary   *Company/Companies*
                                                            of which (s)he is the
                                                            secretary

SECOND SCHEDULE

Company and Subsidiaries

Part I — The Company

Name and Number of Company	*Authorised Capital*	*Issued Capital*	*Held by*	*Beneficially owned by*

Part II — The Subsidiaries

Name and Number of Subsidiary	*Authorised Capital*	*Issued Capital*	*Held by*	*Beneficially owned by*

THIRD SCHEDULE

Warranties[31] and Representations

1 INTERPRETATION

In this schedule where the context admits:

(1) 'the Audited Accounts' means the audited consolidated balance sheet of the Company and the Subsidiaries made up as at the Balance Sheet Date and the audited consolidated profit and loss account of the Company and the Subsidiaries for the year ended on the Balance Sheet Date, true copies of which are annexed to the Disclosure Letter, including the notes thereto;

(2) 'the Balance Sheet Date' means   19   ;

(3) 'encumbrance' includes any interest or equity of any person (including, without prejudice to the generality of the foregoing, any right to acquire, option or right of pre-emption) or any mortgage, charge, pledge, lien, assignment, hypothecation, security interest, title retention or any other security agreement or arrangement;

(4) 'intellectual property' means patents, trade marks, service marks, rights (whether registered or unregistered) in any designs, applications for any of the foregoing, trade or business names and copyright;

(5) 'intellectual property agreements' means agreements or arrangements relating (wholly or partly) to intellectual property or to the disclosure, use, assignment or patenting of any inventions, discovery, improvements, processes, formulae or other knowhow;

(6) 'Listed Intellectual Property' means the Intellectual Property listed in the list annexed to the Disclosure Letter;

(7) 'Listed Intellectual Property Agreements' means the Intellectual Property Agreements listed in the list annexed to the Disclosure Letter;

(8) 'Management Accounts' means the management accounts for the period ended on   19   true copies of which are annexed to the Disclosure Letter;

(9) 'SSAP' means Statement of Standard Accounting Practice in force at the date hereof as issued by the Institute of Chartered Accountants in England and Wales;

(10) any question whether a person is connected with another shall be determined in accordance with the Income and Corporation Taxes Act 1988, s 839, which shall apply in relation to this schedule as it applies in relation to that Act;[32] and

(11) references to 'the Company' include each of the Subsidiaries.

2 WARRANTIES AND REPRESENTATIONS

The Vendors hereby warrant and represent to and for the benefit of the Purchaser in the following terms.

THE COMPANY AND THE VENDORS

(1) Capacity

Each Vendor has full power to enter into and perform this Agreement and this Agreement constitutes binding obligations on the Vendors in accordance with its terms.

(2) Liabilities Owing to or by Vendors

There is not outstanding any indebtedness or other liability (actual or contingent) owing by the Company to any Vendor or any Director or any person connected with any of them, nor is there any indebtedness owing to the Company by any such person, and no promise or representation has been made to any Vendor in connection with the Warranties or the Disclosure Letter in respect of which the Company or any of the Subsidiaries might be liable.

(3) Vendors' Other Interests

No Vendor nor any person connected with any Vendor has any interest, direct or indirect, in any business other than that now carried on by the Company which is or is likely to be or become competitive with the business or any proposed business of the Company.

THE COMPANY'S CONSTITUTION

(4) Share Capital

Part I of the second schedule contains true particulars of the authorised and issued share capital of the Company, all the shares there shown as issued are in issue fully paid and are beneficially owned and registered as set out therein free from any encumbrance.

(5) Memorandum and Articles

The copy of the memorandum and articles of association of the Company annexed to the Disclosure Letter is true and complete and has embodied therein or annexed thereto a copy of every such resolution or agreement as is referred to in the Companies Act 1985, s 380.[33]

(6) Company Resolutions

Neither the Company nor any class of its members has passed any resolution (other than resolutions relating to business at Annual General Meetings which was not special business).

(7) Options etc

No person has the right (whether exercisable now or in the future and whether contingent or not) to call for the allotment, issue, sale or transfer of any share or loan capital of the Company under any option or other agreement (including conversion rights and rights of pre-emption).

THE COMPANY AND THE LAW

(8) Compliance with Laws

The Company has conducted its business in all material respects in accordance with all applicable laws and regulations of the United Kingdom and any relevant foreign country and there is no order, decree or judgment of any Court or any governmental agency of the United Kingdom or any foreign country outstanding against the Company or which may have a material adverse effect upon the assets or business of the Company.

(9) Licences etc

All necessary licences, consents, permits and authorities (public and private) have been obtained by the Company to enable the Company to carry on its business effectively in the places and in the manner in which such business is now carried on and all such licences, consents, permits and authorities are valid and subsisting and the Vendors know of no reason why any of them should be suspended, cancelled or revoked.

(10) Breach of Statutory Provisions

Neither the Company, nor any of its officers, agents or employees (during the course of their duties in relation to the Company) have committed, or omitted to do, any act or thing the commission or omission of which is, or could be, in contravention of any act, order, regulation, or the like in the United Kingdom or elsewhere which is punishable by fine or other penalty.

(11) Litigation

The Company is not engaged in any litigation or arbitration proceedings and so far as the Vendors are aware no litigation or arbitration proceedings are pending or threatened by or against the Company and there are no facts likely to give rise to any litigation or arbitration and the Company has not been a party to any undertaking or assurance given to any court or governmental agency which is still in force.

(12) Insolvency

   (a) No order has been made or petition presented or resolution passed for the winding up of the Company, nor has any distress, execution or other process been levied against the Company or action taken to repossess goods in the Company's possession.

   (b) No steps have been taken for the appointment of an administrator or receiver of any part of the Company's property.

   (c) No floating charge created by the Company has crystallised and, so far as the Vendor is aware, there are no circumstances likely to cause such a floating charge to crystallise.

   (d) The Company has not been a party to any transaction which could be avoided in a winding up.

   (e) The Company has not made or proposed any arrangement or composition with its creditors or any class of its creditors.

(13) Fair Trading

   (a) No agreement, practice or arrangement carried on by the Company or to which the Company is a party:

      (i) is or ought to be or ought to have been registered in accordance with the provisions of the Restrictive Trade Practices Acts 1976 and 1977[34] or contravenes the provisions of the Resale Prices Act 1976 or is or has been the subject of any enquiry, investigation or proceeding under any of those Acts; or

      (ii) is or has been the subject of an enquiry, investigation, reference or report under the Fair Trading Act 1973 (or any previous legislation relating to monopolies or mergers) or the Competition Act 1980; or

(iii) infringes art 85 of the Treaty establishing the European Economic Community or constitutes an abuse of dominant position contrary to art 86 of the said Treaty or infringes any regulation or other enactment made under art 87 of the said Treaty or is or has been the subject of any enquiry, investigation or proceeding in respect thereof; or

(iv) has been notified to the Directorate General of Competition of the Commission of the European Communities; or

(v) is by virtue of its terms or by virtue of any practice for the time being carried on in connection therewith a 'Consumer Trade Practice' within the meaning of the Fair Trading Act 1973, s 13, and susceptible to or under reference to the Consumer Protection Advisory Committee or the subject matter of a report to the Secretary of State or the subject matter of an order by the Secretary of State under the provisions of Part II of that Act; or

(vi) infringes any other competition, anti-restrictive trade practice, anti-trust or consumer protection law or legislation applicable in the United Kingdom or elsewhere and not specifically mentioned in this sub-paragraph.

(*b*) The Company has not given any assurance or undertaking to the Restrictive Practices Court or the Director General of Fair Trading or the Secretary of State for Trade and Industry or the Commission or Court of Justice of the European Communities or to any other court, person or body and is not subject to any Act, decision, regulation, order or other instrument made by any of them relating to any matter referred to in this sub-paragraph.

(*c*) The Company is not in default or in contravention of any article, act, decision, regulation, order or other instrument or of any undertaking relating to any matter referred to in this sub-paragraph.

(14) <u>Defective Products</u>

The Company has not manufactured, sold or supplied products which are, or were, or will become, in any material respect faulty or defective or which do not comply in any material respect with any warranties or representations expressly or impliedly made by the Company or with all applicable regulations, standards and requirements in respect thereof.

(15) <u>Bribes</u>

So far as the Vendors are aware no officer, agent or employee of the Company has paid any bribe or used any of the Company's assets unlawfully to obtain an advantage for any person.

THE COMPANY'S ACCOUNTS AND RECORDS

(16) Books and Records

All accounts, books, ledgers, financial and other records of whatsoever kind ('records') of the Company:

    (*a*)   have been fully, properly and accurately maintained, are in the possession of the Company and contain true and accurate records of all matters entered or required by law to be entered therein;

    (*b*)   do not contain or reflect any material inaccuracies or discrepancies;

and no notice or allegation that any of the records is incorrect or should be rectified has been received. Where any of the records are kept on computer, the Company is the owner of all hardware and all software licences necessary to enable it to use the records as they have been used in its business hitherto and does not share any hardware or software relating to the records with any person.

(17) Accounts Warranty[35]

The Audited Accounts have been prepared in accordance with the requirements of all relevant statutes and generally accepted accounting principles and show a true and fair view of the state of affairs of the Company and the Subsidiaries at the Balance Sheet Date and the profits of the Company and the Subsidiaries for the year ended on the Balance Sheet Date and apply bases and policies of accounting which have been consistently applied in the audited balance sheet and profit and loss accounts for the three financial years prior to the Balance Sheet Date.

(18) Provision for Liabilities

Full provision has been made in the Audited Accounts for all actual liabilities of the Company outstanding at the Balance Sheet Date and proper provision (or note) in accordance with generally accepted accounting principles has been made therein for all other liabilities of the Company then outstanding whether contingent, quantified, disputed or not including (without limitation) the cost of any work or material for which payment has been received or credit taken, any future loss which may arise in connection with uncompleted contracts and any claims against the Company in respect of completed contracts.

(19) Stock Valuation and Accounting Policies[36]

For the purposes of the Audited Accounts, the Company's stock in trade and work in progress has been valued in accordance with SSAP 9 and on a basis in all material respects consistent with that adopted for the purpose of the Company's audited accounts in respect of the beginning and end of each of the three last preceding accounting periods and the value of redundant or obsolete materials and materials below standard has been written down to realisable market value or adequate provision has been made therefor.

(20) Management Accounts[37]

True copies of the management accounts for the period ended on 19   are annexed to the Disclosure Letter. Such management accounts have been prepared in accordance with the

Company's normal practices and the Vendors do not consider them misleading.

(21) Returns

The Company has complied with the provisions of the Companies Act 1985 and all returns, particulars, resolutions and other documents required under any legislation to be delivered on behalf of the Company to the Registrar of Companies or to any other authority whatsoever have been properly made and delivered.

THE COMPANY'S BUSINESS

(22) Business since the Balance Sheet Date[38]

Since the Balance Sheet Date:

- (a) the Company has carried on its business in the ordinary and usual course and without entering into any transaction, assuming any liability or making any payment which is not in the ordinary course of its business and without any interruption or alteration in the nature, scope or manner of its business;
- (b) the Company has not borrowed or raised any money or taken any financial facility;
- (c) the Company has paid its creditors within the times agreed with such creditors and so that there are no debts outstanding by the Company which have been due for more than four weeks;
- (d) there has been no unusual change in the Company's stock levels;
- (e) the Company has not entered into, or agreed to enter into, any capital commitments;
- (f) no share or loan capital has been issued or agreed to be issued by the Company;
- (g) no distribution of capital or income has been declared, made or paid in respect of any share capital of the Company and (excluding fluctuations in overdrawn current accounts with bankers) no loan or share capital of the Company has been repaid in whole or part or has become liable to be repaid; and
- (h) there has been no material deterioration in the financial position, prospects[39] or turnover of the Company.

(23) Working Capital

Having regard to existing bank and other facilities, the Company has sufficient working capital for the purposes of continuing to carry on its business in its present form and at its present level of turnover for the foreseeable future and for the purposes of executing, carrying out and fulfilling in accordance with their terms all orders, projects and contractual obligations which have been placed with, or undertaken by the Company.

(24) Commission

No one is entitled to receive from the Company any finder's fee, brokerage, or other commission in connection with the purchase of shares in the Company.

(25) <u>Consequence of Share Acquisition by the Purchaser</u>

The acquisition of the Sale Shares by the Purchaser or compliance with the terms of this Agreement:

    (*a*)   will not cause the Company to lose the benefit of any right or privilege it presently enjoys or so far as the Vendors are aware, cause any person who normally does business with the Company not to continue to do so on the same basis as previously;

    (*b*)   will not relieve any person of any obligation to the Company or enable any person to determine any such obligation or any right or benefit enjoyed by the Company or to exercise any right whether under an agreement with or otherwise in respect of the Company;

    (*c*)   will not result in any present or future indebtedness of the Company becoming due or capable of being declared due and payable prior to its stated maturity; and

    (*d*)   will not give rise to or cause to become exercisable any right of pre-emption;

and, to the best of the knowledge and belief of the Vendors, the Company's relationships with clients, customers, suppliers and employees will not be adversely affected thereby.

(26) <u>Grants</u>

[The Company has not applied for or received any financial assistance from any supranational, national or local authority or government agency.] [Full particulars of all grants received from any supranational, national or local authority or government agency (and all applications for any such) are contained in the Disclosure Letter and there are no circumstances which might lead to any such grant being refunded or forfeited in whole or in part].

(27) <u>Insurances</u>[40]

    (*a*)   Full particulars of all the Company's insurances are given in the Disclosure Letter and the insurances which are maintained by the Company afford the Company adequate cover against such risks as companies carrying on the same type of business as the Company commonly cover by insurance and in particular:

        (i)   the assets of the Company are insured against fire in their full replacement value; and

        (ii)   the Company is now, and has at all material times been, adequately covered against accident, damage, injury, third party loss (including product liability), loss of profits and other risks normally covered by insurance.

    (*b*)   All the Company's insurances referred to in the Disclosure Letter are in full force and effect, there are no circumstances which might lead to any liability under any of the Company's insurances being avoided by the insurers or the premiums being increased, there are no special or unusual terms, restrictions or rates of premium, all premiums have been paid on time and there is no claim outstanding under any such insurance nor are the Vendors aware of any circumstances likely to give rise to a claim.

THE COMPANY'S ASSETS

(28) Net Asset Value[41]

The value of the net tangible assets of the Company at Completion determined in accordance with the same accounting policies as those applied in the Audited Accounts (and on the basis that each fixed asset is valued at a figure no greater than the value attributed to it in the Audited Accounts or, in the case of any fixed asset acquired by the Company after the Balance Sheet Date, at a figure no greater than cost) will not be less than the value of the net tangible assets of the Company at the Balance Sheet Date as shown in the Audited Accounts.

(29) Assets and Charges

(a)   Except for current assets disposed of by the Company in the ordinary course of its business, the Company is the owner of and has good marketable title to all assets included in the Audited Accounts and all assets which have been acquired by the Company since the Balance Sheet Date and no such asset, nor any of the undertaking, goodwill or uncalled capital of the Company is subject to any encumbrance or any agreement or commitment to give or create any encumbrance.

(b)   Since the Balance Sheet Date, save for disposals in the ordinary course of its business, the assets of the Company have been in the possession of, or under the control of, the Company.

(c)   No asset is shared by the Company with any other person and the Company does not depend for its business upon any assets, facilities or services owned or supplied by any Vendor or any person connected with any Vendor.

(d)   No charge in favour of the Company is void or voidable for want of registration.

(30) Debts[42]

Any debts owed to the Company will realise their full face value and be good and collectable in the ordinary course of business and no amount included in the Audited Accounts as owing to the Company at the Balance Sheet Date has been released for an amount less than the value at which it was included in the Audited Accounts or is now regarded by the Vendor as irrecoverable in whole or in part. The Company has not factored or discounted its debts or agreed to do so.

(31) Title Retention

The Company has not acquired or agreed to acquire any material asset on terms that property therein does not pass until full payment is made.

(32) Intellectual Property Rights

(a)   The Company is the sole beneficial owner of the Listed Intellectual Property and (where such property is capable of registration) the registered proprietor thereof and (save for copyrights) owns no other intellectual property. Save as may appear from the Listed Intellectual Property Agreements no person has been authorised to make any use whatsoever of any intellectual property owned by the Company and the Company has not disclosed (except in the ordinary course of its business) any of its knowhow, trade secrets or list of customers to any other person.

(b)   All the intellectual property used by the Company is owned by it and it does not use any intellectual property in respect of which any third party has any right, title or interest.

(c)   So far as the Vendors are aware, none of the processes or products of the Company infringes any right of any other person relating to intellectual property or involves the unlicensed use of confidential information disclosed to the Company by any person in circumstances which might entitle that person to a claim against the Company and none of the Listed Intellectual Property is being used, claimed, opposed or attacked by any person.

(d)   The Vendors are not aware of any infringement of the Listed Intellectual Property by any third party.

(e)   There are no outstanding claims against the Company for infringement of any intellectual property used (or which has been used) by it and no such claims have been settled by the giving of any undertakings which remain in force.

(f)   Confidential information and knowhow used by the Company is kept strictly confidential and the Company operates and fully complies with procedures which maintain such confidentiality. The Vendors are not aware of any such confidentiality having been breached.

(g)   All application and renewal fees, costs and charges relating to the Listed Intellectual Property have been duly paid on time.

(h)   The Listed Intellectual Property Agreements are all the intellectual property agreements to which the Company is a party and each of them is valid and binding.

(33) Condition of Stock

The Company's stock in trade is in good condition and is capable of being sold by the Company in the ordinary course of its business in accordance with its current price list without rebate or allowance to a purchaser.

(34) Plant

The machinery and plant, including fixed plant and machinery, and all vehicles and office and other equipment used in connection with the business of the Company:

(a)   is in good repair and condition and in satisfactory working order;

(b)   is capable, and will (subject to fair wear and tear) be capable, over the period of time during which it will be written down to a nil value in the accounts of the Company, of doing the work for which it was designed or purchased;

(c)   is not surplus to the Company's requirements; and

(d)   is in the possession and control of, and is the absolute property free from any encumbrance of, the Company save for those items held under hire purchase or rental agreements the value of which items in the aggregate does not exceed £   .

(35) <u>Title to Properties</u>

The particulars of the Properties shown in the list attached to the Disclosure Letter are true and correct and the owner shown therein has good and marketable title to and exclusive occupation of each Property which it is said to own free from any encumbrance, sub-lease, tenancy or right of occupation, reservation, easement, quasi-easement or privilege in favour of any third party and there are appurtenant to each Property all rights and easements necessary for its use and enjoyment and except as shown the Company has no other interest in land and does not occupy any other property.

(36) <u>Matters Affecting Properties</u>

    (*a*)   No Property or any part thereof is affected by any of the following matters or is to the knowledge of the Vendors likely to become so affected:

         (i) any outstanding dispute, notice or complaint or any exception, reservation, right, covenant, restriction or condition which is of an unusual nature or which affects or might in the future affect the use of any of the Properties for the purpose for which it is now used or which affects or might in the future affect the value of the Properties; or

        (ii) any notice, order, demand, requirement or proposal of which the owner has notice or of which the Vendors are aware made or issued by or on behalf of any government or statutory authority, department or body for acquisition, clearance, demolition or closing, the carrying out of any work upon any building, the modification of any planning permission, the discontinuance of any use or the imposition of any building or improvement line; or

       (iii) any compensation received as a result of any refusal of any application for planning consent or the imposition of any restrictions in relation to any planning consent; or

       (iv) any commutation or agreement for the commutation of rent or payment of rent in advance of the due dates of payment thereof.

    (*b*)   Each of the Properties is in a good and substantial state of repair and condition and fit for the purposes for which it is presently used and no high alumina cement, woodwool, calcium chloride, sea-dredged aggregates or asbestos material was used in the construction thereof or of any of them and there are no development works, redevelopment works or fitting out works outstanding in respect of any of the Properties.

    (*c*)   All restrictions, conditions and covenants (including any imposed by or pursuant to any lease) affecting any of the Properties have been observed and performed and no notice of any breach of any of the same has been received or is to the Vendors' knowledge likely to be received.

(*d*)　The use of the Properties and all machinery and equipment therein and the conduct of any business therein complies in all respects with all relevant statutes and regulations including without prejudice to the generality of the foregoing the Factories Act 1961, the Offices Shops and Railway Premises Act 1963, the Fire Precautions Act 1971, the Health and Safety at Work etc Act 1974 and with all rules, regulations and delegated legislation thereunder and all necessary licences and consents required thereunder have been obtained.

(*e*)　There are no restrictive covenants or provisions, legislation or orders, charges, restrictions, agreements, conditions or other matters which preclude the use of any of the Properties for the purposes for which the Properties are now used and each such user is the permitted user under the provisions of the Town and Country Planning Acts 1971 to 1974 and regulations made thereunder and is in accordance with the requirements of the Local Authorities and all restrictions, conditions and covenants imposed by or pursuant to the said Town and Country Planning Acts have been observed and performed and no agreements have been entered into under the Town and Country Planning Act 1971, s 52 in respect of any of the Properties.

(*f*)　All replies by or on behalf of the Vendors or the Company to enquiries relating to any of the Properties made by or on behalf of the Purchaser were when given and are now true and correct.

(37)　Properties Previously Owned

The Company has no existing or contingent liabilities in respect of any properties previously occupied by it or in which it owned or held any interest, including, without limitation, leasehold premises assigned or otherwise disposed of.

The Company's Contracts

(38)　Documents

All title deeds and agreements to which the Company is a party and other documents owned by or which ought to be in the possession of the Company are in the possession of the Company and are properly stamped and are free from any encumbrance.

(39)　Material Contracts

The Company is not a party to or subject to any agreement, transaction, obligation, commitment, understanding, arrangement or liability which:

(*a*)　is incapable of complete performance in accordance with its terms within six months after the date on which it was entered into or undertaken; or

(*b*)　is known by the Vendors or by the Company to be likely to result in a loss to the Company on completion of performance; or

(*c*)　cannot readily be fulfilled or performed by the Company on time and without undue or unusual expenditure of money and effort; or

(*d*)　involves or is likely to involve obligations, restrictions, expenditure or receipts of an unusual, onerous or exceptional nature and not in the ordinary course of the Company's business; or

(*e*)   is a lease or a contract for hire or rent, hire purchase or purchase by way of credit sale or periodical payment; or

(*f*)   is with any trade union or body or organisation representing its employees; or

(*g*)   requires an aggregate consideration payable by the Company in excess of £   ; or

(*h*)   involves or is likely to involve the supply of goods by or to the Company the aggregate sales value of which will represent in excess of [10] per cent of the turnover for the last financial year of the Company; or

(*i*)   is a contract for services (other than contracts for the supply of electricity or normal office services); or

(*j*)   requires the Company to pay any commission, finder's fee, royalty or the like; or

(*k*)   in any way restricts the Company's freedom to carry on the whole or any part of its business in any part of the world in such manner as it thinks fit; or

(*l*)   involves liabilities which may fluctuate in accordance with an index or rate of currency exchange; or

(*m*)   is a contract for the sale of shares or assets which contains warranties or indemnities; or

(*n*)   is in any way otherwise than in the ordinary course of the Company's business.

(40) Defaults

Neither the Company nor any other party to any agreement with the Company is in default thereunder, being a default which would be material in the context of the financial or trading position of the Company nor (so far as the Vendors are aware) are there any circumstances likely to give rise to such a default.

(41) Sureties

No person other than the Company or a Subsidiary has given any guarantee of or security for any overdraft loan or loan facility granted to the Company.

(42) Powers of Attorney

No powers of attorney given by the Company (other than to the holder of an encumbrance solely to facilitate its enforcement) are now in force. No person, as agent or otherwise, is entitled or authorised to bind or commit the Company to any obligation not in the ordinary course of the Company's business, and the Vendors are not aware of any person purporting to do so.

(43) Insider Contracts

(*a*)   There is not outstanding, and there has not at any time during the last six years been outstanding, any agreement or arrangement to which the Company is a party and in which the Vendors, any person beneficially interested in the Company's share capital or any Director or any person connected with any of them is or has been interested, whether directly or indirectly.

(b)   The Company is not a party to, nor has its profits or financial position during such period been affected by, any agreement or arrangement which is not entirely of an arm's length nature.

(c)   All costs incurred by the Company have been charged to the Company and not borne by any other person.

(44) Debts

There are no debts owing by or to the Company other than debts which have arisen in the ordinary course of business, nor has the Company lent any money which has not been repaid.

(45) Options and Guarantees

The Company is not a party to any option or pre-emption right, or a party to any guarantee, suretyship, comfort letter or any other obligation (whatever called) to pay, provide funds or take action in the event of default in the payment of any indebtedness of any other person or default in the performance of any obligation of any other person.

(46) Tenders, etc

No offer, tender, or the like is outstanding which is capable of being converted into an obligation of the Company by an acceptance or other act of some other person.

THE COMPANY AND ITS BANKERS

(47) Borrowings

The total amount borrowed by the Company from its bankers does not exceed its facilities and the total amount borrowed by the Company from whatsoever source does not exceed any limitation on its borrowing contained in its articles of association, or in any debenture or loan stock deed or other instrument.

(48) Continuance of Facilities

Full and accurate details of all overdrafts, loans or other financial facilities outstanding or available to the Company are contained in the Disclosure Letter and true and correct copies of all documents relating thereto are annexed to the Disclosure Letter and neither the Vendors nor the Company have done anything whereby the continuance of any such facilities in full force and effect might be affected or prejudiced.

(49) Off-balance Sheet Financing

The Company has not engaged in any borrowing or financing not required to be reflected in the Audited Accounts.

(50) Bank Accounts

A statement of all the bank accounts of the Company and of the credit or debit balances on such accounts as at a date not more than seven days before the date hereof is annexed to the Disclosure Letter. The Company has no other bank or deposit accounts (whether in credit or overdrawn) and since such statement there have been no payments out of any such accounts except for routine payments and the balances on current account are not now substantially different from the balances shown on such statements.

THE COMPANY AND ITS EMPLOYEES

(51) Directors
The particulars shown in the first schedule are true and complete and no person not named therein as such is a director or shadow director of the Company.

(52) Particulars of Employees
   (*a*)   The particulars shown in the schedule of employees[43] annexed to the Disclosure Letter show all remuneration payable and other benefits provided or which the Company is bound to provide (whether now or in the future) to each officer, employee or consultant of the Company or any person connected with any such person and are true and complete and include particulars of all profit sharing, incentive and bonus arrangements to which the Company is a party whether legally binding on the Company or not.
   (*b*)   Since the Balance Sheet Date no change has been made in the rate of remuneration, or the emoluments or pension benefits of any officer, ex-officer or employee of the Company and no change has been made in the terms of engagement of any such officer or employee, and no additional officer or employee has been appointed.
   (*c*)   No present officer or employee of the Company has given or received notice terminating his employment except as expressly contemplated under this Agreement.
   (*d*)   The Company has not given notice of any redundancies to any employee or government department or started consultations with any trade union pursuant to any statute or regulation.

(53) Service Contracts
There is not outstanding any contract of service between the Company and any of its directors, officers or employees which is not terminable by the Company without compensation (other than any compensation payable by statute) on three month's notice given at any time.

(54) Disputes with Employees
The Vendors are not aware of any outstanding claim against the Company by any person who is now or has been an officer or employee of the Company or any dispute between the Company and a material number or class of its employees and no payments are due by the Company under the provisions of the Employment Protection (Consolidation) Act 1978.

THE COMPANY AND ITS SUBSIDIARIES

(55) Particulars of Subsidiaries
The particulars of the Subsidiaries set out in part II of the second schedule are true and complete and the Company has no other subsidiary undertaking.

(56) Investments, Associations and Branches
The Company:
   (*a*)   is not the holder or beneficial owner of, and has not agreed to

acquire, any class of the share or other capital of any other company or corporation (whether incorporated in the United Kingdom or elsewhere) other than the Subsidiaries;

(*b*)   is not and has not agreed to become a member of any partnership, joint venture, consortium or other unincorporated association or arrangement for sharing commissions or income; and

(*c*)   has no branch, agency or place of business outside England and no permanent establishment (as that expression is defined in the relevant double taxation relief orders current at the date hereof) outside the United Kingdom.

MATERIAL DISCLOSURE

(57)   All Material Matters Disclosed[44]

All information contained or referred to in the Disclosure Letter or in any annexure thereto is accurate in all respects and the Vendors are not aware of any other fact or matter which renders any such information misleading or which might reasonably affect the willingness of a purchaser to purchase the Sale Shares on the terms (including price) of this Agreement.

FOURTH SCHEDULE

Taxation[45]

[Note that this Schedule reflects the law at 1 March 1989 and does not take into account the provisions of the Finance Act 1989.]

1   INTERPRETATION

In this schedule, where the context admits:
- (1)   'Audited Accounts'[46] and 'Balance Sheet Date' have the same meanings as in the third schedule;
- (2)   'event' includes (without limitation):
  - (*a*) any omission, transaction or distribution whether or not the Company is a party thereto;
  - (*b*) the death of any person;
  - (*c*) the failure to avoid an apportionment or deemed distribution of income (whether or not it is or was possible, by taking action after Completion, to avoid such apportionment or deemed distribution);[47]
  - (*d*) the Company ceasing to be a member of any group or associated with any person on or before Completion;[48]
  - (*e*) Completion; and
  - (*f*) any event which is treated as having occurred for the purposes of any legislation;

  and references to the result of events on or before the date of Completion shall include the combined result of two or more events the first of which shall have taken place on or before the date of Completion;
- [(3) 'group relief' has the meaning given to that expression by s 402 Taxes Act 1988;]
- (4)   'relief' means any relief, allowance or credit in respect of taxation or any deduction in computing income, profits or gains for the purpose of taxation;[49]
- (5)   'taxation claim'[50] means a claim for taxation against the Company or the Purchaser, whether made before or after the date hereof, whether satisfied[51] or unsatisfied at the date hereof and whether or not the taxation in question is also chargeable against or attributable to any other person, and includes any assessment, notice, demand or other communication from or action taken by any person, authority or body responsible for the assessment, collection or recovery of taxation in any country which claims:
  - (*a*) payment of taxation;
  - (*b*) to deprive the Company or the Purchaser of any relief whether arising before or after the date hereof;[52] or
  - (*c*) to nullify or cancel any right to the repayment of taxation whether arising before or after the date hereof;

  and which arises from or by reference to:

(i) any income, profits or gains earned, accrued[53] or received on or before the date of Completion or any event on or before the date of Completion, whether alone or in conjunction with other circumstances; or

(ii) a payment under paragraph 2(A);[54]

(6) 'relevant taxation claim' means any taxation claim save to the extent that:

(*a*) provision or reserve in respect thereof has been made in the Audited Accounts or to the extent that payment or discharge of such claim has been taken into account in the Audited Accounts;

(*b*) provision or reserve in respect thereof has been made in the Audited Accounts which is insufficient only by reason of any increase in rates of taxation or change in law after the date hereof having retrospective effect;[55]

(*c*) it is a claim for which the Company is or may become liable as a result of transactions (not including distributions) entered into by the Company in the ordinary course of trading after the Balance Sheet Date and for the purposes of this subparagraph the following shall not be regarded as arising in the ordinary course of trading:

(i) any liability under Part VIII of the Taxes Management Act 1970 (charges on non-residents);

(ii) any liability under Part XVII of the Taxes Act 1988 (anti-avoidance);

(iii) any liability in respect of any distribution (as defined in Part VI of the Taxes Act 1988) or deemed distribution;

(iv) any liability arising from the disposal of or acquisition or deemed disposal or acquisition of any asset other than trading stock; or

(v) [   ];

(*d*) it is a claim against the Purchaser which does not relate to the Sale Shares or the Company or which is for stamp duty or stamp duty reserve tax arising out of this Agreement or Completion; or

(*e*) it is a claim which would not have arisen but for a voluntary act or transaction, which could reasonably have been avoided, carried out by the Purchaser (or persons deriving title from it) or the Company after the date of Completion otherwise than in the ordinary course of business and which the Purchaser was aware could give rise to a claim, but so that this exclusion shall not extend to any voluntary act carried out with the approval, concurrence or assistance of the Vendors;

(7) 'taxation' includes (without limitation) corporation tax, advance corporation tax, income tax, capital gains tax, the charge under the Taxes Act 1988, s 601(2), value added tax, customs and other import duties, excise duties, capital transfer tax, inheritance tax,

stamp duty,[56] stamp duty reserve tax, capital duty, national insurance contributions, foreign taxation and any payment whatsoever which the Company may be or become bound to make to any person as a result of the operation of any enactment relating to taxation and all penalties, charges and interest relating to any claim for taxation or resulting from a failure to comply with the provisions of any enactment relating to taxation;

(8)   'Taxes Act 1970' means the Income and Corporation Taxes Act 1970;

(9)   'Taxes Act 1988' means the Income and Corporation Taxes Act 1988;

(10) references to income or profits or gains earned, accrued or received shall include income or profits or gains treated as earned, accrued or received for the purposes of any legislation;

(11) references to 'the Company' include each of the Subsidiaries; and

(12) any taxation claim arising out of any of the following shall be treated as a relevant taxation claim for all the purposes of this schedule notwithstanding any other provision hereof.[57]

2   TAXATION PAYMENTS

(A) Payments

(1)   Subject to and in accordance with the terms of this schedule the Vendors shall make payments to the Purchaser equal to the amount of each relevant taxation claim.

(2)   For this purpose the amount of any relevant taxation claim shall depend upon whether the claim is of the type described in item (*a*), (*b*) or (*c*) of paragraph 1[(5)]. In the case of a claim of the type described in item (*a*), the amount is the payment claimed; in the case of a claim of the type described in item (*b*), the amount is the amount of taxation (on the basis of rates current at the date of the loss of the relief)[58] which would have been relieved, allowed or credited by the relief of which it is claimed to deprive the Company or the Purchaser, and in the case of a claim of the type described in item (*c*), the amount is the repayment which it is claimed to nullify or cancel.

(3)   Where any relevant taxation claim has been reduced or eliminated by (or where a relevant taxation claim would have arisen but for) some relief available to the Company arising after Completion or some relief available to some person other than the Company, whether arising before or after Completion then such relief shall be disregarded for the purposes of determining whether, in what amount, and on what date any payment should be made by the Vendors hereunder, and accordingly the relevant taxation claim shall be treated as not being reduced or eliminated (or, as the case may be, shall be treated as having arisen).[59]

(B) Date for Payment
The Vendors shall be bound to make payments in respect of relevant taxation claims on the following dates:

(1)   in so far as a relevant taxation claim represents taxation to be borne by the Company but which has not yet become due, the Vendors shall make the payment in respect of that claim (or so much thereof as represents that taxation) on the date on which that taxation becomes due;

(2)   in so far as a relevant taxation claim consists of the nullification or cancellation of a right to repayment of taxation the Vendors shall make the payment in respect of that claim (or so much thereof as represents that nullification or cancellation) on the date on which that repayment would otherwise have become due; and

(3)   in any other case the Vendors shall make the payment fourteen days after the date on which a notice setting out details of the relevant taxation claim is delivered to the Vendors;[60]

and for this purpose references to a date on which taxation becomes due include a reference to the date on which it would have become due were it not for the availability of some relief. Any payment which becomes due on a day which is not a business day shall be paid on the next following business day, and any payment which is made after noon on any day before shall, for the purposes of calculating interest, be deemed to have been paid on the next following business day. No payment shall be treated as made until cleared funds in respect thereof are available to the Purchaser.

(C) Reduction in Consideration
Insofar as the payments made by the Vendors to the Purchaser pursuant to sub-paragraph (A) are less than the consideration for the Sale Shares, they shall constitute a repayment of and a reduction in such consideration, but nothing in this paragraph shall limit the liability of the Vendors to make payments under sub-paragraph (A).

(D) Disclosure not Relevant[61]
The Vendors' obligations to make payments under sub-paragraph (A) shall not be affected by the disclosure, in the Disclosure Letter or otherwise, of the relevant taxation claim giving rise to the payment, or the circumstances giving rise to that relevant taxation claim.

(E) Credits and Reductions
If any relevant taxation claim is disputed by the Company or by either party or represents taxation for which credit is or may become due to the Company at a later date or in respect of which it is subsequently found that there arises a corresponding credit or right to repayment of taxation, the amount of the relevant taxation claim shall nevertheless be payable in full by the Vendors on the due date ascertained in accordance with sub-paragraph (B) but if subsequently any reduction is made in the claim or it is found that the liability in respect thereof falls short of the amount claimed or such credit or repayment is received by the Company the Purchaser shall promptly repay

to the Vendors an amount equal to such reduction, shortfall, credit or repayment up to the amount previously paid by the Vendors in respect of that relevant taxation claim and without interest, save to the extent that interest is included (or allowed) in such credit, repayment, reduction or shortfall. For this purpose, no credit shall be taken to have been received by the Company unless it shall have relieved the Company of a present obligation to pay taxation.

(F)   Over-provisions[62]

If, at the request and cost of the Vendors, the Company's auditors shall certify that any provision for taxation (not being a provision for deferred taxation) contained in the Audited Accounts is an over-provision, the value of such over-provision shall be set against the liability of the Vendors under sub-paragraph (A), except in so far as such over-provision is attributable to the effect of a change in rates of taxation after the date hereof, but no deduction shall be made from any payment which the Vendors shall be obliged to make hereunder unless such certificate is in existence on the due date for that payment. In the event that such a certificate is given after the Vendors have made a payment hereunder, the Purchaser shall refund to the Vendors (without interest) any payment made by the Vendors to the extent that such over-provision could have been set against such payment if the certificate had been in existence on the due date of payment. The Purchaser shall procure that the Company shall co-operate in obtaining any such certificate if the Vendors shall so request.

(G)   Notice and Mitigation
    (1)   If the Purchaser shall become aware of any relevant taxation claim it shall forthwith give written notice thereof to the Vendors setting out reasonable particulars thereof, including the amount and the date on which the Vendors are bound to make a payment in respect of that relevant taxation claim, ascertained in accordance with sub-paragraph (B), but no failure by the Purchaser to comply with this sub-clause shall affect the Vendors' obligations under sub-paragraph (A).
    (2)   Except in a case where fraud is alleged the Purchaser shall take such action and give such information and assistance in connection with the affairs of the Company as the Vendors may reasonably and promptly by notice request to avoid, resist, appeal or compromise a relevant taxation claim provided that:
        (*a*) the Company shall not be obliged to appeal against any assessment, notice, demand or decision if, having given the Vendors notice of the receipt thereof, the Purchaser has not within twenty-one days thereafter received instructions in writing from the Vendors to do so; and
        (*b*) the Company shall not in any circumstances be obliged to pursue any appeal beyond the General Commissioners of Inland Revenue, the Special Commissioners of Inland Revenue, or Value Added Tax Tribunal or any equivalent forum in the United Kingdom or any other jurisdiction.

(3)   The action which the Vendors may request under sub-paragraph (2) shall include (without limitation) the Company applying to postpone (so far as legally possible) the payment of any taxation and allowing the Vendors to take on or take over at their own expense the conduct of all proceedings of whatsoever nature arising in connection with the relevant taxation claim in question. If the Vendors take on or take over the conduct of proceedings, the Purchaser shall, and shall procure that the Company shall, provide such information and assistance as the Vendors may reasonably require in connection with the preparation for and conduct of such proceedings.

(4)   Where the Company is entitled to recover from some other person (including any taxing or other authority) any sum in respect of any relevant taxation claim the Purchaser shall take such action as the Vendors may reasonably and promptly by notice request to enforce such recovery by the Company and shall account to the Vendors for any amount so recovered by the Company (including any interest included in such recovery) not exceeding the amount paid by the Vendors hereunder in respect of that relevant taxation claim.

(5)   Notwithstanding anything in this Agreement, neither the Purchaser nor the Company shall be obliged to take any steps to reduce the amount of any relevant taxation claim or to recover any amount from any other person unless the Vendors shall first indemnify and secure the Company and the Purchaser to their satisfaction against all losses, costs, interest, damages and expenses which may be incurred thereby.

(H)   Interest

The Vendors shall make all payments under this schedule in immediately available funds before noon on the due date for payment without deduction or withholding on any account (save as expressly provided in this schedule) and if any amount is not paid when due the Vendors shall pay to the Purchaser interest on such amount at the rate of   per cent per annum above the base rate of   Bank plc from time to time from the due date until the date of actual payment (as well after judgment as before).

(I)   Deductions and Withholdings

(1)   Any amount payable pursuant to sub-paragraphs (A) or (H) shall be paid free and clear of all deductions, withholdings or set-offs whatsoever, save only as may be required by law.

(2)   If any deductions or withholdings are required by law to be made from any sums, the Vendors shall be obliged to pay the Purchaser such amount as will after the deduction or withholding has been made, leave the Purchaser with the same amount as it would have been entitled to receive in the absence of such requirement to make a deduction or withholding provided that if the Purchaser subsequently receives a credit for such deduction or withholding

then such credit shall be applied in accordance with the provision of sub-paragraph (F).

3   TAXATION WARRANTIES AND REPRESENTATIONS

The Vendors hereby warrant and represent to and for the benefit of the Purchaser in the following terms.

GENERAL TAXATION MATTERS

(1)   Residence

The Company and the Subsidiaries are all resident in the United Kingdom for taxation purposes.

(2)   Tax Provisions

Full provision or reserve has been made in the Audited Accounts for all taxation liable to be assessed on the Company or for which it is accountable in respect of income, profits or gains earned, accrued or received on or before the Balance Sheet Date or any event on or before the Balance Sheet Date including distributions made down to such date or provided for in the Audited Accounts and full provision has been made in the Audited Accounts for deferred taxation in accordance with generally accepted accounting principles.

(3)   Compliance

The Company has properly and punctually made all returns and provided all information required for taxation purposes and none of such returns is disputed by the Inland Revenue or any other authority concerned (in the United Kingdom or elsewhere) and the Vendors are not aware that any dispute is likely, or that any event has occurred which would or might give rise to a payment under paragraph 2(A).

(4)   Payment of Tax

The Company has duly and punctually paid all taxation which it has become liable to pay and is under no liability to pay any penalty or interest in connection with any claim for taxation and has not paid any tax which it was and is not properly due to pay.

DISTRIBUTIONS AND PAYMENTS

(5)   Distributions

    (*a*)   No distribution within the meaning of the Taxes Act 1988, ss 209, 210 and 212 has been made by the Company except dividends shown in its Audited Accounts nor is the Company bound to make any such distribution.

    (*b*)   No securities (within the meaning of the Taxes Act 1988, s 254(1)) issued by the Company and remaining in issue at the date hereof were issued in such circumstances that the interest payable thereon falls to be treated as a distribution under the Taxes Act 1988, s 209(2)(*e*)(iii).

    (*c*)   The Company has not made or received any distribution which is an exempt distribution within the Taxes Act 1988, s 213.

    (*d*)   The Company has not received any capital distribution to which the provisions of the Taxes Act 1988, s 346 could apply.

(e) The Company has not issued any share capital, nor granted options or rights to any person which entitles that person to require the issue of any share capital to which the provision of the Taxes Act 1988, s 249 could apply.

(6) [Group Income] [Membership of Group]62A

[The Disclosure Letter contains particulars of all elections made by the Company under the Taxes Act 1988, s 247 and all such elections are now in force and the Company has not paid any dividend without paying advance corporation tax or made any payment without deduction of income tax in the circumstances specified in sub-section (6) of that section.] [The Company is not and never has been a member of a group of companies for the purposes of any taxation.]

[(7) Surrender of Advance Corporation Tax

The Disclosure Letter contains particulars of all arrangements and agreements to which the Company is or has been a party relating to the surrender of advance corporation tax made or received by the Company under the Taxes Act 1988, s 240 and:

(a) the Company has not paid nor is liable to pay any amount in excess of the advance corporation tax surrendered to it nor for the benefit of any advance corporation tax which is or may become incapable of set-off against the Company's liability to corporation tax;

(b) the Company has received all payments due to it under any such arrangement or agreement for all surrenders of advance corporation tax made by it; and

(c) save in respect of this Agreement, there have not been in existence in relation to the Company any such arrangements as are referred to in the Taxes Act 1988, s 240(11).]

(8) ACT Carry Forward

There has been no major change in the business of the Company within the meaning of the Taxes Act 1988, s 245.

(9) Payments under Deduction

All payments by the Company to any person which ought to have been made under deduction of tax have been so made and the Company has (if required by law to do so) provided certificates of deduction to such person and accounted to the Inland Revenue for the tax so deducted.

(10) Payments and Disallowances

(a) No rents, interest, annual payments or other sums of an income nature paid or payable by the Company or which the Company is under an obligation to pay in the future are wholly or partially disallowable as deductions or charges in computing profits for the purposes of corporation tax by reason of the provisions of the Taxes Act 1988, ss 74, 125, 338, 577, 779 to 784, and 787 or otherwise.

(b) The Company has not used any credit, relief or set-off that may be disallowed pursuant to the Taxes Act 1988, s 237.

Losses

[(11) Group Relief
The Disclosure Letter contains particulars of all arrangements and agreements relating to group relief to which the Company is or has been a party and:

    (*a*)   all claims by the Company for group relief were when made and are now valid and have been or will be allowed by way of relief from corporation tax;

    (*b*)   the Company has not made nor is liable to make any payment under any such arrangement or agreement save in consideration for the surrender of group relief allowable to the Company by way of relief from corporation tax and equivalent to the taxation for which the Company would have been liable had it not been for the surrender;

    (*c*)   the Company has received all payments due to it under any such arrangement or agreement for surrender of group relief made by it; and

    (*d*)   save in respect of this Agreement, there have not been in existence in relation to the Company any such arrangements as are referred to in the Taxes Act 1988, s 410.]

(12) Tax Losses
There has not within the three years preceding the date hereof been a major change in the business of the Company within the meaning of the Taxes Act 1988, s 768.

(13) Dual Resident Companies
The Company is neither a dual resident company nor a dual resident investment company within the meaning of the Taxes Act 1988, s 404.

Close Companies

(14) Close Company[63]

    (*a*)   The Company has never been a close company within the meaning of the Taxes Act 1988, s 414.

    (*b*)   No distribution within the Taxes Act 1988, s 418 has been made by the Company and no such distribution will be made before Completion.

    (*c*)   The Company has not made (and will not be deemed to have made) any loan or advance to a participator or an associate of a participator so as to become liable to make any payment under the Taxes Act 1988, s 419.

    (*d*)   The Company has supplied to the inspector such information and particulars as are necessary to make full and accurate disclosure of all facts and considerations material to be known by him to enable him to make intimations pursuant to the Taxes Act 1988, Sched 19, para 16 that he does not intend to make apportionments in respect of the Company for any accounting period ending on or before the Balance Sheet Date and the Company has received such intimations.

(e) No apportionment pursuant to the Taxes Act 1988, s 423 and Sched 19 has ever been made or could be made against the Company.

(f) The Company has at all times been a 'trading company' or a 'member of a trading group' as defined in the Taxes Act 1988, Sched 19, para 7.

(g) The Company has not expended or applied any sum liable to be regarded as income available for distribution pursuant to the Taxes Act 1988, Sched 19, para 8 (first business loans) and is not bound (contingently or otherwise) to expend or apply any such sum.

ANTI-AVOIDANCE

(15) Taxes Act 1988, s 765
The Company has not without the prior consent of the Treasury been a party to any transaction for which, at the time such transaction was effected, consent under the Taxes Act 1988, s 765 was required.

(16) Controlled Foreign Companies
    (a) No direction has been made by the Board of Inland Revenue under the Taxes Act 1988, s 747 in respect of any controlled foreign companies which are under the control of the Company.

    (b) Section 748(1) of the Taxes Act 1988 applies to all controlled foreign companies controlled by the Company.

(17) Bond Washing
The Company has not since 28 February 1985 transferred any securities with accrued interest as defined in Chapter II of Part XVII of the Taxes Act 1988.

(18) Offshore Funds
The Company does not own nor has owned at any time a material interest in an offshore fund which is or has at any material time been a non-qualifying offshore fund as defined by the Taxes Act 1988, s 760.

(19) Anti-avoidance
    (a) The Company has not at any time entered into or been a party to a transaction or series of transactions either (i) containing steps inserted without any commercial or business purpose, or (ii) being transactions to which any of the following provisions could apply: Taxes Act 1988, ss 703, 729, 730, 737, 739, 770, 774, 776, 779, 780, 781 or 786, without in the appropriate cases having received clearance in respect thereof from the Inland Revenue.

    (b) The Company has never been requested to furnish information pursuant to notices served under the Taxes Act 1988, ss 745 or 778.

CLEARANCES

(20) The Company has not applied for clearance under any of the following provisions:
    (a) Taxes Act 1970, s 215(1) (demergers);
    (b) Taxes Act 1970, s 267(3A) (reconstruction or amalgamation);

(c)   Taxes Act 1970, s 278A (mergers);
(d)   Capital Gains Tax Act 1979, s 88 (share exchanges);
(e)   Taxes Act 1988, s 707 (transactions in securities); or
(f)   Taxes Act 1988, s 776(11) (transactions in land).

ELECTIONS

(21) The Company has not made (and will not be deemed to have made) any elections under the following provisions:
    (a)   Taxes Act 1988, ss 524 and 534 (lump sum receipts for patents and copyright);
    (b)   Finance Act 1985, s 57 (short life assets).

CAPITAL ASSETS

(22) Base Values
    (a)   If each of the capital assets of the Company were disposed of for a consideration equal to the book value of that asset in or adopted for the purpose of the Audited Accounts no liability to corporation tax on chargeable gains or balancing charge under the Capital Allowances Act 1968 or the Finance Act 1971 would arise (and for this purpose there shall be disregarded any relief and allowances available to the Company other than amounts falling to be deducted from the consideration receivable under the Capital Gains Tax Act 1979, s 32).
    (b)   No election under the Finance Act 1988, s 96 is in effect in relation to the Company and full particulars are given in the Disclosure Letter of the first relevant disposal for the purposes of that section.
    (c)   The Disclosure Letter contains full particulars of all assets held by the Company or disposed of by the Company on or after 6 April 1988 in respect of which relief is or would be available under the Finance Act 1988, Sched 9 upon disposal.

(23) Roll-over Relief
The Company has made no claim under the Capital Gains Tax Act 1979, ss 107 to 109 (inclusive), ss 115 to 119 (inclusive) or s 121 and no such claim or other claim has been made by any other person (in particular pursuant to the Capital Gains Tax Act 1979, s 126 or the Taxes Act 1970, s 276) which affects or could affect the amount or value of the consideration for the acquisition of any asset by the Company taken into account in calculating liability to corporation tax on chargeable gains on a subsequent disposal.

(24) Depreciating and Wasting Assets
No asset owned by the Company is a depreciating or wasting asset within the meaning of the Capital Gains Tax Act 1979, s 117 and s 106 and Sched 3 of that Act respectively.

(25) Depreciatory Transactions
No loss which might accrue on the disposal by the Company of any share in or security of any company is liable to be reduced by virtue of any depreciatory transaction within the meaning of the Taxes Act 1970, ss 280

and 281 nor is any expenditure on any share or security liable to be reduced under the Capital Gains Tax Act 1979, s 75.

(26) Transactions Not at Arm's Length
The Company has not disposed of or acquired any asset to or from any person connected with it within the Taxes Act 1988, s 839 or in circumstances such that the provisions of the Capital Gains Tax Act 1979, s 29A could apply to such disposal or acquisition.

(27) Straightline Growth
No asset owned by the Company is subject to a deemed disposal and reacquisition under the Capital Gains Tax Act 1979, Sched 5, paras 11, 14 or 16.

[(28) Intra Group Transfers
The Company has not acquired any asset (past or present) from any other company then belonging to the same group of companies as the Company within the meaning of the Taxes Act 1970, s 272.]

(29) Group Reconstructions
The Company has not been party to any scheme of reconstruction or reorganisation to which the provisions of the Taxes Act 1970, s 267, the Taxes Act 1988, s 703 or to which the Taxes Act 1988, ss 343 and 344 could apply.

(30) Chargeable Debts
No gain chargeable to corporation tax will accrue to the Company on the disposal of any debt owing to the Company not being a debt on a security.

(31) Chargeable Policies
The Company has not acquired benefits under any policy of assurance otherwise than as original beneficial owner.

(32) Claims by the Company
The Company has made no claim under any of the following:
- (a) Capital Gains Tax Act 1979, s 13 (assets situated outside the United Kingdom);
- (b) Capital Gains Tax Act 1979, s 22(2) (assets of negligible value);
- (c) Capital Gains Tax Act 1979, s 40 (tax on chargeable gains payable by instalments);
- (d) Taxes Act 1988, ss 242 and 243 (surplus franked investment income); or
- (e) Taxes Act 1988, s 584 (unremittable income arising outside the United Kingdom).

(33) Gains Accruing to Non-resident Companies or Trusts
No gain has accrued in respect of which the Company may be liable to corporation tax on chargeable gains by virtue of the provisions of the Capital Gains Tax Act 1979, s 15 or the Finance Act 1981, s 80.

[(34) Indexation: Groups and Associated Companies
The Company does not own any debts or shares to which the provisions of the Finance Act 1988, s 114 and Sched 11 could apply.]

MISCELLANEOUS

(35) Assessment of Tax on Lessees
No notice pursuant to the Taxes Act 1988, s 23 has been served on the Company.

(36) Leaseholds
Except insofar as provision has been made in the Audited Accounts the Company is not liable to taxation under the provisions of the Taxes Act 1988, ss 34, 35 and 36 nor does it own any leasehold interest to which the said s 35 may apply.

(37) Quoted Eurobonds
The Company has never at any time issued any quoted Eurobonds as defined in the Taxes Act 1988, s 124(6).

(38) Deep Discount Securities
The Company has not at any time held, owned or issued any deep discount securities as defined in the Taxes Act 1988, Sched 4, para 1.

(39) Stock Lending
The Company has not been a party to any transaction to which the provisions of the Taxes Act 1988, s 129 could apply.

TAXATION OF EMPLOYEES

(40) PAYE
The Company has properly operated the Pay As You Earn system deducting tax as required by law from all payments to or treated as made to employees and ex-employees of the Company and punctually accounting to the Inland Revenue for all tax so deducted.

(41) Benefits for Employees
    (*a*) The Company has not made any payment to or provided any benefit for any officer or employee or ex-officer or ex-employee of the Company which is not allowable as a deduction in calculating the profits of the Company for taxation purposes.

    (*b*) The Company has not issued any shares or conferred any interest in shares in the circumstances described in the Taxes Act 1988, s 138(1) and has complied with the Taxes Act 1988, s 139(5).

    (*c*) The Company has not issued any shares or conferred any interest in shares in the circumstances described in s 77(1) and has complied with the Finance Act 1988, s 85.

    (*d*) The Company has not made any payment to which the Taxes Act 1988, s 313 applies.

    (*e*) The Company does not operate any share scheme approved under the provisions of the Taxes Act 1988, Sched 9 nor a profit related pay scheme to which the provisions of Chapter II of Part V of the Taxes Act 1988 apply.

(42) Payroll Deduction
The Company does not operate and has not operated any such scheme as specified in the Taxes Act 1988, s 202.

(43) National Insurance etc
The Company has paid all national insurance and graduated pension contributions for which it is liable and has kept proper books and records relating to the same.

STAMP DUTIES

(44) Stamp Duty
The Company has not obtained relief from stamp duty under any of the following:

(a) Finance Act 1927, s 55 (reconstructions and amalgamations);
(b) Finance Act 1930, s 42 (intra-group transfers);
(c) Finance Act 1985, ss 78 or 79 (takeovers and voluntary winding up); or
(d) Finance Act 1986, ss 75, 76 or 77 (acquisitions).

(45) Capital Duty
The Company has complied with the provisions of the Finance Act 1973 relating to capital duty and has duly paid all capital duty which it is liable to pay.

(46) Stamp Duty Reserve Tax
The Company has made all returns and paid all stamp duty reserve tax in respect of any transaction in securities to which it has been a party or in respect of which it is liable to account for stamp duty reserve tax.

VALUE ADDED TAX

(47) (a) The Company has complied with all statutory provisions and regulations relating to value added tax and has duly paid or provided for all amounts of value added tax for which the Company is liable.

(b) All supplies made by the Company are taxable supplies and the Company is not and will not be denied credit for any input tax by reason of the operation of the Value Added Tax Act 1983, s 15 and regulations made thereunder.

(c) The Company is not party to any contract under which it may become liable to make or receive supplies the rate of tax applicable to which may change as a result of the proposals announced in HM Customs and Excise News Release dated 21 June 1988.

(d) All input tax for which the Company has claimed credit has been paid by the Company in respect of supplies made to it relating to goods or services used or to be used for the purpose of the Company's business.

(e) The Company is not and has not been, for value added tax purposes a member of any group of companies (other than that comprising the Company and the Subsidiaries alone) and no act or transaction has been effected in consequence whereof the Company is or may be held liable for any value added tax chargeable against some other company except where that other company is a Subsidiary.

(*f*) No supplies have been made to the Company to which the provisions of the Value Added Tax Act 1983, s 7 might apply;

(*g*) The Company has not committed any offence contrary to the Finance Act 1985, s 12 or 13 nor has it received any royalty liability notice pursuant to the Finance Act 1988, s 14A(3), surcharge liability notice pursuant to s 19, or written warranty issued pursuant to s 21A.

(*h*) The Company has not been registered for value added tax otherwise than pursuant to the provisions of the Value Added Tax Act 1983, Sched 1, para 1.

(*i*) The Company has not been required to give security under the Value Added Tax Act 1983, Sched 7, para 5.

INHERITANCE TAX AND GIFTS

(48) Powers of Sale for Inheritance Tax Purposes
There are not in existence any circumstances whereby any such power as is mentioned in the Inheritance Tax Act 1984, s 212 could be exercised in relation to any shares in, securities of, or assets of, the Company.

(49) Gifts

(*a*) The Company is not liable to be assessed to corporation tax on chargeable gains or to inheritance tax as donor or donee of any gift or transferor or transferee of value.

(*b*) The Company has not been a party to associated operations in relation to a transfer of value within the meaning of the Inheritance Tax Act 1984, s 268.

(*c*) No Inland Revenue charge (as defined in the Inheritance Tax Act 1984, s 237) is outstanding over any asset of the Company or in relation to any shares in the capital of the Company.

(*d*) The Company has not received any asset as mentioned in the Capital Gains Tax Act 1979, s 59.

FIFTH SCHEDULE
Adjustment of Consideration

1 INTERPRETATION

In this schedule where the context admits:
(1) 'the Audited Accounts' and 'the Balance Sheet Date' have the same meanings as in the third schedule;
(2) 'the Completion Accounts' means the accounts prepared in accordance with paragraph 2;
(3) 'the Provisional Consideration' means the consideration for the Sale Shares of £   stated in clause 3(A);
(4) 'the Purchaser's Accountants' means Messrs   ; and
(5) 'the Vendors' Accountants' means Messrs.   .

2 COMPLETION ACCOUNTS

(A) Preparation
The parties shall procure that, forthwith after Completion, accounts for the Company and the Subsidiaries shall be prepared and reported on in accordance with this schedule and the parties shall use their best endeavours to secure compliance with this Schedule by their respective accountants.

(B) Description
The Completion Accounts shall consist of a consolidated balance sheet of the Company and the Subsidiaries as at the close of business on the date of Completion and a consolidated profit and loss account of the Company and the Subsidiaries in respect of the period from the day following the Balance Sheet Date to the date of Completion (both dates inclusive).

(C) General Requirements
Subject to sub-paragraph (D), the Completion Accounts shall:
(1) be prepared as if the period from the day following the Balance Sheet Date to the date of Completion were a financial year of the Company;
(2) be prepared in accordance with the requirements of all relevant statutes and generally accepted accounting principles;
(3) show a true and fair view of the assets and liabilities of the Company and the Subsidiaries at the date of Completion and the profits of the Company and the Subsidiaries for the period ended on the date of Completion; and
(4) adopt bases and policies of accounting applied for the purposes of the Audited Accounts.

(D) Specific Requirements[64]
In preparing the Completion Accounts:
(1) no value shall be attributed to goodwill or any other intangible asset;
(2) no value shall be attributed to any assets (including in particular any prepayment or debt) except to the extent that (following

Completion) the Company or a Subsidiary will have the benefit
of the same;
(3)   full provision shall be made for rebates or discounts that will fall
due and fees and commissions that will become payable after
Completion in either case in respect of sales or other transactions
that took place before Completion;
(4)   full provision shall be made for amounts that become due as a
result of the change of control of the Company on Completion;
and
(5)   other fixed assets shall be included at the value at which they were
included in the Audited Accounts, (or, if acquired after the
Balance Sheet Date, their cost) less depreciation on the written
down value, calculated at the following annual rates:

Plant and Machinery	[ ]	per cent
Fixtures and Fittings	[ ]	per cent
Motor Vehicles	[ ]	per cent
Immoveable assets and improvements		
thereto	[ ]	per cent

(6)   [   ]

3   PROCEDURE

(A)   Submission of Draft

Within sixty days after the date of Completion, the Purchaser's Accountants
shall deliver a final draft of the Completion Accounts to the Vendors'
Accountants and, unless the Vendors' Accountants shall notify the
Purchaser's Accountants in writing within twenty-one days after receipt of
such draft that they do not accept that such draft complies with paragraph 2,
the Vendors shall be deemed to have accepted such draft as complying with
paragraph 2.

(B)   Agreement of Draft

If, within the period of twenty-one days referred to in sub-paragraph (A), the
Vendors' Accountants shall notify the Purchaser's Accountants in writing
that they do not accept that the said draft complies with paragraph 2 then the
Purchaser's Accountants and the Vendors' Accountants shall use their best
endeavours to reach agreement upon adjustments to the draft to meet the
objections of the Vendors' Accountants.

(C)   Independent Accountant

In the event that the Vendors' Accountants and the Purchaser's Accountants
are unable to reach agreement as aforesaid, any matter in dispute shall be
referred to the decision of a single independent chartered accountant or an
independent firm of chartered accountants to be agreed upon between them
or, in default of such agreement, to be selected (at the instance of either
party) by the President for the time being of the Institute of Chartered
Accountants in England and Wales, and any such chartered accountant or
firm of chartered accountants (whose costs shall be paid as he or they shall
direct) shall act as expert (and not as arbitrator)[65] in connection with the

giving of such decision which shall, save in the event of manifest error, be binding. In giving such decision, the accountant or firm shall state what adjustments (if any) are to be made to the said draft in order that it shall comply with paragraph 2.

(D) Report

If the Vendors' Accountants accept, or are deemed to accept, that the said draft complies with paragraph 2 the Purchaser's Accountants shall sign a report to the effect that the Completion Accounts comply with paragraph 2 and any Completion Accounts so reported on, or (if sub-paragraph (C) shall apply) the final draft of the Completion Accounts as adjusted by the independent accountant, shall be the Completion Accounts for the purposes of this Agreement and shall be final and binding on the parties.

(E) Information and Explanations

The Purchaser's Accountants shall provide such information and explanations relating to the draft Completion Accounts and their preparation as the Vendors' Accountants, or any independent chartered accountant appointed pursuant to sub-paragraph (C), shall reasonably require.

4   ADJUSTMENT OF CONSIDERATION

(A) Increase or Reduction

When the Completion Accounts have become binding, the Provisional Consideration shall forthwith:

(1) be increased by the amount (if any) by which the net tangible assets of the Company and the Subsidiaries as at the date of Completion as shown by the Completion Accounts are greater than the net tangible assets of the Company and the Subsidiaries as at the Balance Sheet Date as shown by the Audited Accounts; or (as the case may be)

(2) be reduced by the amount (if any) by which the net tangible assets of the Company and the Subsidiaries as at the date of Completion as shown by the Completion Accounts are less than the net tangible assets of the Company and the Subsidiaries as at the Balance Sheet Date as shown by the Audited Accounts.

(B) Payment

Any increase or reduction in the Provisional Consideration shall be paid by the Purchaser or the Vendor (as appropriate) within fourteen days after the Completion Accounts have become binding as aforesaid and any amount not paid when due shall carry interest at the rate of   per cent per annum above the base rate of   Bank plc from time to time from the due date until the date of actual payment (as well after judgment as before).

5   INTERACTION WITH OTHER PROVISIONS[66]

[Subject to the due performance of paragraph 4, if the Purchaser shall have any claim against the Vendors under this Agreement in respect of any liability or deficiency which is taken into account in the Completion Accounts the amount of such liability or deficiency so taken into account shall be deducted from the amount of the Purchaser's claim but, save as aforesaid, preparation and acceptance of the Completion Accounts by the Purchaser shall be without prejudice to any claim which the Purchaser may have against the Vendors under or in respect of any breach of this Agreement.]

SIXTH SCHEDULE[67]

Pensions [Company has own final salary scheme]

1 INTERPRETATION

[(A) Definitions
In this schedule where the context admits:
  (1) 'Actuarial Assumptions' means the actuarial assumptions and methods set out below: ;[68]
  (2) 'Company' means the Company and the Subsidiaries or such one or more of them, as the context requires;
  (3) 'Pension Scheme[s]' means   and   [and 'Pension Scheme' means [any one] [either] of the Pension Schemes, as the context requires;]
  (4) 'Purchaser's Actuary' means the actuary appointed by the Purchaser pursuant to paragraph 2(A);
  (5) 'Relevant Employee' means any past or present employee or officer of the Company or of any predecessor to all or part of its business;
  (6) 'Shortfall' means an amount, calculated as at the close of business on the date of Completion by reference to the Actuarial Assumptions, equal to the amount (if any) by which the aggregate value of the assets of the Pension Scheme (excluding any debts of the Company to the trustees of the Pension Scheme)[69] is exceeded by the value of the liabilities (whether immediate, prospective or contingent) under the Pension Scheme. For this purpose:
    (*a*) when calculating the value of the assets of the Pension Scheme no account shall be taken of any contributions payable to the Pension Scheme after Completion;
    (*b*) when calculating the liability for any benefits no account shall be taken of benefits in respect of pensionable service after the date of Completion but allowance shall be made for projected future increases in earnings up to normal pension age under the Pension Scheme or earlier cessation of pensionable service and increases (whether payable pursuant to a legal obligation or not) to pensions in payment or in deferment; and
    (*c*) any improvements to the benefits under the Pension Scheme which have been announced or are otherwise proposed shall be deemed to have been duly effected under the Pension Scheme and to have come into force before the date of this Agreement; and
  (7) 'Vendors' Actuary' means the actuary appointed by the Vendors pursuant to paragraph 2(A).

[(B) Schedule applies separately to each Pension Scheme
This schedule applies separately to each of the Pension Schemes.][70]

2   CALCULATION OF SHORTFALL

(A)   Appointment of Actuaries

Immediately following Completion the Vendors and the Purchaser shall each appoint an actuary for the purposes of this schedule. For this purpose 'actuary' means a Fellow or a firm of Fellows of The Institute of Actuaries or of The Faculty of Actuaries.

(B)   Data

The Vendors and the Purchaser shall respectively use all reasonable endeavours to procure that all such information as the Vendors' Actuary or the Purchaser's Actuary or any independent actuary appointed under paragraph 2(D) may reasonably request for the purposes of this schedule is supplied promptly to such actuary.

(C)   Agreement of Shortfall

The Purchaser's Actuary shall determine the amount of the Shortfall and shall submit his findings in writing to the Vendors' Actuary for agreement. If the Vendors' Actuary and the Purchaser's Actuary agree the amount (if any) of the Shortfall, the Vendors and the Purchaser shall respectively procure that the Vendors' Actuary and the Purchaser's Actuary jointly certify that amount as the Shortfall.

(D)   Dispute

If the Vendors' Actuary and the Purchaser's Actuary fail to agree the amount (if any) of the Shortfall within two months from the date upon which the Purchaser's Actuary submits his findings to the Vendors' Actuary in accordance with paragraph 2(C), the matter may, at the option of the Vendors or the Purchaser, be referred to an independent actuary to be agreed between the Vendors and the Purchaser or, in default of agreement within fourteen days from the first nomination of an actuary by one party to the other, appointed by the President for the time being of The Institute of Actuaries on the application of either the Vendors or the Purchaser. The certificate of the independent actuary as to the amount (if any) of the Shortfall shall, save in the event of manifest error, be final and binding on the parties and, in so certifying, the independent actuary shall be deemed to be acting as an expert and not as an arbitrator.[71] His costs shall be paid as he directs.

3   PAYMENT OF SHORTFALL

The Vendors undertake to the Purchaser that within a period of fourteen days commencing on and including the date upon which the amount (if any) of the Shortfall is certified as aforesaid the Vendors will, by way of adjustment to the consideration of the Sale Shares,[72] pay to the Purchaser (or to a third party as the Purchaser may direct) a sum in cash equal to the amount shown in the certificate as being the Shortfall together with interest thereon (accruing daily and compounded monthly) from and including the date of Completion to but excluding the date upon which final payment is made in accordance with this paragraph. Such interest shall be at the Agreed

Rate up to and including the last day in the aforesaid fourteen day period and thereafter shall be at   per cent above the Agreed Rate. For this purpose 'Agreed Rate' means   per cent above the base lending rate from time to time of   .

4   WARRANTIES AND REPRESENTATIONS

The Vendors hereby warrant and represent to and for the benefit of the Purchaser in the following terms.

(1)   No Other Pension Arrangements

Save for the Pension Scheme the Company is neither a party to nor participates in nor contributes to any scheme, arrangement or agreement (whether legally enforceable or not) for the provision of any pension, retirement, death, incapacity, sickness, disability, accident or other like benefits (including the payment of medical expenses) for any Relevant Employee or for the widow, child or dependant of any Relevant Employee.

(2)   No Assurances etc

Neither the Company nor any of the Vendors:

(a)   has given any undertaking or assurance (whether legally enforceable or not) to any Relevant Employee or to any widow, child or dependant of any Relevant Employee as to the continuance, introduction, improvement or increase of any benefit of a kind described in (1) above; or

(b)   is paying or has in the last three years paid any benefit of a kind described in (1) above to any Relevant Employee or to the widow, child or dependant of any Relevant Employee.

(3)   All Details Disclosed

All material details relating to the Pension Scheme are contained in or annexed to the Disclosure Letter including (without limitation) the following:

(a)   a true and complete copy of the documents governing the Pension Scheme;

(b)   a true and complete copy of all announcements, explanatory literature and the like which have been issued to any Relevant Employee in connection with the Pension Scheme;

(c)   a true and complete copy of the report on the last actuarial valuation of the Pension Scheme prior to the date of this Agreement and of any subsequent written recommendations of an actuarial nature;

(d)   a true and complete copy of the last audited accounts for the Pension Scheme prior to the date of this Agreement and details of any material change in the investment policy of the Pension Scheme since the date as at which those accounts were made up;

(e)   details of any proposed amendment to the Pension Scheme which has been announced or is being considered;

(f)   details of any discretionary increases to pensions in payment or in deferment under the Pension Scheme granted in the five years prior to the date of this Agreement;

(g)   details of any discretionary practices which may have led any person to expect additional benefits in a given set of circumstances (by way of example, but without limitation, on retirement at the behest of the Company or in the event of redundancy); and

(*h*)   details of the contributions paid to the Pension Scheme by the Company in the five years prior to the date of this Agreement.

(4)   Augmentation

No power under the Pension Scheme has been exercised in relation to any employee or officer of the Company:

(*a*)   to provide terms of membership of the Pension Scheme (whether as to benefits or contributions) which are different from those generally applicable to the members of the Pension Scheme;

(*b*)   to provide any benefits which would not but for the exercise of that power have been payable under the Pension Scheme; or

(*c*)   to augment any benefits under the Pension Scheme.

(5)   Death Benefits Insured

All benefits (other than any refund of members' contributions with interest where appropriate) payable under the Pension Scheme on the death of any person while in employment to which the Pension Scheme relates are insured fully under a policy with an insurance company of good repute and there are no grounds on which that company might avoid liability under that policy.

(6)   Contributions

Contributions to the Pension Scheme are not paid in arrear and all contributions and other amounts which have fallen due for payment have been paid and no fees, charges or expenses referable to the Pension Scheme for which the Company is or may become liable (whether wholly or in part) have been incurred but not paid and the Company has reimbursed any person who has paid any such fees or expenses if and to the extent that the Company is or may become liable to do so.

(7)   Company's Obligations

The Company:

(*a*)   has been admitted to participation in the Pension Scheme;

(*b*)   has observed and performed those provisions of the Pension Scheme which apply to it;

(*c*)   may terminate its liability to contribute to the Pension Scheme without notice, without the consent of any person and without further payment; and

(*d*)   has at all material times held or been named in a contracting-out certificate (within the meaning of the Social Security Pensions Act 1975) referable to the Pension Scheme.

(8)   No Other Employer

The Company is the only employer for the time being participating in the Pension Scheme. No employer which has previously participated in the Pension Scheme has any claim under the Pension Scheme and in respect of any such employer the Pension Scheme has been partially wound up in accordance with its provisions.

(9)   Exempt Approved Scheme

The Pension Scheme:

(*a*) is an exempt approved scheme within the meaning of the Income and Corporation Taxes Act 1988, s 592; and

(*b*) complies with and has at all times been administered in accordance with all applicable laws, regulations and requirements (including those of the Board of Inland Revenue and of trust law).

(10) Data

The data used for the purposes of the last actuarial valuation of the Pension Scheme prior to the date of this Agreement was complete and accurate in all material respects and since the date as at which that valuation was undertaken nothing has happened or has been omitted to be done which may affect materially the level of funding of the benefits under the Pension Scheme.

(11) Litigation

The trustees of the Pension Scheme are not engaged in any litigation or arbitration proceedings and so far as the Vendors are aware no litigation or arbitration proceedings are pending or threatened by or against the trustees of the Pension Scheme and there are no facts likely to give rise to any litigation or arbitration.

(12) Indemnities

In relation to the Pension Scheme or the assets or previous assets thereof neither the Company nor the trustees or adminstrator of the Pension Scheme has given an indemnity or guarantee to any person (other than in the case of the Company any general indemnity in favour of the trustees or administrator under the documents governing the Pension Scheme).

5   Damages for Breach of Pension Warranties

In determining the damages flowing from any breach of the Warranties contained in paragraph 4, the Company shall be deemed to be under a liability:

(1) to provide and to continue to provide any benefits of a kind referred to in that paragraph which are now provided or have been announced or are proposed; and

(2) to maintain and to continue to maintain (without benefits being reduced) the Pension Scheme and any other arrangements of a kind described in that paragraph which are now in existence or are proposed and any discretionary practices of a kind referred to in that paragraph which have hitherto been carried on.[73]

SIXTH SCHEDULE

Pensions [money purchase scheme]

1   INTERPRETATION

(A)   Definitions

In this schedule, where the context admits:

   (1)   'Company' means the Company and the Subsidiaries or such one or more of them, as the context may require;

   (2)   'Pension Scheme[s]' means   and   [and Pension Scheme means [either] [any one] of the Pension Schemes, as the context requires]; and

   (3)   'Relevant Employees' means any present or past employee or officer of the Company or of any predecessor to all or any part of its business.

[(B)   Schedule applies separately to each Pension Scheme

This schedule shall apply separately to each of the Pension Schemes.]

2   WARRANTIES AND REPRESENTATIONS

The Vendors hereby warrant and represent to and for the benefit of the Purchaser in the following terms:

(1)   No Other Arrangements

Save for the Pension Scheme the Company is neither a party to nor participates in nor contributes to any scheme, arrangement or agreement (whether legally enforceable or not) for the provision of any pension, retirement, death, incapacity, sickness, disability, accident or other like benefits (including the payment of medical expenses) for any Relevant Employee or for the widow, child or dependant of any Relevant Employee.

(2)   No Assurances etc

Neither the Company nor any of the Vendors:

   (*a*)   has given any undertaking or assurance (whether legally enforceable or not) to any Relevant Employee or to any widow, child or dependant of any Relevant Employee as to the continuance, introduction, improvement or increase of any benefit of a kind described in (1) above; or

   (*b*)   is paying or has in the last three years paid any benefit of a kind described in (1) above to any Relevant Employee or the widow, child or dependant of any Relevant Employee.

(3)   All Details Disclosed

All material details relating to the Pension Scheme are contained in or annexed to the Disclosure Letter including (without limitation) the following:

   (*a*)   a true and complete copy of the documents governing the Pension Scheme;

   (*b*)   a true and complete copy of all announcements, explanatory literature and the like which have been issued to any Relevant Employee in connection with the Pension Scheme;

(c) a true and complete copy of the report on the last actuarial valuation of the Pension Scheme prior to the date of this Agreement and of any subsequent written recommendations of an actuarial nature;

(d) a true and complete copy of the last audited accounts for the Pension Scheme prior to the date of this Agreement and details of any material change in the investment policy of the Pension Scheme since the date as at which those accounts were made up;

(e) details of any proposed amendment to the Pension Scheme which has been announced or is being considered;

(f) details of any discretionary increases to pensions in payment or in deferment under the Pension Scheme granted in the five years prior to the date of this Agreement;

(g) details of any discretionary practices which may have led any person to expect additional benefits in a given set of circumstances (by way of example, but without limitation, on retirement at the behest of the Company or in the event of redundancy); and

(h) details of the contributions paid to the Pension Scheme by the Company in the five years prior to the date of this Agreement.

(4) Contributions

Contributions to the Pension Scheme are not paid in arrear and all contributions and other amounts which have fallen due for payment have been paid and no fees, charges or expenses referable to the Pension Scheme for which the Company is or may become liable (whether wholly or in part) have been incurred but not paid and the Company has reimbursed any person who has paid any such fees, costs or expenses if and to the extent that the Company is or may become liable so to do.

(5) Company's Obligations

The Company:

(a) has been admitted to participation in the Pension Scheme;

(b) has observed and performed those provisions of the Pension Scheme which apply to it;

(c) may terminate its liability to contribute to the Pension Scheme without notice, without the consent of any person and without further payment [and

(d) has at all material times held or been named in a contracting-out certificate (within the meaning of the Social Security Pensions Act 1975) referable to the Pension Scheme].

(6) Pension Scheme

The Pension Scheme:

(a) apart from the benefits referred to at (b) below provides only money purchase benefits (within the meaning of the Social Security Act 1986, s 84(1));

(b) all benefits (which are not money purchase benefits as aforesaid) payable in the event of death while in employment to which the Pension Scheme relates are insured fully under a policy with an insurance company of good repute and there are no grounds on which that company might avoid liability under that policy;

(*c*)   is an exempt approved scheme (within the meaning of the Income and Corporation Taxes Act 1988, s 592); and

(*d*)   complies with and has at all times been administered in accordance with all applicable laws, regulations and requirements (including those of the Inland Revenue and of trust law).

(7)   Litigation

The trustees of the Pension Scheme are not engaged in any litigation or arbitration proceedings and so far as the Vendors are aware no litigation or arbitration proceedings are pending or threatened by or against the trustees of the Pension Scheme and there are no facts likely to give rise to any litigation or arbitration.

(8)   No Other Employer

The Company is the only employer for the time being participating in the Pension Scheme. No employer which has previously participated in the Pension Scheme has any claim under the Pension Scheme and in respect of any such employer the Pension Scheme has been partially wound up in accordance with its provisions.

(9)   Indemnities

In relation to the Pension Scheme or the assets or previous assets thereof neither the Company nor the trustees or adminstrator of the Pension Scheme has given an indemnity or guarantee to any person (other than in the case of the Company any general indemnity in favour of the trustees or administrator under the documents governing the Pension Scheme).

3   Damages for Breach of Pension Warranties

In determining the damages flowing from any breach of the Warranties contained in paragraph 2, the Company shall be deemed to be under a liability:

(1)   to provide and to continue to provide any benefits of a kind referred to in that paragraph which are now provided or have been announced or are proposed; and

(2)   to maintain and to continue to provide (without benefits being reduced) the Pension Scheme and any other arrangements of a kind described in that paragraph which are now in existence or are proposed and any discretionary practices of a kind referred to in that paragraph which have hitherto been carried on.[74]

SEVENTH SCHEDULE
Vendors' Protection

1   No Other Representations

The Purchaser admits that it has not entered into this Agreement in reliance upon any representation or promise other than those incorporated in the Disclosure Letter or this Agreement.[75]

2   Guarantees

The Purchaser shall use its best endeavours to secure the release of the Vendors from the guarantees and other contingent liabilities listed in the Disclosure Letter for the purpose of this paragraph (offering its own covenant in substitution if requested by the Vendors) and shall in the meantime indemnify the Vendors and keep the Vendors indemnified against any liability (including costs, damages and expenses) thereunder or which may be incurred in relation thereto.

3   Loan Accounts

At Completion the Purchaser shall procure that the Company and the Subsidiaries shall repay to the Vendors the amounts owing to them as specified in the Disclosure Letter.

4   Limitation of Liability[76]

The provisions of this paragraph shall operate to limit the liability of the Vendors under or in connection with the Warranties and the Disclosure Letter and references to 'such liabilities' shall be construed accordingly. The parties agree as follows:
- (1)   no liability shall attach to the Vendors unless the aggregate amount of such liabilities shall exceed the total sum of £   but if such liabilities shall exceed that sum the Vendors shall (subject to the other provisions hereof) be liable for the whole of such liabilities and not merely for the excess;
- (2)   the aggregate amount of such liabilities shall not exceed £   ;
- (3)   claims against the Vendors shall be wholly barred and unenforceable unless written particulars thereof (giving reasonable details of the specific matter or claim in respect of which such claim is made so far as then known to the Purchaser) shall have been given to the Vendors within a period of   years from the date hereof, but this item (3) shall not apply to claims arising under the fourth schedule or to claims which (or delay in the discovery of which) is the consequence of fraud, wilful misconduct or wilful concealment by the Vendors;
- (4)   if the Vendors make any payment by way of damages for breach of the Warranties and within twelve months of the making of the relevant payment the Company, the Subsidiaries or the

Purchaser receives any benefit otherwise than from the Vendors which would not have been received but for the circumstances giving rise to the claim in respect of which the damages payment was made the Purchaser shall, once it or the relevant company has received such benefit, forthwith repay to the Vendors an amount equal to the lesser of (*a*) the amount of such benefit and (*b*) the damages payment in question.

5   AVOIDANCE OF DOUBLE CLAIMS

In the event that the Purchaser is entitled to claim under paragraph 2(A) of the fourth schedule or under the Warranties in respect of the same subject matter the Purchaser may choose to claim under either or both but payments under paragraph 2(A) of the fourth schedule shall *pro tanto* satisfy and discharge any claim which is capable of being made under the Warranties in respect of the same subject matter and *vice versa*.

AGREEMENT FOR SALE—CORPORATE VENDOR

CONTENTS

THIS   AGREEMENT is made the   day of
19

BETWEEN:

(1)   PLC ('the Vendor') a company registered in England
under number   whose registered office is at   ;
and
(2)   PLC ('the Purchaser') a company registered in England
under number   whose registered office is at

WHEREAS:

The Purchaser wishes to acquire the entire issued share capital of
Limited from the Vendor on the terms of this Agreement.

NOW IT IS HEREBY AGREED as follows:

1   INTERPRETATION

(A)   Definitions
In this Agreement where the context admits:

(1)   'the Company' means   Limited a company registered
in England under number   and incorporated on
19   as a private company limited by shares
under the Companies Act(s)   ;
(2)   'Completion' means completion of the sale and purchase of the
Sale Shares;[1]
(3)   'Consideration Shares' means ordinary shares of
each in the Purchaser credited as fully paid;
(4)   'the Directors' means the persons named in Part I of the first
schedule and 'the Continuing Directors' means the persons
named in Part II of that schedule;
(5)   'the Disclosure Letter' means the letter dated the date hereof
written by or on behalf of the Vendor to the Purchaser in agreed
terms;[2]
(6)   'the Properties' means the properties particulars of which are set
out in the list annexed to the Disclosure Letter;
(7)   'the Sale Shares' means the shares to be bought and sold pursuant
to clause 2;
(8)   'the Subsidiaries' means the companies listed in Part II of the
second schedule;
(9)   'the Vendor's Group' means the Vendor and each of its
subsidiaries other than the Company and the Subsidiaries; and
(10) 'the Warranties' means the warranties and representations set out
in paragraph 2 of the third schedule, in paragraph 4 of the fourth
schedule and in paragraph 8 of the sixth schedule.

(B)   Construction of Certain References

In this Agreement where the context admits:

(1)   words and phrases the definitions of which are contained or referred to in Part XXVI of the Companies Act 1985 shall be construed as having the meanings thereby attributed to them;

(2)   references to statutory provisions shall be construed as references to those provisions as amended or re-enacted or as their application is modified by other provisions from time to time and shall include references to any provisions of which they are re-enactments (whether with or without modification);[3]

(3)   where any statement is qualified by the expression 'so far as the Vendor is aware' or 'to the best of the Vendor's knowledge and belief' or any similar expression, that statement shall be deemed to include an additional statement that it has been made after due and careful enquiry;[4]

(4)   references to clauses and schedules are references to clauses hereof and schedules hereto, references to sub-clauses or paragraphs are, unless otherwise stated, references to sub-clauses of the clause or paragraphs of the schedule in which the reference appears, and references to this Agreement include the schedules; and

(5)   references to any document being in agreed terms are to that document in the form signed on behalf of the parties for identification.

(C)   Headings

The headings and sub-headings are inserted for convenience only and shall not affect the construction of this Agreement.

(D)   Schedules

Each of the schedules shall have effect as if set out herein.

2   SALE OF SHARES

(A)   Sale and Purchase

Subject to the terms of this Agreement the Vendor shall sell and the Purchaser shall purchase, free from all liens, charges, equities and encumbrances and together with all rights now or hereafter attaching thereto the entire issued share capital of the Company comprising [ordinary] shares of £   each.

(B)   Simultaneous Completion

The Purchaser shall not be obliged to complete the purchase of any of the Sale Shares unless the purchase of all the Sale Shares is completed simultaneously.

3   CONSIDERATION

(A)   Amount [Consideration Shares]

The total consideration for the Sale Shares shall be the sum of £   , but subject to adjustment as provided in the fourth and fifth schedules. [The total consideration for the Sale Shares shall be the allotment to the Vendor of Consideration Shares].

(B)   Placing[5]

The total consideration for the Sale Shares shall be the allotment to the Vendor of the number of Consideration Shares which, when placed through placees nominated by the Purchaser shall produce payment to the Vendor of aggregate net proceeds of £   . The Purchaser shall arrange a placing to produce such aggregate net proceeds and shall procure the payment of that amount to the Vendor at completion against the renunciation by the Vendor of the allotment of such Consideration Shares as directed by the Purchaser. The Vendor warrants that it will renounce such allotment free from all liens, charges, equities and encumbrances, and together with all rights attaching thereto, agrees to confirm such warranty in favour of   and hereby grants authority to   to place such Consideration Shares on its behalf.

(C)   Dividends etc

The Consideration Shares shall rank pari passu and as a single class with the existing ordinary shares of   each in the Purchaser, and shall carry the right to receive in full all dividends and other distributions declared, made or paid after the date of this Agreement [save that they shall not carry the right to participate in the [interim] [final] dividend of the Purchaser for the year ending   19   [declared on   ]].[6]

4   CONDITIONS AND COMPLETION

(A)   Conditions[7]

Completion is conditional upon:

  (1)   the passing at a general meeting of the Purchaser of a resolution to increase the authorised share capital of the Purchaser to not less than £   and to authorise the directors of the Purchaser to allot the Consideration Shares;[8] and

  (2)   the admission by the Council of The Stock Exchange of the Consideration Shares to the Official List, and such listing becoming fully effective;[9]

and in the event that the above conditions are not satisfied on or before   19   this Agreement shall lapse and no party shall make any claim against any other in respect hereof, save for any antecedent breach.

(B)   Date of Completion

Subject to the provisions of this clause, Completion shall take place on   19   at the offices of Messrs   .

(C)   Vendor's Obligations[10]

On Completion the Vendor shall:

  (1)   deliver to the Purchaser:

    (*a*) duly executed transfers of the Sale Shares by the registered holders thereof in favour of the Purchaser or its nominees together with the relative share certificates;

(*b*) such waivers or consents as the Purchaser may require to enable the Purchaser or its nominees to be registered as holders of the Sale Shares;[11] and

(*c*) powers of attorney in agreed terms.[12]

(2) procure the passing of a resolution of the board of directors of the Company resolving to register the transfers referred to in item (1)(*a*) subject only to due stamping;

(3) cause such persons as the Purchaser may nominate to be validly appointed as additional directors of the Company and the Subsidiaries and, upon such appointment, forthwith cause the Directors (other than the Continuing Directors) and the secretary or secretaries of the Company and the Subsidiaries to retire from all their offices and employments with the Company or the Subsidiaries, each delivering to the Purchaser a letter under seal acknowledging that he has no claim outstanding for compensation or otherwise and without any payment under the Employment Protection (Consolidation) Act 1978;[13]

(4) procure revocation of all authorities to the bankers of the Company and the Subsidiaries relating to bank accounts, giving authority to such persons as the Purchaser may nominate to operate the same;

(5) procure the resignation of the auditors of the Company and the Subsidiaries;[14]

(6) deliver to the Purchaser as agent for the Company and the Subsidiaries:

(*a*) a certificate from Messrs   in the form approved by the Purchaser prior to the signing hereof as to the title of the Company or the Subsidiaries to the Properties;[15]

(*b*) the title deeds to the Properties;[16]

(*c*) all the statutory and other books (duly written up to date) of the Company and each of the Subsidiaries and its/their certificate(s) of incorporation and common seal(s);[17] and

(*d*) certificates in respect of all issued shares in the capital of each of the Subsidiaries and transfer of all shares in any Subsidiary held by any nominee in favour of such persons as the Purchaser shall direct;[18] [and]

(7) deposit the sum of £   with the Purchaser on the terms of clause 7; [and]

(8) comply with clause 3(   ); [and]

(9) procure the discharge of the guarantees and other obligations stipulated in the Disclosure Letter to be discharged at completion.

(D) Service Agreements

On completion the Company and   shall enter into service agreements in the form of the draft(s) in agreed terms.[19]

(E) Purchaser's Obligations

On Completion the Purchaser shall [pay] [satisfy] the consideration for the

Sale Shares as provided by clause 3 [and comply with the provisions of paragraph 3 of the seventh schedule] [any payment in cash to be made] by way of town clearing banker's draft made payable to the Vendor.

(F) Failure to Complete[20]

If in any respect the preceding provisions of this clause (other than sub-clause (A)) are not complied with on the date for Completion set by sub-clause (B) the party not in default (or, in the case of non-compliance with sub-clause (D), the Purchaser) may:

(1) defer Completion to a date not more than twenty-eight days after the date set by sub-clause (B) (and so that the provisions of this sub-clause (F), apart from this item (1), shall apply to Completion as so deferred); or

(2) proceed to Completion so far as practicable (without prejudice to its rights hereunder); or

(3) rescind this Agreement.

5   PURCHASER'S RIGHT OF ACCESS[21]

From the date hereof the Purchaser and its accountants and agents shall be allowed access to all the premises and books of account of the Company and the Subsidiaries, and the Vendor shall supply any information reasonably required by the Purchaser relating to the Company and the Subsidiaries.

6   RESTRICTION OF VENDOR

(A) Covenants

The Vendor undertakes with the Purchaser that it will not and that none of its subsidiaries will:

(1) for the period of   after Completion, either on its own account or in conjunction with or on behalf of any person, firm or company, carry on, or be engaged, concerned or interested (directly or indirectly) in carrying on, the business of
(other than as a holder of less than 5 per cent of any class of shares or debentures listed on The Stock Exchange) within   ; and

(2) for the period of   after Completion, either on its own account or in conjunction with or on behalf of any other person, firm or company, solicit or entice away from the Company or any of the Subsidiaries any person who at the date hereof is an officer, manager, servant, or customer of the Company or any of the Subsidiaries whether or not such person would commit a breach of contract by reason of leaving service or transferring business.

(B) Reasonableness[22]

The restrictions contained in sub-clause A are considered reasonable by the parties, but in the event that any such restriction shall be found to be void but would be valid if some part thereof were deleted, or the period or area of application reduced, such restriction shall apply with such modification as may be necessary to make it valid and effective.

(C) Registration[23]
[Any provision of this Agreement, or of any agreement or arrangement of which it forms part, by virtue of which such agreement or arrangement is subject to registration under the Restrictive Trade Practices Act 1976 shall only take effect the day after particulars of such agreement or arrangement have been furnished to the Director General of Fair Trading pursuant to s 24 of that Act].

7   WARRANTIES AND DEPOSIT

(A) Purchaser's Knowledge[24]
The Warranties are given subject to matters fairly disclosed in the Disclosure Letter, but no other information relating to the Company or the Subsidiaries of which the Purchaser has knowledge (actual or constructive) shall prejudice any claim made by the Purchaser under the Warranties or operate to reduce any amount recoverable.

(B) Warranties to be Independent
Each of the Warranties shall be separate and independent and, save as expressly provided, shall not be limited by reference to any other Warranty or anything in this Agreement.

(C) Damages[25]
Without restricting the rights of the Purchaser or the ability of the Purchaser to claim damages on any basis in the event that any of the Warranties is broken or proves to be untrue or misleading, the Vendor shall, on demand, pay to the Purchaser:

    (*a*)   the amount necessary to put the Company and each of the Subsidiaries into the position which would have existed if the Warranties had not been broken and had been true and not misleading; and

    (*b*)   all costs and expenses incurred by the Purchaser, the Company or the Subsidiaries, directly or indirectly, as a result of such breach.

(D) Pending Completion[26]
The Vendor shall procure that (save only as may be necessary to give effect to this Agreement) neither the Vendor nor the Company nor any of the Subsidiaries shall do, allow or procure any act or omission before Completion which would constitute a breach of any of the Warranties if they were given at any and all times from the date hereof down to Completion or which would make any of the Warranties inaccurate or misleading if they were so given. In particular, without prejudice to the generality of the foregoing, the Vendor shall procure that items (*a*) to (*g*) of paragraph 2(22) of the third schedule shall be complied with at all times from the date hereof down to Completion.

(E) Further Disclosure by Vendor
The Vendor shall forthwith disclose in writing to the Purchaser any matter or thing which may arise or become known to the Vendor after the date hereof and before Completion which is inconsistent with any of the Warranties or which might make any of them inaccurate or misleading if they were given at

any and all times from the date hereof down to Completion or which is material to be known to a purchaser for value of the Sale Shares.

(F)   Right of Rescission[27]
In the event of any such matter or thing as is mentioned in sub-clause (E) becoming known to the Purchaser before Completion or in the event of its becoming apparent on or before Completion that the Vendor is in breach of any of the Warranties or any other term of this Agreement the Purchaser may rescind this Agreement by notice in writing to the Vendor.

(G)   Application of Deposit[28]
Subject to the following provisions of this clause, the Purchaser may apply all or part of the deposit referred to in sub-clause 4C(7) ('the deposit') in recouping any amount lawfully due to it under or by reason of any breach of the terms of this Agreement and any amount so applied shall *pro tanto* satisfy the liability concerned.

(H)   Interest
The deposit shall be deposited by the Purchaser with bankers selected by it and any interest earned thereon shall accrue to and form part of the deposit and shall, accordingly, belong to the Vendor subject to the provisions of this Agreement.

(I)   Release
In the event that the Purchaser shall not have notified the Vendor in writing of any claim hereunder before   19   the deposit and accrued interest shall be released to the Vendor's solicitors Messrs
whose receipt shall be an absolute discharge. In the event that the Purchaser shall have so notified any such claim, it shall use its best endeavours to quantify the amount claimed and any balance shall be so released on that date. Upon final determination of the total amount (if any) falling to be applied by the Purchaser under this clause, any balance of the deposit shall be released to the Vendor's solicitors provided that no amount shall be released before the said   19   .

8   PROVISIONS RELATING TO THIS AGREEMENT

(A)   Assignment
This Agreement shall be binding upon and enure for the benefit of the successors of the parties but shall not be assignable, save that the Purchaser may assign the benefit of the Warranties to any transferee of the share capital of the Company or any of the Subsidiaries.

(B)   Whole Agreement
This Agreement (together with any documents referred to herein) constitutes the whole agreement between the parties hereto relating to its subject matter and no variations hereof shall be effective unless made in writing.[29] This Agreement supersedes   .

(C)   Agreement Survives Completion
The Warranties and all other provisions of this Agreement, in so far as the

same shall not have been performed at Completion, shall remain in full force and effect notwithstanding Completion.

(D) Rights of Rescission
Any right of rescission conferred upon the Purchaser hereby shall be in addition to and without prejudice to all other rights and remedies available to it and no exercise or failure to exercise such a right of rescission shall constitute a waiver by the Purchaser of any such other right or remedy. Completion shall not constitute a waiver by the Purchaser of any breach of any provision of this Agreement whether or not known to the Purchaser at the date of Completion.

(E) Further Assurance
At any time after the date hereof the Vendor shall, at the request and cost of the Purchaser, execute such documents and do such acts and things as the Purchaser may reasonably require for the purpose of vesting the Sale Shares in the Purchaser or its nominees and giving to the Purchaser the full benefit of all the provisions of this Agreement.

(F) Invalidity
If any provision of this Agreement shall be held to be illegal or unenforceable, the enforceability of the remainder of this Agreement shall not be affected.

(G) Notices
Any notice required to be given hereunder shall be in writing in the English language and shall be served by sending the same by pre-paid first class post, telex or telecopy or by delivering the same by hand to the registered office for the time being of the addressee. Any notice sent by post, as provided in this sub-clause, shall be deemed to have been served forty-eight hours after despatch and any notice sent by telex or telecopy, as provided in this sub-clause, shall be deemed to have been served at the time of despatch and in proving the service of the same it will be sufficient to prove, in the case of a letter, that such letter was properly stamped, addressed and placed in the post and, in the case of a telex or telecopy, that such telex or telecopy was duly despatched to a current telex or telecopy number of the addressee.

(H) English Law[30]
This Agreement shall be governed by, and construed in all respects in accordance with, English law.

9   COSTS

Each party to this Agreement shall pay its own costs of and incidental to this Agreement and the sale and purchase hereby agreed to be made, provided that if the Purchaser shall exercise any right hereby conferred to rescind this Agreement the Vendor shall indemnify the Purchaser against expenses and costs incurred in investigating the affairs of the Company and the Subsidiaries and in the preparation of this Agreement.

AS WITNESS the hands of duly authorised representatives of the parties the day and year first before written.

FIRST SCHEDULE

Directors

Part I — Directors

Name of Director

Company/Companies of which (s)he is a director

Part II — (Continuing Directors)

Name of Director

Company/Companies of which (s)he is a director

Part III (Secretary)

Name of Secretary

Company/Companies of which (s)he is the secretary

SECOND SCHEDULE

Company and Subsidiaries

Part I — The Company

Name and Number of Company	*Authorised Capital*	*Issued Capital*	*Held by*	*Beneficially owned by*

Part II — The Subsidiaries

Name and Number of Subsidiary	*Authorised Capital*	*Issued Capital*	*Held by*	*Beneficially owned by*

THIRD SCHEDULE

Warranties[31] and Representations

1   INTERPRETATION

In this schedule where the context admits:

(1)   'the Audited Accounts' means the audited consolidated balance sheet of the Company and the Subsidiaries made up as at the Balance Sheet Date and the audited consolidated profit and loss account of the Company and the Subsidiaries for the year ended on the Balance Sheet Date, true copies of which are annexed to the Disclosure Letter, including the notes thereto;

(2)   'the Balance Sheet Date' means   19   ;

(3)   'encumbrance' includes any interest or equity of any person (including, without prejudice to the generality of the foregoing, any right to acquire, option or right of pre-emption) or any mortgage, charge, pledge, lien, assignment, hypothecation, security interest, title retention or any other security agreement or arrangement;

(4)   'intellectual property' means patents, trade marks, service marks, rights (whether registered or unregistered) in any designs, applications for any of the foregoing, trade or business names and copyright;

(5)   'intellectual property agreements' means agreements or arrangements relating (wholly or partly) to intellectual property or to the disclosure, use, assignment or patenting of any inventions, discovery, improvements, processes, formulae or other knowhow;

(6)   'Listed Intellectual Property' means the Intellectual Property listed in the list annexed to the Disclosure Letter;

(7)   'Listed Intellectual Property Agreements' means the Intellectual Property Agreements listed in the list annexed to the Disclosure Letter;

(8)   'SSAP' means Statement of Standard Accounting Practice in force at the date hereof as issued by the Institute of Chartered Accountants in England and Wales;

(9)   any question whether a person is connected with another shall be determined in accordance with the Income and Corporation Taxes Act 1988, s 839 which shall apply in relation to this schedule as it applies in relation to that Act;[32] and

(10)   references to 'the Company' include each of the Subsidiaries.

2   WARRANTIES AND REPRESENTATIONS

The Vendor hereby warrants and represents to and for the benefit of the Purchaser in the following terms.

THE COMPANY AND THE VENDOR

(1) Capacity
The Vendor has full power to enter into and perform this Agreement and this Agreement constitutes binding obligations on the Vendor in accordance with its terms.
(2) Liabilities Owing to or by Vendor
There is not outstanding any indebtedness or other liability (actual or contingent) owing by the Company to any member of the Vendor's Group or any Director or any person connected with any of them, nor is there any indebtedness owing to the Company by any such person, and no promise or representation has been made to the Vendor in connection with the Warranties or the Disclosure Letter in respect of which the Company or any of the Subsidiaries might be liable.
(3) Vendor's Other Interests
No member of the Vendor's Group nor any person connected with any such member has any interest, direct or indirect, in any business other than that now carried on by the Company which is or is likely to be or become competitive with the business or any proposed business of the Company.

THE COMPANY'S CONSTITUTION

(4) Share Capital
Part I of the second schedule contains true particulars of the authorised and issued share capital of the Company, all the shares there shown as issued are in issue fully paid and are beneficially owned and registered as set out therein free from any encumbrance.
(5) Memorandum and Articles
The copy of the memorandum and articles of association of the Company annexed to the Disclosure Letter is true and complete and has embodied therein or annexed thereto a copy of every such resolution or agreement as is referred to in the Companies Act 1985, s 380.[33]
(6) Company Resolutions
Neither the Company nor any class of its members has passed any resolution (other than resolutions relating to business at Annual General Meetings which was not special business).
(7) Options etc
No person has the right (whether exercisable now or in the future and whether contingent or not) to call for the allotment, issue, sale or transfer of any share or loan capital of the Company under any option or other agreement (including conversion rights and rights of pre-emption).

THE COMPANY AND THE LAW

(8) Compliance with Laws
The Company has conducted its business in all material respects in accordance with all applicable laws and regulations of the United Kingdom and any relevant foreign country and there is no order, decree or judgment of any Court or any governmental agency of the United Kingdom or any

foreign country outstanding against the Company or which may have a material adverse effect upon the assets or business of the Company.

(9) Licences etc

All necessary licences, consents, permits and authorities (public and private) have been obtained by the Company to enable the Company to carry on its business effectively in the places and in the manner in which such business is now carried on and all such licences, consents, permits and authorities are valid and subsisting and the Vendor knows of no reason why any of them should be suspended, cancelled or revoked.

(10) Breach of Statutory Provisions

Neither the Company, nor any of its officers, agents or employees (during the course of their duties in relation to the Company) have committed, or omitted to do, any act or thing the commission or omission of which is, or could be, in contravention of any Act, Order, Regulation, or the like in the United Kingdom or elsewhere which is punishable by fine or other penalty.

(11) Litigation

The Company is not engaged in any litigation or arbitration proceedings and so far as the Vendor is aware no litigation or arbitration proceedings are pending or threatened by or against the Company and there are no facts likely to give rise to any litigation or arbitration and the Company has not been a party to any undertaking or assurance given to any Court or governmental agency which is still in force.

(12) Insolvency

    (*a*) No order has been made or petition presented or resolution passed for the winding up of the Company, nor has any distress, execution or other process been levied against the Company or action taken to repossess goods in the Company's possession.

    (*b*) No steps have been taken for the appointment of an administrator or receiver of any part of the Company's property.

    (*c*) No floating charge created by the Company has crystallised and, so far as the Vendor is aware, there are no circumstances likely to cause such a floating charge to crystallise.

    (*d*) The Company has not been a party to any transaction which could be avoided in a winding up.

    (*e*) The Company has not made or proposed any arrangement or composition with its creditors or any class of its creditors.

(13) Fair Trading

    (*a*) No agreement, practice or arrangement carried on by the Company or to which the Company is a party:

        (i) is or ought to be or ought to have been registered in accordance with the provisions of the Restrictive Trade Practices Acts 1976 and 1977[34] or contravenes the provisions of the Resale Prices Act 1976 or is or has been the subject of any enquiry, investigation or proceeding under any of those Acts; or

   (ii) is or has been the subject of an enquiry, investigation, reference or report under the Fair Trading Act 1973 (or any previous legislation relating to monopolies or mergers) or the Competition Act 1980; or

   (iii) infringes art 85 of the Treaty establishing the European Economic Community or constitutes an abuse of dominant position contrary to art 86 of the said Treaty or infringes any Regulation or other enactment made under art 87 of the said Treaty or is or has been the subject of any enquiry, investigation or proceeding in respect thereof; or

   (iv) has been notified to the Directorate General of Competition of the Commission of the European Communities; or

   (v) is by virtue of its terms or by virtue of any practice for the time being carried on in connection therewith a 'Consumer Trade Practice' within the meaning of the Fair Trading Act 1973, s 13 and susceptible to or under reference to the Consumer Protection Advisory Committee or the subject matter of a report to the Secretary of State or the subject matter of an Order by the Secretary of State under the provisions of Part II of that Act; or

   (vi) infringes any other competition, anti-restrictive trade practice, anti-trust or consumer protection law or legislation applicable in the United Kingdom or elsewhere and not specifically mentioned in this sub-paragraph.

(b)   The Company has not given any assurance or undertaking to the Restrictive Practices Court or the Director General of Fair Trading or the Secretary of State for Trade and Industry or the Commission or Court of Justice of the European Communities or to any other court, person or body and is not subject to any Act, decision, regulation, order or other instrument made by any of them relating to any matter referred to in this sub-paragraph.

(c)   The Company is not in default or in contravention of any Article, Act, decision, regulation, order or other instrument or of any undertaking relating to any matter referred to in this sub-paragraph.

(14) Defective Products

The Company has not manufactured, sold or supplied products which are, or were, or will become, in any material respect faulty or defective or which do not comply in any material respect with any warranties or representations expressly or impliedly made by the Company or with all applicable regulations, standards and requirements in respect thereof.

(15) Bribes

So far as the Vendor is aware no officer, agent or employee of the Company has paid any bribe or used any of the Company's assets unlawfully to obtain an advantage for any person.

THE COMPANY'S ACCOUNTS AND RECORDS

(16) Books and Records
All accounts, books, ledgers, financial and other records of whatsoever kind
('records') of the Company:

(*a*)   have been fully, properly and accurately maintained, are in the
possession of the Company and contain true and accurate
records of all matters entered or required by law to be entered
therein;

(*b*)   do not contain or reflect any material inaccuracies or
discrepancies

and no notice or allegation that any of the records is incorrect or should be
rectified has been received. Where any of the records are kept on computer,
the Company is the owner of all hardware and all software licences necessary
to enable it to use the records as they have been used in its business hitherto
and does not share any hardware or software relating to the records with any
person.

(17) Accounts Warranty[35]
The Audited Accounts have been prepared in accordance with the
requirements of all relevant statutes and generally accepted accounting
principles and show a true and fair view of the state of affairs of the
Company and the Subsidiaries at the Balance Sheet Date and the profits of
the Company and the Subsidiaries for the year ended on the Balance Sheet
Date and apply bases and policies of accounting which have been
consistently applied in the audited balance sheet and profit and loss accounts
for the three financial years prior to the Balance Sheet Date.

(18) Provision for Liabilities
Full provision has been made in the Audited Accounts for all actual
liabilities of the Company outstanding at the Balance Sheet Date and proper
provision (or note) in accordance with generally accepted accounting
principles has been made therein for all other liabilities of the Company then
outstanding whether contingent, quantified, disputed or not including
(without limitation) the cost of any work or material for which payment has
been received or credit taken, any future loss which may arise in connection
with uncompleted contracts and any claims against the Company in respect
of completed contracts.

(19) Stock Valuation and Accounting Policies[36]
For the purposes of the Audited Accounts, the Company's stock in trade and
work in progress has been valued in accordance with SSAP 9 and on a basis
in all material respects consistent with that adopted for the purpose of the
Company's audited accounts in respect of the beginning and end of each of
the three last preceding accounting periods and the value of redundant or
obsolete materials and materials below standard has been written down to
realisable market value or adequate provision has been made therefor.

(20) Management Accounts[37]
True copies of the management accounts for the period ended on
          19   are annexed to the Disclosure Letter. Such
management accounts have been prepared in accordance with the

Company's normal practices and the Vendor does not consider them misleading.

(21) <u>Returns</u>

The Company has complied with the provisions of the Companies Act 1985 and all returns, particulars, resolutions and other documents required under any legislation to be delivered on behalf of the Company to the Registrar of Companies or to any other authority whatsoever have been properly made and delivered.

THE COMPANY'S BUSINESS

(22) <u>Business Since the Balance Sheet Date</u>[38]

Since the Balance Sheet Date:

    (*a*)   the Company has carried on its business in the ordinary and usual course and without entering into any transaction, assuming any liability or making any payment which is not in the ordinary course of its business and without any interruption or alteration in the nature, scope or manner of its business;

    (*b*)   the Company has not borrowed or raised any money or taken any financial facility;

    (*c*)   the Company has paid its creditors within the times agreed with such creditors and so that there are no debts outstanding by the Company which have been due for more than four weeks;

    (*d*)   there has been no unusual change in the Company's stock levels;

    (*e*)   the Company has not entered into, or agreed to enter into, any capital commitments;

    (*f*)   no share or loan capital has been issued or agreed to be issued by the Company;

    (*g*)   no distribution of capital or income has been declared, made or paid in respect of any share capital of the Company and (excluding fluctuations in overdrawn current accounts with bankers) no loan or share capital of the Company has been repaid in whole or part or has become liable to be repaid; and

    (*h*)   there has been no material deterioration in the financial position, prospects[39] or turnover of the Company.

(23) <u>Working Capital</u>

Having regard to existing bank and other facilities, the Company has sufficient working capital for the purposes of continuing to carry on its business in its present form and at its present level of turnover for the foreseeable future and for the purposes of executing, carrying out and fulfilling in accordance with their terms all orders, projects and contractual obligations which have been placed with, or undertaken by the Company.

(24) <u>Commission</u>

No one is entitled to receive from the Company any finder's fee, brokerage, or other commission in connection with the purchase of shares in the Company.

(25) <u>Consequence of Share Acquisition by the Purchaser</u>

The acquisition of the Sale Shares by the Purchaser or compliance with the terms of this Agreement:

(*a*)   will not cause the Company to lose the benefit of any right or privilege it presently enjoys or so far as the Vendor is aware, cause any person who normally does business with the Company not to continue to do so on the same basis as previously;

(*b*)   will not relieve any person of any obligation to the Company or enable any person to determine any such obligation or any right or benefit enjoyed by the Company or to exercise any right whether under an agreement with or otherwise in respect of the Company;

(*c*)   will not result in any present or future indebtedness of the Company becoming due or capable of being declared due and payable prior to its stated maturity; and

(*d*)   will not give rise to or cause to become exercisable any right of pre-emption;

and, to the best of the knowledge and belief of the Vendor, the Company's relationships with clients, customers, suppliers and employees will not be adversely affected thereby.

(26) Grants

[The Company has not applied for or received any financial assistance from any supranational, national or local authority or government agency.] [Full particulars of all grants received from any supranational, national or local authority or government agency (and all applications for any such) are contained in the Disclosure Letter and there are no circumstances which might lead to any such grant being refunded or forfeited in whole or in part.]

(27) Insurances[40]

(*a*)   Full particulars of all the Company's insurances are given in the Disclosure Letter and the insurances which are maintained by the Company afford the Company adequate cover against such risks as companies carrying on the same type of business as the Company commonly cover by insurance and in particular:

(i) the assets of the Company are insured against fire in their full replacement value; and

(ii) the Company is now, and has at all material times been, adequately covered against accident, damage, injury, third party loss (including product liability), loss of profits and other risks normally covered by insurance.

(*b*)   All the Company's insurances referred to in the Disclosure Letter are in full force and effect, there are no circumstances which might lead to any liability under any of the Company's insurances being avoided by the insurers or the premiums being increased, there are no special or unusual terms, restrictions or rates of premium, all premiums have been paid on time and there is no claim outstanding under any such insurance nor is the Vendor aware of any circumstances likely to give rise to a claim.

THE COMPANY'S ASSETS

(28) Net Asset Value[41]

The value of the net tangible assets of the Company at Completion determined in accordance with the same accounting policies as those applied in the Audited Accounts (and on the basis that each fixed asset is valued at a figure no greater than the value attributed to it in the Audited Accounts or, in the case of any fixed asset acquired by the Company after the Balance Sheet Date, at a figure no greater than cost) will not be less than the value of the net tangible assets of the Company at the Balance Sheet Date as shown in the Audited Accounts.

(29) Assets and Charges

(*a*) Except for current assets disposed of by the Company in the ordinary course of its business, the Company is the owner of and has good marketable title to all assets included in the Audited Accounts and all assets which have been acquired by the Company since the Balance Sheet Date and no such asset, nor any of the undertaking, goodwill or uncalled capital of the Company is subject to any encumbrance or any agreement or commitment to give or create any encumbrance.

(*b*) Since the Balance Sheet Date, save for disposals in the ordinary course of its business, the assets of the Company have been in the possession of, or under the control of, the Company.

(*c*) No asset is shared by the Company with any other person and the Company does not depend for its business upon any assets, facilities or services owned or supplied by other members of the Vendor's Group.

(*d*) No charge in favour of the Company is void or voidable for want of registration.

(30) Debts[42]

Any debts owed to the Company will realise their full face value and be good and collectable in the ordinary course of business and no amount included in the Audited Accounts as owing to the Company at the Balance Sheet Date has been released for an amount less than the value at which it was included in the Audited Accounts or is now regarded by the Vendor as irrecoverable in whole or in part. The Company has not factored or discounted its debts or agreed to do so.

(31) Title Retention

The Company has not acquired or agreed to acquire any material asset on terms that property therein does not pass until full payment is made.

(32) Intellectual Property Rights

(*a*) The Company is the sole beneficial owner of the Listed Intellectual Property and (where such property is capable of registration) the registered proprietor thereof and (save for copyrights) owns no other intellectual property. Save as may appear from the Listed Intellectual Property Agreements no person has been authorised to make any use whatsoever of any intellectual property owned by the Company and the Company has not disclosed (except in the ordinary course of its business) any of its knowhow, trade secrets or list of customers to any other person.

(*b*)   All the intellectual property used by the Company is owned by it and it does not use any intellectual property in respect of which any third party has any right, title or interest.

(*c*)   So far as the Vendor is aware, none of the processes or products of the Company infringes any right of any other person relating to intellectual property or involves the unlicensed use of confidential information disclosed to the Company by any person in circumstances which might entitle that person to a claim against the Company and none of the Listed Intellectual Property is being used, claimed, opposed or attacked by any person.

(*d*)   The Vendor is not aware of any infringement of the Listed Intellectual Property by any third party.

(*e*)   There are no outstanding claims against the Company for infringement of any intellectual property used (or which has been used) by it and no such claims have been settled by the giving of any undertakings which remain in force.

(*f*)   Confidential information and knowhow used by the Company is kept strictly confidential and the Company operates and fully complies with procedures which maintain such confidentiality. The Vendor is not aware of any such confidentiality having been breached.

(*g*)   All application and renewal fees, costs and charges relating to the Listed Intellectual Property have been duly paid on time.

(*h*)   The Listed Intellectual Property Agreements are all the intellectual property agreements to which the Company is a party and each of them is valid and binding.

(33) Condition of Stock

The Company's stock in trade is in good condition and is capable of being sold by the Company in the ordinary course of its business in accordance with its current price list without rebate or allowance to a purchaser.

(34) Plant

The machinery and plant, including fixed plant and machinery, and all vehicles and office and other equipment used in connection with the business of the Company:

(*a*)   is in good repair and condition and in satisfactory working order;

(*b*)   is capable, and will (subject to fair wear and tear) be capable, over the period of time during which it will be written down to a nil value in the accounts of the Company, of doing the work for which it was designed or purchased;

(*c*)   is not surplus to the Company's requirements; and

(*d*)   is in the possession and control of, and is the absolute property free from any encumbrance of, the Company save for those items held under hire purchase or rental agreements the value of which items in the aggregate does not exceed £   .

(35) Title to Properties

The particulars of the Properties shown in the list attached to the Disclosure Letter are true and correct and the owner shown therein has good and marketable title to and exclusive occupation of each Property which it is said to own free from any encumbrance, sub-lease, tenancy or right of occupation, reservation, easement, quasi-easement or privilege in favour of any third party and there are appurtenant to each Property all rights and easements necessary for its use and enjoyment and except as shown the Company has no other interest in land and does not occupy any other property.

(36) Matters Affecting Properties

(*a*) No Property or any part thereof is affected by any of the following matters or is to the knowledge of the Vendor likely to become so affected:

(i) any outstanding dispute, notice or complaint or any exception, reservation, right, covenant, restriction or condition which is of an unusual nature or which affects or might in the future affect the use of any of the Properties for the purpose for which it is now used or which affects or might in the future affect the value of the Properties; or

(ii) any notice, order, demand, requirement or proposal of which the owner has notice or of which the Vendor is aware made or issued by or on behalf of any government or statutory authority, department or body for acquisition, clearance, demolition or closing, the carrying out of any work upon any building, the modification of any planning permission, the discontinuance of any use or the imposition of any building or improvement line; or

(iii) any compensation received as a result of any refusal of any application for planning consent or the imposition of any restrictions in relation to any planning consent; or

(iv) any commutation or agreement for the commutation of rent or payment of rent in advance of the due dates of payment thereof.

(*b*) Each of the Properties is in a good and substantial state of repair and condition and fit for the purposes for which it is presently used and no high alumina cement, woodwool, calcium chloride, sea-dredged aggregates or asbestos material was used in the construction thereof or of any of them and there are no development works, redevelopment works or fitting out works outstanding in respect of any of the Properties.

(*c*) All restrictions, conditions and covenants (including any imposed by or pursuant to any lease) affecting any of the Properties have been observed and performed and no notice of any breach of any of the same has been received or is to the Vendor's knowledge likely to be received.

(*d*) The use of the Properties and all machinery and equipment therein and the conduct of any business therein complies in all respects with all relevant statutes and regulations including without prejudice to the generality of the foregoing the Factories Act 1961, the Offices, Shops and Railway Premises Act 1963, the

Fire Precautions Act 1971, the Health and Safety at Work etc Act 1974 and with all rules, regulations and delegated legislation thereunder and all necessary licences and consents required thereunder have been obtained.

(e)   There are no restrictive covenants or provisions, legislation or orders, charges, restrictions, agreements, conditions or other matters which preclude the use of any of the Properties for the purposes for which the Properties are now used and each such user is the permitted user under the provisions of the Town and Country Planning Acts 1971 to 1974 and regulations made thereunder and is in accordance with the requirements of the Local Authorities and all restrictions, conditions and covenants imposed by or pursuant to the said Town and Country Planning Acts have been observed and performed and no agreements have been entered into under the Town and Country Planning Act 1971, s 52, in respect of any of the Properties.

(f)   All replies by or on behalf of the Vendor or the Company to enquiries relating to any of the Properties made by or on behalf of the Purchaser were when given and are now true and correct.

(37) Properties Previously Owned

The Company has no existing or contingent liabilities in respect of any properties previously occupied by it or in which it owned or held any interest, including, without limitation, leasehold premises assigned or otherwise disposed of.

The Company's Contracts

(38) Documents

All title deeds and agreements to which the Company is a party and other documents owned by or which ought to be in the possession of the Company are in the possession of the Company and are properly stamped and are free from any encumbrance.

(39) Material Contracts

The Company is not a party to or subject to any agreement, transaction, obligation, commitment, understanding, arrangement or liability which:

(a)   is incapable of complete performance in accordance with its terms within six months after the date on which it was entered into or undertaken; or

(b)   is known by the Vendor or by the Company to be likely to result in a loss to the Company on completion of performance; or

(c)   cannot readily be fulfilled or performed by the Company on time and without undue or unusual expenditure of money and effort; or

(d)   involves or is likely to involve obligations, restrictions, expenditure or receipts of an unusual, onerous or exceptional nature and not in the ordinary course of the Company's business; or

(e)   is a lease or a contract for hire or rent, hire purchase or purchase by way of credit sale or periodical payment; or (*f*)   is with any trade union or body or organisation representing its employees; or

(*g*)   requires an aggregate consideration payable by the Company in excess of £   ; or

(*h*)   involves or is likely to involve the supply of goods by or to the Company the aggregate sales value of which will represent in excess of [10] per cent of the turnover for the last financial year of the Company; or

(*i*)   is a contract for services (other than contracts for the supply of electricity or normal office services); or

(*j*)   requires the Company to pay any commission, finder's fee, royalty or the like; or

(*k*)   in any way restricts the Company's freedom to carry on the whole or any part of its business in any part of the world in such manner as it thinks fit; or

(*l*)   involves liabilities which may fluctuate in accordance with an index or rate of currency exchange; or

(*m*) is a contract for the sale of shares or assets which contains warranties or indemnities; or

(*n*)   is in any way otherwise than in the ordinary course of the Company's business.

(40) Defaults

Neither the Company nor any other party to any agreement with the Company is in default thereunder, being a default which would be material in the context of the financial or trading position of the Company nor (so far as the Vendor is aware) are there any circumstances likely to give rise to such a default.

(41) Sureties

No person other than the Company or a Subsidiary has given any guarantee of or security for any overdraft loan or loan facility granted to the Company.

(42) Powers of Attorney

No powers of attorney given by the Company (other than to the holder of an encumbrance solely to facilitate its enforcement) are now in force. No person, as agent or otherwise, is entitled or authorised to bind or commit the Company to any obligation not in the ordinary course of the Company's business, and the Vendor is not aware of any person purporting to do so.

(43) Insider Contracts

(*a*)   There is not outstanding, and there has not at any time during the last six years been outstanding, any agreement or arrangement to which the Company is a party and in which the Vendor, any member of the Vendor's Group, any person beneficially interested in the Company's share capital or any Director or any person connected with any of them is or has been interested, whether directly or indirectly.

(*b*)   The Company is not a party to, nor has its profits or financial position during such period been affected by, any agreement or arrangement which is not entirely of an arm's length nature.

(*c*)   All costs incurred by the Company have been charged to the

Company and not borne by any other member of the Vendor's group.

(44) Debts

There are no debts owing by or to the Company other than debts which have arisen in the ordinary course of business, nor has the Company lent any money which has not been repaid.

(45) Options and Guarantees

The Company is not a party to any option or pre-emption right, or a party to any guarantee, suretyship, comfort letter or any other obligation (whatever called) to pay, provide funds or take action in the event of default in the payment of any indebtedness of any other person or default in the performance of any obligation of any other person.

(46) Tenders etc

No offer, tender, or the like is outstanding which is capable of being converted into an obligation of the Company by an acceptance or other act of some other person.

THE COMPANY AND ITS BANKERS

(47) Borrowings

The total amount borrowed by the Company from its bankers does not exceed its facilities and the total amount borrowed by the Company from whatsoever source does not exceed any limitation on its borrowing contained in its articles of association, or in any debenture or loan stock deed or other instrument.

(48) Continuance of Facilities

Full and accurate details of all overdrafts, loans or other financial facilities outstanding or available to the Company are contained in the Disclosure Letter and true and correct copies of all documents relating thereto are annexed to the Disclosure Letter and neither the Vendor nor the Company has done anything whereby the continuance of any such facilities in full force and effect might be affected or prejudiced.

(49) Off-balance Sheet Financing

The Company has not engaged in any borrowing or financing not required to be reflected in the Audited Accounts.

(50) Bank Accounts

A statement of all the bank accounts of the Company and of the credit or debit balances on such accounts as at a date not more than seven days before the date hereof is annexed to the Disclosure Letter. The Company has no other bank or deposit accounts (whether in credit or overdrawn) and since such statement there have been no payments out of any such accounts except for routine payments and the balances on current account are not now substantially different from the balances shown on such statements.

THE COMPANY AND ITS EMPLOYEES

(51) Directors

The particulars shown in the first schedule are true and complete and no person not named therein as such is a director or shadow director of the Company.

(52) Particulars of Employees

(*a*)   The particulars shown in the schedule of employees[43] annexed to the Disclosure Letter show all remuneration payable and other benefits provided or which the Company is bound to provide (whether now or in the future) to each officer, employee or consultant of the Company or any person connected with any such person and are true and complete and include particulars of all profit sharing incentive and bonus arrangements to which the Company is a party whether legally binding on the Company or not.

(*b*)   Since the Balance Sheet Date no change has been made in the rate of remuneration, or the emoluments or pension benefits of any officer, ex-officer or employee of the Company and no change has been made in the terms of engagement of any such officer or employee, and no additional officer or employee has been appointed.

(*c*)   No present officer or employee of the Company has given or received notice terminating his employment except as expressly contemplated under this Agreement.

(*d*)   The Company has not given notice of any redundancies to any employee or government department or started consultations with any trade union pursuant to any statute or regulation.

(53) Service Contracts

There is not outstanding any contract of service between the Company and any of its directors, officers or employees which is not terminable by the Company without compensation (other than any compensation payable by statute) on three month's notice given at any time.

(54) Disputes with Employees

The Vendor is not aware of any outstanding claim against the Company by any person who is now or has been an officer or employee of the Company or any dispute between the Company and a material number or class of its employees and no payments are due by the Company under the provisions of the Employment Protection (Consolidation) Act 1978.

THE COMPANY AND ITS SUBSIDIARIES

(55) Particulars of Subsidiaries

The particulars of the Subsidiaries set out in part II of the second schedule are true and complete and the Company has no other subsidiary undertaking.

(56) Investments, Associations and Branches

The Company:

(*a*)   is not the holder or beneficial owner of, and has not agreed to acquire, any class of the share or other capital of any other company or corporation (whether incorporated in the United Kingdom or elsewhere) other than the Subsidiaries;

(*b*)   is not and has not agreed to become a member of any partnership, joint venture, consortium or other unincorporated association or arrangement for sharing commissions or income; and

(*c*) has no branch, agency or place of business outside England and no permanent establishment (as that expression is defined in the relevant double taxation relief orders current at the date hereof) outside the United Kingdom.

MATERIAL DISCLOSURE

(57) <u>All Material Matters Disclosed</u>[44]

All information contained or referred to in the Disclosure Letter or in any annexure thereto is accurate in all respects and the Vendor is not aware of any other fact or matter which renders any such information misleading or which might reasonably affect the willingness of a purchaser to purchase the Sale Shares on the terms (including price) of this Agreement.

FOURTH SCHEDULE

Taxation[45]

[Note that this Schedule reflects the law at 1 March 1989 and does not take into account the provisions of the Finance Act 1989.]

1   INTERPRETATION

In this schedule, where the context admits:

(1) 'Audited Accounts'[46] and 'Balance Sheet Date' have the same meanings as in the third schedule;

(2) 'event' includes (without limitation):

   (*a*) any omission, transaction or distribution whether or not the Company is a party thereto;

   (*b*) the death of any person;

   (*c*) the failure to avoid an apportionment or deemed distribution of income (whether or not it is or was possible, by taking action after Completion, to avoid such apportionment or deemed distribution);[47]

   (*d*) the Company ceasing to be a member of any group or associated with any person on or before Completion;[48]

   (*e*) Completion; and

   (*f*) any event which is treated as having occurred for the purposes of any legislation;

   and references to the result of events on or before the date of Completion shall include the combined result of two or more events the first of which shall have taken place on or before the date of Completion;

(3) 'group relief' has the meaning given to that expression by the Taxes Act 1988, s 402;

(4) 'relief' means any relief, allowance or credit in respect of taxation or any deduction in computing income, profits or gains for the purpose of taxation;[49]

(5) 'taxation claim'[50] means a claim for taxation against the Company or the Purchaser, whether made before or after the date hereof, whether satisfied[51] or unsatisfied at the date hereof and whether or not the taxation in question is also chargeable against or attributable to any other person, and includes any assessment, notice, demand or other communication from or action taken by any person, authority or body responsible for the assessment, collection or recovery of taxation in any country which claims:

   (*a*) payment of taxation;

   (*b*) to deprive the Company or the Purchaser of any relief whether arising before or after the date hereof;[52] or

   (*c*) to nullify or cancel any right to the repayment of taxation whether arising before or after the date hereof;

   and which arises from or by reference to:

(i) any income, profits or gains earned, accrued[53] or received on or before the date of Completion or any event on or before the date of Completion, whether alone or in conjunction with other circumstances; or

(ii) a payment under paragraph 2(A);[54]

(6) 'relevant taxation claim' means any taxation claim save to the extent that:

(*a*) provision in respect thereof has been made in the Audited Accounts or to the extent that payment or discharge of such claim has been taken into account in the Audited Accounts;

(*b*) provision in respect thereof has been made in the Audited Accounts which is insufficient only by reason of any increase in rates of taxation or change in law after the date hereof having retrospective effect;[55]

(*c*) it is a claim for which the Company is or may become liable as a result of transactions (not including distributions) entered into by the Company in the ordinary course of trading after the Balance Sheet Date and for the purposes of this sub-paragraph the following shall not be regarded as arising in the ordinary course of trading:

(i) any liability under Part VIII of the Taxes Management Act 1970 (charges on non-residents);

(ii) any liability under Part XVII of the Taxes Act 1988 (anti-avoidance);

(iii) any liability in respect of any distribution (as defined in Part VI of the Taxes Act 1988) or deemed distribution;

(iv) any liability arising from the disposal of or acquisition or deemed disposal or acquisition of any asset other than trading stock; or

(v) [   ];

(*d*) it is a claim against the Purchaser which does not relate to the Sale Shares or the Company or which is for stamp duty or stamp duty reserve tax arising out of this Agreement or Completion; or

(*e*) it is a claim which would not have arisen but for a voluntary act or transaction, which could reasonably have been avoided, carried out by the Purchaser (or persons deriving title from it) or the Company after the date of completion otherwise than in the ordinary course of business and which the Purchaser was aware could give rise to a claim, but so that this exclusion shall not extend to any voluntary act carried out with the approval, concurrence or assistance of the Vendor;

(7) 'taxation' includes (without limitation) corporation tax, advance corporation tax, income tax, capital gains tax, the charge under the Taxes Act 1988, s 601(2), value added tax, customs and other import duties, excise duties, capital transfer tax, inheritance tax, stamp duty,[56] stamp duty reserve tax, capital duty, national

insurance contributions, foreign taxation and any payment whatsoever which the Company may be or become bound to make to any person as a result of the operation of any enactment relating to taxation and all penalties, charges and interest relating to any claim for taxation or resulting from a failure to comply with the provisions of any enactment relating to taxation;

(8)   'Taxes Act 1970' means the Income and Corporation Taxes Act 1970;

(9)   'Taxes Act 1988' means the Income and Corporation Taxes Act 1988;

(10)   references to income or profits or gains earned, accrued or received shall include income or profits or gains treated as earned, accrued or received for the purposes of any legislation;

(11)   references to 'the Company' include each of the Subsidiaries; and

(12)   any taxation claim arising out of any of the following shall be treated as a relevant taxation claim for all the purposes of this schedule notwithstanding any other provision hereof:[57]

2   Taxation Payments

(A)   Payments

(1)   Subject to and in accordance with the terms of this schedule the Vendor shall make payments to the Purchaser equal to the amount of each relevant taxation claim.

(2)   For this purpose the amount of any relevant taxation claim shall depend upon whether the claim is of the type described in item (*a*), (*b*) or (*c*) of paragraph 1(5). In the case of a claim of the type described in item (*a*), the amount is the payment claimed; in the case of a claim of the type described in item (*b*), the amount is the amount of taxation (on the basis of rates current at the date of the loss of the relief)[58] which would have been relieved, allowed or credited by the relief of which it is claimed to deprive the Company or the Purchaser, and in the case of a claim of the type described in item (*c*), the amount is the repayment which it is claimed to nullify or cancel.

(3)   Where any relevant taxation claim has been reduced or eliminated by (or where a relevant taxation claim would have arisen but for) some relief available to the Company arising after Completion or some relief available to some person other than the Company, the Vendor or a member of the Vendor's Group whether arising before or after Completion then such relief shall be disregarded for the purposes of determining whether, in what amount, and on what date any payment should be made by the Vendor hereunder, and accordingly the relevant taxation claim shall be treated as not being reduced or eliminated (or, as the case may be, shall be treated as having arisen).[59]

(B) Date for Payment

The Vendor shall be bound to make payments in respect of relevant taxation claims on the following dates:

(1) in so far as a relevant taxation claim represents taxation to be borne by the Company but which has not yet become due, the Vendor shall make the payment in respect of that claim (or so much thereof as represents that taxation) on the date on which that taxation becomes due;

(2) in so far as a relevant taxation claim consists of the nullification or cancellation of a right to repayment of taxation the Vendor shall make the payment in respect of that claim (or so much thereof as represents that nullification or cancellation) on the date on which that repayment would otherwise have become due; and

(3) in any other case the Vendor shall make the payment fourteen days after the date on which a notice setting out details of the relevant taxation claim is delivered to the Vendor;[60]

and for this purpose references to a date on which taxation becomes due include a reference to the date on which it would have become due were it not for the availability of some relief. Any payment which becomes due on a day which is not a business day shall be paid on the next following business day, and any payment which is made after noon on any day before shall, for the purposes of calculating interest, be deemed to have been paid on the next following business day. No payment shall be treated as made until cleared funds in respect thereof are available to the Purchaser.

(C) Reduction in Consideration

Insofar as the payments made by the Vendor to the Purchaser pursuant to sub-paragraph (A) are less than the consideration for the Sale Shares, they shall constitute a repayment of and a reduction in such consideration, but nothing in this paragraph shall limit the liability of the Vendor to make payments under sub-paragraph (A).

(D) Disclosure not Relevant[61]

The Vendor's obligations to make payments under sub-paragraph (A) shall not be affected by the disclosure, in the Disclosure Letter or otherwise, of the relevant taxation claim giving rise to the payment, or the circumstances giving rise to that relevant taxation claim.

(E) Credits and Reductions

If any relevant taxation claim is disputed by the Company or by either party or represents taxation for which credit is or may become due to the Company at a later date or in respect of which it is subsequently found that there arises a corresponding credit or right to repayment of taxation, the amount of the relevant taxation claim shall nevertheless be payable in full by the Vendor on the due date ascertained in accordance with sub-paragraph (B) but if subsequently any reduction is made in the claim or it is found that the liability in respect thereof falls short of the amount claimed or such credit or repayment is received by the Company the Purchaser shall promptly repay to the Vendor an amount equal to such reduction, shortfall, credit or repayment up to the amount previously paid by the Vendor in respect of that relevant taxation claim and without interest, save to the extent that interest is included (or allowed) in such credit, repayment, reduction or shortfall. For this purpose, no credit shall be taken to have been received by the Company unless it shall have relieved the Company of a present obligation to pay taxation.

(F) Over-provisions[62]

If, at the request and cost of the Vendor, the Company's auditors shall certify that any provision for taxation (not being a provision for deferred taxation) contained in the Audited Accounts is an over-provision, the value of such over-provision shall be set against the liability of the Vendor under sub-paragraph (A), except in so far as such over-provision is attributable to the effect of a change in rates of taxation after the date hereof, but no deduction shall be made from any payment which the Vendor shall be obliged to make hereunder unless such certificate is in existence on the due date for that payment. In the event that such a certificate is given after the Vendor has made a payment hereunder, the Purchaser shall refund to the Vendor (without interest) any payment made by the Vendor to the extent that such over-provision could have been set against such payment if the certificate had been in existence on the due date of payment. The Purchaser shall procure that the Company shall co-operate in obtaining any such certificate if the Vendor shall so request.

(G) Notice and Mitigation

    (1) If the Purchaser shall become aware of any relevant taxation claim it shall forthwith give written notice thereof to the Vendor setting out reasonable particulars thereof, including the amount and the date on which the Vendor is bound to make a payment in respect of that relevant taxation claim, ascertained in accordance with sub-paragraph (B), but no failure by the Purchaser to comply with this sub-clause shall affect the Vendor's obligations under sub-paragraph (A).

    (2) Except in a case where fraud is alleged the Purchaser shall take such action and give such information and assistance in connection with the affairs of the Company as the Vendor may reasonably and promptly by notice request to avoid, resist, appeal or compromise a relevant taxation claim provided that:

        (a) the Company shall not be obliged to appeal against any assessment, notice, demand or decision if, having given the Vendor notice of the receipt thereof, the Purchaser has not within twenty-one days thereafter received instructions in writing from the Vendor to do so; and

        (b) the Company shall not in any circumstances be obliged to pursue any appeal beyond the General Commissioners of Inland Revenue, the Special Commissioners of Inland Revenue, or Value Added Tax Tribunal or any equivalent forum in the United Kingdom or any other jurisdiction.

(3) The action which the Vendor may request under sub-paragraph (2) shall include (without limitation) the Company applying to postpone (so far as legally possible) the payment of any taxation and allowing the Vendor to take on or take over at its own expense the conduct of all proceedings of whatsoever nature arising in connection with the relevant taxation claim in question. If the Vendor takes on or takes over the conduct of proceedings, the Purchaser shall, and shall procure that the Company shall, provide such information and assistance as the Vendor may reasonably require in connection with the preparation for and conduct of such proceedings.

(4) Where the Company is entitled to recover from some other person (including any taxing or other authority) any sum in respect of any relevant taxation claim the Purchaser shall take such action as the Vendor may reasonably and promptly by notice request to enforce such recovery by the Company and shall account to the Vendor for any amount so recovered by the Company (including any interest included in such recovery) not exceeding the amount paid by the Vendor hereunder in respect of that relevant taxation claim.

(5) Notwithstanding anything in this Agreement, neither the Purchaser nor the Company shall be obliged to take any steps to reduce the amount of any relevant taxation claim or to recover any amount from any other person unless the Vendor shall first indemnify and secure the Company and the Purchaser to their satisfaction against all losses, costs, interest, damages and expenses which may be incurred thereby.

(H) Interest

The Vendor shall make all payments under this schedule in immediately available funds before noon on the due date for payment without deduction or withholding on any account (save as expressly provided in this schedule) and if any amount is not paid when due the Vendor shall pay to the Purchaser interest on such amount at the rate of   per cent per annum above the base rate of   Bank plc from time to time from the due date until the date of actual payment (as well after judgment as before).

(I) Deductions and Withholdings

(1) Any amount payable pursuant to sub-paragraphs (A) or (H) shall be paid free and clear of all deductions, withholdings or set-offs whatsoever, save only as may be required by law.

(2) If any deductions or withholdings are required by law to be made from any sums, the Vendor shall be obliged to pay the Purchaser such amount as will after the deduction or withholding has been made, leave the Purchaser with the same amount as it would have been entitled to receive in the absence of such requirement to make a deduction or withholding provided that if the Purchaser subsequently receives a credit for such deduction or withholding

then such credit shall be applied in accordance with the provision of sub-paragraph (F).

3   GROUP ARRANGEMENTS AND NEGOTIATIONS

(A) Group Relief and ACT
   (1)   In respect of the accounting period ended on
         19   the [Vendor] and its subsidiaries ('surrendering
         companies') shall surrender group relief or Advance Corporation
         Tax ('ACT') to such of [the Company and the Subsidiaries] as can
         utilise the same ('claimant companies') and the [Purchaser] shall
         procure that   per cent of the amount so surrendered (in the
         case of group relief) and 100 per cent of the amount surrendered
         (in the case of ACT) shall be paid by each relevant claimant
         company to the relevant surrendering company on or before
         19   .
   (2)   The amount of group relief and ACT surrendered shall be
         determined by the surrendering companies but shall not exceed
         the maximum amount which can be utilised by the claimant
         companies by way of relief from liability to corporation tax after
         utilising all other reliefs (including other group relief available to
         them).
   (3)   If any part of the amounts so surrendered shall not be allowed to
         the claimant company by way of a relief from corporation tax the
         surrendering company shall refund to the claimant company
         forthwith the amount paid by the claimant company in respect of
         that part of the amount so surrendered.
   (4)   The parties shall co-operate to secure the agreement with the
         Inland Revenue of the accounts relating to the accounting period
         referred to above and shall take all necessary action to procure
         the surrenders as aforesaid.

(B) Value Added Tax Group Registration
   (1)   On the date of Completion, the Vendor shall procure that an
         application is made to HM Customs & Excise pursuant to the
         Value Added Tax Act 1983, s 29(5), for the exclusion from the
         [Vendor's] group registration of [such of the Company and the
         Subsidiaries as are presently within that group registration] and
         for such exclusion to take effect at the earliest date permitted by
         the said section.
   (2)   Until such application has taken effect, the parties shall furnish or
         procure to be so furnished such information as may be required
         to enable the continuing representative member of the group in
         question to make the returns required in respect of the group and
         the [Vendor] [Purchaser] shall arrange for such returns to be
         made accordingly.
   (3)   Such payments shall be made as may be appropriate to ensure
         that the resulting position between all the companies and bodies

concerned is the same as it would have been if such applications had been granted with effect from the date of [Completion.]

(C)   Conduct of Negotiations
  (1)   The Vendor (which may act through a duly authorised agent for the purposes of this sub-paragraph) shall prepare the Company's tax returns for accounting periods ended on or prior to Completion. The Purchaser shall procure that such returns are authorised, signed and submitted by the Company to the appropriate authority without amendment or with such amendments as the Vendor shall agree (such agreement not to be unreasonably withheld) and that the Vendor is given all such assistance as may be required to agree the said returns with the appropriate authorities. The Vendor shall prepare all documents and deal with all matters (including correspondence) relating to the said returns and the Purchaser shall procure that such access to the books, accounts and records of the Company is afforded as may be required to enable the Vendor to prepare the said returns and conduct matters relating thereto in accordance with the Vendor's rights under this sub-paragraph.
  (2)   Without the prior written approval of the Purchaser the Vendor shall take no action the effect of which is likely to increase the amount of taxation payable by the Company in respect of accounting periods after the Balance Sheet Date or likely to prejudice the business or tax affairs of the Company.

4   TAXATION WARRANTIES AND REPRESENTATIONS
The Vendor hereby warrants and represents to and for the benefit of the Purchaser in the following terms.

GENERAL TAXATION MATTERS
(1)   Residence
The Company and the Subsidiaries are all resident in the United Kingdom for taxation purposes.
(2)   Tax Provisions
Full provision or reserve has been made in the Audited Accounts for all taxation liable to be assessed on the Company or for which it is accountable in respect of income, profits or gains earned, accrued or received on or before the Balance Sheet Date or any event on or before the Balance Sheet Date including distributions made down to such date or provided for in the Audited Accounts and full provision has been made in the Audited Accounts for deferred taxation in accordance with generally accepted accounting principles.
(3)   Compliance
The Company has properly and punctually made all returns and provided all information required for taxation purposes and none of such returns is disputed by the Inland Revenue or any other authority concerned (in the United Kingdom or elsewhere) and the Vendor is not aware that any dispute

is likely, or that any event has occurred which would or might give rise to a payment under paragraph 2A.

(4) Payment of Tax

The Company has duly and punctually paid all taxation which it has become liable to pay and is under no liability to pay any penalty or interest in connection with any claim for taxation and has not paid any tax which it was and is not properly due to pay.

DISTRIBUTIONS AND PAYMENTS

(5) Distributions

(*a*) No distribution within the meaning of the Taxes Act 1988, ss 209, 210 and 212 has been made by the Company except dividends shown in its Audited Accounts nor is the Company bound to make any such distribution.

(*b*) No securities (within the meaning of the Taxes Act 1988, s 254(1)) issued by the Company and remaining in issue at the date hereof were issued in such circumstances that the interest payable thereon falls to be treated as a distribution under the Taxes Act 1988, s 209(2)(*e*)(iii).

(*c*) The Company has not made or received any distribution which is an exempt distribution within the Taxes Act 1988, s 213.

(*d*) The Company has not received any capital distribution to which the provisions of the Taxes Act 1988, s 346 could apply.

(*e*) The Company has not issued any share capital, nor granted options or rights to any person which entitles that person to require the issue of any share capital to which the provision of the Taxes Act 1988, s 249 could apply.

(6) Group Income

The Disclosure Letter contains particulars of all elections made by the Company under the Taxes Act 1988, s 247 and all such elections are now in force and the Company has not paid any dividend without paying advance corporation tax or made any payment without deduction of income tax in the circumstances specified in sub-section (6) of that section.

(7) Surrender of Advance Corporation Tax

The Disclosure Letter contains particulars of all arrangements and agreements to which the Company is or has been a party relating to the surrender of advance corporation tax made or received by the Company under the Taxes Act 1988, s 240 and:

(*a*) the Company has not paid nor is liable to pay any amount in excess of the advance corporation tax surrendered to it nor for the benefit of any advance corporation tax which is or may become incapable of set-off against the Company's liability to corporation tax;

(*b*) the Company has received all payments due to it under any such arrangement or agreement for all surrenders of advance corporation tax made by it; and

(*c*) save in respect of this Agreement, there have not been in existence in relation to the Company any such arrangements as are referred to in the Taxes Act 1988, s 240(11).

(8)   ACT Carry Forward

There has been no major change in the business of the Company within the meaning of the Taxes Act 1988, s 245.

(9)   Payments under Deduction

All payments by the Company to any person which ought to have been made under deduction of tax have been so made and the Company has (if required by law to do so) provided certificates of deduction to such person and accounted to the Inland Revenue for the tax so deducted.

(10)   Payments and Disallowances

    (*a*)   No rents, interest, annual payments or other sums of an income nature paid or payable by the Company or which the Company is under an obligation to pay in the future are wholly or partially disallowable as deductions or charges in computing profits for the purposes of corporation tax by reason of the provisions of the Taxes Act 1988, ss 74, 125, 338, 577, 779 to 784, and 787 or otherwise.

    (*b*)   The Company has not used any credit, relief or set-off that may be disallowed pursuant to the Taxes Act 1988, s 237.

Losses

(11)   Group Relief[62A]

The Disclosure Letter contains particulars of all arrangements and agreements relating to group relief to which the Company is or has been a party and:

    (*a*)   all claims by the Company for group relief were when made and are now valid and have been or will be allowed by way of relief from corporation tax;

    (*b*)   the Company has not made nor is liable to make any payment under any such arrangement or agreement save in consideration for the surrender of group relief allowable to the Company by way of relief from corporation tax and equivalent to the taxation for which the Company would have been liable had it not been for the surrender;

    (*c*)   the Company has received all payments due to it under any such arrangement or agreement for surrender of group relief made by it; and

    (*d*)   save in respect of this Agreement, there have not been in existence in relation to the Company any such arrangements as are referred to in the Taxes Act 1988, s 410.

(12)   Tax Losses

There has not within the three years preceding the date hereof been a major change in the business of the Company within the meaning of the Taxes Act 1988, s 768.

(13)   Dual Resident Companies

The Company is neither a dual resident company nor a dual resident investment company within the meaning of the Taxes Act 1988, s 404.

CLOSE COMPANIES

(14) Close Company[63]

    (*a*)   The Company has never been a close company within the meaning of the Taxes Act 1988, s 414.[63]

    (*b*)   No distribution within the Taxes Act 1988, s 418 has been made by the Company and no such distribution will be made before Completion.

    (*c*)   The Company has not made (and will not be deemed to have made) any loan or advance to a participator or an associate of a participator so as to become liable to make any payment under the Taxes Act 1988, s 419.

    (*d*)   The Company has supplied to the inspector such information and particulars as are necessary to make full and accurate disclosure of all facts and considerations material to be known by him to enable him to make intimations pursuant to the Taxes Act 1988, Sched 19, para 16 that he does not intend to make apportionments in respect of the Company for any accounting period ending on or before the Balance Sheet Date and the Company has received such intimations.

    (*e*)   No apportionment pursuant to the Taxes Act 1988, s 423 and Sched 19 has ever been made or could be made against the Company.

    (*f*)   The Company has at all times been a 'trading company' or a 'member of a trading group' as defined in the Taxes Act 1988, Sched 19, para 7.

    (*g*)   The Company has not expended or applied any sum liable to be regarded as income available for distribution pursuant to the Taxes Act 1988, Sched 19, para 8 (first business loans) and is not bound (contingently or otherwise) to expend or apply any such sum.

ANTI-AVOIDANCE

(15) Taxes Act 1988, s 765

The Company has not without the prior consent of the Treasury been a party to any transaction for which, at the time such transaction was effected, consent under the Taxes Act 1988, s 765 was required.

(16) Controlled Foreign Companies

    (*a*)   No direction has been made by the Board of Inland Revenue under the Taxes Act 1988, s 747 in respect of any controlled foreign companies which are under the control of the Company.

    (*b*)   Section 748(1) of the Taxes Act 1988 applies to all controlled foreign companies controlled by the Company.

(17) Bond Washing

The Company has not since 28 February 1985 transferred any securities with accrued interest as defined in Chapter II of Part XVII of the Taxes Act 1988.

(18) Offshore Funds

The Company does not own nor has owned at any time a material interest in an offshore fund which is or has at any material time been a non-qualifying offshore fund as defined by the Taxes Act 1988, s 760.

(19) <u>Anti-avoidance</u>

    (*a*)   The Company has not at any time entered into or been a party to a transaction or series of transactions either:

        (i) containing steps inserted without any commercial or business purpose, or

        (ii) being transactions to which any of the following provisions could apply: Taxes Act 1988, ss 703, 729, 730, 737, 739, 770, 774, 776, 779, 780, 781 or 786, without in the appropriate cases, having received clearance in respect thereof from the Inland Revenue.

    (*b*)   The Company has never been requested to furnish information pursuant to notices served under the Taxes Act 1988, ss 745 or 778.

CLEARANCES

(20) The Company has not applied for clearance under any of the following provisions:

    (*a*)   Taxes Act 1970, s 215(1) (demergers);

    (*b*)   Taxes Act 1970, s 267(3A) (reconstruction or amalgamation);

    (*c*)   Taxes Act 1970, s 278A (mergers);

    (*d*)   Capital Gains Tax Act 1979, s 88 (share exchanges);

    (*e*)   Taxes Act 1988, s 707 (transactions in securities); or

    (*f*)   Taxes Act 1988, s 776(11) (transactions in land).

ELECTIONS

(21) The Company has not made (and will not be deemed to have made) any elections under the following provisions:

    (*a*)   Taxes Act 1988, ss 524 and 534 (lump sum receipts for patents and copyright);

    (*b*)   Finance Act 1985, s 57 (short life assets).

CAPITAL ASSETS

(22) <u>Base Values</u>

    (*a*)   If each of the capital assets of the Company were disposed of for a consideration equal to the book value of that asset in or adopted for the purpose of the Audited Accounts no liability to corporation tax on chargeable gains or balancing charge under the Capital Allowances Act 1968 or the Finance Act 1971 would arise (and for this purpose there shall be disregarded any relief and allowances available to the Company other than amounts falling to be deducted from the consideration receivable under the Capital Gains Tax Act 1979, s 32).

    (*b*)   No election under the Finance Act 1988, s 96 is in effect in relation to the Company and full particulars are given in the

Disclosure Letter of the first relevant disposal for the purposes of that section.

(c) The Disclosure Letter contains full particulars of all assets held by the Company or disposed of by the Company on or after 6th April 1988 in respect of which relief is or would be available under the Finance Act 1988, Sched 9 upon disposal.

(23) Roll-over Relief

The Company has made no claim under the Capital Gains Tax Act 1979, ss 107 to 109 (inclusive), ss 115 to 119 (inclusive) or s 121 and no such claim or other claim has been made by any other person (in particular pursuant to the Capital Gains Tax Act 1979, s 126 or the Taxes Act 1970, s 276) which affects or could affect the amount or value of the consideration for the acquisition of any asset by the Company taken into account in calculating liability to corporation tax on chargeable gains on a subsequent disposal.

(24) Depreciating and Wasting Assets

No asset owned by the Company is a depreciating or wasting asset within the meaning of the Capital Gains Tax Act 1979, ss 117 and 106 and Sched 3 of that Act respectively.

(25) Depreciatory Transactions

No loss which might accrue on the disposal by the Company of any share in or security of any company is liable to be reduced by virtue of any depreciatory transaction within the meaning of the Taxes Act 1970, ss 280 and 281 nor is any expenditure on any share or security liable to be reduced under the Capital Gains Tax Act 1979, s 75.

(26) Transactions Not at Arm's Length

The Company has not disposed of or acquired any asset to or from any person connected with it within the Taxes Act 1988, s 839 or in circumstances such that the provisions of the Capital Gains Tax Act 1979, s 29A could apply to such disposal or acquisition.

(27) Straightline Growth

No asset owned by the Company is subject to a deemed disposal and reacquisition under the Capital Gains Tax Act 1979, Sched 5, paras 11, 14 or 16.

(28) Intra Group Transfers

The Company has not acquired any asset (past or present) from any other company then belonging to the same group of companies as the Company within the meaning of the Taxes Act 1970, s 272.

(29) Group Reconstructions

The Company has not been party to any scheme of reconstruction or reorganisation to which the provisions of the Taxes Act 1970, s 267, the Taxes Act 1988, s 703 or to which the Taxes Act 1988, ss 343 and 344 could apply.

(30) Chargeable Debts

No gain chargeable to corporation tax will accrue to the Company on the disposal of any debt owing to the Company not being a debt on a security.

(31) Chargeable Policies

The Company has not acquired benefits under any policy of assurance otherwise than as original beneficial owner.

(32) Claims by the Company

The Company has made no claim under any of the following:

- (*a*) Capital Gains Tax Act 1979, s 13 (assets situated outside the United Kingdom);
- (*b*) Capital Gains Tax Act 1979, s 22(2) (assets of negligible value);
- (*c*) Capital Gains Tax Act 1979, s 40 (tax on chargeable gains payable by instalments);
- (*d*) Taxes Act 1988, ss 242 and 243 (surplus franked investment income); or
- (*e*) Taxes Act 1988, s 584 (unremittable income arising outside the United Kingdom).

(33) Gains Accruing to Non-resident Companies or Trusts

There has not accrued any gain in respect of which the Company may be liable to corporation tax on chargeable gains by virtue of the provisions of the Capital Gains Tax Act 1979, s 15 or the Finance Act 1981, s 80.

(34) Indexation: Groups and Associated Companies

The Company does not own any debts or shares to which the provisions of the Finance Act 1988, s 114 and Sched 11 could apply.

MISCELLANEOUS

(35) Assessment of Tax on Lessees

No notice pursuant to the Taxes Act 1988, s 23 has been served on the Company.

(36) Leaseholds

Except insofar as provision has been made in the Audited Accounts the Company is not liable to taxation under the provisions of the Taxes Act 1988, ss 34, 35 and 36 nor does it own any leasehold interest to which the said s 35 may apply.

(37) Quoted Eurobonds

The Company has never at any time issued any quoted Eurobonds as defined in the Taxes Act 1988, s 124(6).

(38) Deep Discount Securities

The Company has not at any time held, owned or issued any deep discount securities as defined in the Taxes Act 1988, Sched 4, para 1.

(39) Stock Lending

The Company has not been a party to any transaction to which the provisions of the Taxes Act 1988, s 129 could apply.

TAXATION OF EMPLOYEES

(40) PAYE

The Company has properly operated the Pay As You Earn system deducting tax as required by law from all payments to or treated as made to employees and ex-employees of the Company and punctually accounted to the Inland Revenue for all tax so deducted.

(41) Benefits for Employees

- (*a*) The Company has not made any payment to or provided any benefit for any officer or employee or ex-officer or ex-employee of the Company which is not allowable as a deduction in calculating the profits of the Company for taxation purposes.

(*b*) The Company has not issued any shares or conferred any interest in shares in the circumstances described in the Taxes Act 1988, s 138(1) and has complied with the Taxes Act 1988, s 139(5).

(*c*) The Company has not issued any shares or conferred any interest in shares in the circumstances described in s 77(1) and has complied with the Finance Act 1988, s 85.

(*d*) The Company has not made any payment to which the Taxes Act 1988, s 313 applies.

(*e*) The Company does not operate any share scheme approved under the provisions of the Taxes Act 1988, Sched 9 nor a profit related pay scheme to which the provisions of Chapter II of Part V of the Taxes Act 1988 apply.

(42) Payroll Deduction
The Company does not operate and has not operated any such scheme as specified in Taxes Act 1988, s 202.

(43) National Insurance etc
The Company has paid all national insurance and graduated pension contributions for which it is liable and has kept proper books and records relating to the same.

STAMP DUTIES

(44) Stamp Duty
The Company has not obtained relief from stamp duty under any of the following:

(*a*) Finance Act 1927, s 55 (reconstructions and amalgamations);

(*b*) Finance Act 1930, s 42 (intra-group transfers);

(*c*) Finance Act 1985, ss 78 or 79 (takeovers and voluntary winding up); or

(*d*) Finance Act 1986, ss 75, 76 or 77 (acquisitions).

(45) Capital Duty
The Company has complied with the provisions of the Finance Act 1973 relating to capital duty and has duly paid all capital duty which it is liable to pay.

(46) Stamp Duty Reserve Tax
The Company has made all returns and paid all stamp duty reserve tax in respect of any transaction in securities to which it has been a party or in respect of which it is liable to account for stamp duty reserve tax.

VALUE ADDED TAX

(47) (*a*) The Company has complied with all statutory provisions and regulations relating to value added tax and has duly paid or provided for all amounts of value added tax for which the Company is liable.

(*b*) All supplies made by the Company are taxable supplies and the Company is not and will not be denied credit for any input tax by reason of the operation of the Value Added Tax Act 1983, s 15 and regulations made thereunder.

(c)　The Company is not party to any contract under which it may become liable to make or receive supplies the rate of tax applicable to which may change as a result of the proposals announced in HM Customs and Excise News Release dated 21 June 1988.

(d)　All input tax for which the Company has claimed credit has been paid by the Company in respect of supplies made to it relating to goods or services used or to be used for the purpose of the Company's business.

(e)　The Company is not and has not been, for value added tax purposes a member of any group of companies (other than that comprising the Company and the Subsidiaries alone) and no act or transaction has been effected in consequence whereof the Company is or may be held liable for any value added tax chargeable against some other company except where that other company is a Subsidiary.

(f)　No supplies have been made to the Company to which the provisions of the Value Added Tax Act 1983, s 7 might apply;

(g)　The Company has not committed any offence contrary to the Finance Act 1985, s 12 or 13 nor has it received any royalty liability notice pursuant to the Finance Act 1988, s 14A(3), surcharge liability notice pursuant to s 19, or written warranty issued pursuant to s 21(A).

(h)　The Company has not been registered for value added tax otherwise than pursuant to the provisions of the Value Added Tax Act 1983, Sched 1, para 1.

(i)　The Company has not been required to give security under the Value Added Tax Act 1983, Sched 7, para 5.

INHERITANCE TAX AND GIFTS

(48)　Powers of Sale for Inheritance Tax purposes
There are not in existence any circumstances whereby any such power as is mentioned in the Inheritance Tax Act 1984, s 212 could be exercised in relation to any shares in, securities of, or assets of, the Company.

(49)　Gifts

(a)　The Company is not liable to be assessed to corporation tax on chargeable gains or to inheritance tax as donor or donee of any gift or transferor or transferee of value.

(b)　The Company has not been a party to associated operations in relation to a transfer of value within the meaning of Inheritance Tax Act 1984, s 268.

(c)　No Inland Revenue Charge (as defined in the Inheritance Tax Act 1984, s 237) is outstanding over any asset of the Company or in relation to any shares in the capital of the Company.

(d)　The Company has not received any asset as mentioned in the Capital Gains Tax Act 1979, s 59.

FIFTH SCHEDULE

Adjustment of Consideration

1 INTERPRETATION

In this schedule, where the context admits:
- (1) 'the Audited Accounts' and 'the Balance Sheet Date' have the same meanings as in the third schedule;
- (2) 'the Completion Accounts' means the accounts prepared in accordance with paragraph 2;
- (3) 'the Provisional Consideration' means the consideration for the Sale Shares of £   stated in clause 3(A);
- (4) 'the Purchaser's Accountants' means Messrs   ; and
- (5) 'the Vendor's Accountants' means Messrs   .

2 COMPLETION ACCOUNTS

(A) Preparation
The parties shall procure that, forthwith after Completion, accounts for the Company and the Subsidiaries shall be prepared and reported on in accordance with this schedule and the parties shall use their best endeavours to secure compliance with this Schedule by their respective accountants.

(B) Description
The Completion Accounts shall consist of a consolidated balance sheet of the Company and the Subsidiaries as at the close of business on the date of Completion and a consolidated profit and loss account of the Company and the Subsidiaries in respect of the period from the day following the Balance Sheet Date to the date of Completion (both dates inclusive).

(C) General Requirements
Subject to sub-paragraph (D), the Completion Accounts shall:
- (1) be prepared as if the period from the day following the Balance Sheet Date to the date of Completion were a financial year of the Company;
- (2) be prepared in accordance with the requirements of all relevant statutes and generally accepted accounting principles;
- (3) show a true and fair view of the assets and liabilities of the Company and the Subsidiaries at the date of Completion and the profits of the Company and the Subsidiaries for the period ended on the date of Completion; and
- (4) adopt bases and policies of accounting applied for the purposes of the Audited Accounts.

(D) Specific Requirements[64]
In preparing the Completion Accounts:
- (1) no value shall be attributed to goodwill or any other intangible asset;
- (2) no value shall be attributed to any assets (including in particular any prepayment or debt) except to the extent that (following

Completion) the Company or a Subsidiary will have the benefit of the same;

(3)   full provision shall be made for rebates or discounts that will fall due and fees and commissions that will become payable after Completion in either case in respect of sales or other transactions that took place before Completion;

(4)   full provision shall be made for amounts that become due as a result of the change of control of the Company on Completion; and

(5)   other fixed assets shall be included at the value at which they were included in the Audited Accounts (or, if acquired after the Balance Sheet Date, their cost) less depreciation on the written down value, calculated at the following annual rates:

Plant and Machinery	[ ]	per cent
Fixtures and Fittings	[ ]	per cent
Motor Vehicles	[ ]	per cent
Immoveable assets and improvements thereto	[ ]	per cent

(6)   [   ]

3   PROCEDURE

(A)   Submission of Draft

Within sixty days after the date of Completion, the Purchaser's Accountants shall deliver a final draft of the Completion Accounts to the Vendor's Accountants and, unless the Vendor's Accountants shall notify the Purchaser's Accountants in writing within twenty-one days after receipt of such draft that they do not accept that such draft complies with paragraph 2, the Vendor shall be deemed to have accepted such draft as complying with paragraph 2.

(B)   Agreement of Draft

If, within the period of twenty-one days referred to in sub-paragraph A, the Vendor's Accountants shall notify the Purchaser's Accountants in writing that they do not accept that the said draft complies with paragraph 2 then the Purchaser's Accountants and the Vendor's Accountants shall use their best endeavours to reach agreement upon adjustments to the draft to meet the objections of the Vendor's Accountants.

(C)   Independent Accountant

In the event that the Vendor's Accountants and the Purchaser's Accountants are unable to reach agreement as aforesaid, any matter in dispute shall be referred to the decision of a single independent chartered accountant or an independent firm of chartered accountants to be agreed upon between them or, in default of such agreement, to be selected (at the instance of either party) by the President for the time being of the Institute of Chartered Accountants in England and Wales, and any such chartered accountant or firm of chartered accountants (whose costs shall be paid as he or they shall direct) shall act as expert (and not as arbitrator)[65] in connection with the giving of such decision which shall, save in the event of manifest error, be binding. In giving such decision, the accountant or firm shall state what adjustments (if any) are to be made to the said draft in order that it shall comply with paragraph 2.

(D) Report

If the Vendor's Accountants accept, or are deemed to accept, that the said draft complies with paragraph 2 the Purchaser's Accountants shall sign a report to the effect that the Completion Accounts comply with paragraph 2 and any Completion Accounts so reported on, or (if sub-paragraph (C) shall apply) the final draft of the Completion Accounts as adjusted by the independent accountant, shall be the Completion Accounts for the purposes of this Agreement and shall be final and binding on the parties.

(E) Information and Explanations

The Purchaser's Accountants shall provide such information and explanations relating to the draft Completion Accounts and their preparation as the Vendor's Accountants, or any independent chartered accountant appointed pursuant to sub-paragraph (C), shall reasonably require.

4 ADJUSTMENT OF CONSIDERATION

(A) Increase or Reduction

When the Completion Accounts have become binding, the Provisional Consideration shall forthwith:

(1) be increased by the amount (if any) by which the net tangible assets of the Company and the Subsidiaries as at the date of Completion as shown by the Completion Accounts are greater than the net tangible assets of the Company and the Subsidiaries as at the Balance Sheet Date as shown by the Audited Accounts; or (as the case may be)

(2) be reduced by the amount (if any) by which the net tangible assets of the Company and the Subsidiaries as at the date of Completion as shown by the Completion Accounts are less than the net tangible assets of the Company and the Subsidiaries as at the Balance Sheet Date as shown by the Audited Accounts.

(B) Payment

Any increase or reduction in the Provisional Consideration shall be paid by the Purchaser or the Vendor (as appropriate) within fourteen days after the Completion Accounts have become binding as aforesaid and any amount not paid when due shall carry interest at the rate of   per cent per annum above the base rate of   Bank plc from time to time from the due date until the date of actual payment (as well after judgment as before).

5 INTERACTION WITH OTHER PROVISIONS[66]

[Subject to the due performance of paragraph 4, if the Purchaser shall have any claim against the Vendor under this Agreement in respect of any liability or deficiency which is taken into account in the Completion Accounts the amount of such liability or deficiency so taken into account shall be deducted from the amount of the Purchaser's claim but, save as aforesaid, preparation and acceptance of the Completion Accounts by the Purchaser shall be without prejudice to any claim which the Purchaser may have against the Vendor under or in respect of any breach of this Agreement.]

SIXTH SCHEDULE[77]

Pensions [Company participates in group final salary scheme]

1   INTERPRETATION

(A) Definitions

In this schedule, where the context admits:

    (1) 'Actuarial Assumptions' means the actuarial assumptions and methods set out below: ;[78]

    (2) 'Adjusted Transfer Value' means an amount equal to [the Transfer Value multiplied by the Investment Adjustment from and including the Membership Transfer Date to and including the Payment Date];

    (3) 'Basic Amount' means an amount, calculated as at the close of business on the date of Completion by reference to the Actuarial Assumptions, equal to the greater of:

        (*a*) an amount equal to the value of the benefits payable under the Pension Scheme to or in respect of the Transferring Employees; and

        (*b*) an amount which bears the same proportion to the amount by which the aggregate value of the assets of the Pension Scheme exceeds the aggregate value of the benefits payable under the Pension Scheme to or in respect of pensioners and deferred pensioners as the aggregate value of the benefits payable under the Pension Scheme to or in respect of the Transferring Employees bears to the aggregate value of the benefits payable under the Pension Scheme to or in respect of all members in pensionable service, including the Transferring Employees;

  for this purpose 'benefits' includes immediate, prospective and contingent benefits and in calculating such benefits:

        (i) in the case of members in pensionable service on the date of Completion no account shall be taken of benefits in respect of pensionable service after the date of Completion but allowance shall be made for projected future increases in earnings up to normal pension age under the Pension Scheme or earlier cessation of pensionable service; and

        (ii) in the case of all members, pensioners and deferred pensioners allowance shall be made for increases (whether payable pursuant to a legal obligation or not) to pensions in payment or in deferment.

  Any improvement to the benefits under the Pension Scheme which has been announced or are otherwise proposed shall be deemed to have been duly effected under the Pension Scheme and to have come into force before the date of this Agreement;

    (4) 'Company' means the Company and the Subsidiaries or such one or more of them, as the context may require;

(5) 'Interest' means, in respect of any period and any principal sum, an amount of interest (accruing daily and compounded monthly) at a rate equal to   per cent above the base lending rate from time to time of   plc;

(6) 'Interim Period' means the period from and including the day next following the date of Completion to but excluding the Membership Transfer Date;

(7) 'Investment Adjustment' means, in respect of each sum to which this definition applies, the formula found by calculating the proportionate change during the period (taking the respective figures published for the close of business on the last business day preceding the commencement of that period and for the close of business on the last business day preceding the day upon which that period ends) specified of an index comprising   per cent of the FT Actuaries All Share Index with gross dividend income reinvested in the same index at monthly intervals and   per cent of the FT Actuaries British Government Fixed Interest Over 15 Year Index with an adjustment on account of accrued interest (as published in *The Financial Times*) at monthly intervals;[79]

(8) 'Membership Transfer Date' means   (or such earlier date as the Purchaser may by not less than one month's notice in writing to the Vendor specify or such later date as the Vendor and the Purchaser may agree in writing);[80]

(9) 'Payment Date' means the earlier of:
  (*a*) the date upon which the Adjusted Transfer Value is paid in full in accordance with paragraph 5(C); and
  (*b*) the date which falls seven days after the later of:
    (i) the date upon which the amount of the Transfer Value is certified in accordance with paragraph 5(B) or 7, as the case may be; and
    (ii) the date upon which the Purchaser notifies the Vendor in writing that the Purchaser's Scheme is an exempt approved scheme (within the meaning of the Income and Corporation Taxes Act 1988, s 592) or that the Inland Revenue have confirmed that the trustees of the Purchaser's Scheme may accept a transfer from the Pension Scheme and (in either case) that if the employment of the Transferring Employees is to be contracted-out by reference to the Purchaser's Scheme the Company holds or is named in a contracting-out certificate in respect of the Purchaser's Scheme;

(10) 'Pension Scheme[s]' means   and   [and Pension Scheme means [either] [any one] of the Pension Schemes, as the context requires];

(11) 'Pensionable Employees' means those persons who are or become employees or officers of the Company and members of the Pension Scheme;

(12) 'Purchaser's Actuary' means the actuary appointed by the Purchaser pursuant to paragraph 2;

(13) 'Purchaser's Scheme' means the retirement benefits scheme or schemes nominated by or at the instance of the Purchaser pursuant to paragraph 4(A);

(14) 'Relevant Employees' means any present or past employee or officer of the Company or of any predecessor to all or any part of its business;

(15) 'Transferring Employees' means those of the Pensionable Employees who:

    (*a*) accept the offer of membership of the Purchaser's Scheme to be made pursuant to paragraph 4(B) and join the Purchaser's Scheme with effect from the Membership Transfer Date; and

    (*b*) consent in writing to a transfer being made in respect of them to the Purchaser's Scheme from the Pension Scheme;[81]

(16) 'Transfer Value' means an amount equal to the sum of:

    [(*a*) the Basic Amount multiplied by the Investment Adjustment for the period from and including the day next following the date of Completion to and including the Membership Transfer Date; plus]

    (*b*) the aggregate contributions paid in respect of the Interim Period to the Pension Scheme by or in respect of the Transferring Employees less   in respect of the cost of insuring the death in service benefits in respect of the Transferring Employees during the Interim Period together with Interest on the balance from the date of payment of each such contribution to the Membership Transfer Date;

reduced, but only if the employment of the Transferring Employees is not to be contracted-out by reference to the Purchaser's Scheme, by an amount equal to the value of the guaranteed minimum pensions (if any) of the Transferring Employees under the Pension Scheme, such value being calculated as at the Membership Transfer Date by reference to the Actuarial Assumptions; and

(17) 'Vendor's Actuary' means the actuary appointed by the Vendor pursuant to paragraph 2.

[(B) Contracting-out Terms

In this schedule, where the context admits, 'contracted-out', 'contracted-out scheme', 'contracting-out certificate', 'guaranteed minimum' and 'guaranteed minimum pension' shall have the same meanings as in the Social Security Pensions Act 1975.]

[(C) Schedule Applies Separately to each Pension Scheme

This schedule shall apply separately to each of the Pension Schemes.][82]

<u>2   Appointment of Actuaries</u>

The Vendor undertakes to appoint an actuary for the purposes of this schedule and the Purchaser undertakes to do likewise. For this purpose 'actuary' means a Fellow or a firm of Fellows of the Institute of Actuaries or of the Faculty of Actuaries.

<u>3   The Pension Scheme</u>

(A) <u>Vendor's Undertakings</u>
The Vendor undertakes to the Purchaser for the Purchaser's benefit and for the benefit of the Company to procure that:

   (1)   subject to the consent of the Inland Revenue being obtained (which consent the Vendor shall use all reasonable endeavours to procure), the Company is permitted to participate in the Pension Scheme throughout the Interim Period;

   (2)   none of the provisions of the Pension Scheme applicable to or capable of applying to the Company or any employee or officer of the Company is amended without the consent in writing of the Purchaser and, save with such consent, no power or discretion under the Pension Scheme is exercised until after the Payment Date which affects any of the benefits payable to or in respect of any employee or officer of the Company; and

   (3)   the Company is not required to make any payment to or in respect of the Pension Scheme except as provided in paragraph 3(B)(1).

(B) <u>Purchaser's Undertakings</u>[83]
The Purchaser shall procure that the Company:

   (1)   pays contributions to the Pension Scheme which accrue during the Interim Period in respect of the Pensionable Employees at the rate of   ; and

   (2)   complies in all other respects with the provisions of the Pension Scheme during the Interim Period.

(C) <u>Contracting-out in Interim Period</u>
The Vendor and the Purchaser undertake to co-operate with each other with a view to procuring that the employment of the Pensionable Employees is contracted-out by reference to the Pension Scheme throughout the Interim Period under a contracting-out certificate in the name of the Company.]

<u>4   The Purchaser's Scheme</u>

(A) <u>Purchaser to Provide Scheme</u>
The Purchaser shall on or before the Membership Transfer Date nominate or procure the nomination of a retirement benefits scheme for the purposes of this schedule which is, or which is designed to be capable of being, an exempt approved scheme (within the meaning of the Income and Corporation Taxes Act 1988, s 592).

(B)   Purchaser to Offer Membership
The Purchaser shall procure that those of the Pensionable Employees who are in pensionable employment by reference to the Pension Scheme immediately prior to the Membership Transfer Date are offered membership of the Purchaser's Scheme with effect from the Membership Transfer Date on terms in respect of service before that date which, when considered as a whole, are substantially no less favourable than those currently applicable to the Pensionable Employees under the Pension Scheme having due regard to whether a transfer is to be made to the Purchaser's Scheme in respect of the accrued rights (if any) of the Transferring Employees under the Pension Scheme to guaranteed minimum pensions (such terms being subject to the transfer or payment being made in full in accordance with paragraph 5(C) or 5(D) and to the powers of amendment and discontinuance under the Purchaser's Scheme).

5   PAYMENT OF TRANSFER VALUE

(A)   Data
The Vendor and the Purchaser shall use all reasonable endeavours to procure that all such information as the Vendor's Actuary or the Purchaser's Actuary or any independent actuary appointed under paragraph 7 may reasonably request for the purposes of this schedule shall be supplied promptly to such actuary.

(B)   Calculation
Immediately following the Membership Transfer Date the Vendor shall procure that the Vendor's Actuary calculates the amount of the Transfer Value and submits his findings in writing to the Purchaser's Actuary. If the Purchaser's Actuary agrees the amount of the Transfer Value, the Vendor and the Purchaser shall respectively procure that the Vendor's Actuary and the Purchaser's Actuary jointly certify that amount as the Transfer Value, If, however, they fail to agree within two months from the date upon which the Vendor's Actuary submits his findings to the Purchaser's Actuary as aforesaid, the matter may, at the option of either the Vendor or the Purchaser, be referred to an independent actuary pursuant to paragraph 7.

(C)   Payment
The Vendor shall use all reasonable endeavours to procure that the trustees of the Pension Scheme transfer to the trustees of the Purchaser's Scheme on the Payment Date the Adjusted Transfer Value in cash (or if the Vendor and the Purchaser so agree transfer assets equal in value to the Adjusted Transfer Value).

(D)   Shortfall
If the sum actually transferred from the Pension Scheme to the Purchaser's Scheme in respect of the Transferring Employees on the Payment Date is less than the Adjusted Transfer Value (the amount of the difference being referred to in this paragraph as the 'Shortfall'), then the Vendor shall forthwith pay to the Purchaser, by way of adjustment to the consideration for the Sale Shares, an amount in cash equal to the Shortfall together with

interest thereon (accruing daily and compounded monthly) from and including the Payment Date to but excluding the date upon which final payment is made in accordance with this paragraph, such interest shall be at per cent above the base lending rate from time to time of

.84

[(E) Payment on Account

If the Purchaser so requests at any time on or after the Membership Transfer Date, the Vendor shall use its best endeavours to procure that as soon as practicable after receiving such request a payment on account of the amount payable pursuant to paragraph 5(C) is made to the Purchaser's Scheme. Such payment shall be equal to [80] per cent of the amount which the Vendor's Actuary, in consultation with the Purchaser's Actuary, reasonably estimates to be the amount of the Adjusted Transfer Value. In the event of a payment on account being made in accordance with this paragraph, the trustees of the Pension Scheme shall be deemed to have transferred on the Payment Date to the trustees of the Purchaser's Scheme (in addition to the amount (if any) they actually transfer on the Payment Date) an amount equal to the payment made in accordance with this paragraph [multiplied by the Investment Adjustment for the period from and including the date upon which that payment is made to and including the Payment Date].]

6 ADDITIONAL VOLUNTARY CONTRIBUTIONS

For the purpose of the foregoing provisions of this schedule there shall be disregarded:
  (1) any benefits under the Pension Scheme which are attributable to additional voluntary contributions made to it by the Transferring Employees and in respect of which the Transferring Employees are not entitled to benefits based on their final pensionable earnings (however defined);
  (2) any such contributions; and
  (3) any transfer in respect of any such benefits.
The Vendor shall, nevertheless, procure that the trustees of the Pension Scheme transfer to the Purchaser's Scheme on the Payment Date for the benefit of the Transferring Employees all such funds or assets of the Pension Scheme which represent any such contributions made by the Transferring Employees and the investment return on them.

7 DISPUTES

Any dispute between the Vendor's Actuary and the Purchaser's Actuary concerning the amount of the Transfer Value or any other matter to be agreed between them in accordance with this schedule may, at the option of either the Vendor or the Purchaser, be referred to an independent actuary to be appointed by agreement between the Vendor and the Purchaser or, in default of agreement within fourteen days from the first nomination of an actuary by one party to the other, by the President for the time being of the Institute of Actuaries on the application of either the Vendor or the Purchaser. The independent actuary shall act as an expert and not as an arbitrator.[85] His decision shall, save in the event of manifest error, be final and binding on the parties and his costs shall be paid as he directs.

8   WARRANTIES AND REPRESENTATIONS

The Vendor hereby warrants and represents to and for the benefit of the Purchaser in the following terms:

(1)   No Other Arrangements

Save for the Pension Scheme the Company is neither a party to nor participates in nor contributes to any scheme, arrangement or agreement (whether legally enforceable or not) for the provision of any pension, retirement, death, incapacity, sickness, disability, accident or other like benefits (including the payment of medical expenses) for any Relevant Employee or for the widow, child or dependant of any Relevant Employee.

(2)   No Assurances etc

Neither the Company nor any member of the Vendor's group:

(a)   has given any undertaking or assurance (whether legally enforceable or not) to any Relevant Employee or to any widow, child or dependant of any Relevant Employee as to the continuance, introduction, improvement or increase of any benefit of a kind described in (1) above; or

(b)   is paying or has in the last three years paid any benefit of the kind described in (1) above to any Relevant Employee or the widow, child or dependant of any Relevant Employee.

(3)   All Details Disclosed

All material details relating to the Pension Scheme are contained in or annexed to the Disclosure Letter including (without limitation) the following:

(a)   a true and complete copy of the documentation governing the Pension Scheme;

(b)   a true and complete copy of all announcements, explanatory literature and the like which have been issued to any Relevant Employee in connection with the Pension Scheme;

(c)   a true and complete copy of the report on the last actuarial valuation of the Pension Scheme prior to the date of this Agreement and of any subsequent written recommendations of an actuarial nature;

(d)   a true and complete copy of the last audited accounts for the Pension Scheme prior to the date of this Agreement and details of any material change in the investment policy of the Pension Scheme since the date as at which those accounts were made up;

(e)   details of any proposed amendment to the Pension Scheme which has been announced or is being considered;

(f)   details of any discretionary increases to pensions in payment or in deferment under the Pension Scheme granted in the five years prior to the date of this Agreement;

(g)   details of any discretionary practices which may have led any person to expect additional benefits in a given set of circumstances (by way of example, but without limitation, on retirement at the behest of the Company or in the event of redundancy); and

(h)　details of the contributions paid to the Pension Scheme by the Company in the five years prior to the date of this Agreement.

(4)　Augmentation

No power under the Pension Scheme has been exercised in relation to any employee or officer of the Company:

(a)　to provide terms of membership of the Pension Scheme (whether as to benefits or contributions) which are different from those generally applicable to the members of the Pension Scheme;

(b)　to provide any benefits which would not but for the exercise of that power have been payable under the Pension Scheme; or

(c)　to augment any benefits under the Pension Scheme.

(5)　Death Benefits Insured

All benefits (other than any refund of members' contributions with interest where appropriate) payable under the Pension Scheme on the death of any person while in employment to which the Pension Scheme relates are insured fully under a policy with an insurance company of good repute and there are no grounds on which that company might avoid liability thereunder.

(6)　Contributions

Contributions to the Pension Scheme are not paid in arrear and all contributions and other amounts which have fallen due for payment have been paid and no fees, charges or expenses referable to the Pension Scheme for which the Company is or may become liable (whether wholly or in part) have been incurred but not paid and the Company has reimbursed any person who has paid any such fees, costs or expenses if and to the extent that the Company is or may become liable so to do.

(7)　Company's Obligations

The Company:

(a)　has been admitted to participation in the Pension Scheme on the same terms as apply to all other employers participating in the Scheme;

(b)　has observed and performed those provisions of the Pension Scheme which apply to it;

(c)　may terminate its liability to contribute to the Pension Scheme without notice, without the consent of any person and without further payment[; and

(d)　has at all material times held or been named in a contracting-out certificate referable to the Pension Scheme].

(8)　Exempt Approved Scheme

The Pension Scheme:

(a)　is an exempt approved scheme (within the meaning of the Income and Corporation Taxes Act 1988, s 592); and

(b)　complies with and has at all times been administered in accordance with all applicable laws, regulations and requirements (including those of the Inland Revenue and of trust law).

(9) <u>Data</u>

The data used for the purposes of the last actuarial valuation of the Pension Scheme prior to the date of this Agreement was complete and accurate in all material respects and since the date as at which that valuation was undertaken nothing has happened or has been omitted to be done which may affect materially the level of funding of the benefits under the Pension Scheme.

(10) <u>Litigation</u>

The trustees of the Pension Scheme are not engaged in any litigation or arbitration proceedings and so far as the Vendor is aware no litigation or arbitration proceedings are pending or threatened by or against the trustees of the Pension Scheme and there are no facts likely to give rise to any litigation or arbitration.

9   DAMAGES FOR BREACH OF PENSION WARRANTIES

In determining the damages flowing from any breach of Warranties contained in paragraph 8, the Company shall be deemed to be under a liability:

(1)   to provide and to continue to provide any benefits of a kind referred to in that paragraph which are now provided or have been announced or are proposed; and

(2)   to maintain and to continue to maintain (without benefits being reduced) the Pension Scheme and any other arrangements of a kind described in that paragraph which are now in existence or are proposed and any discretionary practices of a kind referred to in that paragraph which have hitherto been carried on.[86]

SIXTH SCHEDULE

Pensions [Company has own final salary scheme]

1   INTERPRETATION

[(A) Definitions
In this schedule, where the context admits:
  (1) 'Actuarial Assumptions' means the actuarial assumptions and methods set out below: ;[87]
  (2) 'Company' means the Company and the Subsidiaries or such one or more of them, as the context requires;
  (3) 'Pension Scheme[s]' means   and   [and 'Pension Scheme' means [any one] [either] of the Pension Schemes, as the context requires];
  (4) 'Purchaser's Actuary' means the actuary appointed by the Purchaser pursuant to paragraph 2(A);
  (5) 'Relevant Employee' means any past or present employee or officer of the Company or of any predecessor to all or any part of its business;
  (6) 'Shortfall' means an amount, calculated as at the close of business on the date of Completion by reference to the Actuarial Assumptions, equal to the amount (if any) by which the aggregate value of the assets of the Pension Scheme (excluding any debts of the Company to the trustees of the Pension Scheme)[88] is exceeded by the value of the liabilities (whether immediate, prospective or contingent) under the Pension Scheme. For this purpose:
    (*a*) when calculating the value of the assets of the Pension Scheme no account shall be taken of any contributions payable to the Pension Scheme after Completion;
    (*b*) when calculating the liability for any benefits no account shall be taken of benefits in respect of pensionable service after the date of Completion but allowance shall be made for projected future increases in earnings up to normal pension age under the Pension Scheme or earlier cessation of pensionable service and increases (whether payable pursuant to a legal obligation or not) to pensions in payment or in deferment; and
    (*c*) any improvements to the benefits under the Pension Scheme which have been announced or are otherwise proposed shall be deemed to have been duly effected under the Pension Scheme and to have come into force before the date of this Agreement; and
  (7) 'Vendor's Actuary' means the actuary appointed by the Vendor pursuant to paragraph 2(A).

[(B) Schedule Applies Separately to Each Pension Scheme
This schedule applies separately to each of the Pension Schemes.][89]

2   CALCULATION OF SHORTFALL

(A)   Appointment of Actuaries

Immediately following Completion the Vendor and the Purchaser shall each appoint an actuary for the purposes of this schedule. For this purpose 'actuary' means a Fellow or a firm of Fellows of The Institute of Actuaries or of The Faculty of Actuaries.

(B)   Data

The Vendor and the Purchaser shall respectively use all reasonable endeavours to procure that all such information as the Vendor's Actuary or the Purchaser's Actuary or any independent actuary appointed under paragraph 2(D) may reasonably request for the purposes of this schedule is supplied promptly to such actuary.

(C)   Agreement of Shortfall

The Purchaser's Actuary shall determine the amount of the Shortfall and shall submit his findings in writing to the Vendor's Actuary for agreement. If the Vendor's Actuary and the Purchaser's Actuary agree the amount (if any) of the Shortfall, the Vendor and the Purchaser shall respectively procure that the Vendor's Actuary and the Purchaser's Actuary jointly certify that amount as the Shortfall.

(D)   Dispute

If the Vendor's Actuary and the Purchaser's Actuary fail to agree the amount (if any) of the Shortfall within two months from the date upon which the Purchaser's Actuary submits his findings to the Vendor's Actuary in accordance with paragraph 2(C), the matter may, at the option of the Vendor or the Purchaser, be referred to an independent actuary to be agreed between the Vendor and the Purchaser or, in default of agreement within fourteen days from the first nomination of an actuary by one party to the other, appointed by the President for the time being of The Institute of Actuaries on the application of either the Vendor or the Purchaser. The certificate of the independent actuary as to the amount (if any) of the Shortfall shall, save in the event of manifest error, be final and binding on the parties and, in so certifying, the independent actuary shall be deemed to be acting as an expert and not as an arbitrator.[90] His costs shall be paid as he directs.

3   PAYMENT OF SHORTFALL

The Vendor undertakes to the Purchaser that within a period of fourteen days commencing on and including the date upon which the amount (if any) of the Shortfall is certified as aforesaid the Vendor will, by way of adjustment to the consideration of the Sale Shares,[91] pay to the Purchaser (or to a third party as the Purchaser may direct) a sum in cash equal to the amount shown in the certificate as being the Shortfall together with interest thereon (accruing daily and compounded monthly) from and including the date of Completion to but excluding the date upon which final payment is made in accordance with this paragraph. Such interest shall be at the Agreed Rate up to and including the last day in the aforesaid fourteen day period and thereafter shall be at   per cent above the Agreed Rate. For this purpose 'Agreed Rate' means   per cent above the base lending rate from time to time of   .

4   WARRANTIES AND REPRESENTATIONS

The Vendor hereby warrants and represents to and for the benefit of the Purchaser in the following terms.

(1)   No Other Pension Arrangements

Save for the Pension Scheme the Company is neither a party to nor participates in nor contributes to any scheme, arrangement or agreement (whether legally enforceable or not) for the provision of any pension, retirement, death, incapacity, sickness, disability, accident or other like benefits (including the payment of medical expenses) for any Relevant Employee or for the widow, child or dependant of any Relevant Employee.

(2)   No Assurances etc

Neither the Company nor any member of the Vendor's Group:

(a)   has given any undertaking or assurance (whether legally enforceable or not) to any Relevant Employee or to any widow, child or dependant of any Relevant Employee as to the continuance, introduction, improvement or increase of any benefit of a kind described in (1) above; or

(b)   is paying or has in the last three years paid any benefit of the kind described in (1) above to any Relevant Employee or to the widow, child or dependant of any Relevant Employee.

(3)   All Details Disclosed

All material details relating to the Pension Scheme are contained in or annexed to the Disclosure Letter including (without limitation) the following:

(a)   a true and complete copy of the documents governing the Pension Scheme;

(b)   a true and complete copy of all announcements, explanatory literature and the like which have been issued to any Relevant Employee in connection with the Pension Scheme;

(c)   a true and complete copy of the report on the last actuarial valuation of the Pension Scheme prior to the date of this Agreement and of any subsequent written recommendations of an actuarial nature;

(d)   a true and complete copy of the last audited accounts for the Pension Scheme prior to the date of this Agreement and details of any material change in the investment policy of the Pension Scheme since the date as at which those accounts were made up;

(e)   details of any proposed amendment to the Pension Scheme which has been announced or is being considered;

(f)   details of any discretionary increases to pensions in payment or in deferment under the Pension Scheme granted in the five years prior to the date of this Agreement;

(g)   details of any discretionary practices which may have led any person to expect additional benefits in a given set of circumstances (by way of example, but without limitation, on retirement at the behest of the Company or in the event of redundancy); and

(*h*) details of the contributions paid to the Pension Scheme by the Company in the five years prior to the date of this Agreement.

(4) Augmentation

No power under the Pension Scheme has been exercised in relation to any employee or officer of the Company:

(*a*) to provide terms of membership of the Pension Scheme (whether as to benefits or contributions) which are different from those generally applicable to the members of the Pension Scheme;

(*b*) to provide any benefits which would not but for the exercise of that power have been payable under the Pension Scheme; or

(*c*) to augment any benefits under the Pension Scheme.

(5) Death Benefits Insured

All benefits (other than any refund of members' contributions with interest where appropriate) payable under the Pension Scheme on the death of any person while in employment to which the Pension Scheme relates are insured fully under a policy with an insurance company of good repute and there are no grounds on which that company might avoid liability under that policy.

(6) Contributions

Contributions to the Pension Scheme are not paid in arrear and all contributions and other amounts which have fallen due for payment have been paid and no fees, charges or expenses referable to the Pension Scheme for which the Company is or may become liable (whether wholly or in part) have been incurred but not paid and the Company has reimbursed any person who has paid any such fees, costs or expenses if and to the extent that the Company is or may become liable so to do.

(7) Company's Obligations

The Company:

(*a*) has been admitted to participation in the Pension Scheme;

(*b*) has observed and performed those provisions of the Pension Scheme which apply to it;

(*c*) may terminate its liability to contribute to the Pension Scheme without notice, without the consent of any person and without further payment[; and

(*d*) has at all material times held or been named in a contracting-out certificate (within the meaning of the Social Security Pensions Act 1975) referable to the Pension Scheme].

(8) No Other Employer

The Company is the only employer for the time being participating in the Pension Scheme. No employer which has previously participated in the Pension Scheme has any claim under the Pension Scheme and in respect of any such employer the Pension Scheme has been partially wound up in accordance with its provisions.

(9)   Exempt Approved Scheme

The Pension Scheme:

    (*a*)   is an exempt approved scheme (within the meaning of the Income and Corporation Taxes Act 1988, s 592); and

    (*b*)   complies with and has at all times been administered in accordance with all applicable laws, regulations and requirements (including those of the Inland Revenue and of trust law).

(10) Data

The data used for the purposes of the last actuarial valuation of the Pension Scheme prior to the date of this Agreement was complete and accurate in all material respects and since the date as at which that valuation was undertaken nothing has happened or has been omitted to be done which may affect materially the level of funding of the benefits under the Pension Scheme.

(11) Litigation

The trustees of the Pension Scheme are not engaged in any litigation or arbitration proceedings and so far as the Vendor is aware no litigation or arbitration proceedings are pending or threatened by or against the trustees of the Pension Scheme and there are no facts likely to give rise to any litigation or arbitration.

(12) Indemnities

In relation to the Pension Scheme or the assets or previous assets thereof neither the Company nor the trustees or adminstrator of the Pension Scheme has given an indemnity or guarantee to any person (other than in the case of the Company any general indemnity in favour of the trustees or administrator under the documents governing the Pension Scheme).

5   DAMAGES FOR BREACH OF PENSION WARRANTIES

In determining the damages flowing from any breach of Warranties contained in paragraph 4, the Company shall be deemed to be under a liability:

    (1)   to provide and to continue to provide any benefits of a kind referred to in that paragraph which are now provided or have been announced or are proposed; and

    (2)   to maintain and to continue to maintain (without benefits being reduced) the Pension Scheme and any other arrangements of a kind described in that paragraph which are now in existence or are proposed and any discretionary practices of a kind referred to in that paragraph which have hitherto been carried on.[92]

SIXTH SCHEDULE

Pensions [money purchase scheme]

1 INTERPRETATION

(A) Definitions
In this schedule, where the context admits:
   (1) 'Company' means the Company and the Subsidiaries or such one or more of them, as the context may require;
   [(2) 'Interim Period' means the period from and including the day next following the date of Completion to but excluding the Membership Transfer Date;][93]
   [(3) 'Membership Transfer Date' means   (or such earlier date as the Purchaser may by not less than one month's notice in writing to the Vendor specify or such later date as the Vendor and the Purchaser may agree in writing);][93]
   (4) 'Pension Scheme[s]' means   and   [and Pension Scheme means [either] [any one] of the Pension Schemes, as the context requires;]
   [(5) 'Pensionable Employees' means those persons who are or become employees or officers of the Company and members of the Pension Scheme;][93]
   (6) 'Relevant Employees' means any present or past employee or officer of the Company or of any predecessor to all or any part of its business.

[B *Schedule applies separately to each Pension Scheme*
This schedule shall apply separately to each of the Pension Schemes.]

[2 THE PENSION SCHEME[94]

(A) Vendor's Undertakings
The Vendor undertakes to the Purchaser for the Purchaser's benefit and for the benefit of the Company to procure that:
   (1) subject to the consent of the Inland Revenue being obtained (which consent the Vendor shall use all reasonable endeavours to procure), the Company is permitted to participate in the Pension Scheme throughout the Interim Period;
   (2) none of the provisions of the Pension Scheme applicable to or capable of applying to the Company or any employee or officer of the Company is amended without the consent in writing of the Purchaser;
   (3) the Company is not required to make any payment to or in respect of the Pension Scheme except as provided in paragraph 2(B)(1); and
   (4) benefits are provided under the Pension Scheme for each Pensionable Employee who is in the employment of the Company at the end of the Interim Period but who does not qualify for short service benefits (within the meaning of Sched 16

to the Social Security Act 1973) under the Pension Scheme just as if he had qualified for such short service benefits.[95]

(B) Purchaser's Undertakings

The Purchaser shall procure that the Company:

(1)   pays or procures the payment of contributions to the Pension Scheme which accrue during the Interim Period in respect of the Pensionable Employees; and

(2)   complies in all other respects with the provisions of the Pension Scheme during the Interim Period.

[(C) Contracting-out in Interim Period

The Vendor and the Purchaser undertake to co-operate with each other with a view to procuring that the employment of the Pensionable Employees is contracted-out by reference to the Pension Scheme throughout the Interim Period under a contracting-out certificate (within the meaning of the Social Security Pensions Act 1975) in the name of the Company.]

3   WARRANTIES AND REPRESENTATIONS

The Vendor hereby warrants and represents to and for the benefit of the Purchaser in the following terms:

(1)   No Other Arrangements

Save for the Pension Scheme the Company is neither a party to nor participates in nor contributes to any scheme, arrangement or agreement (whether legally enforceable or not) for the provision of any pension, retirement, death, incapacity, sickness, disability, accident or other like benefits (including the payment of medical expenses) for any Relevant Employee or for the widow, child or dependant of any Relevant Employee.

(2)   No Assurances etc

Neither the Company nor any member of the Vendor's group:

(a)   has given any undertaking or assurance (whether legally enforceable or not) to any Relevant Employee or to any widow, child or dependant of any Relevant Employee as to the continuance, introduction, improvement or increase of any benefit of a kind described in (1) above; or

(b)   is paying or has in the last three years paid any benefit of the kind described in (1) above to any Relevant Employee or the widow, child or dependant of any Relevant Employee.

(3)   All Details Disclosed

All material details relating to the Pension Scheme are contained in or annexed to the Disclosure Letter including (without limitation) the following:

(a)   a true and complete copy of the documentation governing the Pension Scheme;

(b)   a true and complete copy of all announcements, explanatory literature and the like which have been issued to any Relevant Employee in connection with the Pension Scheme;

(c)   a true and complete copy of the report on the last actuarial valuation of the Pension Scheme prior to the date of this Agreement and of any subsequent written recommendations of an actuarial nature;

(*d*) a true and complete copy of the last audited accounts for the Pension Scheme prior to the date of this Agreement and details of any material change in the investment policy of the Pension Scheme since the date as at which those accounts were made up;

(*e*) details of any proposed amendment to the Pension Scheme which has been announced or is being considered;

(*f*) details of any discretionary increases to pensions in payment or in deferment under the Pension Scheme granted in the five years prior to the date of this Agreement;

(*g*) details of any discretionary practices which may have led any person to expect additional benefits in a given set of circumstances (by way of example, but without limitation, on retirement at the behest of the Company or in the event of redundancy); and

(*h*) details of the contributions paid to the Pension Scheme by the Company in the five years prior to the date of this Agreement.

(4) Contributions

Contributions to the Pension Scheme are not paid in arrear and all contributions and other amounts which have fallen due for payment have been paid and no fees, charges or expenses referable to the Pension Scheme for which the Company is or may become liable (whether wholly or in part) have been incurred but not paid and the Company has reimbursed any person who has paid any such fees, costs or expenses if and to the extent that the Company is or may become liable so to do.

(5) Company's Obligations

The Company:

(*a*) has been admitted to participation in the Pension Scheme on the same terms as apply to all other employers participating in the Scheme;

(*b*) has observed and performed those provisions of the Pension Scheme which apply to it;

(*c*) may terminate its liability to contribute to the Pension Scheme without notice, without the consent of any person and without further payment[; and

(*d*) has at all material times held or been named in a contracting-out certificate (within the meaning of the Social Security Pensions Act 1975) referable to the Pension Scheme].

(6) Pension Scheme

The Pension Scheme:

(*a*) apart from the benefits referred to at (*b*) below provides only money purchase benefits (within the meaning of the Social Security Act 1986, s 84(1));

(*b*) all benefits (which are not money purchase benefits as aforesaid) payable in the event of death while in employment to which the Pension Scheme relates are insured fully under a policy with an insurance company of good repute and there are no grounds on which that company might avoid liability under that policy;

(*c*) is an exempt approved scheme (within the meaning of the Income and Corporation Taxes Act 1988, s 592); and

(*d*) complies with and has at all times been administered in accordance with all applicable laws, regulations and requirements (including those of the Inland Revenue and of trust law).

(7) Litigation

The trustees of the Pension Scheme are not engaged in any litigation or arbitration proceedings and so far as the Vendor is aware no litigation or arbitration proceedings are pending or threatened by or against the trustees of the Pension Scheme and there are no facts likely to give rise to any litigation or arbitration.

(8) No Other Employer

The Company is the only employer for the time being participating in the Pension Scheme. No employer which has previously participated in the Pension Scheme has any claim under the Pension Scheme and in respect of any such employer the Pension Scheme has been partially wound up in accordance with its provisions.[96]

(9) Indemnities

In relation to the Pension Scheme or the assets or previous assets thereof neither the Company nor the trustees or adminstrator of the Pension Scheme has given an indemnity or guarantee to any person (other than in the case of the Company any general indemnity in favour of the trustees or administrator under the documentation governing the Pension Scheme).

4   DAMAGES FOR BREACH OF PENSION WARRANTIES

In determining the damages flowing from any breach of Warranties contained in paragraph 3, the Company shall be deemed to be under a liability:

(1) to provide and to continue any benefits of a kind referred to in that paragraph which are now provided or have been announced or are proposed; and

(2) to maintain and to continue (without benefits being reduced) the Pension Scheme and any other arrangements of a kind described in that paragraph which are now in existence or are proposed and any discretionary practices of a kind referred to in that paragraph which have hitherto been carried on.[97]

SEVENTH SCHEDULE

Vendor's Protection

1   NO OTHER REPRESENTATIONS

The Purchaser admits that it has not entered into this Agreement in reliance upon any representation or promise other than those incorporated in the Disclosure Letter or this Agreement.[98]

2   GUARANTEES

The Purchaser shall use its best endeavours to secure the release of the Vendor from the guarantees and other contingent liabilities listed in the Disclosure Letter for the purpose of this paragraph (offering its own covenant in substitution if requested by the Vendor) and shall in the meantime indemnify the Vendor and keep the Vendor indemnified against any liability (including costs damages and expenses) thereunder or which may be incurred in relation thereto.

3   LOAN ACCOUNTS

At Completion the Purchaser shall procure that the Company and the Subsidiaries shall repay to the Vendor [and its subsidiaries] the amounts owing to [them] as specified in the Disclosure Letter.

4   LIMITATION OF LIABILITY[99]

The provisions of this paragraph shall operate to limit the liability of the Vendor under or in connection with the Warranties and the Disclosure Letter and references to 'such liabilities' shall be construed accordingly. The parties agree as follows:

(1)   no liability shall attach to the Vendor unless the aggregate amount of such liabilities shall exceed the total sum of £   but if such liabilities shall exceed that sum the Vendor shall (subject to the other provisions hereof) be liable for the whole of such liabilities and not merely for the excess;

(2)   the aggregate amount of such liabilities shall not exceed £   ;

(3)   claims against the Vendor shall be wholly barred and unenforceable unless written particulars thereof (giving reasonable details of the specific matter or claim in respect of which such claim is made so far as then known to the Purchaser) shall have been given to the Vendor within a period of   years from the date hereof, but this item (3) shall not apply to claims arising under the fourth schedule or to claims which (or delay in the discovery of which) is the consequence of fraud, wilful misconduct or wilful concealment by the Vendor or any officer or employee, or former officer or employee of the Vendor;

(4)   if the Vendor makes any payment by way of damages for breach of the Warranties and within twelve months of the making of the

relevant payment the Company, the Subsidiaries or the Purchaser receives any benefit otherwise than from the Vendor which would not have been received but for the circumstances giving rise to the claim in respect of which the damages payment was made the Purchaser shall, once it or the relevant company has received such benefit, forthwith repay to the Vendor an amount equal to the lesser of (*a*) the amount of such benefit and (*b*) the damages payment in question.

5   AVOIDANCE OF DOUBLE CLAIMS

In the event that the Purchaser is entitled to claim under paragraph 2(A) of the fourth schedule or under the Warranties in respect of the same subject matter the Purchaser may choose to claim under either or both but payments under paragraph 2(A) of the fourth schedule shall pro tanto satisfy and discharge any claim which is capable of being made under the Warranties in respect of the same subject matter and vice versa.

NOTES

Clause 1

1   Retain the definition of 'Completion' even if completion is to be simultaneous with the signature of the agreement.

2   The disclosure letter qualifies the warranties given in Sched 3 (see cl 7(A)). Schedule 3 provides for the following to be included in (or annexed to) the disclosure letter: audited accounts (para 1(1)); memorandum and articles of association (para 2(5)); management accounts (para 2(20)); particulars of insurances (para 2(26)); particulars of intellectual property and intellectual property agreements (para 2(21)); particulars of properties (para 2(33)); statement of bank accounts (para 2(49)); and schedule of employees (para 2(55)). Schedule 4 requires the following: elections for group income (para 4(6)); agreements relating to the surrender of ACT (para 4(7)); agreements relating to group relief (para 4(11)); and details of elections (para 4(21)). Para 4(3) or para 8(3) of Sched 6 requires particulars of pension schemes to be included. The accuracy of the disclosure letter is warranted by Sched 3, para 2(57), and Sched 7, para 2, refers to guarantees and other contingent liabilities of the vendors to be listed in the disclosure letter for the purpose of indemnity. The scheme of the agreement is to oblige the vendors to make all disclosures by way of the disclosure letter (see p 67). A precedent disclosure letter will be found on p 301.

3   Although unlikely to have any adverse effects in the context of this agreement, the combination of items (1) and (2) can produce unlooked-for results when the meaning of a key definition such as 'subsidiary' is changed.

4   Vendors will bear this in mind when considering the warranties and in some cases (eg Sched 3, para 2(57)) they may resist it. If time is short or if secrecy must be maintained during the negotiations vendors will wish to delete or qualify the statement, eg by saying they have enquired only of named individuals.

Clause 3

5   Sub-clause (B) provides for a vendor placing (see p 90). It seems best to specify the consideration as shares, rather than as a sum of money to be satisfied by the issue of shares, as it may be argued on the authority of *Spargo's Case* (1873) 8 LR Ch App 407 that the latter amounts to an issue for cash requiring the authority of a special resolution under the Companies Act 1985, s 95, but see *Stanton (Inspector of Taxes) v Drayton Commercial Investment Co Ltd* [1982] STC 585 where the consideration was stated as a price to be satisfied by the issue of shares at an agreed value and it was held that the consideration was shares, and their value, for tax purposes, was the value agreed between the parties. See also the Companies Act 1985, s 738(2). The purchaser may wish to include a provision restricting the disposal of any of the consideration shares which are not to be placed. The sub-clause contemplates that the vendors have stipulated a fixed cash sum to be realised by a placing as opposed to a fixed number of shares or a number of shares to be ascertained by eg reference to the quoted price. For a precedent vendor placing agreement, see p 312.

6   See, for instance, Table A, reg 104, relating to the apportionment of dividends. The purchaser's articles should be checked.

Clause 4

7   Pre-conditions to completion do normally prevent the vendors ceasing to be the beneficial owners of the shares at the time the contract is signed (see *Wood Preservation Ltd* v *Prior* [1968] 2 All ER 849 and, on appeal, at [1969] 1 All ER 364; and *IRC* v *Ufitec Group Ltd* [1977] 3 All ER 924). Vendors may insist that the purchaser undertakes to convene the necessary meeting and to apply for, and use its best endeavours to obtain, a listing for the consideration shares.

8   Amend if an increase of capital or authorisation of allotment under the Companies Act 1985, s 80, is unnecessary. If the acquisition requires shareholder approval by the purchaser insert this as a condition (this may apply even though the consideration is cash: see p 5). The purchaser will resist a commitment to recommend the acquisition to shareholders as changing circumstances may mean that directors cannot recommend the transaction, bearing in mind their fiduciary duties.

9   If there is a placing the brokers will insist that their obligations are conditional upon the listing of the consideration shares so that the inclusion of this condition in the acquisition agreement itself becomes vital. In any event, the vendors are likely to insist upon it if they are retaining consideration shares. See p 95 as to the implications of including a condition in this form. It is not considered necessary to refer to 'The International Stock Exchange of the United Kingdom and the Republic of Ireland Limited'. Other conditions might include 'the Office of Fair Trading indicating, in terms satisfactory to the [Vendor and] Purchaser that it is not the intention of the Secretary of State for Trade and Industry to refer the proposed acquisition of the Company [or the Subsidiaries] or any matter arising therefrom to the Monopolies and Mergers Commission' (see p 12).

10   Even where completion is simultaneous with signing this clause should be retained as a checklist.

11   Item (*b*) may be necessary if the vendors have granted pre-emption rights to third parties. Pre-emption rights under the target's articles will not be relevant in the case of a single corporate Vendor.

12   Delays in stamping the transfers where adjudication is required will often mean that the purchaser will not be registered for some time after completion and in such a case it is a useful precaution to take a power of attorney. Inclusion of the power of attorney in the agreement would require the agreement to be under seal and, in any event, the power should be granted by the registered holder(s) who are not necessarily the vendor. For a precedent power of attorney see p 311. Notwithstanding delays in registration it is good practice for the board of the target to approve the transfers at completion so as to perfect the purchaser's title as far as possible.

13   See precedent letter of resignation on p 310. Note that the acknowledgement that the director has no claim for compensation does not necessarily bar a claim for redundancy pay or for unfair dismissal (Employment Protection (Consolidation) Act 1978, s 140); hence the concluding words of the sub-clause. In a case where there is any real possibility of a director claiming compensation the conciliation officer procedure should be used (see p 33).

14   Vendors agreeing to this should be aware of the provisions of the Companies Act 1985, s 390, which provides for the form of notices of resignation and their filing at the Companies Registration Office.

15 See p 58. The property warranties are contained in Sched 3, para 2(35) to (37). If time permits, the certificate can be given on exchange (in which case the vendors should refer to it in the disclosure letter so as to qualify the warranties).

16 This may not be possible if the properties are mortgaged.

17 A purchaser may wish the books (other than the register of members which should be checked on completion) to be handed over at the target's offices rather than at completion.

18 The purchaser will certainly wish to change nominees if they are directors who are retiring.

19 Unless it is the vendors themselves who are to enter into the service agreements it will be appropriate to obtain commitments from the executive concerned.

20 If this sub-clause is not included and time is not made of the essence, the party not in default will have to make it so by giving reasonable notice if it wishes to rescind by reason of failure to complete. The sub-clause is obviously unnecessary if completion is simultaneous with exchange. Note cl 8(D) with regard to the right of rescission.

Clause 5

21 Any accountants' investigation should have been concluded before exchange of contracts, but it is always useful for a purchaser to have access to the target's books. Vendors may object to this while the agreement remains conditional.

Clause 6

22 Purchasers sometimes feel that the inclusion of this sub-clause casts doubt upon the reasonableness of the restrictions and prefer a firm statement that they are reasonable for the preservation of the target's goodwill.

23 See p 14.

Clause 7

24 See p 67.

25 See p 69.

26 This is sometimes drafted as a restatement of the warranties at completion, with an exception for breaches outside the Vendor's control.

27 As to the right to rescind, see p 67, and note cl 8(D). Sub-clauses (D), (E) and (F) are not necessary if completion is simultaneous with exchange. Vendors sometimes ask for provision that rescission is not possible after completion.

28 It is difficult to draft these provisions satisfactorily. If the period referred to in subcl (I) is not co-terminous with the limitation period (as reduced, if applicable: see eg Sched 7, para 4) and if the purchaser notifies a claim and withholds a larger amount than that eventually due, any excess will be available against another claim notified after the end of the period stipulated in sub-cl (I). If any of the vendors is a company, it is open to question whether these sub-clauses evidence a charge on intangible moveable property registerable under the Companies Act 1985, s 395 et seq. It is suggested that they do not, but nothing is lost by registration.

Clause 8

29   See p 64. It will be appreciated that the concluding words of the first sentence will not be effective in all circumstances.

29A   See p 75. Although this clause should enable the purchaser to release any one of the vendors without thereby releasing the others, it may not release the vendor in question from his liability to make a contribution if he has acaccepted joint liability (see the Civil Liability (Contribution) Act 1978, s 1(3)). This is, of course, not the concern of the purchaser.

30   If any of the parties is foreign, consider the appointment of a process agent.

Third schedule

Para 1

31   For a general note on warranties, see p 66. The warranties contained in the schedule are extensive and it is unlikely that they would all be appropriate in any particular transaction.

32   The definition of connected persons is wide-ranging and, in relation to an individual, includes relatives, partners, trustees of settlements of which the individual is a settlor and companies controlled by the individual; it also includes companies under common control.

The Company's Constitution

33   The Companies Act 1985, s 380, applies to special resolutions; extraordinary resolutions; resolutions which have been agreed to by all the members of the company, but which, if not so agreed to, would not have been effective for the purpose unless, as the case may be, they have been passed as special resolutions or as extraordinary resolutions; similar resolutions or agreements which have been agreed to by all the members or some class of shareholders; a resolution passed by the directors of a company in compliance with a direction under s 31(2) (change of name on Secretary of State's direction); a resolution of a company to give, vary, revoke or renew an authority to the directors passed under s 147(2) (alteration of memorandum on ceasing to be a public company, following acquisition of its own shares); a resolution conferring, varying, revoking or renewing authority under s 166 (market purchase of company's own shares); a resolution for voluntary winding-up, passed under s 572(1)(a); and a resolution passed by the directors of an old public company under the Companies Consolidation (Consequential Provisions) Act 1985, s 2(1), that the company should be re-registered as a public company.

The Company and the Law

34   See p 14.

The Company's Accounts and Records

35   The vendors will object to warranting that the accounts are 'true and accurate in all material respects' preferring to restrict their warranty to the wording of the auditors' report on the accounts (which, of course, may vary depending upon the type of target).

36   Changes in stock valuation or in the bases and policies of accounting can, of course, affect the recorded profits of the target. Such policies should be stated

by way of note of the accounts (see Statement of Standard Accounting Practice No 2: 'Disclosure of Accounting Policies').

37 The wording of this warranty will frequently be the subject of negotiation. Vendors will be alert to ensure, by appropriate words in the disclosure letter, that they do not indirectly warrant the 'accuracy' of management accounts under warranty (57). This is a point which may also apply to other annexures to the disclosure letter.

The Company's Business

38 Note cl 8(D).

39 The vendors may object to giving warranties as to the 'prospects' of the company and may wish this to be qualified, eg to the best of their knowledge and belief.

40 Vendors who themselves seek insurance against liability under warranties will find insurers wary of this warranty.

The Company's Assets

41 See p 72.

42 Vendors may regard this as an indemnity rather than a warranty. Insurers of warranty liabilities will normally exclude it from cover.

The Company and its Employees

43 It is envisaged that the schedule of employees will show not only remuneration but also length of service, age, position held etc. In the case of a target with a large number of employees, the purchaser may waive the requirement except in respect of employees earning more than a specified amount.

Material Disclosure

44 Vendors who dishonestly conceal material facts may be liable under the Financial Services Act 1986, s 47 (see p 49).

Fourth Schedule

Para 1

45 For a general discussion of this schedule see p 152.

46 'Audited Accounts' may be replaced by completion accounts where the fifth schedule applies and if there is a pound for pound adjustment in the price for a reduction in net asset value of the target (see p 203). If this refers to the completion accounts it is best to change 'this Agreement' to 'the Warranties' in Sched 5, para 5 (see p 208).

47 This item is included to cover close company apportionments, or apportionment pursuant to the controlled foreign companies legislation.

48 This includes the application of the Taxes Act 1988, ss 240 and 410 (arrangements under which the target is deemed to cease to be a member of a group).

49 This includes foreign tax paid for which unilateral double tax relief available.

50 'Taxation claim' includes claims made against the purchaser to cover any

potential liability levied on the purchaser pursuant to the Taxes Act 1988, s 347 and the VAT Act 1983, s 29. See also cl 1(6)(*d*).

51   A satisfied claim is included to prevent the vendor from avoiding liability under the fourth schedule by satisfying a matter that would otherwise be the subject of a taxation claim immediately before completion and reducing the net assets of the target.

52   This allows the purchaser to make a claim where a loss or relief (most commonly trading losses) available to the target is lost. If the purchaser is not paying for the losses, then the vendor may seek to limit the purchaser's right to recover. If the purchaser or his financiers are buying on the basis of profit projections which take into account the availability of tax losses as a tax shelter, then they will require the vendor to indemnify the purchaser for the loss of any losses (and perhaps warrant the existence of the losses). If the purchaser is buying at a price calculated by reference to net asset value, then the vendor may wish to exclude any loss save to the extent that it has been taken into account in computing (and so reducing or eliminating) any provision for deferred taxation.

53   Capital gains that have accrued, but have not been realised, and perhaps for which no deferred tax provision has been made may also be included in the scope of the indemnity. Vendors may wish to make an amendment to cover this point.

54   A grossing up mechanism (see p 154).

55   Vendors may seek to include change in practice. This should be stated to be published practice only. Published practice should not include arrangements to which a tax authority is a party, the text of which is not available to all members of the public.

56   The definition of taxation includes stamp duty, however the schedule is not an indemnity for stamp duty but an adjustment to the price, so the Stamp Act 1891, s 117 should not apply.

57   Any problems which it is agreed will be for the vendor's account should be referred to here, particularly if they could be said to have arisen in the ordinary course of business (see para 1(6)(*c*)).

Para 2

58   The reference to rates of taxation current at the date of the loss of the relief in cl 2(2)(*b*) is arbitrary but to specify or even ascertain when the economic loss is suffered by the target is in practice, impossible.

59   This excludes (*a*) relief from the purchaser's group or (*b*) relief the economic burden of which has been borne by the purchaser (ie which arises after completion) but allows a corporate vendor to satisfy a taxation claim by using group relief.

60   This is again arbitrary; although it is possible to set out a clause which would specify the date when the economic loss is suffered, in practice the date may not be ascertainable.

61   Disclosure should not apply to paras 1 and 2 of the fourth schedule. If there is any matter which the vendor wishes to exclude, then it should be dealt with by express exclusion in para 1(6) referring specifically to the tax liability, ie to the

type of tax involved and the amount in question, rather than the circumstance giving rise to the claim.

62   This does not cover an over-provision for deferred taxation as this is not an over-provision in the amount of taxation that is due, only an over-estimate of the amount which may become due in the opinion of the directors as applied in accordance with SSAP 15.

Warranties

62A   If the company has no subsidiaries delete definition of 'group relief' and warranties (7), (11), (28) and (47)(*d*).

63   If the company is not and has not been a close company omit the remainder of this warranty.

Fifth Schedule

64   These provisions must be discussed with the purchaser's accountants and amplified where necessary. The key question is whether the 'net tangible assets' will be clearly shown.

65   For authority on the words 'act as expert and not as arbitrator', see *Arenson* v *Arenson* [1977] AC 405; *Campbell* v *Edwards* [1976] 1 WLR 403; *Barber* v *Kenwood Manufacturing Co Ltd* [1978] 1 Lloyd's Rep 1975; and *Burgess* v *Purchase & Sons (Farms) Ltd* [1983] 2 WLR 361.

66   The drafting attempts to ensure that the purchaser is not precluded from claiming damages is a result of a breach of warranty because the matter concerned is taken into account in the completion accounts. However, the amount taken into account is deducted from the claim. See note 45.

Sixth Schedule (Pensions [Company has own final salary scheme])

67   There are two alternative sixth schedules to the individual vendor's agreement, to deal with (*a*) a target which has a final salary scheme; and (*b*) a target which has a money purchase scheme.

68   If increased only annually under the pension scheme the purchaser should require the assumed increases in pensionable pay to apply from the last annual review date and not completion. Alternatively the purchaser may require the past service liabilities to be based on actual earnings at completion.

69   The exclusion of debts of the target may be inappropriate if there are to be completion accounts.

70   The vendor may wish to aggregate if the surplus in one scheme can be used to offset a deficit in another.

71   For authority on the words 'act as expert and not as arbitrator', see *Arenson* v *Arenson* [1977] AC 405; *Campbell* v *Edwards* [1976] 1 WLR 403; *Baber* v *Kenwood Manufacturing Co Ltd* [1978] 1 Lloyds Rep 175; and *Burgess* v *Purchase & Sons (Farms) Ltd* [1983] 2 All ER 4.

72   Where the consideration for the acquisition is small, consider wording such as that contained in Sched 4, para 2(C) (see p 192) in place of 'by way of adjustment to the consideration for the sale shares'.

73   See p 39.

Sixth Schedule (Pensions [money purchase scheme])

74   See p 39.

Seventh Schedule

75   See p 64.

76   See p 74.

Sixth Schedule (Pensions [Company participates in group final salary scheme])

77   There are three alternative sixth schedules to the corporate vendor's agreement, to deal with (*a*) a target which participates in a group scheme; (*b*) a target which has its own final salary scheme; and (*c*) a target which has, or participates in, a money purchase scheme.

78   See note 68.

79   The appropriate method of investment adjustment will depend upon how the pension scheme is invested and the number of employees involved. There is no particular justification for either side trying to make a profit out of the transitional arrangements and so the adjustment should be one which can be reasonably obtained by the pension scheme.

80   If pensionable pay is increased annually under the pension scheme the vendor may wish to provide for the Membership Transfer Date to fall before the next annual review date so as to immunise the scheme from pay increases granted after completion.

81   It may be possible to dispense with the need for consents (see p 39). If they are to be obtained the vendor may wish to approve the form in which they are given.

82   The vendor may seek to aggregate the transfers if a deficit in one scheme can be made good by transferring surplus from another.

83   The vendor may require the purchaser to contribute to the administrative expenses either by making a direct payment to the vendor or by making an additional deduction in (*b*) of the definition of 'Transfer Value'. The vendor may also wish to include protective provisions preventing the target increasing the liabilities under the pension scheme during the transitional period (see p 38).

84   The purchaser should ensure that the shortfall provisions do not constitute a penalty (see *Export Credits Guarantee Dept* v *Universal Oil Products Company* [1983] 2 All ER 205 and *Alder* v *Moore* [1961] 1 All ER 1). The vendor may require certain deductions to be made in calculating the shortfall (see p 38). Where the consideration for the acquisition is small, consider wording such as that contained in Schedule 4, para 2(C) (see p 254) in place of 'by way of adjustment to the consideration for the Sale Shares'.

85   See note 4 on p 90.

86   See p 39.

Sixth Schedule (Pensions [Company has own final salary scheme])

87   If increased only annually under the pension scheme the purchaser should require the assumed increases in pensionable pay to apply from the last annual

review date and not completion. Alternatively the purchaser may require the past service liabilities to be based on actual earnings at completion.

88   The exclusion of debts of the target may be inappropriate if there are to be completion accounts.

89   The vendor may wish to aggregate if the surplus in one scheme can be used to offset a deficit in another.

90   For authority on the words 'act as expert and not as arbitrator', see *Arenson* v *Arenson* [1977] AC 405; *Campbell* v *Edwards* [1976] 1 WLR 403; *Baber* v *Kenwood Manufactauring Co Ltd* [1978] 1 Lloyd's Rep 175; and *Burgess* v *Purchase & Sons (Farms) Ltd* [1983] 2 WLR 36.

91   Where the consideration for the acquisition is small, consider wording such as that contained in Schedule 4, para 2(C) (see p 254) in place of 'by way of adjustment to the consideration for the sale shares'.

92   See p 39.

Sixth Schedule (Pensions [Money purchase scheme])

93   Delete if target's own scheme.

94   Schedule relies on statutory transfer power.

95   See p 38.

96   Delete if vendor's group scheme.

97   See p 39.

Seventh Schedule

98   See p 64.

99   See p 74.

Chapter 7

Other Documents

The following precedents and specimens are given in this chapter:
(a) Disclosure Letter;
(b) Completion Board Minutes;
(c) Letter of Resignation by directors of the target;
(d) Power of Attorney;
(e) Vendor Placing Agreement;
(f) Offer Circular complying with the terms of the Financial Services Act 1986 (Investment Advertisements) (Exemptions) (No 2) Order 1988; and
(g) Acquisition Circular to shareholders.

DISCLOSURE LETTER

[On letterhead of the Vendor or Vendor's solicitor]

The Directors
[Purchaser]

[Registered office]

Dear Sirs

[   ] **Limited**

(1)   Interpretation

(*a*) This letter, together with schedules A and B hereto and all documents
expressed to be annexed hereto or delivered herewith or deemed to be
incorporated herein, constitutes the Disclosure Letter as referred to in
clauses [(1) Interpretation] and [(7) Warranties] of the agreement
(the 'Agreement') proposed to be entered into today between
[Vendor] and [Purchaser] relating to the sale and purchase of shares in
[   ] Limited.

(*b*) Unless otherwise defined herein, or unless the context otherwise
requires, words and expressions used in this Disclosure Letter shall
bear the same meanings as are assigned to them in the Agreement and
subject thereto the provisions of clause [(1)   Interpretation] of the
Agreement shall apply to this Disclosure Letter, mutatis mutandis, as
they apply to the Agreement.

(*c*) Documents in schedule A and disclosures in schedule B are listed by
reference to clauses or to sub-paragraphs of paragraph [2 of the third
schedule, paragraph 3 of the fourth schedule and paragraph [4/8] of
the sixth schedule] to the Agreement for ease of reference only. All
disclosures shall be deemed to be made for all purposes of the
Agreement and not merely in relation to any sub-paragraph
specifically referred to.

(2)   General Disclosures

(*a*) This Disclosure Letter shall be deemed to include, and there are
hereby incorporated into it by reference and generally disclosed, the
following:

(i) the contents of all documents listed in schedule A [and of all
other documents referred to herein as being incorporated by
reference];

(ii) all matters contained or referred to in the Agreement and any
documents in, or expressed in the Agreement to be in, [agreed

terms] (whether or not the same are, in fact signed by or on behalf of the parties for identification);

(iii) [all information and all documents available from a search of the public files maintained by the Registrar of Companies in respect of [the Vendor and] the Company at [
19   ;]

(iv) [the statutory registers and books of the Company]; and

(v) [the documents of title in respect of the [Properties]];

(vi) [all matters that would be revealed by searches in relation to the [Properties] at the Land Registry, Land Charges Registry, or any appropriate local authority];

(vii) [all matters which are or would be revealed by a physical inspection of the Properties by a prudent purchaser and his professional advisers;]

(viii) [all matters contained or referred to in the [valuation reports and certificates of title] relating to [certain of] the [Properties] from [   ] to the Purchaser dated [   ]];

(ix) [all information and all documents available to public inspection or in respect of which a search may be made at the Trade Marks Registry];

(x) [all information contained in the report ('the Accountants' Report') on the Company prepared for the Purchaser by [   ] ('the Accountants');]

(xi) [all information, and the contents of all documents, made available to [   ] (as actuaries acting for the Purchaser) by the Vendor or [the Vendor's solicitors/actuaries] in connection with the actuarial review of [the Pension Scheme(s)]]; and

(xii) [the contents of all correspondence passing between the Vendor's solicitors and the Purchaser's solicitors in connection with the negotiation of the Agreement and the acquisition contemplated thereby];

[The provisions and contents of all such documents shall in the event of inconsistency prevail over the provisions and contents of any summary of any document(s) contained in this Disclosure Letter unless otherwise expressly stated in the summary.]

(3) Specific Disclosures

Without prejudice to the generality of the foregoing we disclose the matters set out in Schedule B hereto.

(4) Acknowledgement

Signature by you of the enclosed copy of this letter constitutes an acknowledgment of receipt of this letter (including Schedules A and B hereto) and of copies of the documents specified in Schedule A hereto as annexed hereto, and your acceptance of the terms hereof. Please sign and return the enclosed copy of this letter.

[if on the vendor's solicitors letterhead:]

5 Disclaimer
This letter is written on behalf of the Vendor and is given without liability on the part of this firm or any of its partners or employees.]

Yours faithfully,

....
[For and on behalf of [Vendor]

[ON COPY:
We acknowledge receipt of the letter (including Schedules A and B thereto) a copy of which is set out above and of copies of the documents specified in Schedule A, and accept the terms thereof.

....
For and on behalf of [Purchaser]]

SCHEDULE A

Part I Documents copies of which are annexed hereto

A Documents by reference to particular Clauses and Warranties
Clause/Schedule/Paragraph   Document

1(A)(6)   List of particulars of the Properties.

Third Schedule
1(1)   Audited Accounts.
1(6)   List of Intellectual Property.
1(7)   List of Intellectual Property Agreements.
2(5)   Copy of the memorandum and articles of association of the Company and its Subsidiaries.
2(20)   Copies of Management Accounts.
2(27)   Particulars of all the Company's and the Subsidiaries' insurances.
2(48)   Details of overdrafts, loans and other financial facilities with copies of documents relating thereto.

2(50)	Statement of all the bank accounts of the Company and the Subsidiaries and of the credit or debit balances on such accounts.
2(52)	Schedule of employees.

Fourth Schedule

4(6)	Particulars of all elections made by the Company and the Subsidiaries under Income and Corporation Taxes Act 1988, s 247.
4(7)	Particulars of all arrangements and agreements to which the Company and the Subsidiaries is or has been a party relating to the surrender of advance corporation tax made or received by the Company and the Subsidiaries under Income and Corporation Taxes Act 1988, s 240.
4(11)	Particulars of all arrangements and agreements relating to group relief to which the Company or one of the Subsidiaries is or has been a party.
4(21)	Details of elections under the Income and Corporation Taxes Act 1988, ss 524 and 534 (lump sum receipts for patents and copyright) and the Finance Act 1985, s 57 (short life assets).

Sixth Schedule

	All material details relating to the Pension Scheme including:
4/8(3)(a)	Copy documentation governing the Pension Scheme.
4/8(3)(b)	Copy announcements and explanatory literature issued to any Relevant Employee.
4/8(3)(c)	Copy Report on last actuarial valuation of the Pension Scheme.
4/8(3)(d)	Copy last audited accounts for the Pension Scheme.
4/8(3)(e)	Proposed amendments to the Pension Scheme.
4/8(3)(f)	Discretionary increases to pensions in payment or in deferment under the Pension Scheme granted in the five years prior to the date of the Agreement.
4/8(3)(g)	Discretionary practices which may have led any person to expect additional

4/8(3)(*h*)

benefits in a given set of circumstances. Contributions paid to the Pension Scheme by the Company and the Subsidiaries in the five years prior to the date of the Agreement.

Seventh Schedule

2

List of guarantees and other contingent liabilities.

3

Details of amounts owed to the Vendor by the Company and the Subsidiaries.

B *Other documents*

No	*Date*	*Parties*	*Document*

Initials

For Vendor................. For Purchaser ....

Part II **[Documents copies of which have been delivered to the Purchaser or its financial adviser, solicitors or accountants**

No	*Date*	*Parties*	*Document*

Initials

For Vendor................. For Purchaser ....

SCHEDULE B

Disclosures by reference to particular Warranties (for ease of reference only)

Schedule/Paragraph   *Warranty*   *Disclosure*
[*Third Schedule*]

[*Fourth Schedule*
(for information only)]

[*Sixth Schedule*]

Initials

For Vendor..................   For Purchaser ....

COMPLETION BOARD MINUTES

[These minutes will require to be reproduced and adapted in relation to Subsidiaries.]

[   ] LIMITED

MINUTES of a Meeting of the Board of Directors of the Company held on [   ] 19   at   am/pm at [   ]

PRESENT

being a quorum.

IN ATTENDANCE

1   Transfers
There were produced to the meeting duly executed transfer forms, together with the relative share certificates, in respect of the following transfers:
Transferor   Transferee   Class of Shares   No of Shares

IT WAS RESOLVED that the transfers be and they are hereby approved and (subject to the transfer documents being duly stamped) that the names of the transferees be entered in the register of members of the Company in respect of the shares represented by the respective stock transfer forms and that the common seal of the Company be affixed to certificates issued in respect of the shareholdings of the transferees in accordance with the Articles of Association of the Company and that such certificates be issued to the transferees as appropriate.

2   Appointment of Additional Directors
IT WAS RESOLVED that upon conclusion of the meeting the following persons who have consented to so act be appointed new directors of the Company with immediate effect:

There were produced to the meeting forms 288 duly signed by the above consenting to act as directors.

3   Resignation of Directors
There was produced to the meeting letters of resignation from as directors of the Company and it was resolved that such resignations be and are hereby accepted with effect from the conclusion of the meeting.

4 Appointment of New Secretary

There was produced to the meeting a letter of resignation from
as Secretary of the Company and IT WAS RESOLVED that such
resignation be and it is hereby accepted with effect from the conclusion of the
meeting and that, with effect from the conclusion of the meeting
be appointed as Secretary of the Company in his place.

There was produced to the Meeting a form 288 notifying such resignation
and signed by the above named of consenting to act as Secretary of the
Company.

5 Registered Office

IT WAS RESOLVED that the registered office of the Company be changed
to   and that a duly completed form 287 be completed in respect
thereof.

6 Bankers

IT WAS RESOLVED that the authority of the Company's bankers,
           PLC,   Branch, be revoked and such branch be
notified accordingly forthwith and IT WAS RESOLVED THAT the
Company open a bank account with   Bank PLC,
Branch and that the resolutions contained in the Bank's standard form and
mandate, a copy of which is attached to the original of these minutes, be and
are hereby passed and that any Directors or the Secretary be and are hereby
authorised to sign cheques and all other documents relating to such account
in accordance with such resolutions.

7 Resignation of Auditors

There was produced to the Meeting written resignation of   with
effect from   19   together with their s 390(1) statement as
auditors of the Company and IT WAS RESOLVED that the same be
accepted with effect from the conclusion of the meeting.

8 Appointment of Auditors

IT WAS RESOLVED that   of   be appointed
Auditors of the Company with effect from the conclusion of the meeting.

9 Filings

IT WAS RESOLVED that the Secretary be instructed to submit all forms
and documents to the registrar of companies as necessary.

10 Conclusion

There being no further business, the meeting concluded.

Chairman

LETTER OF RESIGNATION

To the directors
[   ] Limited

I hereby resign as a director/the secretary of your company. I hereby release your company from any claim which I may have on any account whatsoever, including any claim for compensation for loss of office, breach of contract or for redundancy or unfair dismissal and I confirm that no arrangement is outstanding under which your company has or might have any obligation to me.

Dated   19

SIGNED, SEALED and DELIVERED
by
in the presence of

POWER OF ATTORNEY

To whom it may concern:

I, [Vendor] of [address] being the registered holder of 5,000 [ordinary] shares (the 'Shares') in [Target] Limited (the 'Company'), having sold the same to [Purchaser] plc (the 'Attorney') together with all rights now and hereinafter attaching thereto hereby:

(a) irrevocably appoint the Attorney, acting by any director or person acting pursuant to authority conferred by its board of directors, as my attorney to exercise in the Attorney's absolute discretion all rights attaching to the Shares or exercisable by me in my capacity as a member of the Company and declare that without prejudice to the generality of the foregoing the powers exercisable by the Attorney shall include the power to execute, deliver and do all deeds, instruments and acts in my name and on my behalf in pursuance of the foregoing and shall include the power to sub-delegate this power;

(b) declare that such power shall cease and determine upon my ceasing to be a member of the Company but without prejudice to any power exercised prior to such date and shall not, save as may be required by law, terminate on my previous death, bankruptcy or mental disorder and shall in connection with the Shares be accordingly binding upon any personal representation, trustee in bankruptcy or trustee in respect of any mental disorder;

(c) undertake to ratify all deeds, instruments and acts exercised by the Attorney in pursuance of this power; and

(d) undertake not to exercise myself any power exercisable by my Attorney hereunder.

This power of attorney shall be governed by and construed in accordance with English law.

Dated   19

SIGNED, SEALED and DELIVERED
by the said [Vendor]
in the presence of:

VENDOR PLACING AGREEMENT

THIS AGREEMENT is made the   day of   19

BETWEEN:

(1)   PLC ('the Purchaser') a company registered in England
under number   whose registered office is at
and
(2)   ('the Broker') a company registered in England under
number   whose registered office is at   .

WHEREAS:

(A) The Purchaser has entered into an agreement for the acquisition of
the whole of the issued share capital of   Limited.

(B) It is a term of the acquisition that £   of the consideration
is to be satisfied by the allotment, credited as fully paid, of ordinary shares of
     p each of the Purchaser which are to be placed.

(C) The Broker is willing to arrange a placing of shares of the Purchaser
on the terms of this Agreement.

NOW IT IS HEREBY AGREED as follows:

1   INTERPRETATION

(A) In this Agreement where the context admits:

(1) 'the Acquisition Agreement' means the Agreement dated
          19   for the acquisition by the Purchaser from
          of the whole of the issued share capital of
     Limited;

(2) 'the Balance Sheet Date' means   19   ;

(3) 'Consideration Shares' means the   ordinary shares of
     p each of the Purchaser to be allotted to the Vendors under
     clause [3] of the Acquisition Agreement;

(4) 'the Placing' means the placing of the Consideration Shares to be
     made pursuant to this Agreement;

(5) 'the Placing Documents' means the press announcement and the
     circular to the shareholders of the Purchaser in the form signed on
     behalf of the parties for identification;

(6) 'The Stock Exchange' means The International Stock Exchange of
     the United Kingdom and the Republic of Ireland Limited;

(7) 'the Vendors' means the persons named as vendors in the Acquisition
     Agreement;

(8) references to clauses are references to clauses hereof and references to
     sub-clauses or items are, unless otherwise stated, references to sub-
     clauses or items of the clause in which the reference appears.

(B) The headings are inserted for convenience only and shall not affect the
construction of this Agreement

2 CONDITIONS

Completion of this Agreement pursuant to clause 4 is conditional upon:
   (1) the completion of the sale and purchase of the shares of
       Limited in accordance with the Acquisition Agreement and in
       particular (but without limiting the generality of the foregoing) the
       allotment by the Purchaser of   ordinary shares of
                   p each of the Purchaser to the Vendors in accordance
       with the terms of the Acquisition Agreement, such allotment to be on
       terms that the Consideration Shares shall rank pari passu with the
       existing ordinary shares of   p each of the Purchaser and
       shall carry the right to receive in full all dividends and other
       distributions declared, made or paid after the date of this Agreement
       [save that they shall not carry the right to participate in the [interim]
       [final] dividend of the Purchaser for the year ending   19
               declared on   19   ; and
   (2) the admission by the Council of The Stock Exchange of the
       Consideration Shares to the Official List and such listing becoming
       fully effective;
and so that if such conditions are not fulfilled on or before   19
       this Agreement shall lapse save that clause 5(6) and clause 6(B) shall
continue to have effect and neither party shall make any claim against the
other in respect hereof, save for any antecedent breach or any breach of
clause 5(6) or 6(B).

3 BROKER'S OBLIGATIONS

(A) The Broker shall as agent for the Vendors arrange a placing of the
Consideration Shares so as to produce aggregate net cash proceeds of
£   and shall consult the Purchaser as to the identity of the placees
and use its best endeavours to ensure that the Consideration Shares are
placed with not less than   placees.

(B) The Purchaser hereby authorises the Broker to distribute or cause the
distribution of the Placing Documents in connection with the Placing to such
persons as it shall think fit.

4 COMPLETION

On the date on which the conditions referrred to in Clause 2 are satisfied:
   (1) the Purchaser shall deliver to the Broker a fully paid renounceable
       allotment letter in the form signed on behalf of the parties for
       identification in respect of the Consideration Shares duly renounced
       and will arrange for the immediate delivery to the Broker of split
       allotment letters against such allotment letter; and
   (2) subject to compliance with item (1), the Broker shall pay to the
       Vendors by [bankers draft] [cheque] drawn on a city office of a
       London clearing bank and made payable to   the sum of
       £   being the aggregate net proceeds of the placing.

5 PURCHASER'S OBLIGATIONS

The Purchaser undertakes to the Broker that it will:
  (1) forthwith make application through the Broker to the Council of The Stock Exchange for the Consideration Shares to be admitted to the Official List and will use its reasonable endeavours to secure that such listing is granted;
  (2) generally use its reasonable endeavours to ensure satisfaction of the conditions referred to in clause 2;
  (3) procure that the Vendors will renounce their entitlement to the allotment of the Consideration Shares free from all liens, charges, equities and encumbrances and together with all rights attaching thereto and will confirm the terms of such renunciation to the Broker;
  (4) not alter or waive the provisions of the Acquisition Agreement or grant any time for performance except as previously agreed by the Broker;
  (5) not make any public announcement or communication concerning the Placing without the Broker's prior consent; and
  (6) indemnify the Broker against all losses, claims, costs, charges and expenses (other than those specifically contemplated under this Agreement) which the Broker may suffer or incur, or which may be made against the Broker in connection with or arising out of the performance of its obligations under this Agreement and which are not due to the Broker's negligence or wilful default.

6 COMMISSION ARRANGEMENTS

  (A) If this Agreement shall become unconditional the Purchaser shall pay:
  (1) [Broker's commission plus VAT];
  (2) all the legal and out of pocket expenses of the Broker; and
  (3) all other expenses of or incidental to the Placing including (without limitation) any stamp or other duty payable on the issue of the Consideration Shares or otherwise in connection with the Placing.
  (B) In the event that the conditions referred to in Clause 4 are not fulfilled on or before   19   the Purchaser shall pay:
  (1) [minimum commission plus VAT]; and
  (2) the expenses referred to in sub-clauses (A)(2) and (A)(3).

7 WARRANTIES AND REPRESENTATIONS[1]

  (A) The Purchaser hereby warrants and represents to and for the benefit of the Broker in the following terms.
  (1) Subject to the passing of the resolution referred to in clause [4(A)(1)] of the Acquisition Agreement, the Purchaser has power under its Memorandum and Articles of Association to issue the Consideration Shares without any further sanction or consent and the Acquisition Agreement and this Agreement are duly authorised and constitute legally binding obligations of the Purchaser.

(2) All statements of fact contained in the Placing Documents are true and accurate in all material respects and all statements of opinion contained therein represent opinions which are reasonable and are honestly held and there are no other facts the omission of which makes misleading any statement contained in the Placing Documents, whether of fact or opinion, or which are material for disclosure to the Broker in the circumstances of the Placing.

(3) The consolidated audited accounts of the Company and its subsidiaries for the financial year ended on the Balance Sheet Date have been prepared in accordance with the requirements of all relevant statutes and generally accepted accounting principles and show a true and fair view of the assets and liabilities of the Company and its subsidiaries at the Balance Sheet Date and the consolidated profits of the Company and its subsidiaries for the financial year ended on the Balance Sheet Date.

(4) Since the Balance Sheet Date the Company and its subsidiaries have carried on business in the ordinary and usual course without entering into any contract or commitment which is unusual, onerous, or otherwise material for disclosure to the Broker in connection with the Placing.

(5) The Placing Documents, the allotment of the Consideration Shares and the Placing comply and will comply with the provisions of the Companies Act 1985, the Financial Services Act 1986 and the listing rules made thereunder and all other relevant statutes and regulations.

(6) Neither the Company nor any of its subsidiaries is in default under any instrument relating to borrowed money and no indebtedness of any of them has become payable or capable of being demanded before its due date for payment and, so far as the Company is aware, no event has occurred which, with the lapse of time or the giving of notice or both might result in any such indebtedness becoming so payable.

(B) In the event that any of the warranties contained in this clause proves to be inaccurate or misleading, the Broker shall have the right to determine its obligations hereunder in which case clause 6(B) shall apply as if the conditions there referred to had not been fulfilled.

8   Provisions Relating to this Agreement

(A) This Agreement shall be binding upon and enure for the benefit of the successors of the parties but shall not be assignable.

(B) This Agreement (together with any documents referred to herein) constitutes the whole Agreement between the parties hereto relating to its subject matter and no variations hereof shall be effective unless made in writing.

(C) The provisions of this Agreement, insofar as the same shall not have been performed at completion, shall remain in full force and effect notwithstanding completion.

(D) This Agreement shall be governed by and construed in accordance with English law and the parties hereby submit to the non-exclusive jurisdiction of the English courts.

(E) Time shall be of the essence of this Agreement.

AS WITNESS the hands of duly authorised representatives of the parties the day and year first before written.

Notes

1   See p 76. Although breach of these warranties may give rise to a right of rescission, it is unlikely, on the present state in the law, to found a warranty claim.

OFFER CIRCULAR

If you are in any doubt about this offer you should consult a person authorised under the Financial Services Act 1986, who specialises in advising on the sale of shares and debentures.[1]

RECOMMENDED OFFER

by

PURCHASER PLC[2]

to acquire the whole of the share capital of

TARGET LIMITED

The terms of the offer contained

in this document are recommended by all

the directors of

Target Limited[3]

Acceptances should be received by 3.00 pm on Tuesday 7 January 19   .
The procedure for acceptance is set out on page   .

---

[1] Schedule to The Financial Services Act 1986 (Investment Advertisements) (Exemptions) (No 2) Order 1988, para 8.

[2] Schedule, para 6. Schedule, para (2). Note that the offer must be recommended by all the directors.

[3] There is no provision for cases in which some directors are unable to participate.

TARGET LIMITED

(Registered in England No 7654321)

Directors:
A Feather
R Bow
J Quiver

Registered Office:
The Glade
Oakdene
Nottingham NX4 8MB

16 December 1988

To the shareholders

Dear Sir or Madam

Recommended cash offer for your shares

On 13 December 1988 your board and the board of Purchaser PLC ('Purchaser') reached agreement on the terms of an offer to be made by Purchaser for the whole of the share capital of Target Limited ('Target'). Details of this offer are set out in the accompanying letter from Purchaser. As you will see, you are being offered 200p in cash for each ordinary share of £1 of Target. Your directors and their financial advisers, Merchant Bank Limited, consider that the offer is fair and reasonable, having regard to the net asset value of Target and its profit record.

The financial effects of accepting the offer are set out in paragraph 5 of the letter from Purchaser and your attention is also drawn to paragraph 6 headed 'Taxation on Capital Gains'.

Your directors have received assurances from Purchaser that the rights of all employees of Target will be fully safeguarded.

Your directors unanimously recommend shareholders to accept the offer. Your directors, and certain other shareholders who together hold 438,300 shares (representing 43.83 per cent of the issued share capital of Target) have irrevocably undertaken to accept the offer in respect of their entire holdings.

Copies of the accounts of Purchaser for the year ended 31 December 1987 and the letter from Merchant Bank Limited dated 16 December 1988 addressed to the board of Target containing their advice on the financial implications of the offer are enclosed with this letter.[1] A statement by your board is set out in paragraph 2 of Appendix IV of the letter from Purchaser.[2]

Yours faithfully

A Feather
Chairman

[1] Schedule, para 12(*b*).
[2] Schedule, para 12(*c*).

PURCHASER PLC
(Registered in England No 123456789)

Directors:
R Hood (Chairman)
L John
A A Dale
M Marion
F Tuck MA
W Scarlett

Registered office:
Grove House
Sherwood Gardens
Nottingham NX2 3LZ

16 December 1988

To the shareholders of Target Limited

Dear Sir or Madam

RECOMMENDED OFFER BY PURCHASER PLC

1 Introduction

As stated in your chairman's letter set out on page   agreement has been reached between your directors and Purchaser PLC ('Purchaser') for Purchaser to make an offer ('the offer') to acquire, at a price of 200p in cash per share,[1] all the issued ordinary shares of Target Limited ('Target').

This document, which is issued to the shareholders of Target on 16 December 1988,[2] sets out the terms of the offer.

[1] The consideration must be cash, shares or debentures—Schedule, para 2(*f*).
[2] Schedule, para 9.

2 The Offer

Purchaser, as principal, hereby offers to acquire, on and subject to the terms and conditions set out herein, all the 1,000,000 ordinary shares of £1 each of Target ('Target shares') now in issue on the basis of 200p in cash for each Target share.

The Target shares will be acquired free from all liens, charges, equities and encumbrances and together with all rights and advantages now or hereafter attaching thereto, including rights to all dividends and other distributions declared, made or paid hereafter. Signature of the enclosed form of acceptance will constitute a warranty by the accepting shareholder to that effect in respect of the Target shares for which the offer is accepted.

Your directors have agreed to accept the offer in respect of their shareholdings[1] and, as stated in your chairman's letter, unanimously recommend all shareholders to accept the offer.

¹ Schedule, para 12(*d*).

3 Conditions of the Offer

The offer is subject to the following conditions and the further conditions and terms set out in Appendix I:

(*a*) valid acceptances being received by 3.00 pm on 7 January 1989 (or such later date(s) as Purchaser may from time to time decide and notify shareholders subject to paragraph 2(*c*) of Appendix I) in respect of 90 per cent of the shares comprised in the offer or such lesser percentage as Purchaser may decide, provided that the offer will not become unconditional unless Purchaser shall have acquired or agreed to acquire pursuant to or during the offer:

    (i) shares carrying more than 50 per cent of the voting rights then exercisable in general meetings of Target; and

    (ii) shares carrying more than 50 per cent of the votes attributable to the equity share capital of Target;¹ and

(*b*) notification being received that the Board of Inland Revenue are satisfied that the exchange to be effected under the share election referred to in paragraph 4 will be effected for bona fide commercial reasons and will not form part of any such scheme or arrangements as are mentioned in the Capital Gains Tax Act 1979, s 87(1).²

The offer will be open for acceptance by every shareholder for at least 21 days from the date of this document.³ In the event that the conditions set out above have not been fulfilled by the later of the dates referred to in paragraph 1 of Appendix I, the offer will lapse.

The offer is not conditional upon shareholders of Target approving or consenting to any payment or other benefit being made or given to any director or former director of Target in connection with, or in compensation or consideration for, his ceasing to be a director, or loss of any office held in conjunction with any directorship or, in the case of a former director, loss of any office which he held in conjunction with his former directorship and which he continued to hold after ceasing to be director.⁴

The directors of Target have the right to decline to register any transfer of Target shares but have resolved to sanction any transfer of Target shares to the Purchaser made pursuant to the offer. Save as aforesaid there are no restrictions on the transfer of Target shares other than those imposed by law.⁵

---

¹ This follows the wording of para 2(*c*) of the Schedule.
² See p 109.
³ Schedule, para 2(*d*).
⁴ Schedule, para 2(*e*). This is required by para 9 of the Schedule to be stated 'clearly' and is accordingly contained in the letter itself rather than relegated to an appendix.
⁵ Schedule, para 11(*u*).

4 Share Election

Holders of Target shares who validly accept the offer by 3.00 pm on 7 January 1989 may irrevocably elect ('the share election') to receive, subject to the limitation set out below, ordinary shares of £1 each in Purchaser ('Purchaser shares') instead of all or part of the cash consideration which they would otherwise receive under the offer. For the purpose of the share election, the value of each Purchaser share will be taken to be 130p, which is based on the middle market quotation of 130p at the close of business on 13 December 1988 (the latest practicable date for the purposes of finalising the terms of the offer).

The aggregate number of Purchaser shares to be issued under the share election will be limited to a total of 300,000 Purchaser shares, representing in value approximately 19.5 per cent of the total consideration. If share elections cannot be satisfied in full, such elections will be scaled down pro rata and the unsatisfied balance of the consideration will be paid in cash.

No fractions of a Purchaser share will be issued to Target shareholders accepting the offer. Such fractions will be aggregated and sold and the net proceeds will be distributed to the Target shareholders entitled thereto, but so that no individual amount of less than £1 will be distributed.

The Purchaser shares to be issued pursuant to the share election will rank pari passu in all respects with the existing Purchaser shares and will rank in full for all dividends declared, made or paid after the date of their allotment. The first dividend to which Target shareholders accepting the offer and making the share election will be entitled will be the final dividend in respect of Purchaser's financial year ending 31 December 1988 which would normally be paid in June 1989. There are no restrictions on the transfer of fully paid Purchaser shares save those imposed by law.[1]

---

[1] Schedule, para 11(*g*)(iii).

5 Financial Effects of Acceptance[1]

The effects of acceptance as shown below do not take account of the incidence of taxation. Your attention is drawn to paragraph 6.

(a) Capital Value
Target shares have not been quoted on any stock exchange and no meaningful comparison of capital values may therefore be made. On the basis of the statement of the net tangible assets of Target set out in Appendix II, derived from the most recent audited accounts, the net assets attributable to each Target share at 30 September 1988 were 41.2p.

(b) Income
The income available to shareholders of Target who accept the offer is dependent on individual circumstances and the manner in which the cash proceeds are reinvested.

A holder of 100 existing Target shares who accepts the offer and makes the share election would, if the election were satisfied in full, receive 153 Purchaser shares. On the assumptions:

(i) that the cash consideration is reinvested to yield 10 per cent gross (which could be achieved by reinvesting the cash consideration in government securities); and

(ii) of gross annual dividends for Purchaser at the rate announced in respect of its latest financial year ended 31 December 1987;

an accepting shareholder who received consideration (*a*) wholly in cash and (*b*) wholly in Purchaser shares, will benefit from an increase of income as follows:

	All cash consideration £	*All share consideration* £
Income from 100 Target shares	3.43	3.43
Income from £200 cash reinvested	20.00	–
Income from 153 Purchaser shares	–	14.21
Increase in income	£16.57	£10.78

¹ Schedule, para 11(g)(iv).

6 Taxation on Capital Gains

To the extent that they receive and retain their consideration in Purchaser shares Target shareholders will not, under present legislation, be deemed to have made a disposal for the purposes of United Kingdom capital gains tax. To the extent that shareholders receive their consideration in cash, they will be treated for capital gains tax purposes as making a disposal, or part disposal, as the case may be and may, therefore, depending on their circumstances, incur a liability to tax.

If you are in any doubt as to your tax position, you should consult your professional adviser.

7 Business of Target

Target was incorporated in 1894 to acquire a business which had been manufacturing archery targets since shortly before the battle of Agincourt in 1415. It now carries on business from a freehold factory, having a floor area of approximately 12,000 square feet, at Nuthall near Nottingham.

Further information relating to Target is set out in Appendix II.

8 Management and Employees

Purchaser has given assurances that it will have regard to the interests of employees of Target and that the rights of such employees, including existing pension entitlements, will be fully safeguarded.

9 Business of Purchaser

The Purchaser group is an international group with widespread interests in leisure industries. Companies in the Purchaser group are engaged in toxophily, windsurfing and other trivial pursuits. The turnover of the Purchaser group in the year ended 31 December 1987 amounted to some £32.5 million and profits before tax amounted to some £2.6 million. The Purchaser group has approximately 2,000 employees world-wide. Further information on Purchaser is set out in Appendix III.

All companies in the Purchaser group have traded profitably in 1988 and the directors of Purchaser believe that prospects are excellent and intend to continue their policy of expansion.[1]

[1] Schedule, para 11(*g*)(i).

10 Procedure for Acceptance

To accept the offer you should complete and sign part A of the enclosed form of acceptance and transfer in accordance with the instructions thereon.

To exercise the share election you should complete and sign part A and part B of the enclosed form of acceptance and transfer in accordance with the instructions thereon.

You should return the completed form together with your share certificates and any other documents of title for the number of shares for which you wish to accept the offer in the enclosed pre-paid, pre-addressed envelope to Purchaser PLC, Grove House, Sherwood Gardens, Nottingham NX2 3LZ (ref Target Offer) so as to arrive as soon as possible and in any event not later than 3.00 pm on 7 January 1989. The share election ceases to be available at that time.

Even if any document of title is not readily available, the form should nevertheless be completed and returned so as to arrive by the time and date stated and the document of title forwarded to Purchaser as soon as possible thereafter. Purchaser reserves the right to treat as valid any acceptance which is not entirely in order or not accompanied by the relevant documents of title, but in any case the consideration due will not be despatched until the acceptance is completely in order and the remaining documents or satisfactory indemnities have been received.

11 Settlement

No acknowledgement of receipt of documents will be issued but in the event of the offer becoming unconditional in all respects and provided the form of acceptance and transfer and your share certificates and other documents of title (if any) are in order, a cheque and, where applicable, definitive share certificates in respect of Purchaser shares will be posted in accordance with the authority contained in the form within seven days of the offer becoming unconditional in all respects or of the receipt of a valid acceptance (including all necessary documents of title or satisfactory indemnities therefor) whichever is the later.[1]

Application will be made to the Council of The Stock Exchange for the Purchaser shares to be issued pursuant to the offer to be admitted to the Official List. It is expected that dealings in such shares will commence on the first dealing day following that on which the offer becomes or is declared unconditional in all respects. Pending despatch of definitive certificates, transfers will be certified against the register.

If the offer lapses the completed form and share certificates and other documents of title (if any) will be returned to accepting shareholders by first class post not later than seven days thereafter.

All documents and payments sent by or to shareholders or their agents are sent at shareholders' risk.

Settlement of the consideration to which any shareholder is entitled under the terms of the offer will be implemented in full in accordance with the terms of the offer without regard to any lien, right of set-off, counter-claim or other analogous right to which Purchaser may otherwise be or claim to be entitled as against such shareholder.

[1] Schedule, para 11(*f*).

12 Additional Information

The Appendices to this letter contain:

I   Further conditions and terms of the offer.
II Further information relating to Target.
III Further information relating to Purchaser.
IV General information.

13 Documents Available for Inspection

Paragraph 7 of Appendix IV lists certain documents relating to Target and Purchaser which will be available for inspection free of charge at the place and at the time specified therein.[1]

[1] Schedule, para 10.

Yours faithfully

R Hood
Chairman

APPENDIX I
FURTHER CONDITIONS AND TERMS OF THE OFFER

1 Lapse

If condition (*b*) set out in paragraph 3 on page [000] of this document is not fulfilled prior to whichever is the later of 14 February 1989 and the expiration of 21 days after the offer becomes unconditional as to acceptances, then the offer will lapse.

2 Acceptance Period

(*a*) If the offer becomes unconditional as to acceptances, it will remain open until further notice and Purchaser will give not less than fourteen days' notice in writing to shareholders before it is closed.[1]

(*b*) The offer will not be revised or increased.

(*c*) The offer will not be capable of becoming unconditional as to acceptances after 3.00 pm on 14 February 1989 nor will it be kept open after that time unless it has previously become unconditional as to acceptances.[2]

[1] Schedule, para 11(*d*).
[2] Schedule, para 11(*c*).

3 Announcements

On the business day next following the day on which the offer is due to expire, or the day on which the offer becomes unconditional as to acceptances, Purchaser will notify shareholders by letter of the total number of shares (as nearly as practicable) for which acceptances of the offer have been received.

In any announcement of an extension of the offer the next expiry date will be stated. In computing the number of shares represented by acceptances, there may be included for the above purposes acceptances not in all respects in order or subject to verification.

4 Rights of Withdrawal

An acceptance shall be irrevocable.

5 General

(*a*) If circumstances arise in which an offeror is able compulsorily to acquire shares of any dissenting minority under Part XIIIA of the Companies Act 1985, Purchaser intends so to acquire those shares.

(*b*) The form of acceptance and transfer (including the instructions and notes thereon) shall be deemed to be an integral part of this document.

[1] Schedule, para 11(*e*).

APPENDIX II

FURTHER INFORMATION RELATING TO TARGET[1]

1 Secretary and Registered Office

A Quiver
The Glade, Oakdene, Nottingham NX4 8MB

2 Share Capital

The present called up share capital of Target is as follows:

	Authorised	Allotted and fully paid
Ordinary Shares of £1 each	1,500,000	1,000,000

3 Results Summary

The following is a summary of certain results of Target based on the published audited accounts for the five years ended 30 September 1988:

	Year ended 30 September				
	1984 £000s	*1985* £000s	*1986* £000s	*1987* £000s	*1988* £000s
Turnover	474	540	610	750	862
Profit before taxation	110	121	154	188	200
Total amount of dividends paid	18	20	22	24	24
Rate per cent of dividends paid (net)	1.8%	2.0%	2.2%	2.4%	2.4%

4 Net Assets

The following is a summary of the net assets of Target at 30 September 1988 based on the published audited balance sheet at that date:

	£000s	£000s
Fixed assets		
Tangible assets		341
Current assets		
Stocks	95	
Debtors	169	
Cash at bank and in hand	68	
	332	
Current liabilities — Amounts falling due within one year	(163)	
Net current assets		169
Total assets less current liabilities		510
Creditors — amounts falling due after more than one year	30	
Provisions for liabilities and charges	68	
	98	
Net assets attributable to shareholders		412

5   Abridged Accounts

The financial information set out above does not constitute full accounts of Target. Full accounts of Target for the five years ended 30 September 1988 have been delivered to the Registrar of Companies. The auditors of Target have made unqualified reports on all such accounts.[2]

[1] Schedule, para 11(*g*)(ii).
[2] Companies Act 1985, s 255.

APPENDIX III
FURTHER INFORMATION RELATING TO PURCHASER[1]

1   Secretary and Registered Office

F Tuck, MA
Grove House, Sherwood Gardens, Nottingham NX2 3LZ

2 Share Capital

The present called up share capital of Purchaser is as follows:

	Authorised	Allotted and fully paid
Ordinary Shares of £1 each	12,500,000	10,000,000

Purchaser has not issued any share capital since 31 December 1987, the date of the latest audited accounts of Purchaser and Purchaser has no securities in the nature of loan notes or debenture stock in issue at the date of the offer.

3 Results Summary

The following is a summary of certain results of Purchaser based on its published audited consolidated accounts for the five years ended on 31 December 1987.

Year ended on 31 December

	1983 £000s	1984 £000s	1985 £000s	1986 £000s	1987 £000s
Turnover	18,243	20,656	25,755	29,336	32,453
Profit before taxation	2,857	2,861	2,432	2,305	2,593
Profit after taxation	2,097	1,902	1,621	1,202	1,379
Total amount of dividends paid	300	300	337	450	650
Earnings per share	28.0p	25.4p	21.6p	12.0p	13.8p
Rate per cent of dividends paid (net)	4.0%	4.0%	4.5%	4.5%	6.5%

4 Summary of Consolidated Audited Balance Sheet of Purchaser as at 31 December 1987

	£000s	£000s
Fixed assets		
Tangible assets	18,309	
Investments	1,441	
		19,750
Current assets		
Stocks	2,290	
Debtors	4,826	

	£000s	£000s
Investments	613	
Cash at bank and in hand	302	
	8,031	
Creditors—amounts falling due within one year		
Finance debt	1,185	
Other creditors	4,113	
	5,298	
Net current assets		2,733
Total assets less current liabilities		22,483
Creditors—amounts falling due after more than one year		
Finance debt	4,283	
Other creditors	1,777	
		6,060
Provisions for liabilities and charges		657
		15,766
Represented by:		
Capital and reserves		
Called-up share capital		10,000
Share premium account		906
Reserves		4,860
		15,766

5   Half-year Results to 30 June 1988

The following information has been extracted from the announcement on 16 September 1988 regarding the unaudited consolidated results of the Purchaser group for the six months ended 30 June 1988:

	Six months ended 30 June		Year ended 31 December
	1988 £000s	*1987* £000s	*1987* £000s
Turnover	22,175	15,260	32,453
Profit before taxation	1,967	1,240	2,593
Profit after taxation	1,102	678	1,379
Earnings per share	11.0p	6.8p	13.8p

Dividends per share			
Interim	2.5p	2.0p	2.0p
Final			4.5p

In his accompanying remarks the chairman of Purchaser, Mr R Hood, commented on the improved profitability following the acquisition in 1987 of F Tuck & Sons Limited and M Marion & Sons Limited, both of which were now starting to make useful contributions to the group's results. As a consequence of these better prospects for the group, a higher interim dividend had been paid and it is hoped to match this increase again when the final dividend is declared.

6 Abridged Accounts

The financial information set out above does not constitute full accounts of Purchaser. Full accounts of Purchaser for the five years ended 31 December 1987 have been delivered to the Registrar of Companies. The auditors of Purchaser have made unqualified reports on all such accounts.[2]

[1] Schedule, para 11(*g*) (ii).
[2] Companies Act 1985, s 255.

APPENDIX IV
GENERAL INFORMATION

1 Responsibility

(*a*) The directors of Purchaser and Target have each taken all reasonable care to ensure that the facts stated and the opinions expressed in this document and those accompanying it are fair and accurate insofar as they relate to their respective companies and to themselves and that no material fact has been omitted, and each of them accepts responsibility accordingly.[1]

(*b*) The directors of Purchaser hereby state that the information in relation to Purchaser and to Purchaser shares contained in this document by virtue of subparagraph 12(*e*) of the Schedule to The Financial Services Act 1986 (Investment Advertisements) (Exemptions) (No 2) Order 1988, is correct.[2]

[1] Schedule, para 12(*g*)
[2] Schedule, para 12(*e*)

2 Statement of Directors of Target[1]

The directors of Target, acting as a board, hereby state that:
(*a*) There has not been any material change in the financial position or

prospects of Target since 30 September 1988, the date of the latest available accounts of Target.

(b) The interests which the directors of Target have in the securities of Target which are required to be inscribed in the register kept by Target under the Companies Act 1985, s 325 are as follows:

Director	Ordinary shares held beneficially		
	Held Personally	Family Interests	Percentage
A Feather	180,000	32,500	21.25
R Bow	98,000	12,750	11.07
J Quiver	4,000	–	0.4

(c) None of the directors of Target has any interests in the securities of Purchaser which would be required to be inscribed in the register kept by Purchaser under the Companies Act 1985, s 325, if any such director were a director of Purchaser.

(d) Save for the undertaking referred to in paragraph 3 below none of the directors of Target has any material interest in any contract entered into by Purchaser or in any contract entered into by any member of the group of which Purchaser is a member.

[1] Schedule, para 12(c). It is convenient, although slightly odd, to include this in the offer circular. The Schedule only requires the circular to be 'accompanied' by such a statement. It could be included in the letter from the chairman of the target set out at the front of the circular but would look even odder there.

3 Acceptance by Directors of Target[1]

The directors of Target have undertaken to accept the offer in respect of their beneficial shareholders and to procure acceptance in respect of their family shareholdings as set out in paragraph 2(b) above. These shareholdings represent in total 32.72 per cent of the Target shares.

[1] Schedule, para 12(d).

4 Disclosure of Interests[1]

(a) The following dealings in Target shares by the directors of Target and their families have taken place since 16 December 1987:

Director	Date of Transaction	Nature of Transaction	Number of Shares	Price per Share
A Feather	20 Dec 1987	Sale	3,000	£1.50
	14 Feb 1988	Purchase	1,200	£1.60
R Bow	3 March 1988	Purchase	3,000	£1.50

Save as aforesaid, none of the directors of Target nor any person who has been a director of Target since 16 December 1987 has dealt in the share capitals of Target or Purchaser since 16 December 1987.

(*b*) Neither Purchaser nor any person acting on behalf of Purchaser holds any securities of Target.

(*c*) None of the directors of Purchaser has dealt in the share capital of Purchaser or Target since 16 December 1987.

¹ Schedule, para 11(*m*).

5   General

(*a*) It is not proposed in connection with the offer that any payment or other benefit shall be made or given to any director or former director of Target in connection with or in compensation or consideration for his ceasing to be a director or loss of any office held in conjunction with a directorship or, in the case of a former director, loss of any office which he held in conjunction with his former directorship and which he continued to hold after ceasing to be director.¹

(*b*) Following the acquisition of Target, Mr A Feather is to be appointed a director of Purchaser. Save as aforesaid there is no arrangement made between Purchaser or any person with whom Purchaser has an agreement of the type described in the Companies Act 1985, s 204, and any of the directors or shareholders of Target or any persons who have been such directors or shareholders in the period since 16 December 1987 having any connection with or dependence on the offer.²

(*c*) There is no agreement or arrangement whereby any of the shares in Target acquired by Purchaser pursuant to the offer will or may be transferred to any other person. However, Purchaser reserves the right to transfer any of such shares to a nominee on its behalf or any company from time to time a member of the Purchaser group of companies.³

(*d*) All expenses of and incidental to the preparation and circulation of this document and any stamp duty payable on transfers of Target shares pursuant to the offer will be paid by Purchaser.

(*e*) There has not been, within the knowledge of Purchaser, any material change in the financial position or prospects of Target since 30 September 1988, the date of the latest available accounts of Target.⁴

(*f*) Merchant Bank Limited has given (and has not withdrawn) its consent to the issue of this document with the reference to its name in the form and context in which it appears.

¹ Schedule, para 11(*i*).
² Schedule, para 11(*j*).
³ Schedule, para 11(*k*).
⁴ Schedule, para 11(*l*).

6 Material Contracts[1]

The following contracts (not being contracts entered into in the ordinary course of business) are, or maybe, material:
 (i) agreement dated 1 April 1987 for the acquisition by Purchaser of F Tuck & Sons Limited from Mr F Tuck and members of his family for £1,185,000; and
 (ii) agreement dated 17 July 1987 for the acquisition by Purchaser of M Marion & Sons Limited from Miss M Marion for £3,200,000.

[1] Schedule, para 11(*g*).

7 Documents Available for Inspection[1]

Copies of the following documents will be available for inspection free of charge at the offices of Coke & Littleton, 1 Moor Alley, London EC3Z 2FL between 10.00 am and 4.00 pm on weekdays (Saturdays and public holidays excepted) so long as the offer remains open for acceptance:
 (i) the memorandums and articles of association of Target and Purchaser;
 (ii) the audited accounts of Target for the two years ended 30 September 1987 and 1988;
 (iii) the audited consolidated accounts of Purchaser for the two years ended 31 December 1986 and 1987;
 (iv) the letter dated 16 December 1988 from Merchant Bank Limited to the Board of Target;
 (v) the consent of Merchant Bank Limited referred to in paragraph 5 (*f*) above; and
 (vi) the contracts referred to in paragraph 6 above.

[1] Schedule, paras 2(*g*) and 10.

ACQUISITION CIRCULAR

PURCHASER PLC
(Registered in England under No 123456789)

Directors:
R Hood (Chairman)
L John
A A Dale
M Marion
F Tuck, MA
W Scarlett

Registered Office:
Grove House
Sherwood Gardens
Nottingham NX2 3LZ

15 December 1988

To the shareholders

Dear Sir or Madam

Acquisition of Target Limited

It was announced in the press on 25 November 1988, that Purchaser PLC ('Purchaser') had agreed terms for the acquisition by Purchaser from Mr A Feather and Mr R Bow of the whole of the issued share capital of Target Limited ('Target') at the price of £2,000,000 payable in cash on completion.

The acquisition was completed on 12 December 1988.

Business of Target

Target was incorporated in 1894 to acquire a business which had been manufacturing archery targets shortly before the Battle of Agincourt in 1415. It now carries on business from a freehold factory, having a floor area of approximately 12,000 square feet, at Nuthall near Nottingham.

A report by Messrs Profit and Loss, Purchaser's auditors, on the financial position of Target at 30 September 1984 to 30 September 1988 and of its results for the five years ended 30 September 1988 is set out in Appendix I. The report shows that the net tangible assets of Target on 30 September 1988 amounted to £412,000 and Target's profit before tax for the year ended 30 September 1988 was £200,150.

Purchaser sees this acquisition as a logical step in its programme of expansion in the toxophily industry in an area not so far covered by its operations. Purchaser has funded this acquisition from its own resources without recourse to further borrowings. The effect of the reduction in the group's cash balances will be more than offset by the increasing profit contribution which Target is expected to make following acquisition. Budgeted profit for Target in the year ending 30 September 1989 is £260,000.

Management and Staff

Mr Albert Feather (aged 57) has been an executive director of Target since 1966 and is responsible for overall policy and management. Mr Robert Bow (aged 33) joined Target in 1983 and was appointed a director of Target in 1987. He is responsible for export sales. Both have entered into service agreements with Target for a term of two years from 12 December 1988 as directors of Target. The Board of Target now comprises Mr R Hood, Mr L John, Mr F Tuck, Mr A Feather and Mr R Bow. There are some 100 employees of Target and Purchaser intends that their interests will be respected.

General

All companies in the Purchaser group have traded profitably in 1988 and your directors intend to continue their policy of expansion. Although no further acquisitions are currently in contemplation, your directors are alert for opportunities to acquire companies active in the more dangerous leisure activities.

A pro forma statement of net assets of the enlarged group is contained in Appendix II and information with regard to Purchaser and further information with regard to the acquisition is set out in Appendix III.

Yours faithfully

R Hood
Chairman

APPENDIX I

The following is a copy of a report received from Profit & Loss, Chartered Accountants, the auditors of Purchaser.

The Directors	Calculator House
Purchaser PLC	Strand
Grove House	London WC1 4LF
Sherwood Gardens	
Nottingham NX2 3LZ	15 December 1988

Gentlemen

A Introduction

On 12 December 1988, Purchaser PLC ('Purchaser') acquired the whole of the issued share capital of Target Limited ('Target'). The purchase consideration of £2,000,000 was satisfied in cash.

We have examined the audited accounts of Target for the five years ended 30

September 1988. These accounts were audited by Jones & Co, Chartered Accountants in accordance with approved auditing standards. The financial information set out below has been derived from the audited accounts of Target after making such adjustments as we consider appropriate. Our work in connection with this report has been carried out in accordance with the Auditing Guideline: Prospectuses and the reporting accountant.

In our opinion the financial information set out below gives a true and fair view of the results and source and application of funds of Target for the five years ended 30 September 1988 and of its state of affairs at 30 September 1984 to 30 September 1988.

No audited accounts have been prepared for Target subsequent to 30 September 1988.

B   Accounting Policies

The significant accounting policies which have been consistently applied in arriving at the financial information set out in this report are as follows:

1   *Accounting convention*
The accounts are prepared under the historical cost convention.

2   *Stocks*
Stock and work in progress are valued at the lower of cost and net realisable value. Cost represents materials, direct labour and an appropriate proportion of production overheads.

3   *Depreciation*
Fixed assets are depreciated to write-off their cost, which in the case of freehold buildings excludes an estimate by the Directors of the cost of land, by equal annual instalments over their expected useful lives as follows:

Freehold buildings	50 years
Plant and equipment	15 years
Motor vehicles	4 years

4   *Deferred taxation*
Deferred taxation is provided, using the liability method, on all material timing differences which are not expected to continue for the foreseeable future.

C   Turnover and Profits

The results of Target for the five years ended 30 September 1988 are as follows:

Year ended 30 September

	1984 £	1985 £	1986 £	1987 £	1988 £
Turnover (*note 1*)	474,126	540,310	610,222	750,190	862,140
Cost of sales	265,511	286,433	335,622	405,103	478,488
Gross profit	208, 615	253,877	274,600	345,087	383,652
Selling and distribution costs	(30,201)	(52,635)	(60,147)	(93,713)	(114,111)
Administrative expenses	(56,095)	(64,837)	(52,966)	(61,645)	(70,987)
Net operating income (*note 2*)	122,319	136,405	161,487	189,729	198,554
Other income	262	1,140	980	1,504	1,067
Net interest payable (*note 3*)	(12,706)	(16,159)	(8,040)	(3,621)	529
Profit before taxation	109,875	121,386	154,427	187,612	200,150
Taxation (*note 4*)	44,720	48,720	70,124	97,562	105,600
Profit after taxation	65,155	72,666	84,303	90,050	94,550
Extraordinary items (*note 5*)	37,160	–	(10,160)	–	–
Dividends (*note 6*)	(18,000)	(20,000)	(22,000)	(24,000)	(24,000)
Retained profit	£84,315	£52,666	£52,143	£66,050	£70,550

Notes

1 Turnover represents invoiced sales to customers, exclusive of value added tax.

2 Net operating income is stated after charging:

Year ended 30 September

	1984 £	1985 £	1986 £	1987 £	1988 £
Depreciation	19,678	22,450	31,373	33,658	42,300
Directors' remuneration	15,000	15,000	17,500	20,000	25,000
Staff costs	170,318	181,426	187,521	194,378	201,317
Audit fees	1,200	1,400	1,550	1,900	2,700
Hire and leasing charges	660	780	866	912	960

3   Net interest payable comprises:

Year ended 30 September

	1984 £	1985 £	1986 £	1987 £	1988 £
Bank loans and overdrafts repayable within five years	4,487	6,959	3,389	2,948	–
Other loans	8,417	9,451	5,138	1,147	–
	12,904	16,410	8,527	4,095	–
Interest receivable	(198)	(251)	(487)	(474)	(529)
Net interest payable/ (receivable)	£12,706	£16,159	£8,040	£3,621	£(529)

4   Taxation charge comprises:

Year ended 30 September

	1984 £	1985 £	1986 £	1987 £	1988 £
UK Corporation tax	41,800	36,550	64,000	95,000	108,000
Deferred taxation	2,920	12,170	6,124	2,562	(2,400)
	£44,720	£48,720	£70,124	£97,562	£105,600

5   The extraordinary item in the year ended 30 September 1984 related to the profit on sale of property less taxation of £15,926 thereon, and that in the year ended 30 September 1986 represents penalties paid in respect of the cancellation of a contract for capital expenditure.

6   Dividends per ordinary share declared and paid were:

Year ended 30 September

	1984	1985	1986	1987	1988
Rate per share (pence)	72p	80p	88p	96p	96p

D   Statement of Source and Application of Funds

The source and application of funds for each of the five years ended 30 September 1988 are as follows:

Year ended 30 September

	1984 £	1985 £	1986 £	1987 £	1988 £
Funds obtainable from:					
Profit before taxation	109,875	121,386	154,427	187,612	200,150
Depreciation	19,678	22,450	31,373	33,658	42,300
Extraordinary profit on sale of land	57,169	–	–	–	–
Funds generated from operations	£186,722	£143,836	£185,800	£221,270	£242,450
Funds used for:					
Dividends paid	18,000	18,000	20,000	22,000	24,000
Taxation paid	55,009	41,800	36,514	62,362	94,050
Additions to fixed assets	179,043	28,190	43,336	25,695	68,118
Cancellation penalty	–	–	10,160	–	–
Increase/(decrease) in working capital:					
Stocks	6,998	4,099	2,285	3,969	4,543
Debtors	19,870	1,412	22,511	24,039	11,008
Creditors excluding taxation and dividends	(4,005)	6,958	(3,972)	5,893	(6,343)
	22,863	12,469	20,824	33,901	9,208
Increase/(decrease) in liquid funds	(88,193)	43,377	54,966	77,312	47,074
	£186,722	£143,836	£185,800	£221,270	£242,450

E Balance Sheet

The balance sheets of Target at 30 September 1984 to 1988 are as follows:

At 30 September

	1984 £	1985 £	1986 £	1987 £	1988 £
FIXED ASSETS					
Tangible assets (*note 1*)	305,467	311,207	323,170	315,207	341,025

CURRENT ASSETS

Stocks (*note 2*)	80,117	84,216	86,501	90,470	95,013
Debtors (*note 3*)	110,200	111,612	134,123	158,162	169,170
Cash at bank and in hand	–	–	–	21,332	68,406
	190,317	195,828	220,624	269,964	332,589

CREDITORS — amounts falling due within one year (*note 4*)	245,149	191,564	170,056	142,821	163,114
Net current (liabilities)/assets	(54,832)	4,264	50,568	127,143	169,475
Total assets less current liabilities	250,635	315,471	373,738	442,350	510,500
CREDITORS — amounts falling due after more than one year (*note 5*)	30,000	30,000	30,000	30,000	30,000
Provision for liabilities and charges	50,044	62,214	68,338	70,900	68,500
Total assets less liabilities	£170,591	£223,257	£275,400	£341,450	£412,000

CAPITAL AND RESERVES					
Called-up share capital	25,000	25,000	25,000	25,000	25,000
Profit and loss account	145,591	198,257	250,400	316,450	387,000
	£170,591	£223,257	£275,400	£341,450	£412,000

Notes

1 Tangible assets comprise:

	Cost £	Depreciation £	Net Book amount £
Freehold property	208,007	37,920	170,087
Plant, equipment and motor vehicles	399,054	228,116	170,938
	£607,061	£266,036	£341,025

2   Stocks comprise:

	£
Raw materials	10,896
Work in progress	15,796
Finished goods	68,321
	£95,013

3   Debtors are analysed as follows:

	£
Trade debtors	163,975
Other debtors	1,400
Prepayments	3,795
	£169,170

4   Creditors falling due within one year are analysed as follows:

	£
Trade creditors	20,855
Sundry creditors	11,759
Bank loan	8,000
Corporation tax	98,500
Proposed dividend	24,000
	£163,114

5   Creditors falling due after one year comprise a secured bank loan repayable in 1990 on which interest is payable at 12 per cent per annum.

6   Deferred taxation represents:

	Amount provided	Full potential liability
Taxation deferred by capital allowances	£68,500	£80,000

7   The called up share capital at 30 September 1988 comprised:

	Authorised	Allotted and fully paid
Ordinary shares of £1 each	£25,000	£25,000

8   Target had contracted commitments for capital expenditure at 30 September 1988 of £65,000, of which £43,000 is in respect of leased plant, equipment and motor vehicles. The directors had authorised further capital expenditure of £12,000.

9   Target was a close company as defined in the Income and Corporation Taxes Act 1988 for all periods covered by this report. Clearances have been obtained, for all periods up to and including the year ended 30 September 1987, that the Inland Revenue will not seek to apportion Target's income in accordance with the provisions of the Income and Corporation Taxes Act 1988, ss 423 to 430 and Sched 19.

Yours faithfully,

Profit & Loss
Chartered Accountants

APPENDIX II

Pro forma statement of net assets of the enlarged group

An illustrative pro forma consolidated statement of net assets of the enlarged group is set out below. The figures are based on the audited consolidated balance sheet of Purchaser PLC and its subsidiaries at 31 December 1987 and the balance sheet of Target at 30 September 1988 as shown in the Accountants' Report in Appendix I of this document.

	Purchaser PLC	*Target*	*Adjustment*	*Enlarged group pro forma*
	£000	*£000*	*£000*	*£000*
Fixed assets				
Tangible assets	18,309	341	—	18,650
Investments	1,441	—	—	1,441
	19,750	341	—	20,091
Current assets				
Stocks	2,290	95	—	2,385
Debtors	4,826	169	—	4,995
Investments	613	—	—	613
Cash at bank and in hand	302	69	—	371
	8,031	333	—	8,364
Creditors—amounts falling due within one year				
Finance debt	1,185	8	2,000	3,193
Other creditors	4,113	155	—	4,268
	5,298	163	2,000	7,461
Net current assets	2,733	170	(2,000)	903
Total assets less current liabilities	22,483	511	(2,000)	20,994
Creditors—amounts falling due after more than one year				
Finance debt	4,283	30	—	4,313
Other creditors	1,777	—	—	1,777
Provisions for liabilities and charges	657	69	—	726
Net assets	15,766	412	(2,000)	14,178

Notes

1 No adjustment has been made for profits earned by either Purchaser PLC or Target since the respective dates of the above balance sheets.

2 The pro forma statement of net assets excludes any provision for the expenses of the acquisition.

3 The pro forma assumes that the purchase consideration of £2,000,000 was satisfied in cash.

4 No adjustment has been made to reflect the fair value of Target's net assets acquired. Any goodwill arising on pro forma consolidation has been written off against reserves.

APPENDIX III

General Information

1 As at 30 November 1988 Purchaser and its subsidiaries (including for this purpose Target) had outstanding secured bank indebtedness of £38,500, other secured indebtedness amounting to £42,600 and unsecured indebtedness amounting to £5,253. Save as aforesaid and apart from intra group indebtedness neither Purchaser nor any of its subsidiaries had outstanding any borrowings or indebtedness in the nature of borrowing including loan capital issued or unissued bank loans, bank overdrafts, liabilities under acceptances (other than normal trade bills) or acceptance credits, mortgages, charges, hire purchase or finance lease commitments or guarantees or other material contingent liabilities.

2 Shareholders of Target have given to Purchaser the usual indemnities in respect of liabilities for income tax, corporation tax and inheritance tax.

3 The directors of Purchaser are satisfied that, taking into account existing facilities, Purchaser and its subsidiaries have adequate working capital for their present requirements.

4 Save as mentioned in this letter, there has been no significant change in the financial or trading position of the Purchaser group since 31 December 1987 or (the directors of Purchaser are informed) of Target since 30 September 1988, being the respective dates to which the last audited accounts of Purchaser and Target were made up.

5 Neither Purchaser nor any of its subsidiaries (including Target) is engaged in any litigation or arbitration proceedings which may have or have had during the twelve months preceding the date of this letter a significant effect on the financial position on the Purchaser group's financial position nor are there any such proceedings known to the directors of Purchaser to be pending or threatened against any of such companies.

6 The financial information given in this document in respect of profits for the five years ended 30 September 1988 and assets and liabilities at that date does not constitute full accounts of Target as referred to in the Companies

Act 1985, s 255. Full audited accounts of Target for the five years ended 30 September 1988 have been delivered to the Registrar of Companies and unqualified audit reports within the meaning of that section have been given in respect of those full accounts.

7 Messrs Profit & Loss have given and have not withdrawn their written consent to the inclusion in this letter of their report and references thereto in the form and context in which they are included.

Directors' Interests

8 The directors of Purchaser have the following interests in the ordinary share capital of Purchaser as shown in the register of directors' interests as required to be entered in the register referred to in the Companies Act 1985, s 325.

	Shares	
	Beneficial	*Other*
R Hood	28,500	4,000
F Tuck	10,000	–
W Scarlett	–	12,500

The directors of Purchaser are not aware of any interests, direct or indirect, in 5 per cent or more of the issue share capital of Purchaser.

9 There will be no variation in the emoluments of any of the directors of Purchaser arising from the acquisition of Target other than such as may arise under Mr R Hood's service contract with Purchaser dated 12 January 1982 under which he receives an annual commission of 2 per cent of the pre-tax profits of Purchaser and its subsidiaries.

10 Apart from the acquisition of M Marion & Sons Limited (details of which were sent to shareholders on 17 August 1988) none of the directors of Purchaser has had any interest in transactions which are or were unusual in their nature or conditions or significant to the business of the Purchaser group and which were effected since 1 January 1987 or which were effected during an earlier period and remain in any respect outstanding or unperformed.

11 There has been no change in the service contracts of the directors of Purchaser with Purchaser or any of its subsidiaries since 1 April 1988 (the date of the notice convening Purchaser's last annual general meeting).

Material Contracts

12 Save as mentioned in this letter, no material contracts other than the following have been entered into by Purchaser or its subsidiaries (including Target) otherwise than in the ordinary course of business during the two years preceding the date of this letter:

(i) an agreement dated 1 April 1987 for the acquisition of F Tuck & Sons Limited from Mr F Tuck and members of his family for £1,185,000; and

(ii) an agreement dated 17 July 1987 for the acquisition of M Marion & Sons Limited from Miss M Marion for £3,200,000 in cash.

Details of these contracts were sent to shareholders on 1 May 1987 and 17 August 1987 respectively.

Documents for Inspection

13 Copies of the following documents will be available for inspection at the offices of Coke & Littleton, 1 Moor Alley, London, EC3L 2FL, on weekdays (Saturdays and public holidays excepted) during usual business hours up to and including 8 January 1989:

(i) memorandum and articles of association of each of Purchaser and Target;

(ii) the audited consolidated accounts of the Purchaser group for the two years ended 31 December 1987;

(iii) the audited accounts of Target for the two years ended 30 September 1988;

(iv) the agreement for the acquisition of Target;

(v) the report of Messrs Profit & Loss and their written consent to the inclusion of their report in this letter;

(vi) the contracts referred to in paragraph 11 above together with the letters from Purchaser to shareholders giving information relating to those contracts; and

(vii) the service agreements of the directors of Purchaser and the service agreements of Mr Feather and Mr Bow referred to above.

OUTLINE CHECKLIST

1 Consents and Approvals

1.1 Does the acquisition require any consent from creditors of vendors or target (p 4)?

1.2 If consideration is shares, is it necessary to increase purchaser's capital and is any consent needed to issue shares (eg under purchaser's articles, loan stock trust deeds, etc) (p 5)?

1.3 Is consent of purchaser's shareholders required (p 5)?

1.4 If vendor or purchaser is listed, what are The Stock Exchange requirements (p 80)?

1.5 Does the target have any special qualification requiring third party consent to a change in control (p 5)?

1.6 If target is technically public, can dispensation from City Panel be obtained (p 3)?

1.7 Is clearance required under the Capital Gains Tax Act 1979, s 88 (p 109), or under the Income and Corporation Taxes Act 1988, ss 707 (p 111) or 776 (p 116).

1.8 Are there any European or restrictive trade practices implications (p 9)?
1.9 Does the acquisition fall within the criteria of the Fair Trading Act 1973, s 64 (p 12)?

2 Information

2.1 Full company search (p 50).
2.2 Particulars of share capital, names of registered holders and beneficial owners.
2.3 Memorandum and Articles.
2.4 List of directors.
2.5 Latest report and accounts.
2.6 Accountants' Report.
2.7 Details of all borrowing and charges.
2.8 Details of properties.
2.9 Details of guarantees given by or on behalf of the target.
2.10 Details of any intellectual property owned by the target.
2.11 Copies of material contracts.
2.12 Pensions Questionnaire (p 40).
2.13 Other information regarded as important by purchaser.

3 Taxation

3.1 Are there any special reliefs available to the vendors (eg roll-over relief, retirement relief, etc) or are they liable to be subject to any special charge (p 103)?
3.2 Is the target a close company (p 121)?
3.3 Is the target a member of a group (p 129)?
3.4 Are there any first business loan implications (p 126)?
3.5 Does the target have allowable losses (p 141)?
3.6 Are there any inheritance tax implications (p 146)?

4 Preparation of the Agreement

4.1 If the consideration for the acquisition is shares in the purchaser, what are the rights attached to the consideration shares in particular with regard to entitlement to dividend? What are the provisions in the purchaser's articles with regard eg to apportionment of dividends?
4.2 Will all the target's directors retire? Are there to be any service agreements?
4.3 Will the target's auditors change at completion?
4.4 Is the target's title to its property to be investigated or is a certificate to be obtained (p 58)?
4.5 Should completion be conditional upon the obtaining of any necessary consent or approval?

4.6 What special warranties are required?

4.7 Are there any specific matters with regard to taxation (eg continuation of group relief arrangements) which ought to be incorporated in the sale agreement?

4.8 Are there loans by the vendors to the target to be repaid on completion? Are any guarantees given by the vendors on behalf of the target to be released?

5 Procedure

5.1 Title investigation (p 58).

5.2 Investigation of funding of pension scheme (p 33).

5.3 Preparation and agreement of contracts.

5.4 Procurement and agreement of draft disclosure letter.

5.5 Submission of proof circular and any temporary documents of title to consideration shares for Stock Exchange approval (if applicable).

5.6 Exchange of contracts (with press release if desired or required by The Stock Exchange) (p 81).

5.7 Despatch of circular (if shareholder consent required).

5.8 Preparation and agreement of ancillary documents for completion.

5.9 Application for listing of consideration shares (if applicable).

5.10 Completion.

5.11 Despatch of circular (if Class 1).

5.12 Filing at Companies Registration Office.

5.13 Stamp transfers.

Index